Radio Comedy

Radio Comedy

ARTHUR FRANK WERTHEIM

New York   Oxford
OXFORD UNIVERSITY PRESS
1979

Library of Congress Cataloging in Publication Data
Wertheim, Arthur Frank, 1935–
Radio comedy.
Includes bibliographical references and index.
1. Radio programs—United States—History.
2. Comedy programs—United States—History.   I. Title.
PN1991.8.C65W47   791.44'0973   78-10679   ISBN 0-19-502481-8

Printed in the United States of America

For Jason, Our Son

Preface

Kurt Vonnegut, Jr., wrote recently, in a foreword to a book about radio comedians Bob Elliott and Ray Goulding: "It is the truth: Comedians and jazz musicians have been more comforting and enlightening to me than preachers or politicians or philosophers or poets or painters or novelists of my time. Historians in the future, in my opinion, will congratulate us on very little other than our clowning and our jazz." For a cultural historian, radio comedy offers a rich field of exploration. The results of listening to many comedy broadcasts and reading scripts and memoirs lie within these pages.

The book describes the evolution of radio comedy from the fledgling years of the 1920's through the impact of television in the early 1950's. The volume stresses the relationship of radio comedy to American values and society during the Great Depression and World War II. During that time radio became an inexpensive form of home and family entertainment and listening to comedy programs became a national pastime shared by millions of listeners. A major character in radio comedy was the vain, pompous braggart. In her study of American humor, Constance Rourke pointed out that the braggart was a major comic character in frontier legends and tall tales. Radio comedy can be traced back to that tradition of vernacular humor. The book also examines the influences of vaudeville and other stage comedy on

the comedians. Chapters show how Freeman Gosden and Charles
Correll, Jack Benny, and Fred Allen created innovative sound
entertainment. Particular trends, like song and patter and zany
humor, and certain problems, like censorship and commercialism, are also discussed.

Considering the scope of the subject, the author had to be selec-
tive in choosing the most appropriate comedians and comedy
shows. This book is not an encyclopedia of radio comedy programs. Listings of the stars and their broadcasts have already
been published. I primarily chose comedians who helped develop
radio comedy artistically and humorists who had the most popular appeal to listeners. Other shows were selected because the
broadcasts belonged to significant phases of radio comedy. Above
all, I aimed to capture the sounds of American humor on the airwaves.

February 1979   A.F.W.
Jakarta, Indonesia

Acknowledgments

I wish to thank the following librarians for their helpful aid in obtaining research material: Robert Knutson, Department of Special Collections, Doheny Library, University of Southern California; Brooke Whiting, Department of Special Collections, Research Library, University of California, Los Angeles; and Reba Collins, Curator, Will Rogers Memorial Commission, Claremore, Oklahoma. The staff of the Division of Archives and Manuscripts at the State Historical Society of Wisconsin in Madison and that of the Division of Special Collections, William Robertson Coe Library, University of Wyoming, also gave me needed assistance.

The officers and staff of the Pacific Pioneer Broadcasters in Hollywood, California, graciously granted me permission to use their facilities to listen to the tapes and recordings of the comedy broadcasts. In this regard I would like to thank Martin Halperin and Ron Wolf. Mr. Wolf was especially helpful in finding material appropriate to my interests. Les Tremayne provided much information about the history of radio and furnished interviews with radio personalities he had conducted for the Pacific Pioneer Broadcasters. The firm of Needham, Harper, & Steers allowed me to use the *Fibber McGee and Molly* scripts. Ken Greenwald also gave me tapes of comedy broadcasts from his private collection. Evelyn Bigsby let me peruse her copies of *Radio Life* magazine. I would also like to thank Frank Bresee for permitting me to publish photographs from his private collection, the Will Rogers Memorial Commission for granting me permission to quote from material in their archives, and the editors of *The Journal of Popular Culture* for allowing me to use material previously published in that magazine. The permission of the Bob and Dolores Hope Charitable Foundation to quote from *Have Tux, Will Travel* is gratefully acknowledged.

I wish to thank other individuals who gave their time for personal interviews. Pat Weaver spent an afternoon informing me of his experiences in radio. Jim Jordan, William Idelson, and Freeman Gosden helped clear up some points about their careers by way of telephone interviews. Freeman Gosden kindly sent me personal material pertaining to *Amos 'n' Andy*.

A grant from the Graduate School of the University of Southern California assisted in research and typing expenses. Janet Crusius and Clara Harada carefully typed several drafts of the manuscript. Casey Hahn diligently helped research the material on Burns and Allen. I wish to thank Sheldon Meyer and Caroline Taylor of Oxford University Press for their judicious reading and editing of the manuscript.

I am especially grateful to my wife, Carol, for her encouragement and for providing an atmosphere conducive to writing the book. My deceased stepfather, the talent agent Arthur S. Lyons, took me to radio shows as a young boy. I remember watching Jack Benny from a control booth and laughing at the comedy programs coming from my bedside radio. Because of Arthur Lyons I grew up with the radio comedians and learned to appreciate the artistry of show business entertainers. In many ways he has inspired this book.

Contents

In the nation, as comedy moves from a passing effervescence into the broad stream of a common possession, its bearings become singularly wide. There is scarcely an aspect of the American character to which humor is not related, few which in some sense it has not governed.

CONSTANCE ROURKE, American Humor (1931)

The endurance of comedy is merely a symptom of our will to survive, to spite and to overcome death and damnation. Not that man could not live without comedy, but he cannot exist without laughing. He must summon the clown to help him with his public exasperations and private despairs, to soothe his anguish with medication, to make him see the absurdity of his tragedies. And the clown in man will always raise his head to make sure he has the eyes and ears, the mind and heart of an audience with whom he can go on laughing.

WALTER SORELL, Facets of Comedy (1972)

PART ONE

Pioneers in the Fledgling Years

1

Song and Patter

At first radio did not produce much laughter in American homes. In the early 1920's the listeners tuned to crystal sets requiring earphones heard mostly music and talk programs. Static and strange whistling sounds often interfered with the reception. KDKA, the first commercially licensed station, officially opened on November 2, 1920, with news bulletins announcing the results of the Harding-Cox presidential election and with recorded music. Located in a rooftop shack above Westinghouse's East Pittsburgh plant, KDKA at first broadcast primarily music and information programs. WJZ, another Westinghouse station, began operations eleven months later from a shack above the company's red-brick factory in Newark, New Jersey, and, shortly after the opening, from a section of the building's ladies "cloak room." The orchestra leader, Vincent Lopez, remembered climbing a "rickety stairway" to the sparsely furnished studio to do his first broadcast in 1921:

> The small room was decorated with some absorbent material dyed an ugly shade of red to give it some semblance of uniformity. There were also some second-hand lamps as well as some rugs to help deaden studio sounds. Somehow an old upright piano had been squeezed in. Even Casey's in Brooklyn had owned a better one.[1]

In its early years radio was primarily a cultural and educational medium broadcasting music and information. A typical WJZ radio log featured live concerts by bands and orchestras, violinists and pianists, and operatic recitals by sopranos, contraltos, and tenors. Informative talks on the home, business, and health, as well as children's bedtime stories, were also broadcast. The musical groups on WJZ were often sponsored by companies, including the Rheingold Quartet, Schrafft's Tearoom Orchestra, and the Wanamaker Organ Concert. The most popular programs in the 1920's featured such orchestras as the Ipana Troubadours, Harry Horlick's A & P Gypsies, Harry Reser's Cliquot Club Eskimos, and the Goodrich Silvertown Orchestra.[2]

There were several reasons why comedy programs were not a regular feature in the early 1920's. Before network radio and sponsored income-producing programming, local stations run on shoestring budgets lacked the finances to pay popular entertainers. Some stars eager to experience the novelty of radio worked for nothing, like Eddie Cantor, who appeared on WJZ in 1921. Vaudeville headliners found the broadcasting conditions primitive, and talking into a microphone without an audience awkward. Comedians earning lucrative salaries in vaudeville and Broadway musical comedies were not about to risk their careers to be heard over a strange-sounding box in exchange for free dinners, publicity, or merchandise. By contrast, amateur musicians and budding professionals anxious for any opportunity came in droves to the studios. Musical programs, especially those with soloists or a small group of instrumentalists, were relatively inexpensive to produce. Vaudeville producers and booking agents were also reluctant to have their stars broadcast on radio even before the medium began to affect box-office business. They reasoned that listeners would not pay admission to a theater if they could hear the same entertainment at home. E. F. Albee, the autocratic vaudeville showman, had a policy that performers under his contract could not appear on radio.

It is difficult to pinpoint when the first joke was told on radio. Perhaps one day an anonymous individual decided to break the monotony of music and serious talk by relating an amusing story. Certainly comedy developed on radio because of the need to produce diversified programming and entertainment. A 1926 poll of 2800 radio fans concluded that listeners thought there was too much music on the dial. Owners of sets wanted more variety programs, especially comedy shows.[3]

In the mid-1920's certain members of radio orchestras on local stations, in order to enliven their programs, started to toss impromptu jokes back and forth. These musicians were among the airwaves' first jesters. The Coo-Coo Club Orchestra was noted for its music and comedy format on Cleveland's WTAM from 1924 to 1927. Listeners in the Midwest regularly tuned into their three-hour Saturday night broadcast. Everett (Ev) Jones, a member of the twelve-man band, recalled their style:

> Most of the "script" was ad-libbed. I would write down a lot of jokes, and as we were playing a tune the announcer would look them over and select the ones he liked. We would go into whatever gags he had selected at the end of a number. We went through this procedure after every dance tune. There were no rehearsals. There was no real script as we know it today.

Many puns and cheap Scotsman jokes were told by the musicians:

> What is the difference between a Scotsman and a coconut?
> You can get a drink out of a coconut.
>
> What is a drydock?
> A doctor out of prescriptions.

The announcer also cracked jokes about the orchestra and introduced one soloist from Chicago as "the pride of the stockyards." Similar programs included Chicago's Coon-Sanders Nighthawks and Detroit's Red Apple Club.[4]

The chief station announcer also became one of the first comedians on radio. In radio's early years the announcer often managed the station and did all types of duties, from janitor to program director. In order to fill in the program schedule he often told jokes he had pirated from *Joe Miller's Complete Jest*

Book and humor magazines such as *Judge, College Humor, Whiz Bang*, and *Madison's Budget*. The last, published annually between 1898 and 1921 by the former vaudevillian James Madison, was the stage comedian's "Bible," containing one-liners, monologues, and routines. The station announcer might have stolen these from *Madison's Budget:*

> My friend made a fortune in the boat-renting business. He put up a sign: RIDES ON THE LAKE. MARRIED MEN 10 CENTS, WIVES THROWN IN.

> I heard your mother-in-law was dangerously sick. Yes, but now she's dangerously well again.[5]

The announcer sometimes enlisted friends, studio hands, and unemployed performers to play in amusing skits in "jamboree" sessions. He also had no difficulty finding amateurs anxious to try out their routines over radio. Some walked into the studio unannounced, and they were permitted to relate a few jokes—provided the gags were clean. Many Pat and Mike jokes and laundered versions of stories about the farmer's daughter were related by unknowns. Patrick Barnes, chief announcer at Chicago's WHT, was the host of a "jamboree" midnight program of comedy skits called *Your Hour* in 1925, and listeners heard the volunteer performers rehearse their skits live over the air. In fact, the rehearsals for such programs were considered to be more entertaining than the actual performance.

Aspiring comedians appeared frequently on local stations in the mid-1920's, but except for scattered reviews their names and routines remain mostly unknown. *Radio Broadcast* magazine did publish a favorable review of a woman comedian who did a monologue over Denver's KOA:

> KOA—Monologue by a Mrs. (or was it Miss?) Harrison. First rate, and in excellent style for radio delivery. Mrs. (Miss?) Harrison is acquainted with one of the principal secrets of success in humorous broadcast, to wit—that of not pausing after each wisecrack for a laugh. Nobody laughs out loud at a radio joke anyway so such pauses are simply flat. This monologist rushed

through with her lines at top speed and without under-
scoring her jokes by a changed inflection of the voice.
The ludicrous laugh which punctuated her remarks
lost nothing of its mirth in the broadcasting. The sketch
was original and had to do with a club woman's busy
day.

These would-be comedians rarely went on to become well-known
humorists. Radio mainly borrowed comedy stars from the theater, and for commercial reasons it was reluctant to take chances
with newcomers. There were exceptions—Charlie Cantor, a shoe
salesman, tested his dialect comedy routines on his customers
and told the best ones over New York's WHN at night. He eventually became a successful radio comedy character actor and in
the 1940's starred as Clifton Finnegan on *Duffy's Tavern*.[6]

Nightclub comics could also be heard on the airwaves in the
1920's. Since remote broadcasts of orchestra music were very
popular, program managers, like WHN's Nils T. Granlund, believed that live broadcasts of nightclub entertainment would also
attract listeners. WHN broadcast twice weekly from the Village
Grove Nut Club on Sheridan Square in Greenwich Village. Listeners who liked to stay up until two o'clock in the morning
heard insult jokes and skits by "Nutsy" Fagan, Lou Dolgoff,
Buddy Walker, and a "dumb" comic named "Lehigh Vallee, dis-
tant brother of Rudy." The star was a female impersonator who
imitated a shrieking soprano. The entertainers threw pots, pans,
and pies, and yelled "Cuckoo! Horsefeathers!" into the microphone. Similar "nut acts" were then common in vaudeville; but
the radio listener had to imagine much of the slapstick on the
WHN broadcast.[7]

The most popular form of early radio humor was the song and
comedy patter team. Two-man acts performing piano or ukulele
numbers, harmony singing, joke exchanges, and skits had been
billed frequently in small-time vaudeville houses. Their format
of popular music and amusing chatter was suited to radio's early
years. They cost less than a full orchestra and added diversity to
programming. They also helped make comedy a regular feature
on the radio.

Billy Jones and Ernie Hare were radio's most renowned song

and patter team. Jones, a talented tenor discovered by Lew
Fields, had performed in musical comedies and on the concert
stage. He also made records for the Victor Company under the
name Victor Roberts. One day in the recording studio he met
baritone Ernie Hare, a former salesman who since 1909 had been
singing in Broadway musicals. The two teamed to do several
popular records for Victor and Pathé. They learned proper microphone technique and voice inflection and made records which
later helped them in broadcasting. For publicity purposes Pathé
Records sent Jones and Hare to WJZ on October 18, 1921, to do
their first broadcast. They received considerable fan mail for this
ninety-minute unrehearsed program of song and patter and were
very enthusiastic about the new medium.[8]

In 1923 the pair signed with the Happiness Candy Company
to broadcast a song and patter program. Jones and Hare were
then called the "Happiness Boys," an indirect form of linkage
product advertising common in early radio. Considered to be the
first regular comedy show on radio, the "Happiness Boys" premiered over local New York station WEAF on August 22, 1923.
Listeners liked their harmony singing and funny chatter, and
they remained with the candy company for five and a half years.
In 1927 their extremely popular thirty-minute program began to
be aired on the NBC network at 8 p.m. on Friday night. The
"Happiness Boys" were a nationwide sensation during the late
1920's, when they averaged 700 fan letters a week.

A major key to their success was their ability to create recognizable trademarks or "signatures" for their programs. Jones and
Hare became especially noted for their catchy opening and closing theme songs. They began their broadcast with the following
greeting:

> How do you do, everybody, how do you do?
> How do you do, everybody, how are you?
> We are here we must confess just to bring you happiness
> Hope we please you more or less, how do you do?
> How do you do, oh, how do you do?
> How do you doodle-doodle-doodle-doodle-do?
> Billy Jones and Ernie Hare wish to say to you out there
> How do you doodle-doodle-doodle-doodle-do?

Their closing song reminded listeners to tune in next week:

> Goodnight, everybody, goodnight.
> Goodnight, everybody, goodnight.
> Don't forget you have a date.
> Every Friday night at eight,
> So watch out and don't be late.
> Goodnight.

These ditties generated in the listener's mind a sense of consistency and continuity.[9]

Between songs Jones and Hare told jokes and performed short skits. One witty routine that showed their talent as impersonators parodied early radio. Using an English accent, Jones played a stuttering announcer who made fluffs over the air:

> Pardon me, this is station OUCH of the New Writers Broadcrest—Brood—Breath—Broadcasting Company— pardon me again—operating on a wave length of 600 motorcycles by the authority of the Federal Prohibition Agents. The first number on the program for this evening will be rendered—to be rendered meaning to be torn apart—by the Silent Dozen Orchestra. They will play as their opening selection "People Who Live in Glass Houses Shouldn't." There will be an interrupted vocal chorus sung by those famous entertainers "Pete and Repeat."

The skit also lampooned station breaks:

> Station ICH New York. We will now give you the correct time. When you hear the beautiful chimes it will be exactly six and seven-eighths split seconds past eight o'clock Eastern Daylight Standard Railroad Western Mountain Central Time. Get ready now. Listen for the chime. Attention. Forward March (sound of a cuckoo clock).

Their satire on radio programs concluded with a bedtime horror story for children and an operatic aria by "Howl & Bellow"— "the silver-plated tenor and gold-filled baritone." Many of the routines came from a joke file and notebooks in which they jotted down ideas for their broadcasts. They laughed out loud after a

The Happiness Boys, Billy Jones and Ernie Hare, with Helen Hann, WEAF hostess-accompanist, at the piano.
(Courtesy of the National Broadcasting Company, Inc.)

joke and used a small studio so that their guffaws could be heard distinctly by listeners. One reviewer praised their style and delivery:

> They can make you laugh at a veteran joke. They laugh at each other and their hearty laughter is contagious. They never permit a deadly silence after they have sprung one of their "gags," nor do they laugh too loud and long. When one tells a story that does not go over, his teammate taunts him and carries the radio audience along. Never for an instant do they miss the radio audience's reactions, either consciously or subconsciously.[10]

Other song and patter teams were heard on the airwaves in the 1920's. One popular pair was Scrappy Lambert and Billy Hillpot, who had a Wednesday night program beginning in 1926 over the NBC Red network. The show was sponsored by Smith Brothers Cough Drops. Known as "The Smith Brothers" or "Trade and Mark," the names of the two men on the cough drop package, they sang songs and told jokes for eight years under the same sponsor. Other popular acts were Breen and Derose, Brome & Llewellyn, the Raybestos Twins, and the blackface Gold Dust Twins (Goldy and Dusty), who broadcast over the WEAF chain in 1925. Phil Cook also did a single song and patter act, strumming the ukulele and singing the news in rhyme. Cook was later known as "The Quaker Oats Man" on NBC in 1930.

Gene and Glenn also had a large following in radio's fledgling years. Glenn Rowell first teamed with Ford Rush in a piano and singing act at Cincinnati's WLW in the mid-1920's. The team became a trio when Gene Carroll joined them. When Rush left to become an orchestra conductor, Gene and Glenn decided to do the act themselves. They moved to Cleveland, where the manager of WTAM suggested they add comedy to their routine. They asked a friend to write their dialogue and soon they were earning $600 a week doing a successful song and patter act over WTAM. Gene and Glenn became well known in the late 1920's as stars of NBC's *Quaker Early Birds Program*, a daily fifteen-minute early morning situation comedy. Gene, a talented voice imitator, took the roles of Lena, a boarding house owner, and

Jake, the handyman, while Glenn played himself. The dialogue between the characters was often hilarious. Gene and Glenn were on radio until 1943 when Glenn retired from show business. Gene continued as a character actor; he did Lena the maid on *Fibber McGee and Molly*.[11]

The mixture of humor and music on the song and patter programs was a forerunner of future developments in radio comedy. Industry spokesmen like Edgar Felix, publicity director of WEAF, believed that comedy was best presented between musical interludes:

> The apparent limit for which any voice, no matter how good, can be heard without interruption is ten minutes and, in most cases, less than that. Humor needs musical backing. The song-and-humor program offers enough relief against voice monotony to be effective. Radio humor is a highly appealing feature and, when the dignity of the sponsor is not an essential factor, has excellent possibilities as a commercial broadcasting feature.[12]

Most radio comedy shows in the 1930's had orchestral music and singing between the comedy spots. The song and patter programs were eventually unable to compete against the slick comedy variety shows starring vaudeville headliners.

During the 1930's Jones and Hare were sponsored by a sock manufacturer and by a baking company; they were known as the "Interwoven Pair" and the "Taystee Loafers" for their respective employers. Their simple format, which had delighted listeners in the mid-1920's, sounded old-fashioned compared with the professional routines of Fred Allen and Jack Benny. By the late 1930's Jones and Hare were doing a local radio program at New York's WMCA with a limited audience. When Hare died in 1939 and Jones in 1940, much of the listening public were not aware of how important they had been in the evolution of radio comedy.

Vaudeville entertainers began entering the medium with the development of network radio. Several well-known comedians appeared on the historic inaugural broadcast of the National Broadcasting Company, a four-and-a-half-hour program beamed over a hookup of twenty-four stations on November 15, 1926. Approximately five thousand miles of AT & T telephone wire was leased for the broadcast, which was carried live on twenty-five stations in twenty-one cities. The star-studded program cost approximately $50,000, a phenomenal figure at the time. Broadcast from the Grand Ballroom of the old Waldorf-Astoria, the extravaganza featured a variety of excellent entertainment, including the New York Symphony Orchestra conducted by Walter Damrosch, the Vincent Lopez and Ben Bernie orchestras, the Goldman Band, and the opera stars Titta Ruffo and Mary Garden, who sang by remote hookup from Chicago. The German-Jewish dialect comedy team of Joe Weber and Lew Fields, a famous two-man vaudeville act, also performed a skit, and humorist Will Rogers spoke over a microphone placed backstage in a theater in Independence, Kansas. The presence of Rogers and of Weber and Fields showed the importance the new network gave to comedy. Heard over two million radios and transmitted by short wave to Europe and South America, the NBC inaugural program also signaled radio's debut as a powerful medium. Although whistling sounds interfered with the clarity of the remote hookups, there was general enthusiasm for radio's ability to bridge the awesome distances in the nation and to give listeners a sense of sharing a common experience. As a dowager excitedly told her husband when leaving the Waldorf-Astoria, "My dear, I had no idea! We simply must get one of these radios the first thing tomorrow."[13]

Sponsored variety programs on NBC were among the first regularly scheduled broadcasts to present Broadway headliners. Sponsorship created large budgets, so that lucrative salaries became available to lure well-known entertainers. Advertising agencies also began entering the radio field, producing programs for their clients that were sold to the networks for a 15 per cent commission. Vaudeville comedy stars made frequent guest appearances on the National Carbon Company's *Eveready Hour*, broadcast over NBC beginning in 1926. This weekly variety program, produced by the N. W. Ayer Advertising Agency, had a budget ample enough to give listeners a variety of quality entertainment, including drama, poetry readings, lectures, operas, classical music, jazz, minstrel shows, and comedy monologues and skits. Will Rogers was paid $1000 for a single appearance on the *Eveready Hour*. Weber and Fields and the vaudeville piano and singing team of Gus Van and Joe Schenck also appeared on the program. Another important network variety program was produced by Samuel "Roxy" Rothafel, the famous theater manager and show business entrepreneur. "Roxy" presented the first live broadcast from a theater in 1923 when a variety show was aired from the stage of his Capitol Theatre on Broadway. He was also the host of a regular Sunday night broadcast from the theater which became a permanent program on the NBC Blue network in 1927. *Roxy and His Gang* mainly featured talented musicians and popular singers, but listeners also heard poetry, lectures, and comedy. Frank Moulan was the star comedian on *Roxy and His Gang*, a series that continued until 1931.[14]

At first, vaudeville comedians viewed radio with trepidation. They had spent their professional lives perfecting their comic stage act before different live audiences in hundreds of cities and towns. The stage entertainers used the same time-tested material for years. Radio, by contrast, had regular listeners, so comedians needed new jokes every week. The sound medium devoured comedy material at a much faster rate than vaudeville did. In the theater, a performer *knew* the makeup of his audience, but on radio the comedian was heard by a faceless mass of listeners. Unable to tailor his material to a particular audience, the radio comedians had to develop humor that appealed to a wide cross section of the American public. Vaudeville comedian Billy B. Van remarked on radio's uniqueness in 1926:

> The radio comedian is considerably hampered by this very diverse audience. He can not tell witticisms that appeal locally, he can not tell stories that hold a race, a class or a religion up to ridicule, he cannot jest of things which are not familiar to the every day life of his hearers.[15]

Thus radio comedians catered to a large, invisible, middle-class public.

From its inception, radio was considered family home entertainment, so lewd jokes and double entendres were taboo. The broadcast of a Broadway musical, *Tangerine*, over WJZ in 1921 was canceled when the producers refused to delete certain risqué material. "Only the cleanest of clean humor, entirely free of suggestion, is permissible" over radio, wrote Van. "Considering the millions of people that may be listening in and the little children that are probably part of the audience, this is right and proper."[16]

The stage comedian often relied on facial gestures, bizarre costumes, make-up, and props in his routine. Radio, a non-visual form of entertainment, depended largely on voice inflections, sound effects, and dialogue to incite laughter. "The hardest thing for the comedian to bear in mind when talking over the radio . . . is that the audience is looking at him through ears and that he must appeal to them through their mental eyes," declared Van:

> This means that he can't shamble out with an awkward gait and look around him with a bewildered expression while the spectators take in the details of his baggy trousers, enormous shoes, red nose and absurd little hat cocked on one side of his head. He can't depend on any stage properties to bring out an obscure point.

The radio performer also had to clearly enunciate his words so that listeners could hear his jokes distinctly. Instead of being able to move freely about the stage he had to stand still with script in hand in front of a microphone.[17]

Stage comedians often suffered from "mike fright" when they first appeared on radio. There were no studio audiences in the early years, and, to a comic who relied on laughter and applause for his timing and delivery, the silence was deadening. Especially perturbed by the lack of an audience was the veteran vaudeville comedian and musical comedy star Frank Tinney, whose monologue over Detroit's WJR "suffered . . . because of the absence of applause." Joe Cook, an experienced Broadway showman who had entertained audiences for years on stage, felt uncomfortable during his radio debut in 1926:

> At first I found myself talking too fast because I was
> rather nervous. . . . Throughout the whole time I was
> on the air, I was deathly afraid I was mechanical, that
> I sounded as though I were talking into a record instead
> of joking with a real flesh and blood audience.

Cook was unable to use the stage props he employed in his variety act. "On the stage, I can juggle with balls, bottles, ladders, musical instruments; on the radio, I can juggle only with my voice and play the musical instruments." Although Cook later had his own program and did frequent guest appearances, he never became a major radio comedy star.[18]

Approximately ten months after the inaugural broadcast of NBC, the Columbia Phonograph Broadcasting System began broadcasting—on September 18, 1927. The new network began with a sixteen-station hookup and ten hours of weekly programming. Conductor Howard Barlow opened the premier broadcast with an afternoon concert, followed by a program featuring popular music by Donald Voorhees and his dance orchestra. In the evening Barlow conducted Deems Taylor's new opera, *The King's Henchman*, sung by Metropolitan Opera stars, an innovative program unfortunately spoiled by technical difficulties. The network lacked financial resources, and within a year the phonograph company sold its controlling interest to new backers, who renamed the network the Columbia Broadcasting System. In September 1928 the new CBS owners appointed William Paley, a young cigar executive, as president. The dynamic Paley soon made CBS a serious rival of NBC by improving the network's financial position and programming.

The debuts of CBS and NBC corresponded to a growing interest in radio by the American public. The number of purchased sets escalated during the 1920's. In 1922, three million homes had receivers, while sales of radio equipment amounted to close to sixty million dollars. By 1929, with a radio in every third home in America, sales totaled $842,548,000, an increase of approximately 1400 per cent. Nor was the price of a set out of reach for the middle class. Montgomery Ward's 1922 Fall Catalogue advertised a crystal radio receiving outfit for $49.50, with more expensive living-room consoles available on installment. Radios, refrigerators, vacuum cleaners, and automobiles were among the many new consumer items Americans purchased on credit in the 1920's. Like the automobile, radio lessened the isolation of farms and small towns. Network programming allowed rural and urban listeners to hear the same shows and vicariously experience news events like the aviator Charles Lindbergh's triumphant return to Washington, D.C. in 1927. Even in the 1920's radio was a powerful agency of cultural homogenization and showed tremendous potential in the entertainment field, but it was clear that the medium needed more original comedy shows. In the mid-1920's two pioneers named Gosden and Correll were broadcasting a program that was to have an important bearing on the development of radio comedy.[19]

2
Sam 'n' Henry

Freeman Gosden and Charles Correll were early radio comedy's most significant innovators. In 1925 they began their career on radio as an ordinary harmony team. A year later they changed to a situation comedy format in the groundbreaking series *Sam 'n' Henry*, a forerunner of *Amos 'n' Andy*. The influences on their creation of *Sam 'n' Henry* are crucial for an understanding of the evolution of radio comedy.

Correll was born in Peoria, Illinois, on February 3, 1890, and at an early age displayed an inclination for show business. In the basement of his home the boy and his friends staged plays, charging the neighbors five pins for admission. At the circus the chubby, jovial youngster enjoyed watching the various acts as he sold lemonade to the spectators. He also worked as an usher at the local playhouse, and after the performances he and the other employees met to mimic the actors. Correll learned to be a stonemason like his father and labored for a time as a bricklayer. His ambition, however, was to be a hoofer, and he won several dance contests. He also took up the piano and was employed nightly at a motion picture theater playing background music for silent movies. The talented Correll also sang in a barbershop quartet and in amateur minstrel shows.[1]

In the summer of 1918 Correll was hired as a rehearsal coach by the Joe Bren Producing Company, which staged amateur talent shows for clubs, fraternal organizations, and church groups.

A company employee had seen Correll perform in an amateur show in Peoria and had hired him to help produce the theatricals. The Bren Company supplied the script, music, costumes, and scenery to the local organizations, and they in turn provided the talent for the productions. Correll was soon promoted to stage director and traveled throughout the South staging shows. He met his future partner, Freeman Gosden, in August 1919, while directing a home talent show for the Elks Club in Durham, North Carolina.

Gosden, who had been born in Richmond, Virginia, on May 5, 1899, was also a natural-born entertainer. The scrappy, curly-haired boy liked to do daring stunts. At age ten he entered a diving contest in Annette Kellerman's swimming and diving show. He enjoyed performing simple magic tricks and once assisted Howard Thurston, the famous magician, during a performance in Richmond. Gosden pretended he was a sloppy assistant by dropping the eggs Thurston took from a hat. That bit on stage was probably his first attempt at comedy. He also imitated Charlie Chaplin by putting on an oversized pair of shoes and derby and walking bowlegged with a cane. Even as a child Gosden liked to imitate people, and his skill at impersonation would become fundamental to doing the many roles on *Amos 'n' Andy*. He also became proficient in playing the ukulele and singing and tap dancing, and he occasionally performed as a song-and-dance man in local amateur musical comedies and minstrel shows. After a stint as a Navy radio operator during World War I, he was employed as an automobile salesman and a traveling agent for the American Tobacco Company.

In 1919, Gosden also obtained a position as a director with the Bren Producing Company. His initial assignment was to stage an amateur night at Elizabeth City, North Carolina. Gosden first went to Durham to get advice from Correll on directing the show and to obtain a copy of the script and music. They liked each other immediately. Gosden taught Correll's amateurs a dance routine, while Correll worked all night informing Gosden of the production's details. "That was the beginning of a very strong friendship that has proven itself many times during the ensuing years," recalled Gosden.[2]

For six years they worked together for the Bren Company, traveling from town to town and directing amateur talent musical comedy and minstrel shows. Gosden rehearsed the performers and occasionally acted as an endman in the minstrel productions. Correll was in charge of the costumes and scenery, played the piano, and conducted the orchestra. The pair learned how to adapt material to different audiences all over the country. The experience of staging amateur shows proved to be an invaluable training for radio. "Coaching gave us the 'feel' of an audience," said Gosden. "In directing a show your personal reactions are, or should be, those of an auditor, and believe me, this helps a lot in radio."[3]

Gosden and Correll made their first broadcast during the fall of 1920 from New Orleans, where they were directing a talent show for the Shriners. The manager of an experimental station asked them to try the new medium. Curious about radio, the two accepted, though they knew that they might not be heard more than a mile away. They sang the popular song "Whispering" into a large microphone resembling a loudspeaker. Both wondered if anyone had listened, but then a woman several blocks from the studio telephoned to say she had heard them clearly on her crystal set.

Five years elapsed before Gosden and Correll next appeared on radio. The two had been assigned to the production company's Chicago home office, where Correll managed the organization's show division and Gosden administered the circus department. In the mid-1920's Chicago was becoming a major center of early radio, and the many local stations, eager to fill their program schedules, were willing to let amateurs perform. In a bachelor apartment, which they shared, the two roommates sang harmony songs. Correll played the piano and Gosden strummed the ukulele. In 1925 a friend suggested they perform on radio, so the two did a program at WQGA. Although they were having as much fun singing on radio as at home, they were not ready to resign their jobs for an uncertain broadcasting career.

Shortly thereafter, Bob Boneil, manager of WEBH, asked them to broadcast a late-night program over his station. WEBH was located in Chicago's Edgewater Beach Hotel in a small room next to the main dining room. Like most pioneer stations, WEBH was run on a small budget. They jokingly asked Boneil how much it would cost them to do the program. The station could not afford to pay a salary, replied Boneil, but they could have a free Blue Plate Special dinner. In March 1925 they started broadcasting once a week, yet their program was so entertaining the pair was soon performing every night but Monday from 11:30 to 12. (Monday was Silent Night in Chicago—all stations went off the air to enable listeners to pick up long-distance broadcasts.) Gosden and Correll's format consisted of harmony singing, with Correll at the piano and Gosden on the ukulele. They sang "Yes, Sir, That's My Baby," and "The Red, Red Robin Goes Bob, Bob, Bobbin Along." Listeners liked their lively style, but they did not differ greatly from a typical harmony team of the 1920's. The stint at WEBH was nonetheless an important turning point in their lives. Soon they were announcing programs and "doing everything but sweeping up the studio."[4] Gosden and Correll were gradually gaining a local following and thinking of radio as a permanent career.

Another opportunity soon arose that had an important bearing on the evolution of radio comedy. They were offered a full-time position in November 1925 at WGN, a station owned by the Chicago *Tribune*. A lucky set of circumstances led to their hiring. Ben McCanna, in charge of radio at the *Tribune*, asked Henry Selinger, manager of WGN, to employ a harmony team to do a regular program. McCanna hoped to attract a well-known vaudeville act and gave Selinger the unheard of sum of $3000 a week to spend. Despite the attractive salary Selinger was unable to find any headliners who wanted to go into radio permanently. He began instead to canvass the local area for talent. The station manager could have signed Jim and Marian Jordan (later *Fibber McGee and Molly*), who were then obscure entertainers doing a piano and singing program on a Chicago station, but McCanna wanted a two-man act. Selinger next called the manager of the Chicago Theater for recommendations and was advised to telephone Will Harris, the theater's booking agent. "There are a couple of fellows sitting here who might consider

Freeman Gosden (ukulele) and Charles Correll (piano) began on radio as a harmony team in 1925.
(Courtesy of the Department of Special Collections, Doheny Library, University of Southern California, Los Angeles. *Amos 'n' Andy* Collection.)

it," Harris told Selinger. "Their names are Correll and Gosden."
Before engaging the team, Selinger heard them on WEBH and
watched their harmony act on stage at the McVickers Theater in
the Paul Ash revue "Red Hot." Impressed by their talent, he offered them $250 a week for six months. The partners went out
into the hall to discuss the offer because they could not believe
the high salary. They also needed the money to pay off debts.
"Are they really going to pay us that?" Correll exclaimed to his
partner. The pair agreed to Selinger's terms, knowing it was an
excellent opportunity to join a more prestigious station. They
then quit their jobs with the Bren Company in order to devote
themselves exclusively to radio.[5]

Gosden and Correll, as they were then known, broadcast six
times a week on WGN. They also helped around the studio,
which was located in the Drake Hotel, doing spot announcing
and writing program material. Because their broadcast usually
lasted several hours they had to expand their repertoire. The
partners chatted between numbers and impersonated various
characters in short skits. One of the songs they sang was "Who'll
be the Papa?":

> Who'll be the Papa?
> I'll be the Papa.
> And oh what a Papa you'll be.
> Tell me, who'll be the Mama?
> I'll be the Mama.
> And oh what a Mama for me. . . .

They also made several stage appearances in the Chicago area
and records for the Victor Talking Machine Company. Despite
the publicity their singing style still differed little from that of
other harmony teams. McCanna told Selinger: "You better get
rid of those two guys. They stink." Gosden and Correll also realized that their song and patter routine had a limited future on
radio.[6]

The team had been at WGN for a few months when the station management suggested they try a different type of program.
Selinger asked them if they were interested in doing a radio
adaptation of Sydney Fisher's *The Gumps*, a family comic strip

syndicated by the *Tribune* chain. The newspaper had pioneered
in making comic serials like *The Gumps* a clever sales device.
Every day, newspaper readers looked forward to reading about
their favorite characters. The WGN management believed that
serialization could also be an attractive radio format and increase
the number of listeners. Gosden and Correll liked the idea of dra-
matizing a comic strip, but they had never played such character
types as the bumbling Andy Gump and his independent son
Chester. Nor did they feel capable of writing the family serial
since neither was married and had children. The two thus declined WGN's proposal.[7]

They had a more exciting idea for a program and presented it
to the station. Gosden and Correll wanted to broadcast a serial
based on two Southern blacks named Sam and Henry. Because of
their background the pair felt they knew enough about the
South and Negro life to write the series. Correll's grandparents
had been born and raised in the Deep South, and his grandfather
had spent the Civil War in a Union prison camp. After that war
his father had moved from the South to Peoria. Gosden came
from an old Virginia family which had lived in that state for
three generations. His father had fought for the Confederacy as a
member of Mosby's Rangers, an independent cavalry unit which
had refused to surrender at the Civil War's conclusion. Gosden
was raised by a "mammy," and he had frequently heard other
black people talk in the household.

His parents raised a black youngster, Garrett Brown, until
Brown was about sixteen years old. Gosden's sister-in-law remembered Brown, who was nicknamed "Snowball." He had an
amusing jargon and "everyone laughed at his quibbles." One of
his pet sayings was said to be, "ain't dat sumpin'," an expression
later made famous on *Amos 'n' Andy*. Gosden and Brown were
playmates in the household, and they had staged impromptu
minstrel shows for Freeman's invalid father. With Brown as
endman and Gosden as interlocutor, the boys had exchanged
jokes, had done imitations, and had put on imaginative skits.
When he wrote the early episodes of *Amos 'n' Andy* Gosden modeled Sylvester, a minor character, on Brown. He once said that
Amos was also partly based on his childhood friend.[8]

Their experience in minstrel shows also had a major influence on their desire to create a radio program concerning two black characters. Whenever the minstrel show came to Richmond, Gosden attended the performances. As mentioned earlier, Gosden was a clog dancer in amateur minstrel shows and often played the part of the blackface endman. Correll had also sung and told Negro dialect jokes in amateur minstrels before joining the Bren Company. They staged minstrel-style entertainment for that organization and wrote a Negro dialect number called "The Kinky Kids' Parade" for a 1925 Paul Ash musical revue in Chicago. They also enjoyed doing comic Negro dialogue routines at parties.

The minstrel show, an extremely popular nineteenth-century form of variety theater, had first been performed by white entertainers in blackface who mimicked Negro dances, songs, jokes, and dialect. The comedy largely derived from exaggerated Negro speech and racial caricatures. The foolish, "ignorant" endmen, Tambo and Bones, chatted back and forth in a heavy patois replete with malapropisms, and they exchanged one-liners, puns, riddles, and amusing stories. Their personalities contrasted with the pompous, well-spoken interlocutor, or master of ceremonies. Audiences laughed whenever the endmen mocked the interlocutor's affectations or the interlocutor ridiculed the endmen for their bad grammar and stupidity. In the radio serial the vain and lazy Andy contrasted with the simple-minded and diligent Amos, characterizations that drew upon the stereotyped simplistic caricatures of minstrel shows. The comic dialogue in *Amos 'n' Andy* also contained abundant malapropisms and wordplay.[9]

Although those stage shows had lost much of their popularity by the time Gosden and Correll created *Sam 'n' Henry* in 1926, there were still minstrel traveling companies and many renowned vaudeville blackface comics and singers. Lew Dockstader, a blackface comic, owned a successful minstrel show in the early twentieth century. Al Jolson was a featured performer with Dockstader's minstrels from 1907 to 1911 before becoming a blackface vaudeville and Broadway musical comedy star. Eddie Cantor wore burnt-cork makeup while appearing in Florenz Ziegfeld's *Midnight Frolics* and in the musical show *Whoopee*

(1928). In the 1920's blackface comic routines were both an acceptable and a popular form of stage entertainment. Few people questioned comics making fun of the speech and behavior of ethnic groups, including Irishmen and Jews, who were the butts of many routines. Joke books like *Minstrel Jokes*, *Coon Jokes*, and *Darky Jones*, lampooning exaggerated Negro traits, sold widely in dime stores. An amateur group desiring to stage a minstrel show could still buy such guide books as *The Amateur Minstrel* and *Burnt Cork*. Gosden and Correll created their radio serials in an environment that readily accepted the comic portrayal of blackface Negro stage stereotypes.[10]

A notable two-man blackface comedy team in the 1920's was George Moran and Charlie Mack, known as the *Two Black Crows*. Mack had started in minstrel shows and then had gone into vaudeville and musical comedy revues, doing a blackface act with different partners, including Bert Swor. He had eventually teamed up with Moran, who played the straight man in their Negro dialect routines. In the 1920's they became Broadway comedy stars, and made several best-selling phonograph records and movies. The team did guest radio appearances on the *Eveready Hour* and were featured on the 1928 CBS *Majestic Theater Hour*, a Sunday night variety program. The basis of their act lay in setting up an ignorant character (Mack) against a boastful one (Moran). Moran's role was to scoff at Mack's stupidity. One routine, a preposterous takeoff on "the early bird catches the worm," typifies their style:

> MORAN   . . . Always remember, that the early bird catches the worm.
>
> MACK   The early bird catches what worm?
>
> MORAN   Why, any worm.
>
> MACK   Well, who cares about that?
>
> MORAN   Everybody knows that the early bird catches the worm.
>
> MACK   Well, what of it? What about it?
>
> MORAN   He catches it, that's all.
>
> MACK   Well, let him have it. Who wants a worm anyhow? What's his idea in catching a worm?
>
> MORAN   Why, he catches the worm because he wants it.
>
> MACK   Well, what does he want with it?
>
> MORAN   How do I know what he wants?

MACK   Well, how do you know he wants it? How do you know that?

MORAN   Well, what's his idea in catching it, if he don't want it?

MACK   Well, what's the worm's idea in bein' there?

MORAN   Why the worm lives there.

MACK   He lives where?

MORAN   He lives where he is.

MACK   Doggone, I don't even know where he is. I don't know that.

MORAN   Well, he's at home. That's where he is!

MACK   Well, I'd rather not hear any more about it. Which is the early bird? Which bird is early?

MORAN   Why the first bird gits there is the early bird.

MACK   What causes that?

MORAN   Because he's the first bird there.

MACK   Yeah. Well, suppose some other bird got there ahead of him?

MORAN   Oh boy, you don't seem to know anything! . . .[11]

A similar piece of dialogue is found in an early *Amos 'n' Andy* episode. A conversation between Andy and his "lazy" uneducated employee Lightnin' is likewise highlighted by colloquial expressions.

ANDY   Well now Lightnin', let's git down to brass tacks an' let's start hittin' de nail on de head, git yo' nose up to de grindstone, yo' shoulder to de wheel, an' all dem things.

LIGHTNIN'   Whut'd you say, Mr. Andy?

ANDY   In other words, keep a stiff uppeh lip, keep yo' eyes open. You is gittin' bad as a hoss, you kin sleep standin' up.

LIGHTNIN'   Yessah. I aint goin' do it no more though.

ANDY   Remembeh dat dey didn't burn down Rome in a day, an' all dat stuff.

LIGHTNIN'   You say dey DIDN'T burn down Rome?

ANDY   Not in one day dey ain't.

LIGHTNIN'   I'se crazy 'bout fires. When was it?

ANDY   When was whut?

LIGHTNIN'   Dis heah fire 'bout burnin' sumpin' down.

ANDY   Well, it ain't no use to go into dat wid yo'—dat's a slogan like "nine stitches save a lot of time," or sumpin. . . .[12]

Sam 'n' Henry and *Amos 'n' Andy* also revolved around two con-trasting characters speaking a thick Negro dialect.

Other blackface comedy acts and minstrel-style entertainment were featured on early radio, among them *Honey Boy and Sassafras* (George Fields and Johnnie Welsh) and *Molasses 'n' January* (Pick Malone and Pat Padgett), who were regulars on the series *Show Boat* (1932). *The Burnt Cork Review*, a one-hour weekly variety program featuring instrumentalists, singers, and comedians, was broadcast over Cincinnati's WLW in 1926. Chicago listeners heard the *Haymaker's Minstrels* over WLS. Two popular programs on NBC were the *Sealey Air Weavers* (1927–28) and the *Dutch Masters Minstrels* (1928–32). The NBC schedule in the 1930's included *Sinclair Weiner Minstrels* (1932–36) *Mollé Minstrels* (1934–35), *Minstrel Show* (1937–38), and *Plantation Party* (1938–43). In 1929 Gosden and Correll broadcast a Thursday night minstrel show on Chicago's WMAQ, and they starred on a *Mystic Knights of the Sea Friday Night Minstrel Show* in December 1936. In fact, the airwaves were full of banjo music, sentimental Southern ballads, and blackface routines until the late 1930's.[13]

Gosden and Correll also got some ideas for their radio programs from newspaper comic strip serials. *Sam 'n' Henry*, and its successor, *Amos 'n' Andy*, had continuous story lines centered upon regular characters. The simple and easily recognizable characterizations in comic strips also influenced the radio pioneers. They thought of using two major contrasting personalities like *Mutt and Jeff* (1907), the tall scheming dupe and the foolish little fellow. Sam (Amos) was the small, kinder man, while the heavyset Henry (Andy) was boisterous and domineering. In real life Correll, who played Andy, was short and stocky, while Gosden, who played Amos, was tall and lanky. Comic strips, however, were a graphic art. Correll and Gosden realized that on radio characterization largely depended on voice inflection and that the two characters had to *sound* different rather than look different:

> It was decided that, on account of the character of Amos being excitable, sympathetic, kind, and younger than

>Andy, Amos should have the high, thin voice. With a
>voice of this type, Amos can more easily excite the
>listener or play on his sympathy, as the different situa-
>tions present themselves. In contrast to him, it was de-
>cided that Andy should have a deep voice, thus portray-
>ing his domineering, boastful, and conceited nature.

Radio listeners held mental pictures of the personalities through
the tones of the characters' voices. Correll believed that this
"mental impression" would

>be much more acute than one conveyed in printers' ink.
>And because of its acuteness it stimulates listeners to
>exercise their imaginations.
>
>Our voices, of course, help make the action and the
>situations vigorous and true. We try to make everything
>as human as possible through emotional rather than
>graphic picturization.

Gosden and Correll were one of the first entertainers to make artistic use of radio's assets as a sound medium.[14]

At first the WGN management rejected their proposal for a
series based on two black characters. When the station finally
decided to try it out, Gosden and Correll had to do their first
broadcast on short notice. *Sam 'n' Henry*, considered the first situation comedy on radio, debuted over WGN on January 12,
1926. Bill Hay, WGN's sales manager, was the program's announcer. The soft-spoken Hay opened the broadcast with the
words "10:10. WGN. *Sam 'n' Henry*." Broadcast six evenings a
week, each episode ran ten minutes and was written by the two
actors. Gosden played Sam and Correll Henry, and they also did
the voices of the minor characters.

The partners chose an historically significant subject for their
series. After World War I many black Southerners had migrated
to Northern cities, seeking employment. Sam Smith and Henry
Johnson hailed from Birmingham, Alabama, and the first program depicted them riding on the buckboard of a mule-driven
wagon en route to the train depot. They had decided to spend
their savings on train tickets to Chicago, where they hoped to
find employment with a construction company:

SAM   Henry, did you evah see a mule as slow as dis one?

HENRY   Oh, dis mule is fas' enough. We gonna git to de depot alright.

SAM   You know dat Chicago train don't wait fo' nobody—it jes' goes on—jes' stops and goes right on.

HENRY   Well, we ain't got but two mo' blocks to go—don't be so 'patient, don't be so 'patient.

SAM   I hope dey got fastah mules dan dis up in Chicago.

HENRY   You know some o' de boys said dey was goin' to be down dere to de depot to tell us go'bye and take dis mule back.

SAM   Not only some o' de boys—but Liza goin' to be down dere too—and she's gonna kiss me go'bye she said. You know, Henry, I kin'-a hate to leave dat dere gal.

HENRY   Dere you go—wimmen on de brain—how we gonna evah be millionaries in Chicago when you always talkin' 'bout wimmen?[15]

The early broadcasts, which portrayed the innocent characters' troubles in Chicago, mirrored the difficulties Southern blacks had in adjusting to life in the Northern cities. They were unable to find the construction company offices, and they became lost in the Windy City. The pair hired a taxi and were overcharged for the ride. Thinking the driver would return to give them back their change, the two sat forlornly on the street-corner waiting for the taxi driver. They also got lost on the subway and found themselves back at the train depot. The two newcomers, especially the gullible Sam, are taken advantage of by hucksters. Sam bought a fountain pen from a "street fakir" and was fleeced by a fortune teller and quack doctor. Using money he intended for his girl friend's birthday present, he purchased a life insurance policy from a fast-talking salesman. The two were employed by the construction company but were soon fired for loafing on the job. Sam and Henry had trouble finding work and were arrested for shooting craps. Victimized by con men and stranded in the big city, the two characters moved from one predicament to another.

The humor of *Sam 'n' Henry* mainly derived from their comic misadventures, foolish naïveté, and ignorance. It is fashionable now to view these characters as cardboard stereotypes, and to a certain degree that interpretation has some validity. Their child-like innocence resembled Negro theatrical stereotypes and "Sambo" images of blacks held by white society. Like the "Dandy" stage character, they enjoyed crap games and liquor. Henry was especially characterized as an indolent individual. As in the humor of the minstrel shows, the characters' ignorance is the object of amusement. Sam believed Lake Michigan to be the Atlantic Ocean and the League of Nations "de league wid de Chicago Cubs." He did not understand that one has to buy a special "slug" to make a telephone call:

> SAM   . . . Look heah, Henry, dis thing must be out of ordah.
> HENRY   W'y don' you read the signs?
> SAM   Whut do de signs say, Henry?
> HENRY   W'y de sign dere say, "Buy a Slug."
> SAM   Whut it say?
> HENRY   It say, "Buy a Slug."
> SAM   A slug of what?[16]

On the other hand, the characters were never consciously pre-sented in any demeaning manner. Sam was loyal, honest, and industrious. Gosden and Correll also portrayed the parts sympa-thetically, and they understood the plight of the black man in the Northern city. The characters of Sam and Henry were un-doubtedly shaped by the minstrel shows, but they had a human dimension that went beyond mere stereotyping.

The broadcast was also an important forerunner of *Amos 'n' Andy*. The personalities of Amos and Andy were quite similar to those of Sam and Henry. The plots in the early *Amos 'n' Andy* scripts followed the same story lines. Only the names of the lo-cales and characters were changed. The Jewels of the Crown, a fraternal lodge joined by Sam and Henry, was known as the Mystic Knights of the Sea in *Amos 'n' Andy*. There were many malapropisms in both series, and much wordplay. Well-known expressions from *Amos 'n' Andy*, like "awah, awah, awah" and "ain't dat sumpin'," first appeared in *Sam 'n' Henry*. The pace and tone of the *Sam 'n' Henry* and early *Amos 'n' Andy* broad-casts are also comparable, for both are slow moving, melodra-matic, and sentimental.

During the first few weeks *Sam 'n' Henry* failed to attract many listeners. Gosden and Correll thought of quitting, but Selinger urged them to broadcast for several more weeks. By the end of five weeks listeners began talking about the series, and its continuous story line kept them tuned to their radios every night. Listening to the show gradually became a habit in the Chicago area. "You've started something there that it will be hard to stop," a fan wrote. "Sam 'n' Henry are to WGN what Andy Gump is to the *Tribune.*" One writer complained he could never see a complete motion picture show because his wife had to be home to hear the broadcast. Another listener, who called *Sam 'n' Henry* the end of a perfect day, could not wait to tell her children about the broadcast every morning. Gosden and Correll soon had a large local following in the Chicago area, where they made personal stage appearances in blackface. They performed *Sam 'n' Henry* on WGN until December 18, 1927, doing a total of 586 episodes. A comic strip about the characters was also published in the Chicago *Sunday Tribune*, and *Sam 'n' Henry* records were sold by the Victor Company.[17]

During 1926 and 1927 Gosden and Correll pioneered in evolving a new form of radio comedy, in part using ideas borrowed from the minstrel show and the comic strip. They broke away from their limited song and patter repertoire to create the first radio situation comedy. Any evaluation of *Sam 'n' Henry* must consider both its positive and negative features. It perpetuated clichés about Negroes and reassured white listeners that their new neighbors from the South were less intelligent and less diligent than themselves. If the series gave whites a feeling of false superiority, it also mirrored the difficult life of rootless Southern blacks in a Northern metropolis. Like D. W. Griffith's film *The Birth of a Nation* (1915), *Sam 'n' Henry* showed the artistic potential of a new entertainment medium using the subject matter of American blacks. Griffith's pioneering movie had demeaned the Negro with insulting caricatures and an inaccurate picture of Reconstruction in the South. But that was not the case with *Sam 'n' Henry*. It paved the way not only for *Amos 'n' Andy*, but for the great explosion of radio comedy during the Great Depression.[18]

PART TWO

The Great Depression

3
Amos 'n' Andy

During their second year of broadcasting *Sam 'n' Henry* Gosden and Correll wanted to record their program for other stations. This would be done six weeks in advance on two separate records containing five-minute sections of the nightly show. These discs would be shipped to stations around the country and played on double turnstiles on the night of the live broadcast on WGN. They believed that this innovation in radio syndication, known as a "chainless chain," would vastly increase their audience. The Chicago *Tribune* opposed the idea, claiming contractual ownership rights to the title *Sam 'n' Henry* and the exclusive right for WGN to broadcast the show. Anxious to distribute their program nationally, Gosden and Correll decided to leave WGN after expiration of their second-year contract. An advertising executive urged them to join the Chicago *Daily News* station, WMAQ, whose management was more receptive to the "chainless chain" idea. The two "jumped" to WMAQ and made an agreement with the station allowing them to send recordings to other outlets.[1]

They had to invent a new title for the WMAQ series, since the *Tribune* held the rights to the name *Sam 'n' Henry*. When they wrote the first script, the two characters were called Jim and Charlie, but their names were changed to Amos and Andy by the time of the premier broadcast on March 19, 1928. Legend has it

35

that the comedians chanced on the title on the way up to the studio to do the first program. Supposedly, they encountered two men named Amos and Andy in the elevator. The story is not true, for the week before their WMAQ debut newspaper publicity articles already announced the title as *Amos 'n' Andy*. Gosden and Correll actually worked hard to find the best names. Amos and Andy were chosen partly because they were both short, four-letter words beginning with A and sounding euphonious. They were also names listeners could easily remember. Amos, a biblical name, was a good choice for a character described as a "trusting, simple, unsophisticated" individual, while Andy characterized a "domineering" and "lazy" personality.[2]

During 1928–29 *Amos 'n' Andy* was an immediate hit in the Chicago area. It was also a success in other parts of the country, which broadcast the recorded program. Because the comedians leased their series to over forty stations they were practically able to control the ten o'clock time slot. Their popularity in Chicago was noticed by William Benton, then assistant general manager of the Lord & Thomas advertising agency, which handled the Pepsodent toothpaste account. He suggested to Albert Lasker, president of Lord & Thomas, that *Amos 'n' Andy* should be sponsored by Pepsodent on a network. Excited by the idea, Lasker phoned NBC and learned that the network was anxious to sign the comedians rather than compete against them. The new network was also experiencing financial difficulties and needed a popular program on its schedule. NBC offered Gosden and Correll a lucrative contract, and they started broadcasting *Amos 'n' Andy* over the company's Blue network on August 19, 1929, approximately ten months before the stock market crash. A year later the Pepsodent-sponsored program was a national craze.

In many comedy shows, especially *Amos 'n' Andy*, the Depression was often the subject of a joke or a comic routine. Max Eastman has suggested in his study of humor that laughter can be interpreted as a "specific adaptation to . . . shocks and frustrations," and that a joke is often "composed of unpleasant experiences playfully enjoyed."[3] Since the transference of a serious matter to comedy tends to allay its consequences, joking about the crisis temporarily mollified the Depression's tragic implica-

tions for the listener. In their broadcasts radio comedians sometimes suggested simplified explanations for the economic collapse
that made the Depression's complexity suddenly understandable
to the average person.

References to the Depression appeared very frequently in the
early *Amos 'n' Andy* programs. On October 30, one day after
the stock market crash, the first Depression gag was used on the
show. Lightnin', an unemployed young man, has asked Andy for
a job with his taxi company:

ANDY   Well Lightnin', 'course I would like to give you a job
        but de bizness repression is on right now.

LIGHTNIN'   Whut is dat you say Mr. Andy?

ANDY   Is you been keepin' yo' eye on de stock market?

LIGHTNIN'   Nosah, I aint never seed it.

ANDY   Well, de stock market crashed.

LIGHTNIN'   Anybody git hurt?

ANDY   Well, 'course Lightnin', when de stock market crashes,
        it hurts us bizness men. Dat's whut puts de repression
        on things. . . .[4]

Their conversation suggests several ways in which the Depression gag could temporarily lessen the impact of the economic
crisis. First, a national calamity, the Great Crash, was the subject
of a joke: Lightnin's belief that an actual building collapsed and
injured people. By joking about a serious incident, Gosden and
Correll reduced its implication to a comic level. Second, Andy's
explanation of bad business conditions simplified a very complex
phenomenon—the exact reasons for the Depression. The Freud-
ian term "repression" in reference to the economic crisis was employed regularly on their programs and became a famous catch
phrase used by the public when speaking of the crisis. One newspaper editorial suggested that due to the collapse of private en-
terprise, "Amos and Andy's term 'repression' is a better one than
the one generally used—'depression.' "[5]

Four days later, the two devoted their entire broadcast to the
stock market crash. Margin, pooling, stock manipulation, and
tips were some of the subjects discussed. George (Kingfish) Stevens, a confidence man who had befriended the "boys," had lost
$800 in the crash. "Dey wiped me out," the Kingfish exclaimed

to Andy. "Yo' see, a week ago Thursday, de big crash started. De
bulls an' de bears was fightin' it out an' de bears chased de
bulls." The small investor was depicted as a victim of business
manipulation:

ANDY   Dem tips is hard to fit, aint dey?
KINGFISH Dey is hard to stay away from. Ev'ybody's got a tip.
ANDY   Good ones?
KINGFISH Bad ones. Ev'ybody knows de inside on de stocks, yo'
         see—dat's whut dey tell yo', so den you buy it an' it just
         look like dey waitin' fo' you to buy it, 'cause de minute
         you buy it, it goes down.
ANDY   Down where?
KINGFISH Well, if you buy a stock fo' so much money, de fust
         thing you know it gits cheaper, den you lose.
ANDY   Well, whut makes de stock go up?
KINGFISH Well, some o' dese big mens down on Wall Street git in
         a pool, an' when dey git behind de stocks, dey say dat's
         whut make it go up.[6]

Another major event of the Great Depression, President Roosevelt's closing of the banks, was the subject of an *Amos 'n' Andy*
program. After taking office Roosevelt issued a proclamation declaring a bank holiday. The banking crisis and the issuance of
scrip puzzled most Americans, who feared that their savings
were jeopardized. Gosden's and Correll's treatment of the situation on March 7, 1933, aimed to restore confidence in the government and the banking system. "Whut is dat new money?"
Lightnin' asked about scrip. "New money?" replied Andy. "I
cant even git ahold of none o' de OLD money." The Kingfish and
Andy convinced Lightnin' not to panic and believe in rumors.
Amos also confidently informed his friends that the bank holiday was "goin' bring back prosperity quicker dan ever." He
closed the program by declaring that

> de president of de United States is fightin' fo' more dan
> just 'mergency bankin' relief—he is workin' out a plan
> to have a system in de banks dat will not only he'p 'em
> now but will he'p 'em fo' all time to come, an' dis
> banker says dat dat's zackly whut's goin' happen an'
> Mr. Roosevelt means bizness, an' he's gittin' action, so

yo' see, dis bank holiday is really ⸱
country.

This humorous, reassuring explanation of ⸱
must have allayed listeners' fears. "People be⸱
den remarked. "When the banks closed in 19⸱
the situation, and we soon got a letter from ⸱⸱⸱⸱⸱
thanking us." The two performers aimed to cheer people up during the Depression.[7]

An optimistic belief that the crisis would soon be over was
voiced in the early *Amos 'n' Andy* programs. On the eve of Roosevelt's inauguration, Amos described the newly elected President
as a great leader who had the potential to end the Depression
and who was "goin' in office an' give ev'ything he's got to his
country." The program ended on a note of confidence:

KINGFISH An' if all de people will have de confidence in de country dat dey ought to have, ev'ything goin' be alright
pretty quick.

ANDY Yo' right about dat.

AMOS Tonight 'fore I go to bed I'se gonna pray dat Mr. Roosevelt will even do more fo' de country dan he's promised
to do.

The Roosevelt inauguration broadcast reaffirmed faith in the
country and its political process.[8]

The comedians also poked fun at the idea that the economic
crisis would be of short duration. When the purchase of a new
suit and pair of shoes convinced Andy that the business "repression" was over, Amos reminded his friend that business was still
bad at the taxi company. The false optimism of Hoover and the
bankers that "prosperity is just around the corner" was the subject of several gags on their program. In one episode Andy prepared a speech to be delivered before the Mystic Knights of the
Sea. "I might talk about de repression an' good times bein'
around de corneh," he said, "soon as I check up wid somebody
an' find out whut corneh 'tis. . . ."[9]

Radio comedy also relieved the decade's social tensions by the
reaffirmation of traditional American values. Faith in the work
ethic and individual success were often voiced on the programs.

ular form of home entertainment, radio acted as a strong
ale booster, supporting mores associated with the family and
raditional morality. Radio comedy reassured listeners that values identifiable with the American way of life were still vital
even though faith in the country's institutions was declining.
The Depression was depicted as a moral lesson, teaching and
reminding Americans of ideas associated with their heritage.[10]

Success, failure, and the problems of money were major
themes in the early *Amos 'n' Andy* scripts. As in *Sam 'n' Henry*,
the two leading characters had moved from the rural South
(where they had worked on a farm outside Atlanta, Georgia) to
a large Northern urban ghetto (first Chicago, then Harlem) in
order to obtain better jobs. We are going North, Andy told Amos,
where we can "make a lot o' money." They had an extremely
difficult time finding employment until Andy thought of an
idea to strike it rich:

ANDY De thing we gotta do is to git in some kind o' bizness so
we kin work fo' ourselves.

AMOS Whut kind o' bizness is we goin' git in?

ANDY I been tellin' yo—if we kin git a second hand automobile an' make a taxi-cab out of it, dat's de thing to do.

AMOS De trouble is though is to find dat second hand car.
Whut kind o' car would yo' buy?

ANDY Well, lemme see—

AMOS Yo' know-a—if you git a closed car, dey cost almost
twice as much as an open car cost.

ANDY You is right about dat, a'right.

AMOS I was talkin' to Sylvester today an' he say dat he knows
where we kin git a open car—but it aint got no top on it.

ANDY Aint got no top on it huh?

AMOS He say dat it's in good shape—got tires on it an' ev'y-
thing.

ANDY How much do de thing cost?

AMOS He say it dont cost much an' we kin buy it on time.

ANDY Well, dat sounds pretty good.

AMOS He say we might be able to git it widout payin' anything down on it.

ANDY But it aint got no top on it huh?

AMOS No, he say it aint got no top on it—dat's de trouble.

ANDY   Wait a minute—I got a idea.

AMOS   Whut is it, whut is it—'splain it to me.

ANDY   We kin start sumpin' new—be diff'ent dan anything else in de country—we kin clean up a fortune—make barrels o' money—be millionaires—have de biggest comp'ny in de world.

AMOS   Wait a minute—wait a minute—'splain dat to me—how we goin' do it?

ANDY   You say de car aint got no top on it.

AMOS   Dat's de trouble wid it—it aint got no top on it—but we kin git de car on time.

ANDY   We'll buy dat automobile an' start up a comp'ny called de Fresh Air Taxi Comp'ny.

AMOS   Boy, dat's a idea—Um—Um—de Fresh Air Company— Um—Um.[11]

Like so many small businesses during the Depression, the "Fresh Air Taxi Company of America, Incorpulated," was a precarious venture depending on one dilapidated convertible taxi bought for $25.00. A daily profit of $4.00 or $5.00 was a cause for celebration, but most often the two were in debt. Economic problems caused Amos to reflect nostalgically on his earlier life: "Sometime Andy, I wish I was back down in Georgia workin' fo' Mr. Williams, yo' know it. We didn't have a worry in de world den."[12] A major reason for the series' enormous popularity was that Amos's and Andy's worries reflected the problems of many Americans afflicted with unemployment and hunger during the Depression.

The serial's daily plots frequently concerned the pair's endeavors to make ends meet. Risky investments in a lunchroom, garage, hotel, and furniture store led to constant harassment by creditors. They became involved in law suits and failed to pay their income tax because they did not understand the form. Andy, a sucker for a fast buck, was victimized by phony salesmen and hucksters, especially by the Kingfish, who spent their money on wild schemes. The Kingfish, played by Gosden, first appeared on the broadcast of May 25, 1928, when he talked Amos and Andy into joining his fraternal lodge, the Mystic Knights of the Sea:

STEVENS   Well, gent'mens, I was talkin' to Brother Fred heah, yo' lan'lord, an' he was tellin' me dat you two boys ain't been in Chicago for long an' I thought it would be a nice thing to git you two boys in dat great fraternity known as Mystic Knights of de Sea.

ANDY   Whut is de name o' dat thing again?

STEVENS   De name of de fraternity, brothers, is de Mystic Knights of de Sea, of which I is de King-fish. . . . We all stick together so dat de Mystic Knights of de Sea is like one big family. Dey is all brothers.

AMOS   Dey is all brothers—Um—Um—ain't dat sumpin'.

ANDY   How many brothers is yo' got?

STEVENS   Well, we is got over 200 brothers dat we call sardines— den we has de officers—we has de Whale, de Sword-fish, de Cat-fish, an' de Shad.

ANDY   Ev'rybody's a fish huh?

STEVENS   Yes, every brother's a fish. We call de members sardines an' den each officer is a big fish. Now, de Whale, de Mackeral an' de catfish swims around de three chairs. I swim around de head chair—de big chair.

AMOS   Where do yo' hold de meetin's—in a swimmin' pool?

ANDY   Dont pay no 'tention to him Kingfish.

STEVENS   No, we talks jus' like we was in de water. De secketary of de lodge is known as de Shad an' de brother dat guards de door is de Swordfish.

ANDY   Do dey have meetin's an' ev'ything?

STEVENS   Oh brother—we has great meetin's. Whenever a sardine gits sick, de Jellyfish sees dat he gits plen'y to eat an' in case any of de Sardines die dey is buried wid fishly honors.

AMOS   Certainly do sound good to me—how much it cost?

ANDY   Wait a minute Amos—wait a minute.

STEVENS   Well, brothers I brought two application blanks wid me an' if you brothers would like to come into de Mystic Knights of the Sea, just sign dese two applications blanks an' gimme two dollars a piece down an' you kin pay de balance when you comes in fo' 'nitiation.[13]

The fast-talking Kingfish was one of the most memorable small-time swindlers in broadcasting history.

How to earn money and how to keep it out of the hands of

confidence men like the Kingfish dominated the early plots. Listeners facing similar problems in the 1930's readily identified with Amos's and Andy's predicaments. The way that the characters' hopes for monetary success were turned into business failures mirrored the lives of many Americans.

The serial was largely based on a clever contrast of the two central characters' opinion of work. On the first program Amos was introduced by the announcer as a "hard working little fellow who tries to do everything he can to help others and to make himself progress," while Andy was characterized as "not especially fond of hard work." The pompous Andy appointed himself president of the taxi company, while the industrious Amos was given the job as "chief mechanic's mate, fixer of automobile, head driver . . . and chief bizness gitter." Amos had a difficult time getting Andy to do any labor:

> AMOS   I thought you knowed by now dat if you is goin' git any money you is gotta work fo' it.
>
> ANDY   Well, Amos, I got so much on my mind, I just can't drive dat taxicab now.
>
> AMOS   Well, if you wanna make money, you better go to work den.[14]

Amos believed in the traditional American work ethic, an ideal he had inherited from his father: "My papa used to tell me dat yo' ain't never goin' git nuthin' dat yo' dont work fo'. Dis heah thing o' bein on Easy street might be alright—I dont know —but I always remember whut he say—if I ever git anything, I goin' have to work fo' it." Amos had an entirely different outlook than Andy on how to end the Depression:

> ANDY   People is comin' around wid a long face talkin' 'bout bizness an' when dey see me sittin' heah like dis all dressed up, dey goin' think de repression oveh—den dat news is goin' spread an' if I sit heah long enough I'll have ev'ybody thinkin' dat it IS oveh.
>
> AMOS   Yeh, but if you goin' sit heah an' aint goin' do nuthin' it aint goin' git over. Dont think it's goin' git over by hopin'—you gotta do sumpin' to he'p it git over.[15]

Amos viewed the Depression as a moral lesson reminding Americans of the basic values of diligence, saving, and generosity:

> Times like dese does a lot o' good 'cause when dis is over, which is bound to be, an' good times come back again, people's like us dat is livin' today is goin' learn a lesson an' dey goin' know whut a rainy day means. People is done always used de repression "I is savin' up fo' a rainy day" but dey didn't even know whut dey was talkin' bout. Now, when good times come back again people is gonna remember all dis an' know what a rainy day is—so maybe after all, dis was a good thing to bring people back to dey're senses an' sort a remind ev'ybody dat de sky AINT de limit.[16]

Many Americans shared Amos's belief that the carefree spending of the 1920's had precipitated the Depression and that the crisis would bring the country back to its senses.

The Thanksgiving broadcasts in 1930 and 1931 especially urged the importance of generosity during a time of economic hardship. Thanksgiving, said Amos, was a time to reflect on the "little things of life." One should be thankful that you have "a place to sleep" and "got sumpin' to eat" for "a lot o' people aint got dat right now." One should have faith that the Depression will soon be over: "Ev'ybody knows dat things is goin' git better an' dey WILL git better 'cause dis happens ev'vy few yeahs. . . ." Through the figure of Amos, Gosden and Correll reasserted the values of generosity, diligence, and unpretentiousness, mores many Americans wanted to return to at the time.[17]

The annual Christmas program, a popular feature, also stressed the importance of giving and sharing. Programs depicted Amos and Andy decorating their tree, buying presents, and celebrating the holiday in a convivial spirit:

> AMOS   Yo' know it's sumpin' bout Xmas time dat kind-a gits under yo' skin, yo' know it—sumpin' sweet about it.
>
> ANDY   Yeh, I like Xmas. . . . An' let's wish ev'ybody a merry Xmas.
>
> AMOS   An' a lot o' happiness 'cause if they have happiness

dey'll have a merry Xmas an' health an' ev'ything else.[18]

A highlight of the Christmas Eve program was Amos's recitation of the *Lord's Prayer* by the bedside of his daughter. Good will toward others was a perennial theme on the holiday broadcasts.

The importance of friendship was another value stressed in the series. Despite their disagreements, Amos and Andy were close friends and assisted one another in times of crisis. Their brotherly relationship was revealed in an early broadcast in which Amos criticized Andy for calling him stupid:

AMOS   De way you talks to me sometimes, makes me feel like I ain't nothin'. If I lissen to you all day long, I'll feel like jumpin' out de window or sumpin'. Why don't you say sumpin' good about me sometime?

ANDY   Come yere, Amos—come on now—don't feel that way. Ain't I yore buddy?

AMOS   You is my buddy a'right, Andy, an' I is yore buddy too, I hopes. . . .

ANDY   Amos, from now on, I goin' be better to you.

AMOS   I don't wants you to be better—I jest don't want you to call me no more names or say nothin' to me to hurt me, dat's all. I'll try to learn ev'ything as fast as I kin an' I'll work my haid off. I don't know whut is de matter wid me today—I'se jest kind of homesick, an' lonesome—I'se jest kind of down in de dumps, dat's all.

ANDY   Come on—put on yore hat—let's go out an' git some fresh air.

AMOS   I don't care—I'll walk around wid you an' git a little fresh air. But don't be mad wid me now 'cause I said dat—I jest had to git it off my chest, dat's all.

ANDY   Come on—we'll go down an' see a movin' pitcher show or sumpin'—dat'll make you feel better—put yore arm around me.

AMOS   I'se wid you—come on.[19]

The amity of Amos and Andy carried a special meaning during the time when hungry and unemployed Americans turned to friends and family for aid.

Radio comedy quickly became a popular form of middle-class

entertainment closely associated with the home. Comedy programs were generally aired during the evening hours when the
family gathered around its set to hear favorite shows. For millions of families, listening to *Amos 'n' Andy* was a nightly ritual.
In their first study of Middletown in 1929, the Lynds discovered
that radio was becoming an important necessity of family life
and "another means of standardizing many of Middletown's
habits." In their second study, made in 1937, the authors reported that radio had increased in popularity. Forty-six per cent
of Middletown homes had owned sets in 1930. The Lynds found
radio to be a "mild cohesive element in family life" because of
common listening participation. People across the country actually bought radios just to listen to *Amos 'n' Andy*. By January
1935 approximately 70 per cent of American homes had receivers, and radio had become a national pastime shared by millions
of listeners.[20]

One reason for the boom was that radio manufacturers realized
consumers had less money to spend during the Depression and
began producing inexpensive smaller sets called cathedral, compact, or Depression radios. In 1930 most of the 3.8 million receivers sold were costly consoles. Three years later 74 per cent
of the radios purchased were low-priced table models. In 1931,
the International Radio Corporation of Ann Arbor, Michigan,
introduced the Kadette, an inexpensive AC-DC set with a plastic
exterior. A deluxe Kadette model, advertised as "the world's
smallest 5-tube super-heterodyne chassis," cost $25 in 1933. One
could also buy a less expensive pocket-sized Kadette, Jr., for
$12.50—the "world's smallest AC-DC radio." Manufacturers
promoted low-cost radios for every room in the house. In May
1933 RCA listed a cathedral set (model R-28) for $19.95, and
General Electric advertised an AC-DC compact radio (model
K-40) for $17.95. The buying public with limited budgets were
attracted to the cheaper sets, which helped boost sales to 7.6 million in 1937.[21]

The low prices enabled middle-class families to purchase radios. In 1935, receivers were found in 90 per cent of homes having an annual family income over $10,000, but 85 per cent of
homes with incomes between $5000 to $10,000 also had sets.

Surveys taken between 1931 and 1933 showed that people in the
middle class *used* their radios more than people in upper-level
income brackets did. The wealthy, who could afford to go to
nightclubs or the theater, viewed the radio as just another household consumer item. The middle class, by contrast, depended
more heavily upon their sets for entertainment. That group
made up most of the mass audience for *Amos 'n' Andy*, a program that was closely associated with middle-class moral values.[22]

Newspaper editorials and articles praised the broadcast for its
"clean and wholesome patter" that presented lessons in the difference between right and wrong. Amos epitomized the virtues
of thrift and diligence, while Andy and the Kingfish indulged in
the vices of idleness and scheming. One editorial lamented that
the nation had too few Amos Joneses who put their money in
savings banks and too many Andy Browns who speculated in un-
sound business ventures. As long as *Amos 'n' Andy* is broadcast,
suggested another writer, "we can rest assured that the community is going to remain clean." A minister in a Middlewestern
church delivered a sermon drawing lessons from the two characters. The program's announcer, Bill Hay, once called Amos and
Andy "nationally loved characters with a homey philosophy that
attacks life problems in a way that interests, amuses, and in so
many cases helps."[23]

Listening to a program on a coast-to-coast hookup gave the
listener a sense of sharing a common experience with a national
audience. Network broadcasting, according to the Lynds, carried
"people away from localism" and gave "them direct access to the
more popular stereotypes in the national life." During the Depression loneliness was widespread, and radio tended to mitigate
the feeling of solitude. People shared with their friends the previous night's comedy jokes, and they often adopted the new language of radio comedy, especially catch phrases, in their everyday conversation. A popular, inexpensive form of entertainment
appealing to both urban and rural audiences, radio helped knit
the nation together.[24]

One result of this phenomenon was a strong listener identification, which propelled radio comedy personalities to national

fame. Gosden and Correll were among the new success heroes of the 1930's. A 1931 newspaper article listed them, along with Will Rogers, Charles Lindbergh, and boxer Gene Tunney, as the country's "public gods." During the Depression they fulfilled a need among Americans for new heroes. In 1929 the comedians were guests of Herbert Hoover, an avid fan of their program, and they exchanged jokes with the President at the White House for over an hour. Syndicated biographies of their lives extolled their sudden rise from obscurity to fame. Their annual income— over $125,000 each, which included royalties from an *Amos 'n' Andy* candy bar and from a toy model of the Fresh-Air Taxicab —was phenomenal, considering the hard times. Known as "the great America disease," the *Amos 'n' Andy* craze was not limited to their broadcasts. They were greeted by thousands on coast-to-coast tours in cities that staged lavish welcoming parades, and their stage performances were sold out nightly. Wherever they went people crowded around them to shake hands. "The reasons for the overwhelming success of *Amos 'n' Andy* are not hard to find," stated one editorialist. "They combine in simple manner, the fundamental appeals to the human heart and mind. . . . The average radio listener recognizes in the day-by-day affairs of *Amos 'n' Andy* shades of his own triumphs and defeats, joys and sorrows, reactions and reasonings."[25]

Amos 'n' Andy was the most popular show on the air during the 1930–31 and 1931–32 seasons, when it was estimated that its audience reached as many as forty million listeners. Approximately one-third of the nation was then listening to the broadcast. Because of its enormous popularity the program affected various aspects of American life. The telephone company claimed that calls declined during the show's fifteen minutes on the air (7 to 7:15 p.m.). Motion picture theaters installed loudspeakers in lobbies and stopped whatever film was being shown so that fans could hear the program over a radio placed on the stage. On warm summer evenings the voices of Amos and Andy were heard from open windows. Lowell Thomas believed his initial popularity as a newscaster was due to the fact that his program preceded *Amos 'n' Andy*. "America would tune me in to wait for *Amos 'n' Andy*," Thomas admitted. Between 1929 and

1935 the entire nation seemed addicted to the program, from the poor, who listened in front of store windows, to the wealthy Vincent Astor and Henry Ford, each of whom sat listening to it in his plush living room. "There are three things which I shall never forget about America—the Rocky Mountains, Niagara Falls, and *Amos 'n' Andy,*" said the playwright George Bernard Shaw.[26]

The program dramatically boosted Pepsodent sales and had a major effect on convincing sponsors that radio advertising could increase consumption of marketable items. Bill Hay, who used a low-key style, became noted for the toothpaste plug: "Use Pepsodent twice a day, see your dentist twice a year." "I wish I had a penny for every tube that sold," the announcer joked. One Friday night he wanted to test the slogan so he reversed the plug: "Use Pepsodent twice a year, see your dentist twice a day." The sponsor received thousands of letters on Monday morning. After the opening theme ("The Perfect Song," from *The Birth of a Nation*) played on an organ, Hay introduced the performers: "Here they ah, Amos 'n' Andy." The popularity of Pepsodent and *Amos 'n' Andy* was the subject of a 1931 *New Yorker* illustration by the artist Reginald Marsh. Marsh showed a mass of people praying under a clock tower at 7. Above them were Amos and Andy dressed as angels. Over the two characters' heads was a banner with the words "Brush Your Teeth Night & Morning, Consult Your Dentist Twice a Year." The success of *Amos 'n' Andy* helped NBC financially. The network grossed $150 million in 1929, mostly from advertising. In 1930 NBC began charging sponsors $3350 an hour on the Blue network and $4980 an hour on the Red network.[27]

When NBC moved the broadcast from 11 p.m. to 7 p.m. Eastern Standard Time a massive protest erupted. The network made the change in 1929 because East Coast listeners complained that eleven o'clock was too late to hear their favorite program and that children would not go to bed until they heard *Amos 'n' Andy.* The new time angered listeners in the Midwestern, Rocky Mountain, and Far Western states. They sent telegrams and letters opposing the rescheduling. California listeners wrote that they missed the broadcast because they were still working at 4 p.m.

Kansas City citizens welcomed Gosden and Correll on June 14, 1929, with a Fresh-Air Taxicab Parade. A prize of $100 was awarded to the winning entry.

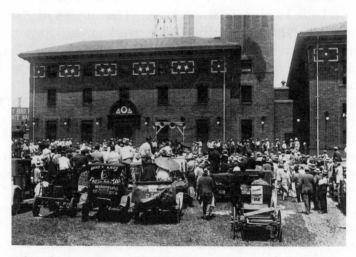

After the parade Gosden and Correll broadcast *Amos 'n' Andy* from the *Kansas City Star*'s office building, headquarters of WDAF. The crowd heard the show over loudspeakers in the courtyard.

Long lines gathered in front of the Los Angeles Pantages Theatre in 1929 to see Gosden and Correll impersonate Amos and Andy on stage. (All three photographs courtesy of the Department of Special Collections, Doheny Library, University of Southern California, Los Angeles. *Amos 'n' Andy* Collection.)

The Secretary of State of Colorado, Charles M. Armstrong, sent
the following telegram to the Pepsodent Company:

> On behalf of the 115 employes of the secretary of
> state's office, and several hundred other employes of the
> state of Colorado, I ask you to reconsider the time of
> broadcasting Amos and Andy which under the new
> schedule, brings it to the Rocky Mountain region at 5
> p.m. This does not allow them to enjoy this program,
> and one hour later would be greatly appreciated by all
> who have followed this most interesting entertainment
> and program.[28]

Other angry fans telephoned their local station and some threatened not to buy Pepsodent toothpaste. Because of the furor Gosden and Correll decided to do a second live broadcast three hours
later for listeners on the West Coast. It eventually became common practice for radio comedians to do two live programs.

Fans were constantly caught up in the soap opera plots of the
daily broadcasts. When Amos's fiancée, Ruby Taylor, lay ill with
pneumonia the performers received thousands of letters praying
for her recovery. For days listeners did not know if she would
live. When she started improving and was finally fully recovered, listeners sent in letters of congratulations. Sacks of telegrams were received at the Pepsodent offices urging Amos not to
deposit his life savings into the Kingfish's Great Home Bank,
which invested money in horse races. Some threatened never to
listen to the program again and to boycott Pepsodent toothpaste.

In October 1931 Amos was falsely charged with murder and
put on trial. Fans avidly followed the trial nightly on their radios
and read about it in the daily newspapers. Amos was probably
going to be convicted, to the great worry of forty million listeners. Albert Lasker told the comedians: "The country's mad! The
Parent-Teacher Association is going to boycott the program if
Amos is found guilty." On the broadcast of October 22, an alarm
clock suddenly sounded just as the jury foreman was delivering
the verdict. Amos had been dreaming the entire episode. "That's
how we got out of that," Correll remarked. It "was a dirty trick
but we had to do it—we had to get out of it someway." Gosden

and Correll were masters at creating suspenseful situations that got listeners involved with the characters.[29]

The comedians liked inventing two- and three-week story lines with surprise endings. The most publicized episode concerned Madame Queen's breach of promise suit against Andy. Madame Queen, the owner of a Harlem beauty shop, sued Andy for breaking their agreement to marry. During December 1931 listeners sat glued to their sets waiting to hear the outcome of the trial, which lasted for two weeks on the air. The daily proceedings provided diversion for a nation trapped in the worst economic disaster in its history. In order to make the trial as realistic as possible the comedians read law books and newspaper trial accounts, and they received advice on trial procedure from A. L. Ashby, vice president and general counsel of NBC. The courtroom scenes, in which Gosden and Correll played all the parts, kept the huge radio audience in suspense. Just as Andy was about to be convicted, Madame Queen screamed and fainted. The broadcast then went off the air for the weekend. On Monday anxious listeners learned that she had spotted her husband, whom she believed had been lost at sea, sitting in the back of the courtroom. The judge dismissed the breach of promise suit, to the satisfaction of millions across the country who did not want Andy to go to jail.[30]

The fifteen-minute broadcasts were written by Gosden and Correll, a phenomenal feat considering that the show was aired five or six times a week and totaled 4090 episodes. (Not until 1943, when the program became half an hour in length, did they hire writers.) They either wrote the script the day of the broadcast or two or three days in advance. The comedians preferred working under pressure of a deadline, and the pair felt the material sounded more spontaneous if written at the last minute. They wrote the scripts in an office located in Chicago's Palmolive Building. Their personalities contrasted well. Correll was easygoing and patient, while Gosden was a quick thinker and full of nervous energy. He would pace up and down the floor dictating the dialogue, nervously flipping coins in the air. Gosden drew on the Negro dialect he had heard in Virginia and other parts of the South. Sitting at a desk with his coat off and tie loosened,

Correll, who had once been a stenographer, typed the script, making an original and a carbon copy, approximately four pages long and containing 1500 to 2000 words. The time it took to complete a script varied considerably. They once wrote an episode in twenty-five minutes, but a script session generally averaged three or four hours, while a difficult passage of dialogue sometimes took longer.[31]

Because they knew the characters so well, the two felt it was unnecessary to rehearse the script. They also believed that rehearsals might make their delivery mechanical. The dialogue was written as it was pronounced over the air, so the two mainly followed the script and rarely ad-libbed. "We read every word we ever said," Correll once remarked. The studio was located in Chicago's Merchandise Mart and furnished like a comfortable living room with stuffed chairs and a fireplace. There was no live audience for their broadcasts in Chicago, nor was anyone allowed in the studio. "We did not want people sitting with long faces in front of us," said Correll.[32]

During the broadcast they sat at a table opposite one another. The microphone was placed near Correll's right elbow, and to imitate Andy the actor spoke in a low voice approximately one inch from the mike. When he was impersonating Amos, Gosden sat about two feet from the microphone, using a high-pitched voice. To do Sylvester he inched closer to the microphone and spoke in an extremely soft tone. Gosden not only did the Kingfish but also Lightnin' and other minor parts. Correll played Henry Van Porter, Brother Crawford, and most of the white characters. In order to avoid laughing, they tried not to look at one another during the program. The comedians were not always successful, and, at one broadcast, Gosden had to pour a glass of water on himself to stop giggling.[33]

In the early days Gosden and Correll did their own sound effects. The comedians went to great lengths to recreate the proper noises, including breaking glasses and dishes and lighting cigarettes. On one show they had to pretend that Amos and Andy were being chased by robbers, so before air time they ran around the studio for three minutes until they were out of breath. For the closing fadeout the two slowly walked away from the table as they said their final lines.[34]

The program's catch phrases and malapropisms became national sayings used by millions of people. "I'se regusted" was often employed by Americans during the Depression when facing a difficult situation. At company meetings executives discussed "propolitions" and the possibility of being "Incorpulated." Other terms used in daily conversations were "check and double check," "ain't dat sumpin'," "sitchiation," "sho, sho," and "awah, awah, awah." The characters had pet expressions, like Andy's "Buzz me, Miss Blue" and Kingfish's "Holy Mackerel, Andy." The names of well-known people were mangled— "J. Ping-Pong Morgan" and "Charles Limburger." Amos 'n' Andyisms became part of everyday speech. One newspaper article published in 1930 suggested that the program was changing the American language.[35]

Letters from listeners reveal that *Amos 'n' Andy* had become an integral part of their daily lives. People depended on the broadcast for uplift and amusement. One particular letter illustrates how the program could alleviate personal and economic problems:

> For nearly a year we have tuned in every night except Wednesday on the joys and sorrows of the two belovedest of all radio stars, and there never has been a time when our hearts have not been a little lighter and our sleep a bit sweeter for having listened.
>
> Last winter over a stretch of days when life was a rather grim thing indeed, Amos and Andy provided the one "High Spot" of the struggle. We always knew that however bewildering the day might be, there was a momentary escape from it all at 10 P.M. when for ten delicious minutes we could lose ourselves utterly in the antics of this delightful pair.
>
> Amos and Andy have truly been part of our lives. In fact we can hardly conceive of a schedule of living in which they fail to figure. Each member of the family religiously chose Wednesday night for "stepping out" as otherwise it only meant having to tear frantically away from some other "doings" in order to reach home

in good time to hear The Boys. No event was sufficiently
thrilling to warrant passing up an episode.

We cannot soon forget how much Amos and Andy have
contributed to our happiness. There is no service higher
than that which helps take the drudgery out of difficult
lives. We have chuckled over Andy's never-failing mag-
nificence and his colossal ability as a business man. We
have been inspired by the high aims and rigid honesty
of Amos, and we have all been close to tears at times
when real trials and tribulations beset either of our beloved friends.[36]

Another letter to Gosden and Correll suggests that *Amos 'n'
Andy* was a frequent topic of conversation among fellow listeners. The writer wrote down the various comments she had heard
at work the day after a broadcast:

> Say Bill did you hear Amos & Andy last night? Hell yes
> I'm glad Amos is finely [*sic*] waking up.
>
> Hello Grace, did you wait up for the two funny guys?
> Sure we always turn the radio off after they are through.
>
> You know, I was so darn tired last night I went to bed
> at 8:30, but I got up & turned the radio on at 10 o'clock
> to hear Amos & Andy.
>
> Say who the Hell is this Amos & Andy your all talking
> about, guess I'll have to buy one of them infernal ma-
> chines & find out.
>
> You know I get so—dam mad. I like to hear Amos &
> Andy at 10 o'clock but that dam man of mine always
> wants to tune on the Tribune at that time. I've a notion
> to buy another radio & put it in the cellar where I can
> tune it where I dam please.[37]

Sharing the previous night's *Amos 'n' Andy* broadcast gave listeners a feeling of common participation.

In radio's early years a show devoted to describing black life
was a major breakthrough, even if white impersonators were

used. Gosden and Correll made research trips to Harlem, where
they talked to people on the streets and visited poolrooms, barber
shops, and cigar stores in search of subject matter. Dots on a map
of Harlem in their office indicated the exact location of important places in the show.[38]

Newspaper publicity articles described *Amos 'n' Andy*'s appeal to a cross section of the black population. The comedians
were invited to address black professional organizations such as
the Urban League and Chicago's Du Sable Club. At 7 p.m. in
Harlem many people rushed home to turn on their set or listened
in front of radio stores. The next day listeners gathered on Harlem street corners to discuss the broadcast. In a letter to the
Chicago *Daily News*, a black writer defended the program:

> I have never yet been able to detect anything of a preju-
> dicial or harmful nature in any of their skits. . . .
>
> I have traveled extensively to all parts of this country
> and at the present time I spend five days each month in
> some city among my own Negro people. So I think I am
> qualified to state that all of the characters portrayed by
> Correll and Gosden are true to life.[39]

Like *Sam 'n' Henry*, *Amos 'n' Andy* did perpetuate certain
negative caricatures of black Americans. The central characters
were usually depicted as gullible and foolish individuals who got
into ridiculous predicaments. The minor characters particularly
had stereotyped traits: there was the scheming Kingfish, the lazy
and stupid Lightnin', and the domineering Madame Queen.
However, as in *Sam 'n' Henry*, the characters were presented
sympathetically, and Gosden and Correll had no conscious inten-
tions of insulting black listeners. Some blacks certainly felt the
series mocked their race, but it was too early for a massive protest. The widespread popularity of the serial partly served to
make the show initially acceptable.

Only the most vocal and outraged critics attacked the serial's
stereotypes in the 1930's. One critique resulted in an unsuccess-
ful attempt to censor the program in 1931. The Pittsburgh *Courier*, a black weekly newspaper, led a campaign to have the Fed-

eral Radio Commission ban the show. Three basic reasons were
given for the action:

1. Exploitation of Negroes for white commercial gain.
2. Portrayal of characters detrimental to the self-respect
   and general advancement of the race.
3. Placing business activities among Negroes in a harm-
   ful light.[40]

Although supporters claimed to have up to three hundred thousand signatures on their petition, the *Courier*'s campaign failed
to draw mass support. Most members of the black community
rallied behind Gosden and Correll. The Chicago *Defender*, another black newspaper, attacked the *Courier*'s position, declaring
that *Amos 'n' Andy* was a valuable program for all races. The
Defender invited the two performers to entertain 30,000 black
children at a city picnic. The *Courier* lashed out at the *Defender*
for its Uncle Tomism, but by late 1931 it was clear that most
black people wanted *Amos 'n' Andy* to remain on the air. Not
until the rise of the civil rights movement in the early 1950's
was the program denounced by a majority of black people.

Amos 'n' Andy* served more positive social and psychological
needs than negative ones during the Great Depression. Humorous references to the economic crisis allowed listeners to laugh at
their problems. *Amos 'n' Andy* reaffirmed the traditional values
of the work ethic, success, and friendship. The program was
closely associated with middle-class morality, and people viewed
it as clean family entertainment. During the troubled times
Americans needed to be reassured that time-honored values still
existed. Listening to *Amos 'n' Andy* temporarily helped to relieve personal and economic hardships.

4

Radio's Court Jester

Will Rogers's radio talks were also popular during the Great Depression. The cowboy humorist had become interested in radio in the 1920's. His first broadcast was from the Pittsburgh *Post* studio of station KDKA, probably some time in early 1922. A photograph of Rogers, standing casually in front of a microphone with his hands in his pockets, with his wife, Betty, at the piano, was printed on the front cover of KDKA's newspaper, *Radio Broadcasting News*, on March 26, 1922. Several *Ziegfeld Follies* girls, who also appear in the photograph, presumably joined Rogers in the broadcast. Since KDKA often used the photograph for publicity purposes and no transcript of Rogers's remarks exists, the humorist's first broadcast might have occurred earlier. He probably delivered a monologue discussing the day's headlines, a routine similar to his vaudeville repertoire. Rogers's informal chat was heard only in a small area by listeners owning crystal sets. His appearance on KDKA at the dawn of early broadcasting signaled his interest in the new form of entertainment.[1]

In the 1920's Rogers, a *Ziegfeld Follies* headliner, was famous for his topical monologue, and because of his popularity he was frequently engaged as a banquet speaker. Several of his after-dinner talks in New York City were broadcast. Newark's pioneer station, WJZ, aired his remarks at the 1923 Newspaper Publishers Association banquet at the Waldorf-Astoria. His next speech

59

was scheduled for September 16, 1925, but there were difficulties. The entertainer had planned to address the second annual
Radio Industries banquet over a twelve-station hookup. Officials
learned a few hours before the dinner, however, that he could
not perform. Two representatives of the organization rushed to
New York City's New Amsterdam Theatre, where Rogers was
appearing on stage. Feeling the humorist had withdrawn because of lack of payment, they offered him a large sum for his
fifteen-minute talk. Rogers explained that the problem was not
financial, for he had signed a concert-tour contract empowering
his manager to prevent public appearances. But he did not want
to disappoint the organizers and promised to find a way out of
the situation. Rogers thought for a moment, scratched his head,
rubbed his cheek, and grinned. He would attend the broadcast
as scheduled and explain why he was not permitted to speak.[2]

Rogers's talk, heard by over one thousand guests at the Com-
modore Hotel and thousands more on the radio, lampooned the
incident preventing his appearance:

> I have been forbidden to make a speech to you over
> the radio by my manager who I am soon to start on a
> concert tour for. He figures if you ever heard me once
> you would never want to hear me again. But I wanted
> to come and explain to you in person and show you that
> it is a bigger disappointment to me than to you because
> when you make an actor keep his mouth shut he is in
> pain. It's like an after-dinner speaker going to a banquet
> and not being called upon.

He then began to needle the members of the radio trade by poking fun at the strange whistling sounds heard over the airwaves
during the medium's fledgling years:

> I don't know what this dinner is for. Somebody stung
> some sucker with a new radio set and said let's have a
> dinner. Never mind a dinner, get rid of the static. A
> dinner is all right for those of you here, but how about
> the millions that tune in and all they hear is—whistle—
> ooooooooo—whistle. . . .

He ended the talk by ribbing political dignitaries and jesting about national affairs. The humorist received an ovation when he concluded his remarks.[3]

Rogers appeared on other programs during radio's first decade. Several stations carried his comments on current events during the broadcast of the Coolidge–Davis 1924 presidential election results. He also did guest spots on the *Eveready Hour* and on the premier broadcast of the National Broadcasting Company. His monologue on the latter program, entitled "Fifteen Minutes with a Diplomat," described his travels in Europe and the West, and his visit with President Coolidge at the White House. The NBC inaugural broadcast spectacular impressed him tremendously. The entertainer realized that over a national hookup he could reach audiences who had never seen him on stage. "Radio is too big a thing to be out of," he remarked after the broadcast.[4]

On January 4, 1928, Rogers was involved in an even more ambitious broadcasting project—he performed on the *Dodge Victory Hour*, a transcontinental hookup of forty-five stations. (It cost $1000 a minute.) The humorist broadcast from his home in Beverly Hills, where as master of ceremonies he introduced Paul Whiteman's orchestra in New York City, the actor Fred Stone in Chicago, and Al Jolson in New Orleans. Since Chicago was the center of the hookup, Rogers's family, sitting in the next room, heard his voice transmitted there and back in less than a second. Rogers also wore headphones so he could listen to Whiteman play George Gershwin's "Rhapsody in Blue" and Jolson croon "Mammy" and "California, Here I Come." The entertainer surprised thousands of listeners by delivering a talk imitating Calvin Coolidge's State of the Union message. The President had just returned from a trip to the Midwest, where farmers were asking for relief from falling prices. Puckering his lips to mimic Coolidge's Vermont twang, Rogers reported on the nation's economic state:

> Ladies and Gentlemen: It's the duty of the President to deliver a message to the people on the condition of the country. I am proud to report that the condition of the country as a whole is prosperous. I don't mean by that

the whole country is prosperous. But as a Hole it's prosperous. That is it is prosperous for a Hole. There is not a "hole" lot of doubt about that.[5]

Rogers's play on "whole" delighted listeners, and his imitation was so effective that many believed Coolidge had actually been on the air.

In his talk Rogers also commented on various issues of the day. On farm relief: "Fill a Farmer up, that will stop him from hollering quicker 'n anything." On Prohibition: "Prohibition is GOING DOWN about as well as usual." On foreign debts: "I am sorry to state that they are just as Foreign as ever, if not more so." On Secretary of the Treasury Andrew Mellon: "Mellon has saved some money, for the country, and done very well for himself. He is the only Treasury that has saved faster than Congress could divide it up."[6]

Although Rogers's imitation of Coolidge was generally well received, a few listeners criticized him for mimicking the President. The humorist sent a note to Coolidge explaining that his talk should be taken as good fun. The President's reply indicated he was not perturbed by the issue:

> I hope it will cheer you up to know that I thought the matter of rather small consequence myself though the office was informed from several sources that I had been on the air. I wish to assure you that your note makes it all plain that you had no intention save harmless amusement.
>
> I hope you will not give the affair another troubled thought. I am well aware how nicely you have referred to me so many times.

Rogers publicly thanked the President for his gracious letter in his newspaper column:

> I knew my man before I joked about him. It's as I have often said: You can always joke goodnaturedly a big man, but be sure he is a big man before you joke about him.

Famous for his jibes at leading politicians, Rogers believed that important people in the limelight liked to feel themselves capable of accepting a little ribbing.[7]

Although Rogers was enthusiastic about radio, he felt awkward in the new medium. On stage he relied on lasso tricks and other props and devices to break up his monologue, but in the broadcasting studio he had to stand still in front of the mike. The microphone reminded him of an automobile radiator cap: "I was afraid the thing was going to bite me all the time." Rogers was also troubled by the lack of a live audience in early radio. He was a trained stage performer, dependent on audience response for the timing of his jokes and to measure his effectiveness. His infectious grin, casual manner, and other stage mannerisms were indispensable to his repertoire. In the theater a performer knew his public, said Rogers, but "you got every known specie in the world" in radio's invisible audience. For those reasons he called the medium "the toughest test a comedian has."[8]

On his broadcasts Rogers often poked fun at the radio entertainer's inability to discern his audience. "I don't know whether I am any good until I see whether they have sold any gas or not," jested the humorist, whose programs were sponsored by the Gulf Oil Company from 1933 to 1935. "Imagine some performer standing up in front of the radio broadcasting, you know, for one of these cemetery associations, see, and he don't know how funny he is until he finds out how many people died and bought lots that week." In order to overcome those difficulties Rogers insisted that live audiences attend his Gulf broadcasts, and in them he continued to use facial expressions to prompt laughter. When some listeners at home complained that they missed the jokes, Rogers apologized for playing to the studio audience, explaining how important they were to his style.[9]

Rogers did not worry about the length of his repertoire on stage, even though programs were planned according to tight schedules. Accustomed to talking in a rambling style, he had difficulty in timing his radio monologue. *The Gulf Show* was a half-hour Sunday evening program which began at 9 p.m. After musical entertainment by the Al Goodman Orchestra and the singing of the Revelers Quartet, Rogers was allotted twelve to fifteen minutes for his comic monologue. In order to finish on time the humorist started using an alarm clock on his second Gulf broadcast on May 7, 1933:

> The hardest thing over this radio is to get me stopped.
> I never know when to stop. So, tonight, I got me a clock
> here. . . . I have the alarm clock timed. When that
> alarm goes off, I am going to stop, that is all there is to
> it. I don't care whether I am in the middle of reciting
> Gunga Din or the Declaration of Independence, I am
> going to stop when that rings.

For some reason the alarm never sounded. He joked about the
blunder on the next program:

> If the thing don't go off today, I am through with Big
> Bens, that is all. In fact, I got two alarm clocks. I got
> another one. I am the only radio man that carried his
> own spare—alarm clock.[10]

The clock eventually became a running gag on his Gulf broadcasts. Often the alarm went off in the middle of a joke: "Oh,
Lord! There goes that thing. Darn that thing. I wasn't through
yet. The darn thing worked today." At other times he would an-
ticipate the alarm sounding before he finished his monologue:

> This thing is going to go off in a minute, and I'd like to
> finish with a joke before it went off, but I think it's go-
> ing to go off before I can think of a joke. (Laughter—
> alarm.) See—there it goes. I know it would. Well, so
> long anyhow. Good-bye. (Applause.)

The humorist joked that the timepiece, which became known as
"Will Rogers's famous alarm clock," woke up listeners who had
fallen asleep during his monologue.[11]

Rogers enjoyed posing as a natural comedian whose wit was
spontaneous. On the program he talked about his ad-lib style and
how he did not need a prepared script:

> I just gab away here. I don't have anything written
> down, you know, like I should have. All my friends,
> they come here all prepared with their stuff written
> down. I know it is the proper way to do, and you can do
> it better. I repeat and forget, and everything. That is
> what I do.

"Another reason I do not write it down—if I ever read what I
wrote down, I would be ashamed to read it," he further re-

marked. Although Rogers had attended school for approximately ten years, and he wrote books, magazine articles, and a daily newspaper column, he conveyed to the public the image of an uneducated cowboy.[12]

Rogers's casual appearance at his broadcasts suggested that his routine was extemporaneous. Dressed in a rumpled blue serge suit, with his hair slightly disheveled, he stood nonchalantly before the microphone with his hands in his pockets and talked in an informal, friendly manner. In front of him was an empty stand that would have normally contained a script. He often chewed gum, a habit he had developed on the stage. During one broadcast he asked "Has anybody got any chewing gum? Any of the choir got any chewing gum? You are going to get a rotten act if you haven't got any gum."[13]

His reputation for appearing at the studio a few minutes before broadcast time also contributed to Rogers's seemingly impromptu style. He once missed the opening minutes of a show because he was playing in a polo match. When a friend reminded him of the broadcast Rogers replied, "I believe it is, sure enough. Say! I guess I'd better get downtown and see what I can do about it." J. Franklin Drake, president of the Gulf Oil Company, was in the audience and volunteered to substitute for Rogers. The executive was relating a story on the air when the entertainer rushed through the theater door, thanked Mr. Drake, and started delivering his monologue as if nothing out of the ordinary had happened. Rogers's easygoing attitude added to his reputation as an ad-lib comedian whose humor was off the cuff.[14]

In fact, he devoted considerable time and preparation to his radio program because he was concerned about entertaining an invisible audience. Rogers wrote his own material in advance of the broadcast and was reluctant to hire comedy writers. When a prominent gag man offered to write his show for $1000 a week the humorist rejected the offer, stating that he would write the comedy writer's material for the same salary. Rogers would spend a week developing topics for his Sunday talk. On Monday morning, he read many newspapers and magazines representing different editorial opinions in order to obtain contrasting ideas on current affairs. In the studio on Wednesday he tested a tenta-

66

tive repertoire before several groups of friends in order to judge their reactions. He then sat down at his typewriter and, in a slow hunt-and-peck system, typed out his monologue. That rough draft, which never appeared at his broadcasts, served as the basis for his talk. His remarks over the air sometimes closely followed the draft; at other times Rogers ad-libbed from subjects in his notes. Thinking the quips came from the entertainer's hip pocket, the audience never knew that he had prepared all week for the broadcast.[15]

Rogers's style might have seemed improvised, but he was actually an experienced professional comedian. He had been in show business since 1902, when he had joined Texas Jack's Wild West Show in South Africa as a trick roper and rider. In 1916, as a *Ziegfeld Follies* star, he had discovered he could make audiences laugh by cracking timely jokes. In the early twentieth century the writer Finley Peter Dunne had created "Mr. Dooley," an Irish saloonkeeper who shrewdly satirized contemporary affairs. Stage comedians, however, had not yet achieved wide success with topical humor. At the 1916 Friars Club Frolic, Rogers had jested about Woodrow Wilson's order dispatching United States troops into Mexico in pursuit of Pancho Villa's forces. The President, who attended the affair, had laughed with the rest of the audience. Rogers was pleased by the success of this response, and, at the suggestion of his wife, he began using topical jokes in his routine at the *Midnight Frolics* on the New Amsterdam Roof and as a regular performer with the *Ziegfeld Follies*.

The entertainer's monologue was not highlighted by one-liners, but by wry insightful comments on the day's news.

> Personally, I don't like the jokes that get the biggest laughs. . . . I like one where, if you are with a friend, and hear it, it makes you think, and you nudge your friend and say, "he's right about that."

The headlines were an endless source of comedy material, an asset to the radio comedian who could not repeat well-worn jokes to a regular listening audience. "Now tonight all I know is this—just what little I read in the papers during the day," Rogers stated often on his programs.[16]

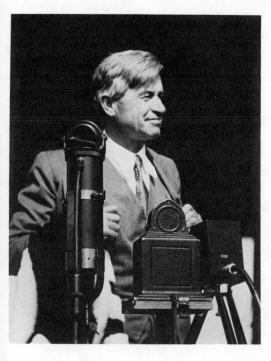

Will Rogers speaking on radio at the dedication of the Kellogg Arabian Horse Ranch, May 17, 1932. He called the large microphones "hub caps." "I was afraid the thing was going to bite me all the time," the humorist said.

(Courtesy, Will Rogers Memorial Commission, Claremore, Oklahoma.)

Will Rogers broadcasting for Gulf in the early 1930's. Although the empty script stand suggests that Rogers's jokes were extemporaneous, he actually prepared all week for his broadcast.

A typical radio monologue consisted of a potpourri of ironic commentaries on current events. Rogers liked to roam from topic to topic, jesting on one broadcast about the New Deal, farm relief, international debts, the Hoover Dam, Mother's Day, and Greta Garbo. He also could get considerable mileage out of a controversial subject. Governmental plans to improve the economy during the Great Depression became a "running topic" on consecutive programs in 1935.

He occasionally devoted an entire broadcast to a single subject, as he did in his famous Mother's Day program on May 12, 1935. In an earlier (1930) broadcast, Rogers had praised American mothers for their hard work, but his later program poked fun at the holiday's commercialism. Florists, he stated, were "keeping open this evening just to accommodate late consciences." Although flowers were a nice gesture, "you can't eat 'em," he joked. He instead recommended giving a more practical gift—a ham or some pork chops. A family man, Rogers liked the idea of honoring mothers, and he suggested sending them a different present monthly instead of annually. His Mother's Day address illustrated his habit of discoursing at length on topics having wide appeal.[17]

One reason for the humorist's enormous popularity was his ability to select subjects that were interesting to the average listener. Sports was one of Rogers's favorite topics. He enjoyed riding horses, roping calves, and playing polo, and he talked about those activities on his program. He also often made references to the athletic skills of such sports heroes as Dizzy Dean and Jim Thorpe, and he participated in a special memorial tribute to the football coach Knute Rockne over a national hookup. On several programs he discussed the players in the 1935 Alabama-Stanford Rose Bowl contest. Another popular broadcast described a mock football game between the United States and Europe. Imitating sports announcer Graham McNamee, Rogers used the game to comment about current financial problems, especially the questions of international debt payments and the gold standard. According to Rogers, economic rivalry between nations was like a football contest. "Ah, the Americans are in a huddle now!" he exclaimed:

> They're singing the blues. Now they're out of the huddle. They shift over to the left. It's a pass! No it ain't! It's a fake play! It's a variation of the old inflation crisscross, but Europe's diagnosed the play. Europe's got 'em figured out, and we can't gain an inch. We were held when the gold was changing hands.

Rogers ended the broadcast with Senator Carter Glass running for a touchdown:

> There's little Carter Glass. He's got the ball and he's in the open. Oh boy, he's streaking it down that field! Look at him go! He's shaken out England. He's dodged France. It's a touchdown! And the whistle blows for the end of the game!

Among the many letters Rogers received praising the talk was one from the Senator, who had written to say how much he had enjoyed the program.[18]

Over the years the entertainer had developed certain devices to make audiences laugh. His carefully timed delivery, alternating between short and long pauses, had a certain rhythm. Rogers often chuckled after a joke to stimulate the audience. He also liked to surprise listeners by appearing serious about a topic and then suddenly making the subject the butt of a jest. Subtlety was another key to his style. The best "thing about a joke is to make it look like it was not a joke," Rogers declared.[19]

By underplaying his comic remarks he was at liberty to comment upon any sacrosanct subject. This stance enabled him to play the role of the nation's court jester, who could freely rib famous personalities and satirize public issues. Rogers's ability to make fun of pomposity and hypocrisy appealed to the average listener, who enjoyed hearing "big men" cut down to size. "Will in his day could ridicule anything . . . to death," Fred Allen recalled. Rogers's dry humor was laced with a sharp sense of irony that could expose the absurdity of governmental bureaucracy:

> I see by the papers this morning that they are going to change the name of Hoover Dam. That is the silliest thing I ever heard of in politics. They are going to take

the name of Hoover away from that dam. Lord, if they
feel that way about it, I don't see why they don't just
transfer the two names.[20]

Rogers's pose as a wise country philosopher capable of shrewd
judgments was in the crackerbox oracle tradition of American
humor. That tradition dates back to Benjamin Franklin's literary
characters, Poor Richard and Silence Dogood, two witty, eighteenth-century, commonsense sages. Several nineteenth-century
writers also invented comic characters who were crackerbox philosophers. The most well known were Seba Smith's Major Jack
Downing, James Russell Lowell's Parson Hosea Biglow, Henry
Wheeler Shaw's Josh Billings, and Charles Farrar Browne's Artemus Ward. Those characters also posed as sagacious wits and
wise innocents who were short on book learning but renowned
for instinctive insights. They also had several characteristics that
reappeared in Rogers's style of horse-sense humor: rural dialect;
the homely metaphor, simile, and pun; hyperbole; and commonsense aphorisms, proverbs, and quips.[21]

In one- or two-sentence remarks Rogers could satirize a public
institution or celebrity:

> But with Congress, every time they make a joke, it's a
> law. . . . And every time they make a law it's a joke.

> When a Republican turns Democrat that is just like a
> horse thief going to church.

> He [Roosevelt] swallowed our depression. He has in-
> haled fear and exhaled confidence.

> Jim Thorpe . . . could kick a Ford car over a goal post
> 20 years away.

> Compared to Hollywood, Sodom and Gomorrah were a
> couple of babes in the woods.[22]

Those witticisms were repeated by listeners long after they were
stated on the air.

Rogers's sayings accentuated vivid, incongruous metaphors
and similes. He liked to draw absurd parallels, such as comparing war to bill collecting:

> You can't go out and git a war like you used to could
> . . . just on a minute's notice, you know. Wars is
> gittin' kind of hard to arrange. You got to bill them way
> ahead.

Another time he likened the Great Depression to a train accident:

> In 1928 and 1929, you remember? That's when the
> train hit all of us. . . . We're so scared now that we
> drive up to the track and we won't do anything.
> (Laughter.) We just stand there. We just stand there
> and look, and look, and we won't cross. . . . We're so
> scared. We think it might turn around and come back
> and hit us again. (Laughter.)

The laughter Rogers received largely stemmed from the preposterous images he conjured up in the listeners' minds.[23]

Another of his trademarks was taking complex topics and exaggerating their implications to the point of ridiculousness. On
one broadcast he defined the term "inflation":

> Well, inflation doesn't mean a thing in the world only
> to inflate. You never thought of that before. Or if you
> want it explained more thoroughly than just inflate,
> why, well, it is the old system of supply and demand,
> plus the economic theories of minus production and plus
> the manufacturing potentialities, etc., etc., etc. When
> you reach the point of etc., why you are practically all
> etcetra, etcetra [sic].

Using hyperbole, Rogers once made fun of President Roosevelt's
complicated New Deal legislation:

> What we are trying to do is elevate the commodity
> prices, plus the cost of production, and increase the pur-
> chasing power within the means of the purchaser, or
> plus the cost of production (laughs) (general laughter)
> and thereby enhance the buying power plus liquidation
> and receiving fees, etcetra, etcetra [sic]—and—distri-
> bution will naturally seek its level, and when—capital
> versus labor minus recognition of Russia—and (laugh-
> ter) and Mr. Ford cuts his wages down to the NRA
> level, (laughter) and—and (applause) and—etcetra,

> etcetra, [sic] E Pluribus Unum (laughter) and—which
> about covers the whole situation as Mr. Einstein laid it
> out to us (laughter)—the whole thing, you know, was
> laid out by Mr. Einstein.

Economic theory might still be an enigma to the radio audience
after Rogers's ludicrous explanation, but joking about a perplex-
ing subject made the listeners feel good.[24]

Rogers believed that he could communicate with more people
if he spoke naturally, with little concern for good grammar. "I
had listened to so many announcers trying to talk correctly that
I thought you had to do it," he commented on a broadcast. "Now
I find you can get up here and use bum English just like everybody else can, and you don't have to speak correctly at all, and
you are understood by everybody." He often used colloquialisms
such as "hot dog" and "wait a minute" in his talks. He liked to
coin new words or employ familiar words in unusual contexts.
Rogers habitually added "er" and "a" to words and expressions,
and "kinder," "sorter," "woulda," and "coulda" appeared frequently in his broadcasts. His informal, unaffected style enabled
Rogers to talk on a plane listeners could understand. "With his
ungrammatical approach to his subject matter he was never
above the heads of the man in the street," Fred Allen remarked.
"The little man in the street accepted Will as a voice that he
would like to say the things that Will was saying for him."[25]

Like the tall-tale humorists of the nineteenth-century frontier,
Rogers colored his talks with many Western expressions. Slang
had been used widely on the Western frontier; it had been a
friendly and casual means of communication. Backwoodsmen,
hunters, trappers, farmers, and cowboys assembled around camp-
fires relating farfetched stories in local jargon. Rogers also enjoyed telling yarns over the radio, especially tales and anecdotes
about ranch life and his travels. Born on a ranch near Claremore, Oklahoma, on November 4, 1879, the cowboy humorist
spoke in a Southwestern drawl, frequently using such contractions as ropin', jokin', gittin', and ain't. He sometimes cracked a
joke employing the terminology of farm life: "He [Huey Long]
didn't hatch out with any new plans during the week, he's just
sittin' on the same eggs."[26]

To many Americans Rogers stood for the old agrarian values of neighborliness and self-reliance. He conveyed the image of an unaffected Westerner not only on radio, but also in motion pictures and the stage. In his private life he preferred living "close to the soil," and from 1928 until his death in 1935 he lived on a large ranch in Santa Monica, California, where he had a stable, corrals, a riding ring, a roping arena, and a polo field. In an increasingly impersonal urbanized industrial country, Rogers's values carried strong nostalgic appeal to people who disliked the large metropolis and wished to return to the "good old days." This was particularly true during the Great Depression, when many Americans were questioning machine technology. Rogers's popular rural image corresponded to other cultural manifestations of the 1930's: the Southern Agrarian writers' glorification of farm life, Midwestern regional painting, the revival of folk art and music, and the theme of the dignified tenant farmer in documentary photography. He seemed to represent the traditional values Americans wished to return to during the economic crisis.

Rogers felt that ranchers, cowboys, and farmers were virtuous, industrious people, while city slickers were not. During one broadcast he commented: "Country folks are smarter than city folks. You never have to explain a joke to country folks." The cowboy humorist shared with the Populists of the 1890's a suspicion of Eastern bankers, whom he believed often manipulated wealth and profits on the Stock Exchange. Newspapers, he claimed, devoted too much attention to the New York stock market and not enough space to the common citizen's problems: "They don't know that there are 120,000,000 people more interested in how much milk the old cow is going to give tonight or how much bushels of potatoes they are going to raise to the acre than there is interested in what U.S. Steel closed at or American Can. . . ."[27] A Populist suspicion of urban financial speculation caused him to champion the farmer.

One could learn more about life working with one's hands than by reading books, said Rogers. He supported the New Deal's Civilian Conservation Corps because the program allowed youngsters to work close to nature, constructing hiking trails and planting trees. He feared, however, that city folks in the program might lack a "green thumb." "With city men and women planting the trees, you know, they are liable to get the wrong end in the ground and in our forest of the future, the roots will be in the air and limbs in the ground." Rogers felt that the CCC gave youngsters "a pick and shovel instead of a golf pick or tennis racket . . . and then in the CCC Camp you don't have to hear some Professor lecture on the advantages of Russia." Because he preferred innate intelligence to learned knowledge, he enjoyed poking fun at intellectuals. This moderate anti-intellectualism was part of his stance as a natural-born comedian who extolled farm life.[28]

Rogers proudly discussed his ancestry over the radio. "You know I am an Indian. My folks are Cherokees and I am very proud of the fact. . . ." He was especially bitter about the white man's treatment of the Indians and blamed the government for abrogating treaties and settling his people "on land where the grass won't grow and the water won't flow." A strong note of irony always underscored his remarks when he discussed his heritage:

> Our record with the Indians is going to go down in history. It is going to make us might proud of it in the future when our children of ten more generations read of what we did to them. Every man in our history that killed the most Indians has got a statue built for him.

Proud to be descended from the nation's first settlers, Rogers commented that if it were not for the "extreme generosity of the Indians the Pilgrims would never have been able to land."[29]

Rogers basically admired the rugged individual who toiled with his hands or piloted a plane alone across vast distances; even though his support of the aviation industry and an Army Air Corps conflicted with his agrarian ideals. Yet he admired individual courage, whether in bulldogging steers, riding wild horses, or experimenting with solo airplane flights. On his broadcasts he hailed the aviation feats of Charles Lindbergh, Amelia Earhart, and Wiley Post. An avid adventurer and traveler, Rogers had flown with his friend Lindbergh in Mexico, and Rogers and Wiley Post were killed in an airplane accident on August 15, 1935, near Point Barrow, Alaska. They had planned to survey a transpacific mail-passenger air route via Alaska and Russia.

The humorist represented the self-made man who presumably had risen from humble beginnings to become a world-renowned celebrity. He appeared to remind Americans that the rags-to-riches ideal was still possible during the Great Depression. In actuality his father was a prosperous cattle rancher, and Rogers had never experienced deprivation as a youngster. As a star in radio, theater, and the movies the humorist mingled with royalty and screen stars and he was invited to the White House by four Presidents. His payment of $77,000 for the Squibb broadcasts, which Rogers gave to charity, made headlines. One newspaper claimed that he received $200 for every broadcast minute and that his total earnings for six and one-half hours on the air exceeded President Hoover's annual salary. The Gulf Oil Company paid him $50,000 for his seven programs in 1933, a phenomenal sum, considering the nation's financial state. Rogers had been such a popular folk hero to the American people that few had noticed the paradox between his actual wealth and fame and his public image as a humble cowboy.[30]

In his 1930 Squibb radio talks, Rogers's first series of regular weekly programs, he praised the self-made man from rural background who had achieved success in American society. "Each Sunday I'll take some big person I've met and tell folks about him as he strikes me with little jokes to keep it from being too serious," Rogers stated about his upcoming series. His fifteen-minute biographical portraits included descriptions of Henry Ford, Charles Lindbergh, and Herbert Hoover. Those audio biographies revealed Rogers's admiration for the self-reliant individual. He lauded Ford as the perfect self-made man who practiced the virtues he had learned as a farm boy—diligence, honesty, and common sense. Herbert Hoover's character had likewise been influenced by his boyhood on an Iowa farm. From humble beginnings Hoover "had worked his way through school and was really a self-made man that way." Although the humorist lampooned his subjects, he basically admired their individualism and industriousness. The popular Squibb broadcasts were aired approximately six months after the stock market crash, when faith in the rags-to-riches ideal had been severely shaken. Rogers had said what many Americans wanted to hear: self-reliance and the natural values of rural life still had meaning in Depression America.[31]

During the early 1930's thousands of businesses went bankrupt and millions of Americans joined bread lines. A sense of inferiority and loss of self-confidence gripped the unemployed. Some turned to socialism and communism; others felt a need to rediscover traditional American values that had been lost in the "roaring twenties." Rogers's friendly, confident remarks over the radio reassured listeners that the nineteenth-century codes of integrity, neighborliness, and individual initiative were still vital during those critical years.

His next important broadcast after the Squibb programs was a nationwide address on the unemployment situation on October 18, 1931, a talk that stressed the importance of the work ethic. The industrialist Owen D. Young asked Rogers if he would join President Herbert Hoover on a program devoted to restoring confidence in the American economy. Rogers joked about his appearance with Hoover:

> I looked everything up about him, and inquired, and found that after discounting about two-thirds that the Democrats said about him, I had nothing much to lose by appearing with him, so I took the chance. So if we do all right today, there's liable to be a new team on the radio.

Speaking from Los Angeles, the entertainer interpreted the Great Depression as a moral lesson reminding Americans to appreciate the basic necessities of life. People had lost their perspective in the 1920's by indulging in installment buying and financial speculation:

> We are the first nation in the history of the world to go to the poorhouse in an automobile. We been so busy in the last few years getting radios and bathtubs and facial creams, and straight eights, that we forgot to see if we had any bacon or beans.

Americans had also become fat, lazy, and indifferent to hard work. "The trouble with us in America," he asserted, "is we are just muscle bound from holding a steering wheel, the only place we are calloused from work is the bottom of our driving toe." Rogers urged Americans to keep busy while waiting for a job to turn up:

> Now everybody has got a scheme to relieve unemployment,—there is just one way to do it and that's for everybody to go to work. *Where?* Why right where you are, look around you will see a lot of things to do, weeds to cut, fences to be fixed, lawns to be mowed, filling stations to be robbed, gangsters to be catered to. There is a million little odds and ends right under your eye that an idle man can turn his hand to every day. Course he won't get paid for it, but he won't get paid for not doing it. My theory is that it will keep him in practice in case something does show, you can keep practicing so work won't be a novelty when it does come.

In that broadcast Rogers took the role of a commonsense philosopher urging a return to the basic American ideals of self-reliance and the work ethic. Hundreds of telegrams were sent to Rogers praising the speech. His talk carried great appeal in a critical time when belief in the American system was declining.[32]

Throughout the hard times of the Great Depression Rogers empathized with the underdog. On his broadcasts he often praised the courage of the poor and belittled the callousness of the rich:

> This nation needs a more equal distribution of wealth. . . . The big fellow has more money, but the little fellow's got more nerve. . . . The little fellow can look starvation in the face and smile, but the big guy can't look uncertainty in the face and do the same thing.

Rogers never made fun of the "little fellow" on his broadcasts. Indeed, he felt the poor were a forgotten class:

> But nobody ever asked a poor guy what he thinks of the New Year. Just read your paper, and it's always what Mr. So and So said. Nobody says—Bud, what do you think of it? You know. They never get his opinion.

Although at times he spoke as if he were a socialist, Rogers's social philosophy derived from frontier egalitarianism, a belief in giving everyone an equal opportunity.[33]

Rogers confidently expressed over the radio the opinion that the Depression would soon end. During the fall of 1933, when the unemployment rate was at its lowest and industrial production had been sharply curtailed, he commented that the nation was in a "convalescent period now, following a severe illness," but it would soon recover and return to normal. A year later he stated optimistically: "I know that everythin' is pickin' up from what I see all over. . . . Of course, I don't lay that to me bein' off for five weeks, but anyhow things is pickin' up." The humorist's jokes about the Great Depression also enabled listeners to laugh momentarily at their problems: "We got quite a bunch of notables in here tonight on account of its being free," he jested. "That's one thing the Depression has done. It's made all free entertainment popular." The Depression was hardly a laughing matter to the unemployed, but since comedians were rarely taken seriously they could make the most tragic event appear less ominous.[34]

Because he was idolized and respected as a popular oracle of commonsense wisdom, Rogers gave people confidence to face hard times. The radio was an important morale booster for the financially insecure. A 1939 Princeton University Radio Research Report, sponsored by the Rockefeller Foundation, concluded that "To the morale of an unemployed family, a radio is an important bolster. It is the chief recreation of the group. . . . Loss of the radio from unemployed homes in most cases was considered a final, crushing misfortune." Like listening to *Amos 'n' Andy*, hearing a Rogers program was a household ritual. A fan letter to the humorist illustrates the significance of his Sunday night broadcasts:

> I am somewhat of a shut-in and my radio means a great deal to me. But on Sunday nites I find myself not alone at the radio. At 7:00 o'clock p.m. M.S.T. my mother and dad draw up their chairs close to [the radio] and we all wait for that voice which will come to us in a few minutes and which we enjoy listening to so much.

> There is only one trouble with your talks, Mr. Rogers.
> They are not nearly long enough.

Another letter from a man who had considered suicide reveals
how Rogers could help relieve the tensions of everyday life:

> Chalk it down on your slate that you put new hope in
> one poor devil, last night. Of course in my business we
> have not had any income for three years and this
> Christmas I thought would bring something. So I put
> all the creditors off until after the first of the year. Then
> there wasn't any business and the deluge reached me. I
> thought I would listen to you last night and later on
> start the car motor with the door shut. Well I listened
> and I found myself actually gaining hope and courage
> to carry on. It was fine. I turned to my wife and said "I
> am going to write Will Rogers and thank him and even
> if he never gets to read the letter I will feel better for
> having written it." Someday I am going to have your
> autographed photograph to take pride in as the man
> who helped me.[35]

Because of his warmth and sincerity Rogers's informal talks
resembled President Roosevelt's friendly radio fireside chats.
Both spoke in an intimate tone, conveying confidence in the
American economy. Rogers described his Squibb broadcasts as
neighborly chats: "I'll just talk to folks like I'd dropped in for a
Sunday night call." He also noted that Roosevelt was a "plain
spoken man" who "doesn't mess around with a lot of big words."
The humorist praised the President's unaffected speaking style:
"He showed these radio announcers and our public speakers
what to do with a vocabulary—leave it right in the dictionary
where it belongs."[36]

During Roosevelt's first hundred days in office Rogers strongly
backed the chief executive's actions to improve the economy. On
his broadcast of May 7, 1933, he praised Roosevelt's speech announcing a temporary nationwide closing of banks and emergency banking legislation.

> That speech will, when history is written, go down some
> day as being the detour sign where depression turned

back. It was a speech of the people, for the people, delivered so that confidence would not perish from the
earth.[37]

After the program the White House telephoned NBC asking for
a copy of his talk. The transcript was read over the telephone so
that the President would know the humorist's remarks before
making his own fireside chat, which was scheduled to follow
Rogers's broadcast.

The entertainer talked extensively about the new Administration in his President's Day broadcast on April 30, 1933. He
viewed the chief executive as a charismatic leader who would
pull the country out of the Depression:

> That bird has done more for us in seven weeks than
> we've done for ourselves in seven years. We elected him
> because he was a Democrat, and now we honor him be-
> cause he is a magician. (Laughter.) He's the Houdini of
> Hyde Park. And maybe this Houdini of Hyde Park
> can't do everything. He may not get our hands out of
> all the handcuffs which we have foolishly stuck our
> mitts out and got 'em into ourselves, but even if he can
> just git one hand loose—you know what I mean and
> leave the handcuff hanging on the other, he will have
> accomplished a great deal. He's a fast worker. He was
> nominated—I mean—well no—I was there when he
> was nominated—I ought to know that. He was inaugu-
> rated at noon in Washington, and they started the in-
> augural parade down Pennsylvania Avenue and before
> it got half way down there, he closed every bank in the
> United States. (Laughter.)

At the broadcast's conclusion Rogers addressed a personal message to the President:

> Now I understand Mr. Roosevelt—somebody told me
> was listenin' in. Now Mr. Roosevelt, we've turned
> everything over to you. We've given you more power
> than we have ever given any man—any man was ever
> given in the history of the world. We don't know what
> it's all about. We tried to run the country individually
> and collectively, and along the Democrat line, but boy

we've gummed it so—so you take it, and run it if you want to, you know, and deflate, or inflate, or complicate, or you know insulate—Do anything so long as you get us a dollar or two every now and again. So you're our lawyer. We're going to turn the whole thing over— Things are moving so fast in this country now that we don't know what it's all about. The whole country's cock-eyed anyhow, and we're just appointing you, and you take it—we don't know what it's all about, but God Bless You.[38]

In other talks Rogers enthusiastically supported Roosevelt's early New Deal recovery legislation. On August 27, 1933, the humorist delivered a special radio talk urging companies to join the Blue Eagle drive program by adopting the National Recovery Act codes on hiring and fair business practices. He endorsed other proposals that relieved unemployment, commenting: "If this Administration ever goes under, it should have written on its tombstone: 'Perished through trying to give the little fellow a square deal.' " He once defined F.D.R.'s pragmatic style of experimenting with various economic solutions and hiring many different personal advisers:

The minute he pumps one dry, he turns him loose and turns on another. (Laughter.) He brings them in there fast, and soaks up all they know, and then crosses out all he doesn't want, then takes out the theories and adds a little common sense himself. (Laughter.)[39]

Rogers eventually began to question certain New Deal programs because he distrusted costly federal projects that did little for the unemployed. A staunch advocate of do-it-yourself individualism, he was suspicious of bureaucracy and believed that government projects sometimes became corrupted by graft. He also thought some programs did not put enough people to work: "Trouble is the government will loan ten million to build some project, and ten men working some levers, or steering wheels will build it." In "the good old days" before mechanical conveniences people worked harder:

The difference in this country between employment and unemployment is the wheelbarrow. When we traded

the old wheelbarrow for a three ton truck, and old Nellie
for a 2 door sedan, thats the day the government started
into the relief business. When Ma traded the old skillet
for a bridge deck, and Pa his ax for a putter, thats the
day their congressman started asking for relief.

A believer in the work ethic, Rogers opposed handouts and relief
programs that made people lazy and less self-reliant: "We're
living in a peculiar time," he remarked. "You get more for not
working than you will for working, and more for not raising a
hog than raising it."[40]

The humorist's skepticism was best revealed in his 1935 broadcasts. At that time he satirized the number of impractical plans
which had been devised to improve the economy. Rogers's famous Plan Day radio talk on April 21, 1935, lampooned several
programs, including the Townsend Plan, which was supposed to
give elderly people a monthly allowance:

> Today is—today's Plan Day. I'm sort of going to give
> an inkling of the Rogers' Plan to agonize the world.
> But you know the Townsend plan and various others of
> a similar nature went down in Congress with a tremen-
> dous majority, so it looks like a kind of a bad day for
> plans. I think Townsend was conscientious, well-mean-
> ing, humanitarian old gentleman. I believe if he had
> lowered his sight and called for maybe fifty dollars in-
> stead of two hundred a month, and took out the clause
> where they had to spend it. . . . Old people, you know,
> are naturally kind of conservative.

The trouble with these proposals, said Rogers, was that they
failed to appeal to a large majority: "If they're milk and honey
to you, they are poison ivy to somebody else. . . ." Huey Long's
Share-the-Wealth plan to redistribute income was too utopian:
"I know a lot of tremendously rich people that should share
their wealth with me, but they just don't see it my way."[41]

A week after the Plan Day address Rogers jested about Henry
Morgenthau's proposal to levy increased taxes on estates. Under
the Secretary of the Treasury's inheritance tax legislation, he
suggested, the government might take every penny an entrepre-
neur earned and then notify the heirs "your father died a pau-

per here today." Instead of a lavish funeral a banker would be buried by "the Millionaires' Emergency Burial Association." According to Rogers, the wealthy would have to die on schedule to keep the government solvent: "In order for Mr. Morgenthau's plan to work out . . . he's got to bump those wealthy guys off, or something." J. P. Morgan would be "scheduled to die on a certain year. And you can bet, if they can arrange it, they'll have him die while the Democrats are in . . . so they can get the benefit of the estate." Rogers believed that if a business leader earned his money by working hard and honestly his heirs should be entitled to his earnings.[42]

There was only one good place for a plan and that was on paper, said Rogers. "The minute you get it off the sheet of paper and get it out in the air it blows away." On one broadcast he announced his own proposal to abolish plans:

> My plan to state it in a nut-shell, and in fact that's where all plans come from. . . . (Laughter.) And the nuts should never be cracked. But here is my plan in a nut-shell. My plan is to end all plans. It's to do away with all plans. That's what it is. This country has been planned to death.[43]

Politics was an amusing spectacle to Rogers, and his stance as a nonpartisan observer enabled him to jest about both Democrats and Republicans. Leading politicians rarely took offense because they accepted Rogers as the country's court jester. "I never met one of 'em that I didn't like," said Rogers about the nation's chief executives. "If I didn't like one, you'd never hear me jokin' about him." Rogers poked fun at the Democrats spending too much money and the Republicans for ignoring the needs of the ordinary citizen. He particularly enjoyed ribbing the Republicans about their defeat in the 1934 congressional elections in a broadcast called the "Death of the Republican Party." His comments about the failings of the Grand Old Party became a running gag on other programs. The "children wouldn't go to bed until they had heard what had happened to the Republicans every Sunday night," the humorist joked.[44]

Rogers also liked to needle members of Congress. His *Congres-*

sional Record talk, given on May 12, 1935, satirized the Representatives. "The way our Congressional business is being carried
on nowadays, being a Senator—or a Congressman—is not much,"
he jested. "It just really consists in receiving telegrams. That's
about all it is." Instead of addressing one another in an artificial
manner during debates a Congressman should speak plainly and
honestly. Why not refer to a Representative as "the coyote from
Maine" or "the pole cat from Oregon"? One Congressman had
suggested that Rogers's proposal to abolish plans be inserted in
the *Congressional Record:*

> I feel pretty good about that. It—the highest praise that
> a humorist can have is to get yourself into the Congres-
> sional Record. (Laughter–applause.) Just—just think,
> my name will be right in there along side of Huey
> Long's, and all those other big humorists. You see, ordi-
> narily you got to work your way up as a humorist and
> first get into Congress. Then you work on up into the
> Senate, and if your stuff is funny enough it goes into
> the Congressional Record.[45]

In an earlier program Rogers had parodied the proceedings of
the Senate by pretending he was presiding over a session of that
body. He told Vice President John Nance Garner that

> you will have nothing to do with the running of this
> meeting. I am running this outfit here. I don't want you
> to go to sleep as usual, either. . . . After this meeting
> is over, I have some very good news for you, you can get
> right back to your regular business. There is going to be
> a poker game as soon as this is over.

He then ordered Huey Long to sit down: "If you can't find your
place to rest, I am sure there is people in your home state of
Louisiana that will be glad to dig you a place to rest." Rogers
called the Senate "the highest priced bunch of Yes-men we know
in America." He then went on to describe the manner in which
legislation was passed:

> We will vote on this bill in the usual way. It won't be
> read. I don't know what it is. All in favor say "Aye";
> all those opposed say "No." The bill is passed. . . . I

don't know whether it will interest you senators or not
to know what was in the bill we just passed a few moments ago. You are usually not interested in it. . . .
The one you passed a few moments ago, that was to
cancel all of the debt, to pay Europe any expense they
have been out in getting us to cancel it, and also to make
them a loan equal to the debt. That is what you have
done.

Since his contract with Gulf was to expire after that talk, Garner
and other Senate members wired Rogers, urging the continua-
tion of his broadcasts:

> What is this we hear about your radio retirement
> (STOP) Does this mean that you will not preside over
> Senate again (STOP) We have enjoyed your recent talks
> on the air and want your assurance that you will soon
> return with your humorous and wholesome comment
> on national affairs.[46]

Only occasionally did Rogers receive letters and telegrams
criticizing his remarks over the air. Once some listeners felt he
was joking about the Lindbergh kidnapping. Another time he
received letters criticizing him for using the term "darkies."
Rogers apologized on both occasions, stating that he did not mean
to offend any listeners. Such incidents never diminished his reputation as a popular entertainer whose humor was closely associated with national values and morale.[47]

Rogers stood for traditional American beliefs in a critical time
of economic problems and social change. Like the *Amos 'n' Andy*
programs, his broadcasts supported mores associated with the
national heritage, and they reassured listeners that values identifiable with the American way of life were still vital during the
Great Depression, when faith in our institutions was declining.
"There was something infectious about his humor," said President Roosevelt in 1938:

> His appeal went straight to the heart of the nation.
> Above all things, in a time grown too solemn and som-
> ber he brought his countrymen back to a sense of pro-
> portion.[48]

Listeners thrived on his commonsense philosophy, and his deflation of pomposity appealed to the "little fellow." By the time of his death Rogers had become a folk hero, and he was mourned by millions of Americans. He was the first great radio comedy monologuist and court jester. Bob Hope later became radio's second noted monologuist and jester, but Hope's rapid-fire delivery appealed to the more sophisticated urban society of the 1940's. By contrast, Rogers's casual style and oracular wit reflected the early days of radio, when listeners living in the midst of the Great Depression treasured a humorist who embodied the values of rural America.

5

The Fire Chief

After the pioneer radio comedians of the 1920's came a new wave of entertainers from vaudeville who entered radio in the early 1930's. Ed Wynn, Fred Allen, Jack Benny, Jack Pearl, and George Burns and Gracie Allen all had their first radio series during the 1932–33 season. Because of the popularity of radio and sound motion pictures, vaudeville had declined as a major American entertainment form by 1930. There had been approximately two thousand vaudeville theaters in the country in 1900. By 1930 there were fewer than a hundred, and in that year the premier showcase for vaudeville, the Palace Theatre on Times Square, was equipped for sound movies. In November 1932 the last regularly scheduled vaudeville show was presented at the Palace. In the 1890's vaudeville houses had first booked movie shorts to "clear the house," but by the early 1930's live acts were being used as audience "chasers." Listeners remained home to hear their favorite entertainer on radio rather than go out to a theater. Once well-known performers entered radio, vaudeville was truly "dead." Comedians were soon cracking jokes over the air about radio "killing" vaudeville.[1]

Former vaudeville comics practicing a clean form of humor found radio appropriate to their routines. Risqué acts catering to male audiences in concert saloons, beerhalls, and variety theaters had at first dominated vaudeville, but during the 1880's theater owners and producers, especially the impresario Tony Pastor, changed the nature of vaudeville by emphasizing whole-some family entertainment. Vaudeville comedy routines were far different from the homespun humor of the comic Yankee and country yokel, major character stage types in the eighteenth and nineteenth century. With its slapstick, stooges, he-she jokes, punch-line monologues, and ethnic characterizations, vaudeville revolutionized stage comedy. Some vaudevillians continued to do this type of humor on radio. The airwaves also became a re-spectable middle-class entertainment form for the family. Gov-ernment licensing of stations, sponsorship pressure, and network censorship kept the airwaves clean. Most radio comedians came from vaudeville rather than the burlesque, hotel-club, and "borscht" circuits where performers entertained audiences with off-color material.

Vaudeville had other marked influences on early radio. Variety programs such as Rudy Vallee's *Fleischmann Hour*, Eddie Can-tor's *Chase and Sanborn Hour*, and the *Ziegfeld Follies of the Air* were modeled on vaudeville's bill of fare. Those hour-long shows featured an assortment of musical and singing numbers and comedy routines. Many vaudeville comics made their first radio appearances on such programs. The standard radio comedy pro-gram emphasized variety entertainment, with the show divided into various "spots": comedy monologue, skit, guest star, orches-tra number, and singer. The first radio comedy writers, including David Freedman, Billy Wells, and Harry Conn, had written material for vaudeville performers. The writers often gave the radio entertainers jokes that had proven to be successful on stage.

Eddie Cantor's Sunday night *Chase and Sanborn Hour*, which premiered on September 13, 1931, was an innovative variety show. A famous vaudeville and *Ziegfeld Follies* headliner in the 1920's, Cantor was signed for the program after he made a guest appearance on Rudy Vallee's broadcast in February 1931. Pro-duced by the J. Walter Thompson advertising agency, *The Chase and Sanborn Hour* offered listeners lively musical and comedy entertainment. The program was written by a staff of talented writers, including Carroll Carroll and David Freedman. Cantor was one of the first radio stars to use his announcer (Jimmy Wallington) as a straight man. The format of using the announcer to set up jokes for the comedian eventually became common practice on comedy broadcasts. The popular program also featured regular stooges whom listeners enjoyed hearing every week. The funniest were Bert Gordon as the Mad Russian and Harry Einstein as Parkyakarkus. The stooges often heckled Cantor, who personified the underdog to his listeners. The versatile Cantor could also play straight man to his bit characters and do comedy parts in sketches. Rubinoff was the star violinist on the show, and singers Bobbie Breen and Deanna Durbin, discovered by Cantor, were also regulars. Cantor was also the first headliner to give a serious curtain speech for charity at the program's end. He also concluded his show with his famous sign-off song, "I love to spend this hour with you." Unlike the two-man song and patter programs and standard orchestra broadcasts in the 1920's, *The Chase and Sanborn Hour* brought Broadway entertainment into American living rooms.[2]

According to the Cooperative Analysis of Broadcasting (C.A.B.) rating system, over 50 per cent of the listening public were hearing the Cantor show. It led all programs in the rating charts in January 1933 and 1934. The entertainer and the sponsor were besieged by fan letters. On the occasion of his fortieth birthday the singer jokingly told his listeners his shirt and sock sizes and that he liked chocolate cake. Cantor subsequently received 15,000 packages from his ardent admirers. On another program Jimmy Wallington remarked that the eighteenth-century English author Samuel Johnson drank twenty-four cups of coffee daily and would have consumed more if Chase and Sanborn had been available. Hundreds of listeners telephoned NBC to point out Wallington's error. Much to the embarrassment of Chase and Sanborn executives, Johnson had not drunk coffee, but tea.

Listeners worshipped Cantor on radio in the early 1930's. The microphone transmitted his sparkling personality and friendly voice into millions of living rooms. "On this program you had a feeling of being friends with almost everyone," wrote Cantor. "Let's make a date for next Sunday night," he told his radio audience in his sign-off song. Listening to the entertainer at 8 p.m. EST on Sunday night became a regular habit of radio owners.[3]

Cantor represented important values to the American people

during the economic crisis. By singing patriotic songs and praising America Cantor gave his listeners renewed faith in their country at a critical time. The singer-comedian personified a charitable, unselfish man who urged helping the needy on his broadcasts. Cantor was the successful "little guy" who had started as a poor immigrant boy on New York's Lower East Side singing on street corners and in a saloon. After spending several years in small-time vaudeville he had risen to stardom in the *Ziegfeld Follies*. He also epitomized the family man who spoke fondly of and joked lightheartedly about his wife and five daughters on the air.

Cantor's Depression era broadcasts carried a tone of optimism and patriotism. In 1932 he announced his candidacy for President. He even wrote a book, *Your Next President*, outlining his platform and his plans to end the Depression. Cantor's bid "gave him a chance to be funny about the political situation and get off a few patriotic goodies that classed him as 'A Great American.' " Chants of "We want Cantor! We want Cantor!" were heard over the airwaves. On one broadcast in December 1931 Cantor played a Depression doctor who advised a sick Uncle Sam (who is ill because of the economy) not to lose confidence in America. "Seriously, Uncle Sam, you've got everything!" said the singer.

> You've got the people, the natural resources, the power and the wealth to be the biggest nation on earth. . . . You've become a little too high hat—you're not working as hard as you used to. Do the chores around the house. Plain, honest work can't hurt you. And keep cheerful. Get out of the shadows and into the sunshine. Face the sun and the shadows will fall behind you. . . . Don't look back, look ahead, the view that way is a whole lot pleasanter. . . . Why, Uncle, You're the richest, strongest man on earth and you don't know it!

Like Will Rogers, Cantor's charismatic personality and faith in America lifted the spirits of millions of listeners who were worried about the hard times.[4]

Despite his enormous popularity, Cantor treated radio as if he were still performing on stage. At first he had problems understanding the mechanics of the medium and the need to time a broadcast. The producer had trouble convincing him to cut and edit lines. Cantor continued to use vaudeville material and jokes pilfered from humor magazines and books. He dressed in bizarre costumes for the broadcasts. On one Halloween program the announcer described the star as "wearing one golf shoe and one lady's slipper, one silk stocking and one plaid golf sock, tweed knickers and a tutu, a woman's blouse with a man's vest over it, a necktie, a blond curly wig and a Sherlock Holmes fore-and-aft cap." Carroll Carroll recalled that "sometimes the costume dictated the subject of the jokes, sometimes it had to be planned to fit the jokes." He did slapstick routines and sight gags on the air. During one routine Cantor broke an egg over a character actor's head. He jumped into the arms of a stooge after a joke and made funny faces to the studio audience. People at home wondered why the audience was laughing. Cantor forgot that the home listeners could not *see* him.[5]

The true test of a radio comic lay in redesigning his routine for an aural rather than visual medium. Comedians who depended largely on facial expressions, props, costumes, and slapstick had the most difficult time adjusting to radio. There was the problem of finding the right format. Listeners quickly grew tired of programs consisting mainly of corny jokes between a straight man and the comic. Comedians who created a new style, like Jack Benny, survived the longest on the airwaves, while entertainers who largely kept to their vaudeville repertoire, like Ed Wynn, were unable to sustain their popularity over a long period.

The influence of vaudeville on early radio comedy can be illustrated best by examining the career of Ed Wynn. Wynn, whose real name was Isaiah Edwin Leopold, was born on November 9, 1886, in Philadelphia, Pennsylvania. His stage name was derived from his middle name, "Ed—Win." Wynn's father, a wealthy hat manufacturer, wanted him to enter the millinery business, and he employed his teenage son as a hat salesman. The youngster did not like the work and instead wanted to enter show business. According to Wynn's son, Keenan, "he was funnier

with the hats than he was at selling them." His father's occupa-
tion had one lasting influence on Wynn. In vaudeville the comedian became known for wearing funny hats, including a trick
Panama hat, made in his father's factory, that he could fold into
twenty-eight different shapes. Even on radio he wore several hats
to get laughs from the studio audience.[6]

A born comic, Wynn had liked playing the fool as a young
boy. He was expelled from school several times for his tomfool-
ery. The entertainer used to clown on the beach at Atlantic City,
a seaside resort where his family summered. A large crowd gathered in the morning to watch him and his friends perform stunts.
"I will never forget it," the comedian recalled.

> At Virginia Avenue where the Steel Pier is, they would
> hang on the boardwalk and go on the pier and watch us.
> That I know for a fact because those were my first press
> notices. I was twelve, thirteen, fourteen years of age. I
> had a sense of the ridiculous when I was a child. A great
> sense of fun.[7]

Wynn ran away from home at sixteen and obtained a job as a
child actor at $12.00 a week with the Thurber Nash Repertory
Company in New England. Wynn first acted on August 8, 1902,
in Norwich, Connecticut, where he played an elderly Methodist
minister in *Jim Bledsoe*. The company folded several months
later, and the apprentice actor was left stranded in Bangor,
Maine, without a cent in his pocket. He earned his fare home
by playing piano in a whorehouse. Wynn tried working for his
father again, but after seven months he left home and headed for
New York.

Manhattan was then the center of vaudeville, and it offered
opportunity for a young, talented performer. Wynn rented a
room for $2.50 a week in a theatrical boardinghouse on West 44
Street. One evening in the back room at Kid McCoy's Broadway
rathskeller, an actors' hangout, he met Jack Lewis, the vaudevillian. Wynn talked to Lewis about a two-man college act he
had written called "The Freshman and the Sophomore," satirizing wealthy college boys. Lewis agreed to perform the sketch
and they tried out the act successfully at a benefit in a theater

on West 125 Street. The team joined Percy Williams's vaudeville chain at $200 a week and for nearly two years they performed the college sketch. Wynn wore pegtop trousers and a ludicrous Panama hat. The funnyman walked on stage smoking a meerschaum pipe and with a bulldog on a leash. He looked at the audience and said: "Rah, rah, rah. Who pays my bills? Pa and Ma." Wynn already showed signs of becoming a visual clown. The performer got laughs by the way he talked and looked and the facial expressions he made. When the pair disbanded in 1904, Wynn teamed with several other performers in joke and musical sketches that he wrote.[8]

Around 1910 Wynn decided to do a single, and by 1912 he had gained a reputation as a promising stand-up comic known for telling funny stories and joke toppers. In 1913, he appeared at the Palace in a sketch called "The King's Jester." Wynn's role was to make the dour king laugh—if the jester failed he was subject to death. After trying several gags without success he whispered a dirty joke into the king's ear and the monarch burst out laughing. "Why didn't you tell me you wanted to hear that kind of a story?" the entertainer quipped.[9]

Wynn was destined to become a vaudeville headliner and musical comedy star. Florenz Ziegfeld signed him for the *Ziegfeld Follies of 1914*. In 1917 he performed in two musical comedies, *Doing Our Bit* at the Winter Garden and *Over the Top* at the Nora Bayes Theater. For his starring role in the *Shubert Gaieties of 1919* at the 44 Street Theatre, built on the site where he had rented a room in 1902, Wynn earned $1750 a week.[10] During the next fifteen years he starred in many Broadway shows, including *The Perfect Fool*, *The Grab Bag*, *Manhattan Mary*, *Simple Simon*, *The Laugh Parade*, and *Hooray for What!*

Wynn's role as a buffoon in *The Perfect Fool* led to his first appearance on radio. The Broadway hit was aired live over Newark's pioneer station WJZ on February 19, 1922. It was the first stage show ever to be broadcast. Wynn had never suffered from stage fright, but he was petrified by the new medium and in the studio approached the microphone nervously. He began to tell some sure-fire jokes, but all he heard in response was silence because there was no live audience to measure his effectiveness and timing. He started to worry and perspire. Frustrated, he turned desperately to the announcer and confessed, "I can't do anything." The announcer quickly assembled an impromptu audience from a variety of people in the studio: electricians, cleaning women, telephone operators, studio hands, and other performers in the cast. As soon as the makeshift audience began laughing hysterically the comedian started to feel more comfortable before the microphone. Although Wynn later overcame his initial awkwardness, he was never as relaxed in the studio as he was in the theater. "Why there isn't a Tuesday that I'm not as nervous as a man who faces the death sentence," he admitted.[11]

After *The Perfect Fool* broadcast Wynn did not return to radio for ten years. During the 1920's famous performers avoided the medium because of its low pay and non-professionalism. Wynn was lured back into radio by the high salaries being offered headliners by sponsors anxious to have name entertainers sell their products. French singer Maurice Chevalier, for example, received $5000 a week to star on *The Chase and Sanborn Hour* in 1931. Noticing a drop in the number of evening listeners in 1932, advertisers turned to established vaudeville personalities to attract listeners. Borrowing stars from the stage rather than developing new talent was a major step that marked the industry for years. Texaco officials, including George Vos, the company's advertising executive, saw Wynn perform in the Broadway comedy, *The Laugh Parade.* It is said that they sat through the show with their eyes closed to get an idea of how Wynn would sound on radio. His clowning impressed them, and they asked the funnyman to do a radio show for the oil company. Remembering his first experience on the air, Wynn initially balked at their offer. His buffoonery, he insisted, was largely visual and depended on such props as hats and costumes. Wynn finally agreed to do the series, but only if live audiences attended the broadcasts. Texaco budgeted $14,450 for each half-hour program, with $5000 going to Wynn and $8000 to NBC. The era of radio comedy as big business had begun.[12]

The Fire Chief program premiered on April 28, 1932, over the NBC Red network on Tuesday night. It immediately became one of the most popular shows on the air. The program was initially broadcast from New York City's New Amsterdam Theater and later originated from NBC's Times Square headquarters and from various theaters on the East Coast. Before air time Wynn greeted the audience in the lobby and talked with them in the aisles. He also charged admission to the broadcasts and donated the proceeds to charity.

The use of a live audience was a daring innovation. Spectators had previously either been prohibited in the studio or had viewed broadcasts behind a large "glass curtain" that prevented noise from going over the air. They heard the program over loudspeakers and were cautioned to be as silent as possible. Eddie Cantor was probably the first major radio entertainer to have a live audience. On *The Chase and Sanborn Hour* the audience was initially instructed by Jimmy Wallington not to applaud or laugh for fear of distracting home listeners. That policy was changed accidentally in 1932, when the singer, spotting his wife in the audience, grabbed her hat and fur to use as props in a routine. The audience applauded Cantor's action and laughed hysterically throughout the broadcast. The program was a hit and Cantor received letters praising the show. He then decided to let the spectators freely applaud and laugh. The singer discovered that studio audiences not only improved his timing, but laughter stimulated home listeners. "They were no longer alone in the empty living room; they were part of the show," he recalled. A survey of listeners' tastes published in 1935 concluded that most set owners felt radio humor was improved by audience laughter and applause.[13]

Audiences at a *Fire Chief* broadcast had the feeling they were attending a stage show. Huge gasoline pumps flanked each end of the stage at the New Amsterdam Theatre. The program began with an elaborate fanfare. A fire engine siren sounded and was followed by a musician ringing a large bell. Louis Witten, the program's director, stepped up to the microphone and delivered the opening commercial. He introduced the orchestra and then the announcer, Graham McNamee, Wynn's straight man. McNamee's introduction was accompanied by the sound of auto horns. Witten next introduced Ed Wynn as the Fire Chief and the Perfect Fool. The comedian ran onto the stage as a trombonist, stood up, and reproduced the comedian's zany laughter on his instrument. Wynn wore a funny costume and hat, including an old miniature topper derby which he had used since his vaudeville days. As in the theater, he wore facial makeup and light tortoise-shell glasses. His ludicrous garb, infectious grin, and arching eyebrows made people laugh even before he said a word. Wynn went to the front of the stage and stood before a stand holding the script. He opened the program with one of his familiar chuckles, and in a high-pitched voice delivered his standard opening line: "I'm the chief, Graham, tonight the program's going to be different.[14]

The show's format reflected the influence of variety theater. A typical *Fire Chief* broadcast consisted of joke routines between Wynn and McNamee followed by musical numbers from the orchestra or singing by the Fire Chief Quartet. The idea of alternating humor and music on a comedy program prevented the listener from getting tired of the comedian. A smooth transition between the comedy routine and the musical entertainment was necessary. On other shows besides Wynn's the band sometimes played music that tied in with the comedian's routine, or the conductor or singer had an important speaking part in the script. Wynn did not have a lead-in to the musical number; instead, the orchestra music began immediately after a comedy section. The music on *The Fire Chief* broadcast was lively and cheerful and contributed to the program's brisk mood.

Between musical selections Wynn went backstage and, aided by his valet, Al Baron, changed into another costume and applied new facial makeup. Wynn is known to have used seven different outfits during his broadcasts, including an orange pea jacket with a black and orange collegiate cap and a zebra-striped blazer and straw hat. For his closing routine as Texaco's Fire Chief he put on a miniature fire helmet. On his broadcasts Wynn wore the same oversized funny shoes he had been wearing on stage since 1906, when he bought them for $3.50. They had been repaired and resoled over a dozen times, at a cost of over $1400. Home listeners missed the full effect of a Wynn performance because they were unable to see the laughgetter's costumes and clowning.

The Fire Chief programs were written by Wynn and a "silent partner." The comedian had a file containing eighty thousand to one hundred thousand gags, and indexed alphabetically by subject matter, from acrobats to xylophone. Like other former vaudevillians on radio, Wynn found that he could not repeat the same jokes to an audience that listened in weekly. "There is this distinct difference between playing the clown on stage and on the air," he commented.

> The comedian has an opportunity to test his material in the theatre. . . . But the joke that floats across the stage can never be recalled and never be repeated, even though it may have convulsed the audience with laughter.

Wynn thus carefully selected jokes for his radio program. He and his collaborator, Eddie Preble, had the gags chosen for an upcoming broadcast typed on small cards and tacked on a wall. Wynn then walked up and down the line of cards picking appropriate jokes for particular spots and dictating a rough draft to a secretary as he went along. Two or three times a week he stayed up until five or six in the morning perfecting the script, and he often spent all day Sunday rewriting. Several rehearsals were held before the program was ready to be broadcast on Tuesday night.[15]

The funnyman aimed for approximately fifty laughs on each show. On a thirty-minute *Fire Chief* program Wynn and McNamee had about seventeen minutes of comedy dialogue. In radio's early years comedians had a theory that to be a success one had to get off three or four "sock" jokes a minute. Laughs were graded fair, good, or "belly." As the show progressed writers and directors marked the script by giving a fair laugh a check, a good joke a star, and a large guffaw a goose egg. Wynn tried to get three sure-fire jokes a minute, or a laugh every twenty seconds. The remaining time was spent in building up to the punch line, a process called "feeding." The timing had to be perfect. Too many gags on top of each other could smother an audience.[16]

Wynn was a master at timing his delivery and setting up his jokes. He instinctively knew how long to pause before a punch

Ed Wynn in costume as the Texaco Fire Chief in 1933. He is wearing his famous oversized shoes.

Ed Wynn and Graham McNamee broadcasting *The Fire Chief* program from the stage of New York's New Amsterdam Theater. The comedian was one of the first radio performers to have a live audience.

Ed Wynn emphasized bizarre costumes and facial expressions during his broadcasts.
(Courtesy, Society for the Preservation of Variety Arts, Los Angeles, California.)

line and to ad-lib when necessary to increase the humor of a particular routine. He listened carefully to the studio audience's reaction for his timing, and could adjust his pace to fit their response. A typical Wynn–McNamee routine was once analyzed to illustrate the comedian's technique:

WYNN   I've got a friend who is a boxer. Once he hung up his coat in a restaurant, but he was afraid someone would run off with it. (*This was the beginning of the joke, but since the audience began to titter the pace became slower.*)

GRAHAM   They do that. (*Philosophically.*)

WYNN   What do you mean, "They do that?" (*Wynn is stalling now.*)

GRAHAM   They run off with them. I recognize that coat you've got on. (*Pause for laughs. Continues giggling. Then Wynn continues with the joke as he started.*)

WYNN   This friend of mine was afraid someone would run off with his coat so he put a sign on it. He hung a sign on it saying, "This coat belongs to the champion boxer of the world and I'll be back." (*Here Wynn slows up in pace and makes funny noises, then continues.*)

WYNN   Do you know what happened, Graham? Do you know what happened? (*Pause until the audience grasps the full meaning of the repetition.*)

GRAHAM   No. (*Chuckling, which is an accepted device in timing.*) What happened?

WYNN   When he came back, Graham, he found another sign hanging where the coat had been. This sign said—"This coat was taken by the champion runner of the world, and I *won't* be back." (*The audience roars with laughter, but Wynn, listening carefully, decides he is not getting quite the laugh he wants. He waits for the first lull and then swiftly adds:*)

WYNN   You know, Graham, I'm really surprised they laugh at some of these. (*At the finish laughter breaks out again. The unexpected touch makes the joke seem twice as funny.*)[17]

McNamee was the perfect stooge for Wynn. The comedian had never met him until the afternoon prior to the evening of their first broadcast. From the beginning they worked together as a successful team. McNamee gave Wynn confidence and often encouraged him before broadcast time. "Boy, oh boy, Ed, we're gonna slay 'em tonight," he often said to his partner. McNamee occasionally broke out into hysterics during Wynn's funny lines and was also a good ad-libber, but his best role was as a foil. The comic liked to kid his announcer on the program:

> The wife has an accident. She is overcome by escaping gas. It seems she turned on the radio while Graham Mc-Namee was talking.

Known as "The Father of Sportscasting," McNamee later became radio's first important sportscaster, and he introduced techniques still used today.[18]

The stooge-comedian routine was a holdover from two-man stage comedy. In vaudeville, one partner played the comic who delivered the jokes while the other, who fed lines to the comedian, talked "straight" and thus was called a "straight man." The comic ridiculed his straight man with insult jokes and hit him on the head with a bladder. There were several variations on the routine. Sometimes the stooge was planted in the audience, where he heckled his partner by constantly interrupting him. Sometimes the vaudeville comic used the orchestra leader in the pit as his stooge. In radio's early years orchestra leaders and program announcers doubled as straight men. The announcer Jimmy Wallington served as Eddie Cantor's straight man on *The Chase and Sanborn Hour*. Joe Cook was probably the first comedian to have a stooge on radio: he used John S. Young as a straight man in 1929.

The repartee between Wynn and McNamee was similar to vaudeville format. McNamee set jokes up for the Fire Chief by asking questions or making a statement. The exchange between Wynn and his straight man revolved around a series of questions and answers. It took four to six lines of dialogue to reach the punch line:

GRAHAM   Say Chief, I read in the papers that you had an explosion on the farm.

WYNN   Oh, I had a terrible explosion on the farm, Graham.

GRAHAM   Well, how did it happen?

WYNN   My pet hen ate some popcorn and then sat on a stove.

After a large guffaw from the audience the process was repeated:

WYNN   Graham, I had a friend of mine down to my farm the other day and I served him some beer. I served him some beer, Graham, and do you know what he said?

GRAHAM   No, Chief, what did he say?

WYNN   He said, "I don't want that! Bring me a whole stein. Bring me a whole stein!" So you know what I brought him?

GRAHAM   What did you bring him, Chief?

WYNN   A cow![19]

At the program's end McNamee read fictitious letters from listeners, asking questions of the Fire Chief. Wynn always had a funny reply:

GRAHAM   Here's one from Southern Pines, North Carolina.

WYNN   Oh, I love Southern Pines.

GRAHAM   Dear Fire Chief: As you know everything, can you tell me what does it mean when a married man dreams he's a bachelor? Signed, Hotsie Totsie.

WYNN   Dear Hotsie Totsie: When a married man dreams that he's a bachelor it's a sign he's going to meet with a great disappointment when he wakes up.[20]

On the stage the entertainer had earned a reputation as a talented story-telling comedian. Wynn's story jokes were no doubt inane and corny, but on radio he told them in a hilarious manner, chuckling and giggling between sentences and varying the pitch of his voice. "It is not the story so much as the way it is told that draws the laugh," he commented. Wynn once related a yarn about a father who told his son to write an essay on milk:

> The father says "you still have to write a ten page essay on milk." And the boy said "I'm too tired Papa, I'm only going to write one page on milk." The father says: "How can you do that?" He says, "well, I'm making it *condensed* milk."[21]

Longer versions of story-telling jokes were Wynn's preposterous descriptions of operas, fairy tales, and novels. On many shows he poked fun at the melodramatic plots of operas. *The Fire Chief* broadcast of May 31, 1932, was highlighted by Wynn's takeoff on *Carmen*.

WYNN   As the curtain goes up on the opera *Carmen*, you see Carmen, the heroine of the opera. She is very pretty but very thin. She is so thin she's just like a bone; in fact her own dog buried her three times in one week. The opera is all about gypsies, and gypsies, as you know, are not very clean people.

GRAHAM   What do you mean, Chief? Don't they wash themselves?

WYNN   Oh, yes, they wash clean but they dry dirty. And in the first scene Carmen says to her father, "Papa your wash is back; the laundry refused it." Her father is the king of the gypsies and he is a very old man. He's so old he gets winded playing checkers. He decides to go fishing. It seems he can only eat soft foods as he has a pullman mouth.

GRAHAM   A pullman mouth?

WYNN   Yes, a pullman mouth. My goodness, Graham, don't you know what a pullman mouth is—no lowers and very few uppers. . . . The next scene is the bull fight. The arena is gaily decorated. Royalty and peasants are turning out for the great battle of the year. A carriage drives up to the entrance. A nobleman steps out. He is the pillar of society. The crowd knows this and they lean on him. He is the Earl of Wintergreen. He buys five bags of peanuts to take in the royal box with him. He hates peanuts but loves to blow up the bags and break them. Carmen too is in the royal box. It is a day when rich and poor mingle. In fact you see Carmen, the cigarette girl, rubbing shoulders with the Earl of Wintergreen. SoOoOoOo—in his dressing room, Escamillio is pacing the floor. His toreador's costume hasn't come back from the cleaners. The spectators are yelling for Escamillio. He cannot wait for his costume to come, so he rushes into the arena in his underwear and the bull sees red. Escamillio wins the fight and so he will not also win Carmen. Hosay shoots her but she does not die. That night she calls up Escamillio and says, "Did you read in the papers that I have been killed?" And he says, "Yes, I know you're dead. Which place are you calling from?"[22]

Wynn enjoyed spoofing the Texaco gas commercials on the broadcasts. He and other radio personalities began joking about products in the early 1930's. In 1932, Pabst Blue Ribbon beer sponsored orchestra leader Ben Bernie, who gave his version of the commercial: "The old Alma Malta, preferred by the maltitudes. Blue Ribbon Malta is the mosta of the besta." Ray Perkins jested that Jergens lotion "is of no use whatsoever in improving your poker hands." Wynn made kidding the sponsor a permanent part of his program. The power of Texaco Fire Chief gasoline was the subject of several jokes:

> WYNN   I spilt some Fire Chief gas in the field where I keep my horse, you know, . . . Some grasshoppers were on the field and they got hold of some of this Fire Chief gasoline.
>
> GRAHAM   What happened?
>
> WYNN   Well, it was so powerful. . . . When I got back the grasshoppers had eaten the horse and were pitching horseshoes to see who would eat the saddle.

Wynn sometimes needled McNamee when the announcer was delivering the Texaco commercial. The comedian interrupted him with such remarks as "is that so," "fancy that," "my goodness," or "starting up again." Wynn especially ribbed McNamee about his exuberant praise of Fire Chief gasoline: "Don't talk to me about gas, Graham. If a doctor ever operated on you for appendicitis, he'd find himself opening a gas station." At first sponsors did not like their products spoofed, but companies soon learned that it was a humorous, effective way to advertise. Sponsors also aimed to associate their product with a popular comedian. Calling Wynn "The Fire Chief" was an example of this device.[23]

McNamee once made a blooper during a commercial, and it became the subject of a national joke. On the August 9, 1932, program, he inadvertently mispronounced gasoline "gasoloon." Wynn, a good ad-libber, quickly caught the blunder:

WYNN   Ah, ah, ah. He says "gasoloon" (much laughter). Maybe that's the trouble, Graham (laughter).

GRAHAM   I guess it is.

WYNN   Yes, my uncle uses a different "gasoloon."

Believing he might have offended McNamee, Wynn went backstage after the broadcast and apologized to the announcer. McNamee good-naturedly accepted the comedian's apology. "You're the first star I know who has ever given a tumble to anyone's feelings," the announcer said. The word "gasoloon" soon became a running gag and catch phrase on the program:

WYNN   What cost the most, Texaco Fire Chief gasoline or Texaco Fire Chief "gasoloon"?

GRAHAM   Chief, are you going to keep after me just for one little mistake?

WYNN   Well you shouldn't make a mistake, Graham. I'm not keeping after you for that.

The blooper was publicized in newspapers and people started using the word "gasoloon" in everyday conversation.[24]

"A comedian," Wynn once said, "is not a man who says funny things. A comedian is a man who says things funny." His visual clowning was lost on the home listening audience. To offset that handicap he emphasized an amusing speaking voice on the air. "It was radio that converted Dad from a classical clown into a stand-up comic," admitted Keenan Wynn. He continued to use several speech affectations he had used on stage, particularly an occasional lisp and giggling in the middle of a joke. The laugh-getter had an hilarious sounding delivery that suggested the character of a foolish clown on the radio.[25]

On the first *Fire Chief* program Wynn began talking in a high-pitched voice because he was nervous:

> When I rushed out and started to speak, it was in that high register, and unconsciously I stayed with it throughout the broadcast. It wasn't until afterward that I realized what I had done. And do you know I had the devil's own time duplicating that pitch for a while? I had to play back the recordings of that first broadcast and listen to it several times before I had it down to the

point where it became second nature to me. And I've
broadcast in that voice range ever since.

On radio Wynn concentrated on making his lines sound funny.
"In my broadcasts," he stated, "I doubt if I really tell more than
two or three real jokes or gags. The rest is made up of lines. And
the success of those lines depends not so much in how they look
as in how I say them."[26]

Wynn used other devices to stimulate laughter on his broadcasts, including a long-drawn-out so-o-o-o-o injected in his story-
telling jokes to make them sound funnier. There are two versions
describing the origins of that particular artifice. One evening
while performing on stage he got a swelling in his throat and by
mistake blurted out so-o-o-o-o. The audience burst out laughing.
Realizing he might have discovered a good gimmick, he repeated
the expression and received more laughter. Eventually the word
became a permanent part of his routine. A more frequently
quoted story suggests that he first used the phrase in the musical
revue, *The Laugh Parade*, in 1931. His mother had the habit of
employing the expression whenever she stopped to think. One
night while she was attending *The Laugh Parade* the comedian
mimicked his mother. She and her friends and the rest of the
audience laughed at the imitation. From then on he used the device on stage and radio.[27]

As a vaudeville comedian, Wynn's repertoire had included
many puns. Wordplay appeared quite frequently in early radio
humor, because vaudevillians had largely depended on them in
their comedy stage routines. Wynn was a master at punning and
used many such gags on radio. "I love puns," he once remarked
on the air. "You notice tonight I'm almost pun struck." His wordplay gags sound trite today, but back in radio's early years audiences thrived on these typical Wynn puns:

> The darnest thing happened. I was just carrying a jar
> of jelly wrapped in a newspaper when it fell on the floor
> and broke. You should see the *jam* [*italics mine*] Dick
> Tracy is in today!

> He said he wants one tooth pulled he said to the dentist.
> And then the Judge said to him, he said, "do you swear

you'll pull the tooth, the whole tooth, and nothing but the tooth?"

On radio a pun had to be carefully delivered so that the home listener would catch the double meaning. Although puns never completely disappeared from radio comedy, these types of jokes decreased as shows became more professional and innovative.[28]

Known as The Perfect Fool on stage and radio, Wynn's broadcasts were farcical and farfetched. He once commented that "humor is the truth and wit is the exaggeration of truth." A typical Wynn gag was based on an extreme exaggeration of truth. The comedian enjoyed jokes that were comically absurd and even joked about his style. "Some of these, Graham, are absolutely ridiculous," said Wynn. "But I love them when they're silly." His nonsensical gags had little basis in reality. As a result he was the ultimate escapist comedian for the Great Depression.[29]

Wynn's comic idiocy carried great appeal during the economic crisis. His buffoonery temporarily took listeners' minds off their problems. "I'd rather make a nation laugh than cry," he stated. Like other early radio comedians, Wynn cracked jokes about the Depression. He had the ability to clown about any subject, including bread lines:

GRAHAM   Here's one from Metropolis, Illinois. . . . Dear Fire Chief . . . I would like to be a baker when I grow up. Is there such a thing as a course in college which teaches the art of baking. Signed . . . Domestic Science.

WYNN   Dear Domestic Science . . . There must be a course in college which teaches baking because I know a fellow who went to college and after a four year loaf went into a bread line.

Gags poking fun at the naïve hope that good times were "just around the corner" also appeared on *The Fire Chief* broadcast:

GRAHAM   Things are improving, undoubtedly. The darkest hours are over.

WYNN   Oh, I agree with you Graham, the darkest hours are over. You can tell that because the pay envelopes are getting lighter all the time.[30]

Newspaper articles praised *The Fire Chief* program as an important morale booster for the nation. An article in the *Milwaukee Journal*, published on August 6, 1932, was headlined "Ed Wynn Leading Fans Away from Depression." Wynn's humor was so infectious, the reporter suggested, that he made "landlords forget their rent." Listening to Ed Wynn had become such a household ritual by 1932 that NBC received hundreds of telephone calls from fans complaining of missing the broadcast because a campaign speech by President Hoover ran overtime. *The Nation* magazine reported on Hoover's blunder:

> Even Americans will rebel if things go too far. At eight-thirty on a recent evening the populace of the United States, respectful if dubious, tuned in on Mr. Hoover's portentous speech in Iowa. At nine-thirty, accustomed to the prompt intervention of the omnipotent announcer, the listeners confidently awaited the President's concluding words. Confidently and also impatiently; for at nine-thirty on every Tuesday evening Mr. Ed Wynn comes on the air. But Mr. Hoover had only arrived at point number two of his twelve-point program. The populace shifted in its myriad seats; wives looked at husbands; children, allowed to remain up till ten on Tuesdays, looked in alarm at the clock; twenty thousand votes shifted to Franklin Roosevelt. Nine-forty-five: Mr. Hoover had arrived at point four; five million Americans consulted their radio programs and discovered that Ed Wynn's time had not been altered or canceled; two million switched off their instruments and sent their children to bed weeping; votes lost to Mr. Hoover multiplied too fast for computation. Ten o'clock: the candidate solemnly labored point number seven; too late to hope for even a fragment of Ed Wynn. What did the N.B.C. mean by this outrage? Whose hour was it anyhow? Ten million husbands and wives retired to bed in a mood of bitter rebellion; no votes left for Hoover. Did the Republican National Committee pay for the half hour thus usurped by its candidate? If so, we can assure it that $5,000 was never less well spent.

"I never thought President Hoover would play a trick like this on me," joked Wynn. One reporter suggested that "if President

Hoover loses the election by a small majority . . . it may well be that the revenge of Ed Wynn fans will be responsible."[31]

Wynn's success on the radio peaked during the 1932–33 season, when the nation was paralyzed by unemployment, business failures, and bank closings. In 1933 *The Fire Chief* program had a C.A.B. rating of 44.8, meaning that nearly one-half of the homes in which ratings were taken listened to Ed Wynn. The next year, however, his rating declined to 31.6, and by 1935 it was down to 25.6. *The Fire Chief* program went off the air in May 1935, when Texaco, noticing the declining ratings, withdrew its sponsorship.[32]

Shortly thereafter Wynn starred in a new series called *Gulliver*, broadcast on Thursday night over the NBC Blue network during the 1935–36 season. The comedian, who played Jonathan Swift's Gulliver, called his role "a titular device by which I am enabled ; . . to travel hither and yon, while tossing around gags in the manner of my regular routine." Although the format resembled *The Fire Chief* broadcasts, the program failed to attract a wide audience. Not only was Wynn's brand of humor becoming less popular, but the show lacked sparkle. John S. Young, Wynn's new straight man, did not compare with Graham McNamee, who was unavailable for the series. The program lasted less than a year.[33]

In November 14, 1936, Wynn returned to the airwaves on *The Perfect Fool* broadcast, heard over the NBC Blue network on Saturday evening at 8 p.m. The show was based on the character the star had developed on stage. Wynn continued to parody plots of operas and novels and played musical instruments, including the piano. He often used guest stars as foils, ribbing the celebrities and interrupting them in the middle of a song or performance. McNamee returned as Wynn's straight man, doing similar question-and-answer gags. Although the program had some entertaining features, its mood of inane nonsense did not attract a large audience. It had a low Hooper rating—11.5—in January 1937—and by the end of the year the show was off the air. The listening public had tired of Wynn's clowning.[34]

By 1937, radio comedy was entering a new phase, with character comedians and cleverly written situation comedy. The character comedian, Jack Benny, and the situation comedy,

Fibber McGee and Molly, represented an innovative humor that took full advantage of radio's strength as a sound medium. Old vaudeville jokes, puns, and one-liners were being used less frequently. Wynn's routines were too dependent on stale vaudeville gags, and he failed to develop a new repertoire or radio character to sustain his popularity. His corny puns appeared dated by 1937. Wynn was also handicapped by the fact that he was mainly a visual clown, so that on radio much of his humor was lost. Due to the poor reception of the *Gulliver* and *Perfect Fool* programs, he decided to forgo radio for a time except for occasional guest spots.

Wynn's disillusionment with radio also stemmed from a financial misfortune in the medium. In 1933 he had formed a national broadcasting chain of twenty-three stations called the Amalgamated Broadcasting Company. He wanted the network to broadcast quality programs in music, the arts, politics, and popular entertainment. He hoped that the chain could also hire unemployed actors and actresses during the Great Depression. The call letters of the major outlet in New York City, WNEW, was named after Wynn. The network's inaugural program, broadcast on September 25, 1933, featured celebrities in politics, business, and the arts. Wynn had invested a quarter of a million dollars to start the network, but after six weeks the chain went bankrupt. Busy in Hollywood making a movie, Wynn had let the new company become mismanaged. He had to sell his holdings at a loss to pay off creditors.[35]

During the mid-1930's Wynn also had considerable family problems. The comedian's public image as a clown contrasted sharply with his unhappy private life. Wynn was so involved with his career in radio, movies, and the theater that he had little time to spend with his family. His son remembered his father returning home exhausted from work and unable to play with him. "He gave to people but there was nothing left when he came home," Keenan Wynn recalled. Ed's relationship with his son was often strained and was not helped by Keenan, who felt that he had to live up to his father's reputation.[36]

During the time *The Fire Chief* program was on the air Wynn was also having marital difficulties. His marriage to Hilda

Keenan, the daughter of the actor Frank Keenan, had been shaky for a number of years. Wynn separated from his wife in 1934, and in December 1936 she sued him for divorce on grounds of cruelty. She accused him of having an adulterous relationship with Frieda Mierse, an ex-Follies beauty and former Miss America of 1927. His wife also claimed that her husband had kept her a prisoner in New York's Doctors Hospital. The comedian stated that she had been confined to the hospital because of drinking problems. His wife rose habitually at two o'clock in the morning and had the chauffeur drive her to nightclubs, from which she returned intoxicated. Wynn was also sued in 1935 by his aunt and uncle, Mr. and Mrs. Samuel Greenberg, for $115,000—a sum they claimed Wynn owed them for taking care of his alcoholic wife for two years. The court eventually settled this suit in favor of the comedian, awarding the Greenbergs a token sum of $1000. The Wynns were legally divorced in May 1937, but instead of the $3500-a-week alimony his wife had requested, the court granted her $300 a week. Later that year Wynn married Frieda Mierse, but their marriage lasted only two years. Depressed about his private life, Wynn lived for several years as a recluse in a Manhattan hotel apartment, leaving only occasionally at night for a stroll down Fifth Avenue.[37]

In September 1944 Wynn returned to radio on *The Happy Island* program, which was broadcast Monday evening on the new American Broadcasting Company. The comedian played the part of King Bubbles, the lovable monarch of a mythical kingdom, Happy Island. The broadcast resembled a stage show. The cast wore funny costumes and facial makeup and elaborately decorated sets were used. The program had many character parts played by excellent performers and funny skits written by an able writing staff. One amusing spot featured Wynn reading bedtime stories to a young girl. But as a whole the broadcasts failed to click. During January 1945 the show had a very low Hooper rating—4.4—and in early 1945 Borden Milk dropped the program. *Happy Island*, which lasted only twenty-six weeks, was another disappointment to Wynn. In 1946, he briefly returned as the Fire Chief on the *Texaco Star Theatre*.[38]

Except for *The Fire Chief* program, Wynn's career in radio

never was as great a success as it had been on stage, television, and the movies. Wynn nonetheless contributed to early radio comedy. He was one of the first entertainers to use a live audience, and his nonsensical humor let people temporarily forget their troubles during the critical years of the Great Depression. Television later gave Wynn the opportunity to show the full range of his talent that had been partly inhibited on radio. When he died on June 19, 1966, he was mourned by the entertainment industry as a great artist—a comedian's comedian. He was "undoubtedly the greatest comedian and the man who taught all of us something," Jack Benny said.[39]

6

Zanies

During the critical years of the Great Depression zaniness was fashionable on the airwaves. Other comedy buffoons besides Wynn entertained listeners, chiefly Joe Penner, Jack Pearl, Raymond Knight, and Stoopnagle and Budd. Their madcap style was the perfect anodyne for the troubled economic times and mirrored the period's turmoil. But, like Wynn, they peaked in popularity in the early 1930's and then slowly faded from the limelight. Two great slapstick comics, Bert Lahr and Groucho Marx, also tried radio at the time. The difficulties those visual comedians encountered in a sound medium were similar to the problems Wynn faced.

Joe Penner had been an unknown comedian on the burlesque circuit before he became an overnight sensation on radio. His rise to stardom resembled a rags-to-riches story. Born Josef Pinter in a village near Budapest in 1904, young Penner emigrated to the United States around 1916. He grew up as a poor boy in Detroit, Michigan. At age fourteen he left school and worked in many odd jobs—as a newspaper and magazine salesman, a foundry worker, and a lens grinder. Penner was a talented child. He sang in the church choir, imitated Charlie Chaplin at amateur vaudeville nights, and earned money giving fiddle lessons.[1]

When Penner was about sixteen he decided to enter show business. He had to begin at the bottom. He was fired as an

assistant to a magician and mind-reader when he mistakenly
revealed a magic act by exposing the rigging supporting a float-
ing woman. But Penner's main ambition was to be a comedian.
Once he replaced a comic in a nightclub burlesque show. The
manager liked his act so much that he hired him for $35 a week.
The aspiring showman later picked up occasional nightclub and
burlesque jobs, mainly one night stands. Most of the time he was
broke and hungry. In 1923 he joined a traveling carnival doing
a comedy act with a Greek straight man. Then he turned to playing second-rate nightclubs, called "toilets" in the trade, and to
working on the burlesque circuit. Sometimes he got roles in
musical revues. At the eve of the stock market crash very few
people had heard of Joe Penner.

Penner played a dumb fool in his burlesque act. He imitated
a wide range of ethnic characters and did female impersonations.
The stand-up comic hollered, cackled, and mugged his lines, pep-
pering the audience with a barrage of inanities. Dressed in a
derby hat and smoking a cigar, he asked questions such as
"Wanna buy an ashcan?" or "Wanna buy a rhinoceros?" One
night in 1931, while appearing in a revue in Birmingham, Alabama, Penner ad-libbed the line "Wanna buy a duck?" and the
audience laughed hysterically. Soon radio listeners across the
nation would be repeating the expression.

Penner made his radio debut on Rudy Vallee's *Fleischmann
Hour*, a popular early variety program which had premiered on
NBC in 1929. Responsible for developing the show's variety format was John Reber, who was then in charge of radio at J.
Walter Thompson, the advertising agency handling Vallee's
sponsor, Standard Brands. Radio departments in advertising
agencies were creating shows for clients who were anxious to sell
their products on the air. Ideas for programming were generated
in the departments rather than the networks, which would buy
the package (writers, performers, staff) from the agency. A king-
pin of early radio, Reber aimed to give the listening public a
variety of excellent entertainment and to discover new talent for
the Vallee program. Vallee himself recalled that the producers
"were scurrying everywhere beating the bushes to fish out possible performers." In addition to Penner, the Vallee show intro-

duced ventriloquist Edgar Bergen and his dummy, Charlie Mc-
Carthy, comedian Bob Burns, and impersonator Tommy Riggs to
radio. Penner, who was offered $750 to go on *The Fleischmann
Hour* in 1933, was worried about how his stage act would sound
on radio. Vallee introduced him as "a really great comedian"
who should be better known to the public. Penner replied "Hello,
Rudy; wanna buy a duck?" When Vallee answered that he did
not want to buy a duck, the comedian retorted shrilly, "you
nah-h-sty man!" That remark later became another well-known
Penner expression. The comic's debut was so successful he returned to make other guest spots on the Vallee program. Those
appearances made Penner a national sensation.[2]

Standard Brands signed the funnyman to host *The Bakers'
Broadcast* in 1933. Penner received $7500 for each thirty-minute
Sunday night program on the CBS network. *The Bakers' Broadcast* emphasized farcical comedy, and it also provided musical
entertainment with Ozzie Nelson's orchestra and vocals by Harriet Hilliard, later Nelson's wife. Penner did comedy exchanges
with a straight man and played roles in farfetched skits. His
act, which depended on funny-sounding lines, at first transferred
well to radio. He relied on repeating foolish catch phrases on
every program. Listeners waited eagerly to hear him say
"Wanna buy a duck?" "Iz dat so?" "Don't ever doooo that!" and
"You nah-h-sty man!" The funnyman also became noted for his
"yuk yuk" laugh. A Penner radio routine exuded uninhibited
craziness:

JOE	Iz zat so? I'm a bird and animal lover. Did you ever see my cat?
STRAIGHT	No. I never saw your cat.
JOE	Well, every one says I've got the funniest puss you ever saw.
STRAIGHT	I agree with that.
JOE	Oh, you nasty man.
STRAIGHT	Listen, is there something you want to ask me?
JOE	Just one question—but it's very important.
STRAIGHT	What is it?
JOE	Do you wanna buy a duck?
STRAIGHT	What?

> JOE   Do you wanna buy a duck?
> STRAIGHT No, I don't want any ducks. The nearest thing I have to
>   it is a swan. . . .
> JOE   Well, do you wanna buy a duck's egg.
> STRAIGHT I don't eat duck eggs.
> JOE   These ain't for eating—they're for throwing.
> STRAIGHT I'm not interested.
> JOE   Aw, just take a look at this duck. Margie, say hello to
>   the big bad man.
> DUCK   Quack! Quack! Hello.[3]

Penner's style caught on with the fun-hungry Americans, who were experiencing the worst economic crisis of their lives. His lunacy, which had little relation to reality, provided escapist entertainment. Penner bought a live duck, posed with it for publicity photographs, and named it "Goo-Goo." The duck became a national craze, a symbol of the times. In 1934, Penner's show, which had a C.A.B. rating of 35.2, was rated the second most popular comedy program on the air. In June 1934, he was voted the best comedian on radio.[4]

By 1935, however, there were signs that his style was losing appeal. He was overworking his catch phrases, and audiences were tiring of the blabbermouth routines. He blamed the program's slump in ratings on the advertising agency, which wanted him to keep the same repertoire. But there were other problems besides the agency's reluctance to change the format. Penner's portrayal of the ignorant, pitiful, and arrogant fool did not wear well, and listeners were discovering other comedians who were offering a new type of character comedy, entertainers like Jack Benny. After two years on the air Penner's program sounded stale. He left the show after the 1934–35 season, blaming the program's demise on the Thompson agency. In fact, Penner's sponsors probably felt the comedian's act was not versatile enough to survive on radio.

After the initial success of his first radio series, Penner's career went downhill. During the 1936–37 season he did a Sunday night situation comedy series over the CBS network. Penner played a bungling, ne'er-do-well member of a wealthy family called the Park Avenue Penners. Although the role was made for Penner, the scripts varied in quality. The program, which registered a 16.1 Hooper rating in January 1938, did not have a large following. Two other situation comedies he tried flopped badly. Those failures convinced Penner to leave radio in 1940 and return to the stage.[5]

While in Philadelphia, appearing on stage in the production *Yokel Boy*, Penner dropped dead of a heart attack on January 10, 1941. He was only thirty-six years old. The comedian's fame was so brief that he remains a relatively unknown personality, and his radio shows, which are rarely replayed, sound dated. Penner's style appealed to listeners in the early 1930's, when "perfect fools" were in vogue.

Another popular radio buffoon at that time was Jack Pearl, who grew up during the turn of the century in New York City's Lower East Side. The young boy was surrounded by all the color of Jewish immigrant life. The environment undoubtedly influenced the direction of Pearl's comedy, because he later became famous for German dialect routines, ethnic characterizations, and funny stories about the old country. He entered show business as a child actor in Gus Edwards's children's revue, *School Days*, which also had young George Jessel and Walter Winchell in the cast. Pearl then worked as a comic in burlesque shows and appeared in a two-man act with Ben Bard in vaudeville. When the team split up Pearl began doing a single in vaudeville and Broadway musicals. By the mid-1920's he was a headliner, playing the Palace on several occasions and starring in *Artists and Models* (1927), a Broadway show, and in the last *Ziegfeld Follies* (1931).[6]

The demise of vaudeville prompted Pearl to turn to radio. He did a guest spot on Ed Sullivan's radio program and starred on the 1932 *Ziegfeld Follies of the Air*. He was such a sensation on the Ziegfeld broadcast that Lucky Strike signed him for the 1932–33 season to star in a sixty-minute Thursday night variety program on the NBC Red network. That show received one of the highest ratings in radio in 1933.[7]

Pearl played the role of Baron von Munchausen. One of radio's first comic braggarts, the Baron was based on an eighteenth-century German cavalry officer who had exaggerated his deeds and travels in writing. Pearl's characterization also derived from ethnic stage comedy. German dialect comics, or "Dutch acts," as they were called, had been popular on the vaudeville stage. Even before vaudeville minstrel comics had mimicked German accents and mannerisms. Over the air Pearl spun preposterous tall tales about the Baron. When his straight man, Cliff Hall, known as "Sharlie," questioned his farfetched stories, the Baron would retort, "Vas you dere, Sharlie?" Pearl's writer, Billy Wells, thought Hall's first name was Charlie, and he had the Baron say the line after every colossal lie. Like Penner's "Wanna buy a duck?" it became a popular catch phrase, repeated by listeners.[8]

The repartee between Pearl and Hall resembled standard vaudeville straight-man and comic routines. Hall played an intelligent type, while Pearl impersonated the stupid, egocentric Baron. The stooge fed lines to the comedian:

> PEARL   I went to correspondence school.
> HALL   I didn't know they had correspondence schools on the Continent.
> PEARL   Sure. . . . They threw me out from there.
> HALL   They threw you out of the correspondence school?
> PEARL   I played hooky.
> HALL   You played hooky from a correspondence school. How is that possible?
> PEARL   I sent them an empty envelope.[9]

The full range of Pearl's talent can only be appreciated by listening to a broadcast. He had a hilarious German accent, a ludicrous laugh, and a fine sense of timing and delivery that made him an overnight sensation. The character of the Baron was so popular that Pearl made an MGM movie, *Meet the Baron*, in 1933.

Pearl started a rage for ethnic characters on radio. In the mid-1930's Bert Gordon, an ex-vaudevillian, played the Mad Russian on Eddie Cantor's show. The Mad Russian became known for his expression "How doo you doo?" Harry Einstein, a former advertising copy writer, did a Greek character called Parkyakarkus on Cantor's program. Like the Baron, these ethnic stereotype characters spoke in exaggerated dialect and resembled stock stage types.

Joe Penner: "Wanna buy a duck!"
(Copyright by Frank Bresee.)

Jack Pearl and Muriel Evans in a
publicity still for the movie *Meet the
Baron* (1933).

Stoopnagle and Budd (Frederick
Chase Taylor and Wilbur Budd
Hulick)

Since Pearl's act lacked versatility, his popularity plummeted as fast as it had risen. After his successful 1932–33 program he did a thirty-minute Wednesday night show for Royal Gelatin, but it received mediocre ratings. A 1936–37 Monday night show for Raleigh cigarettes likewise had little appeal. There are several explanations for Pearl's demise. His routine was too derivative of vaudeville, and audiences gradually tired of his set routine, which he repeated constantly on every program. Jack Benny warned Pearl that he was overusing the "Vas you dere, Scharlie?" expression. He urged him to drop the catch phrase and try something else for a few weeks. "Then when you hit the audience with the line, it will be even funnier," Benny recommended. "Are you out of your mind?" Pearl replied. " 'Vas you dere' is the biggest thing on my show . . . the listener can't wait for it . . . they expect it. If I don't do it each time, they'll be disappointed." Like Penner's routine, Pearl's act did not have enough credibility to remain on the air for a long time. Although Pearl tried several comebacks on radio and television, he never regained the fame he had had as Baron von Munchausen in 1932–33.[10]

Listeners could find other zany comedy shows on their radio dial. Riotous "nut" acts and "dumb" monologuists were featured on the popular CBS *Nit Wit Hour* in 1930–31. Another uproarious broadcast was the *Cuckoo Hour*, starring Raymond Knight. A former lawyer, playwright, and actor, Knight became a radio fan while confined to bed with pleurisy in 1928. Shortly afterward he obtained a position with NBC as a continuity writer, preparing program introductions, commercials, news bulletins, and interviews. Bertha Brainard, a network program executive, asked Knight to create a comedy show for a thirty-minute opening in the schedule. "What kind of a program?" inquired Knight. "Something zany, something cuckoo," she suggested.[11]

Knight's brainchild was the popular *Cuckoo Hour*, which started as a Wednesday night feature on January 1, 1930. The comedian, who had studied playwriting in George Pierce Baker's "47 Workshop" at Harvard University and had won a Drama League writing award, found that experience helpful in radio. "Usually I would start with a phrase or a snatch of dialogue on some topic and develop the program from there," he remarked. The fact that Knight did not come from the vaudeville stage helped him create a more original show for radio. "I didn't write gags and I didn't have any gag files. So I had to depend on my own imagination." Sheer lunacy reigned on the *Cuckoo Hour*. A brash announcer set the tone of the program at the beginning:

> Good evening, friends—and what of it? The next fifteen minutes are to be devoted to a broadcast of the Cuckoo Hour, radio's oldest network comedy program, and if you don't think that's something—well maybe you're right. The Cuckoos feature Raymond Knight, the radio humorist, as Station KUKU's Master of Ceremonies, and Ambrose J. Weems, and there are a lot of other disreputable things about the Cuckoo Hour which are too numerous to mention at this time. Are you still with us? Ho hum, there's no accounting for tastes. We now turn you over to Station KUKU.

Knight then started jesting about the number of stale jokes on radio:

> Good evening, fellow pixies, this is Raymond Knight, the Voice of the Diaphragm e-nun-ciating. I thought up the Knight plan for old joke pensions one evening while listening to a phonograph record which was made recently of one of the Cuckoo programs. And it suddenly occurred to me, how many old jokes there were on the radio which really ought to be pensioned. Now here's the way my plan works. After a joke has been in use on the radio for sixty years, and this takes in ninety-nine and forty-four hundredths of them, then it becomes automatically entitled to an old joke pension. The last person to use the joke immediately begins to receive an income of two hundred dollars per month. The comedians will naturally seize the opportunity for three square meals a day, and half of them will overeat on the first meal and die from digestion. This will leave only twenty-five per cent of the radio comedians alive. I think by now you are beginning to get the idea.[12]

One of radio's first satirists, Knight spoofed all types of subjects. No topic was out of bounds for his humor. He poked fun at news headlines, women's fashions, bankers, department stores, the weather. During a hot spell in August 1933 Knight wrote a program about a winter sports carnival in which "almost every fourth word in the script was 'snow.' " Several times during the broadcast Knight asked his listeners if they were any cooler. Knight was also one of the first comedians to parody radio programs. He wrote takeoffs on morning exercise shows, lecture programs, and classical music hours, calling the last "music depreciation." One skit concerned the radio home economist Mrs. Pennyfeather, who ran a "Personal Service for Perturbed People." Believing babies caught cold because they had little hair, Mrs. Pennyfeather invented a tiny toupee, which she tried on a baby during a broadcast. The reluctant infant cried when she put the toupee on his head. "Don't you want nice hair on your head like mine?" she inquired. Suddenly the baby pulled at her hair, and the home economist's wig came off. "This concludes Mrs. Pennyfeather's demonstration of her Baby Toupee," said Knight. The baby "is now using it as a beard, which now leads me to call him the *Heir apparent.*"[13]

The madcap horseplay on the program delighted the public in the early 1930's. Knight was named the "No. 1 radio wit in the United States" in a 1932 New York *World-Telegram* poll of radio editors. After the *Cuckoo Hour* went off the air in the mid-1930's Knight tried other programs, but with limited success. In 1938, he left radio in order to devote himself to playwriting. Three years later he returned to NBC as a writer, and eventually he became a director and program executive. A pioneer of radio satire, Knight influenced Bob Elliott of Bob and Ray and was respected by other entertainers. Groucho Marx, for example, once called him "the best comedian on the air."[14]

The irreverent comedy on the *Cuckoo Hour* hour can be compared with the Marx Brothers movies, *The Cocoanuts* (1929), *Animal Crackers* (1930), *Monkey Business* (1931), and *Horse Feathers* (1932). Appearing during the depths of the Great Depression, those Marx Brothers classics have been called "anarcho-nihilist laff riots." According to film historian Andrew Bergman, "the most desperate years of our national experience produced our most desperate comedy, one that rang some hilarious and savage changes on a hundred conventions." Knight's comedy was too inane to suggest social anarchy, but he and the other radio zanies shared with the Marx Brothers a style of buffoonery reflective of the turmoil of the economic collapse.[15]

During the 1932–33 season Groucho and Chico Marx starred in *Flywheel, Shyster and Flywheel*, a Monday evening broadcast of horseplay on the NBC Blue. Despite a good 22.1 C.A.B. rating, the sponsor, Esso gasoline, dropped the show after only one season. Groucho resented being taken off the air by a petroleum company:

> Company sales, as a result of our show, had risen precipitously. Profits doubled in that brief time, and Esso felt guilty taking the money. So Esso dropped us after twenty-six weeks. Those were the days of guilt-edged securities, which don't exist today.[16]

Until 1947 Marx had difficulty finding the right type of radio format for his talent. He and Chico played Hollywood agents in a series that did not remain long on the air. *The Circle* (1939), a spontaneous and sophisticated round-table discussion broadcast with many stars, including Groucho and Chico, Basil Rathbone, and the master of ceremonies, Ronald Colman, lasted less than a season. Although the critics raved about the show, it did not draw enough listeners. Groucho tried several other programs, but they all failed dismally. He performed best as the comedy star of *Blue Ribbon Town* in 1943–44, a variety show buttressed by singers and guest stars. Groucho's problems in radio were similar to Ed Wynn's, in that Marx was primarily a visual physical comic, and much of his talent was lost in a sound medium. Radio allowed him to flaunt his superb talent as a punster, but he disliked reading "canned" or prepared script material and was best in an extemporaneous format. In 1947 Marx began *You Bet Your Life* on radio, a comic quiz show in which he could ad-lib with contestants. The television version permitted him to use the full range of his talent. A brilliant movie and television comedian, Marx found the sound medium of radio confining, and consequently he never became a major radio comedy star.

Bert Lahr, another great visual clown, also was inhibited by

radio. A famous comedian on Broadway, Lahr depended on slapstick, funny costumes, and mugging to get laughs on stage. Attracted by the high salaries offered headliners to go on radio,
Lahr signed for a series in 1932. He recalled how awkward he
felt standing stationary in front of a mike:

> When I got in front of that microphone and had to hold
> a paper in my hand, I had fear. If I did it today, things
> would be different. But standing there, trying to read,
> I'd fluff something, and then I'd fight it.

Lahr read his script too fast, was overly self-conscious, and tried
to do raucous burlesque comedy. He had trouble finding the correct intonation for his lines and tended to play to the studio audience rather than to the radio listener. Instead of a physical
gesture he substituted an awkward "huh, huh" to signal the
punchline. It was not entirely Lahr's fault. The director of his
1932 broadcast told him to do his program as if he was appearing
in a Broadway musical. "It was awful. I had a thirteen-week
deal, and after four weeks they paid me off for all thirteen," Lahr
recalled. "The first experience was so painful that I think it gave
me a mental block." The entertainer later became more accustomed to radio by concentrating on punning and verbal pratfalls
in guest spots on the Rudy Vallee, Bing Crosby, and Fred Allen
shows. Yet, like Groucho Marx, Lahr never made it big on
radio.[17]

Some early radio comedy zanies did not come from the vaudeville stage. The two-man comedy team of Stoopnagle and Budd
(Frederick Chase Taylor and Wilbur Budd Hulick) were radio
originals. Taylor was born in Buffalo on October 4, 1897, and,
after a stint in the U.S. Naval Reserve during World War I, he
joined his father's lumber company and later became a stock-
broker. At night he did a comedy act called "Nip and Tuck"
over Buffalo's WMAK in 1925. After the stock market crash
Taylor left the brokerage business and obtained a permanent job
with the Buffalo Broadcasting Corporation, owners of WMAK,
and did everything around the station, including writing, acting,
directing, and announcing. There he met his future partner,
Budd Hulick, the station announcer and a former band leader
and radio disc jockey.[18]

A fortuitous event on October 30, 1930, was responsible for their debut as a comedy team. Because of weather interference WMAK was unable to switch to a scheduled network program. Hulick rushed over to Taylor, who was busy typing at his desk. "The CBS line has broken," Hulick exclaimed anxiously. "There's a hurricane along the coast. We have fifteen minutes to fill. What are we going to do?" Taylor looked bewildered and had no suggestion. "Let's just talk," urged Hulick. "Whatever we say will be better than silence—I hope." For fifteen minutes they ad-libbed without a script or notes, cracking jokes and relating witty stories. They received many fan letters praising their broadcast and asking them to go on the air again.[19]

Encouraged by the listeners' response, the station management decided to broadcast them on a regular basis. Stoopnagle and Budd soon began to attract a large audience in the Buffalo area. Listeners enjoyed their impromptu satirical humor and bizarre skits, which included an eyewitness account of a stunt man walking up a building and a person delivering a kangaroo to a housewife. The comedy team often surprised listeners. Stoopnagle once asked Budd to scratch his back in the middle of a broadcast. Another time Stoopnagle told his partner, "I can't think of anything to say." "Don't worry, Stoop, you always think of something," replied Budd. Physically they resembled Abbott and Costello. Stoopnagle was short and plump, while Budd was tall and lean.[20]

In the 1930's they were heard on network radio first on a fifteen-minute evening program called *The Gloom Chasers*, and then on several variety programs between 1932 and 1937. Instead of using a prepared script, Stoopnagle and Budd worked from notes. "A program built on plain jokes has no flavor, no tone," declared Taylor. "Anyone can tell a joke if it is handed to him in a script." Sometimes their programs lacked sponsors and were broadcast on a sustaining basis. Stoopnagle and Budd liked to make fun of this on the air. "They haven't got a sponsor! They haven't got a sponsor!" the pair shouted. Taylor felt they were better off without a sponsor:

> First we built up a reputation for doing our stuff— stuff we thought funny on the air. Then a sponsor

would come along and hire us for his show. Right away
he would start to change our act. He would insist on our
doing what he thought was funny. Naturally, when we
did this we weren't funny at all because we weren't ourselves.[21]

Stoopnagle and Budd became known for their preposterous
parodies and witty comments on all types of subjects. One was
promotional advertising gimmicks: "Just tear off the top of the
Empire State Building, mail it in and it's yours." Budd played
the straight man, while Colonel Stoopnagle concocted ludicrous
stories:

BUDD   Colonel, what was all that pounding I heard the other
              day in that vacant lot you own?
STOOPNAGLE   That isn't a vacant lot, Budd; that's my new building
              going down.
BUDD   Your new building going up, you mean.
STOOPNAGLE   No, no, no. It's a new kind of a building. It starts at the
              surface of the ground and goes down. You see, it's going
              to have the reputation of being the lowest building in
              New York, like the Empire State Building being the
              highest.
BUDD   What are you going to call the building?
STOOPNAGLE   The Lbiny.
BUDD   Lbiny, huh. How do you spell that word?
STOOPNAGLE   L-b-i-n-y. Lowest-Building-In-New-York. Not bad, eh?
BUDD   No, and not good, either.
STOOPNAGLE   You see, when a visitor comes to my building, I meet
              her at the door and I say: "You are now entering the
              portals of the Lbiny Building, the lowest building in
              New York. As we step into the subtivator—"
BUDD   What's a subtivator?
STOOPNAGLE   It's the opposite of an elevator. It takes you down first,
              instead of up first, like an elevator. . . .
BUDD   And what would you do in case of an earthquake?
STOOPNAGLE   Earthquake? Why, naturally, we'd just let the building
              shake like a bowlful of.
BUDD   Bowlful of what?
STOOPNAGLE   Jelly! What did you think we were building it out of?[22]

Stoopnagle became noted for promoting odd inventions on the
radio, such as the Stoopnagle bed, "with a live snapping turtle

attached to the bottom . . . designed for people who like a quick bite before going to bed." Or a "shoe with a built-in bad taste . . . soaked in vinegar and red pepper . . . to cure people who every time they open their mouth put their foot in it." He coined funny words such as "majamas" (mother's pajamas) and "porcupone" (a porcupine lying face down). He also made up new definitions:

BUDD   Colonel, before you go back to your cell, I wish you'd give me a couple of definitions . . . what is *summer?*
STOOPNAGLE Summer is between spring and fall to make you sorry you complained of the cold last winter, when you were sorry you complained of the heat last summer.
BUDD   Now, what's *winter?*
STOOPNAGLE *Winter* is stuff that rich people go South during.
BUDD   And *spring?*
STOOPNAGLE *Spring* is a thing that when it's snowing out and cold as the dickens, it won't be long until but usually is.
BUDD   One more, Colonel, and we're through, What is *fall?*
STOOPNAGLE *Fall* is something that when a guy likes a girl he hopes she will for him.[23]

Like Penner, Pearl, and Knight, Stoopnagle and Budd were a big comedy hit in the early 1930's and then suddenly went out of fashion. They broke up in 1938 and never achieved similar success alone. Taylor was master of ceremonies for *Music and Manners* on the Mutual network and then returned to local radio. Stoopnagle was the host of a quiz show, *Quixie Doodle*, in 1939, and in the 1940's he made frequent guest appearances on various programs. The zanies were undoubtedly funny for a time, but compared to the new radio comedians, Jack Benny and Fred Allen, they could not attract listeners over a long time span. By 1935 listeners were tuning in to Benny, whose innovative style of character comedy was entirely different.

PART THREE

The New Radio Comedy

7

The Fall Guy

Between 1932 and 1937 Jack Benny created a new program format that changed the nature of radio comedy. The comedian's first five years in broadcasting are crucial for understanding the form's development. Benny's shows de-emphasized timeworn vaudeville routines by reducing the number of puns, he-she jokes, and "feed lines" by the stooge. Unlike Wynn and Penner, Benny's humor relied less on zaniness and more on comic situations derived from his radio persona as a braggart and skinflint. The comedian pretended to be a virtuoso violin player, a handsome movie star, and an ageless bon vivant. Those characteristics were evident in Benny's vaudeville stage personality, but they did not dominate his act until he entered radio. The regular appearance of a radio family, or "gang" (Don Wilson, Phil Harris, Dennis Day, Eddie Anderson, and Mary Livingstone), was another innovation. Benny shifted the focus of his program away from the star to his cast, who got laughs by deflating Benny's ego. As the target of the jokes he gained the sympathy of listeners, who viewed him as a lovable fall guy. Benny played a character easily recognizable in everyday life. "I represent everything that's wrong with anybody," the comedian commented. "The minute I come on, even the most hen-pecked guy in the audience feels good."[1]

Like several other radio comedians (George Burns, Jack Pearl,

Fanny Brice), Benny was the son of Jewish immigrant parents. The jester and the fiddler had been important figures in Yiddish culture. For centuries Jews had turned to humor as a survival mechanism. They laughed off their problems and used wit as a form of self-parody and social commentary. "No other people on earth, whether in the past or the present time, has taken itself so mercilessly as the butt of its own jokes as the Jewish people," wrote the psychoanalyst Martin Grotjahn in *Beyond Laughter:*

> It almost seems as if the Jewish joke in its unbelievable superiority shows the cruel enemy how to be hostile and still remain human. The Jewish joke is only a masochistic mask; it is by no means a sign of masochistic perversion. The Jewish joke constitutes victory by defeat. The persecuted Jew who makes himself the butt of the joke deflects his dangerous hostility away from the persecutors onto himself. The result is not defeat or surrender but victory and greatness.

Unlike other Jewish performers (Eddie Cantor, George Jessel, Al Jolson, Fanny Brice) Benny did not employ Jewish dialect or material in his routine. One reason may have been that he did not grow up in New York's Lower East Side, as did the other entertainers. Benny's reliance on self-disparagement, his portrayal of the victimized fall guy and patsy (a *shnook* and *schlemiel*), his parody of violin playing and his use of the cheapskate stereotype suggests, however, that his ethnic background had an importance on the development of his humor.[2]

Benny's father, Meyer Kubelsky, had grown up in a Lithuanian *shtetl* in the 1880's. Because of pogroms and economic hardships Kubelsky emigrated to the United States in his early twenties. He arrived in New York City in 1889. He traveled to Chicago, where a fellow countryman helped him find a job in a sweatshop, working twelve hours a day. He saved enough money to purchase a horse and wagon, and for several years he peddled kitchenware in small towns bordering Lake Michigan. Whenever he visited Waukegan, Illinois, Kubelsky stayed with a prosperous Jewish tailor, Solomon Schwartz, who convinced him to settle in the growing town. Kubelsky wanted to be a saloonkeeper as his father had been, and so he opened a tavern in Waukegan. In 1893 a matchmaker arranged a marriage between Kubelsky and Emma Sachs, a young Lithuanian Jewish immigrant. A year later Emma was expecting a baby, and she went to Chicago to be with her parents and near a good hospital. The baby, named Benjamin, was born on St. Valentine's Day, February 14, 1894. Forty years later Benjamin, known to Americans as Jack Benny, was the most popular comedian on radio.[3]

The family first lived in a small modest apartment on Glendon Street, located above a butcher shop. Although the saloon business earned Kubelsky a satisfactory income, his wife felt the trade lacked respectability. When her husband was injured in a brawl she convinced him to sell the business. He then opened a small haberdashery shop, which at first barely made enough profit to support the family. The Kubelskys moved to a four-room apartment on Genessee Street, across from the shop. Benny remembered his parents talking late at night around the dining room table, which was covered with an old lace tablecloth. They always seemed to be worried about sales and inventory at the store. Their conversation bored him because he had no desire to follow his father's trade.

As a young boy Benny had a love for music. He liked hearing his mother play the piano and tried imitating her on the keyboard. When he was six his father bought him a small violin. Like most immigrant fathers, Kubelsky wanted his son to achieve success in American society; he hoped Benny would become a famous musician:

> It always seemed to me we owed a debt to America, and I wanted very hard to pay some of it back. Yet I was only a small haberdasher, a nothing. But when I gave my son a violin, I thought if he could be a great musician, if he could make beautiful music. . . .[4]

After taking violin instructions from local teachers, Benny, then eight years old, began weekly lessons under Dr. Hugo Kortschak, a professor at the Chicago School of Music. The distinguished teacher, who was later a music professor at Yale University and founder of the Berkshire String Quartet, charged $15 a lesson, a

large sum for the Kubelskys. Benny easily mastered the finger-
ing positions and exercises. Soon he was giving impromptu concerts at home for visiting relatives. His teachers admitted that
he had a natural gift for the violin, but the young boy disliked
playing the required scales and practicing a minimum of two
hours a day to fully develop his talent.

In Waukegan he was considered a child prodigy, and he
played in various town orchestras. On an imitation Amati violin
purchased by his father, Benny played in a trio at his grammar
school graduation exercises. He joined the Farmer's Orchestra,
a six-piece children's ensemble, which entertained at weddings,
bar mitzvahs, parties, and special engagements. During one orchestral performance at the Waukegan Opera House Benny fell
asleep, missing his cue for a solo. The stage manager, Julius H.
Sinykin, woke him up and admonished the young violinist. Sinykin, who later became Benny's best friend, helped the teenager
obtain a job at Joe Howard's Barrison Theatre, playing the violin
with the band in the pit during vaudeville performances.

The Barrison was Benny's introduction to the world of show
business. He was captivated by the aura of the footlights and
occasionally met the headliners. The vaudeville stage offered
talented Jewish youngsters a promising career. Because many
vaudeville theaters were owned by Jews, budding entertainers
did not encounter the prejudice found in other fields. In 1911
the Marx Brothers played the Barrison, and Minnie Palmer,
their mother, asked Benny to join their act as a violinist in the
pit. Benny wanted to go, but his father felt he was too young to
travel. Kubelsky also wanted his son to be a concert violinist, not
a vaudeville entertainer. Benny enjoyed playing at the Barrison
so much that he neglected his studies. He was not a diligent student, played truant, and was reputed to be a classroom cut-up.
He told jokes to his friends during history class, put a piece of
limburger cheese near the schoolroom radiator, and did a prat-
fall with an armful of empty shoe boxes in the aisle. After being
expelled from high school in the ninth grade because of poor
marks Benny worked for his father. He also studied bookkeeping
at the Waukegan Business College. Neither bookkeeping nor the
clothing business interested him. What he liked most was playing at night at the Barrison.

Benny's job at the theater gave him the chance to enter vaudeville in 1912. When the Barrison suddenly closed, Cora Salisbury, the orchestra pianist, decided to return to the vaudeville
stage. She was impressed by eighteen-year-old Benny's talent
and asked him to join her in a violin and piano act. Benny
wanted to go, but his parents disapproved until Mrs. Salisbury,
who was in her mid-forties, convinced them she could take care
of their son. The duo, called "Salisbury and Kubelsky—From
Grand Opera to Ragtime," opened at the Majestic Theater in
Gary, Indiana, in September. They entertained audiences in
small-time Midwestern vaudeville theaters, offering a repertoire
of classical numbers and popular melodies. The young showman
gained valuable experience by playing to different audiences
four or five times a day. Dressed in a formal tuxedo from his father's haberdashery shop, he always received a good ovation for
his solo, "The Rosary." For a year he slept in cheap boarding-
houses and on station benches while waiting for the train to take
him to the next town.

After a few weeks on tour Benny—or Kubelsky, as he was then
known—received a letter from a lawyer threatening to sue because he was capitalizing on the name of a well-known violinist,
Jan Kubelik. Benny was reluctant to change his name, but he
was advised to do so in order to avoid a lawsuit. He thought a
euphonious surname would be catchy, so he changed his name
to Ben K. Benny. Salisbury and Benny broke up as a team in
1913, when his partner had to return home to take care of her
ailing mother.

The young performer next teamed up with the pianist Lyman
Woods in a piano and violin act called "Bennie and Woods."
Benny felt that the "ie" at the end of his name had more flair.
During their first year together they played small-town theaters,
but soon the talented pair got bookings in larger cities on various
circuits. In September 1917 they were booked into the Palace
Theatre on the number two spot on the bill. The audience generally did not arrive at the Palace until the third spot, so they received limited applause for their eleven-minute act and had to
be content with a good review in *Variety*. The two sometimes inserted humor in their performances by doing funny musical
numbers, exaggerating popular melodies and mimicking serious

concert musicians. Benny often fooled about with his violin and held the fiddle in an amusing manner. He would roll his eyes, pretend that he was having a hard time playing a difficult number, and wave his little finger during an easy passage. Those pantomime stunts were his first attempts at comedy.

The act disbanded in early 1918 when Benny enlisted in the United States Navy. He was then stationed at the Great Lakes Naval Station. His participation in Navy camp shows actually contributed to his comedy career. On one program he played a serious violin piece and received boos and whistling from the sailors. David Wolff, a friend, quickly walked on stage and whispered to Benny to stop fiddling and talk. Benny told a story about an argument he had with Wolff about the "Irish Navy." "You see, I claim the Swiss Navy is bigger than the Irish Navy . . . but that the *Jewish* Navy is bigger than both of them put together." The audience roared. Benny told more Navy jokes and jested about the bad food at the Station. He was good at telling jokes, and the experience gave him confidence.[5]

He and another sailor, Zez Confrey, who later became a well-known songwriter, teamed up to do a violin and piano act in *The Great Lakes Revue*. During a rehearsal the director, David Wolff, asked Benny to do some comedy lines as an admiral's orderly in a skit. He liked Benny's reserved style so much he decided to enlarge the role. The songwriter, Bob Carleton, who acted in the sketch, remembered: "We'd all toss out gags like they were something we had in our pockets and didn't want any more. But Jack would pounce on each joke, lasso it, improve it and find a spot to squeeze it into the script." When the show opened at Chicago's Great Northern Auditorium Benny was playing the comedy lead, "Izzy There, the Admiral's Disorderly." *The Revue* toured the major cities of the Midwest.[6]

After the tour Benny was discharged from the Navy and decided to return to vaudeville as a single. His act, called "Ben K. Benny—Fiddle Funology," featured violin playing and gags and was billed on the number two spot on small-time circuits. As the curtain opened Benny would be playing the violin with his back to the audience. Suddenly, he would turn around and, with a surprised look, say, "Oh, I guess I'm on."[7] He sometimes sang

and did ragtime tunes on the violin. By then kidding with the
fiddle was becoming a major part of his repertoire. He liked to
imitate a pig's squeak or a cat's meow and rolled his eyes whenever he made a mistake or struck a disharmonious note. Those
mistakes and notes were planned. His routine was somewhat
similar to the fiddle and patter act of Ben Bernie, who was then
a star performer on the Orpheum circuit. When Bernie accused
him of trying to use his name, Benny changed his first name to
Jack after Jack Osterman, a comedian Benny admired. Now he
called his act "Jack Benny: Fun with a Fiddle" and later "A
Few Minutes with Jack Benny" and "Jack Benny: Aristocrat of
Humor."

By the early 1920's the violin had become only a prop in his
comic monologue. His father could not believe that he had given
up serious violin playing and was using the fiddle solely for
laughter. "The violin . . . is funny?" Kubelsky asked his son.
"I'm sorry, Benny, but I couldn't laugh." When Benny became
a popular radio comedian his father finally admitted he had
made the right choice.[8]

On the vaudeville stage he began to develop a comic stage
character and certain mannerisms that had a marked influence
on his style of humor. Vaudeville monologuists had short snappy
routines lasting ten to twenty minutes. Perfect timing and delivery were essential to keep audiences laughing continually. That
training later proved invaluable for mastering the fast pace of a
thirty-minute radio comedy program. Benny studied some
vaudeville comedians, especially Frank Fay and Julius Tannen.
On stage Benny pretended he was a suave debonair type with a
touch of conceit. His style differed from that of slapstick comics.
Benny did not wear zany outfits; he dressed fashionably in a coat
and tie and spoke in a sophisticated and slightly bored manner.
His opening lines would reveal his cocky personality. "How's
the show going up till now?" he would ask the orchestra leader.
"Fine," the conductor would reply. "Well, I'll fix that!" Benny
would say. During a 1927 performance at the Los Angeles Orpheum, Benny came on stage and announced, "Ladies and gentlemen, on my way to the theater this evening nothing happened." The dapper comedian stared at the audience for a

moment, wished them good night, and sauntered off the stage. Benny's monologue also included topical jokes on the day's head-lines and comments on the city where he was playing. And he related funny stories about himself and his girl friends. The source of his success was not punch-line jokes and belly laughs, but his suave stage personality, a precursor of his vain radio character.[9]

As a vaudeville entertainer Benny sometimes told stingy jokes, although those gags did not yet dominate his routine. Many were "cheap" Scotsman stories that were popular at the time, and he occasionally characterized himself as a skinflint. George Burns recalled Benny telling the audience about taking his date to dinner. "She got so excited she dropped her *tray*." Eddie Can-tor remembered doing a routine with him at the Miami Beach Floridian Club in 1930, when Benny cracked a joke about going to the greyhound races and "betting two dollars on the rabbit— to *show*."[10]

He was then booked into major vaudeville houses in large cities, where his style appealed to urbane tastes. Benny appeared on the next-to-closing headliner spot doing about seventeen min-utes of monologue. In 1924 he was the star attraction at the Pal-ace Theatre, and in 1926 the Schuberts hired him for the bawdy revue, *Great Temptations*, noted for its nude chorus girls. Benny did a violin solo and several other spots, including a twelve-minute monologue which received good reviews. In 1928, he became master of ceremonies at the Palace, introducing acts with witty remarks. He began to get a national reputation as a flippant master of ceremonies-monologuist noted for city jokes and jibes at personalities. Benny's increasing popularity earned him a movie contract with Metro-Goldwyn-Mayer. He played small roles in two undistinguished films, *Hollywood Revue of 1929* and *Chasing Rainbows* (1930). He then joined Earl Car-roll's lavish and risqué Broadway revue, *The Vanities of 1930*, as a monologuist and skit performer. At that time Benny began pondering his future as an entertainer. His movie debut had been a flop, and vaudeville was a dying institution because of the new appeal of sound movies and radio. Theater business was also off because of the Great Depression.

Benny thought about a career in radio at the time sponsors were offering large sums to vaudeville stars. Several of his colleagues from the stage were entering radio, including Eddie Cantor and George Burns and Gracie Allen, who had signed with Robert Burns Cigars for their first radio series in early 1932. Benny was also very interested in the medium's potential and listened regularly to *Amos 'n' Andy* and the team Gene and Glenn.

In early 1932 Benny encountered Ed Sullivan, columnist for the New York *Daily News*, at Lindy's restaurant. Sullivan was the host of an entertainment news and interview show on WHN, a local New York station, and he asked Benny to be a guest on the program. "But I don't know a thing about radio," Benny told Sullivan. "Nobody does," the columnist replied. After agreeing to appear, the comedian asked gag writer Al Boasberg to write a five-minute monologue. Like most stage performers, Benny worried about sitting in a silent studio without a live audience and was unable to sleep well. He kept repeating to his wife, Mary: "Am I going to flop! Am I going to flop!" Sullivan recalled that Benny was as "nervous as a goat" for his March 29, 1932, debut. The comedian pretended he was a Hollywood film writer and actor on the Sullivan broadcast:

> Ladies and gentlemen, this is Jack Benny talking. There will be a slight pause while you say, "Who Cares?" I am here tonight as a scenario writer. There is quite a lot of money in writing for the pictures. Well, there would be if I could sell one. I'm going back to pictures in about ten weeks. I'm going to be in a new film with Greta Garbo. They sent me the story last week. When the picture opens I'm found dead in the bathroom. It's sort of a mystery show. I'm found in the bathtub on a Wednesday night. . . . You'd really like Garbo. She and I were great friends in Hollywood. She used to let me drive her car around town. Of course, she paid me for it. . . .[11]

After his appearance on the Sullivan program Benny thought of doing a broadcast like the "old maestro," Ben Bernie. Since 1931 Bernie had been doing a network musical comedy variety program and had become a popular orchestra leader–comedian radio personality. Like Benny, he had a suave style, although he talked much more affectedly, like a pseudo-aristocrat. Bernie's standard opening line was "Yowsah, yowsah. Greetings and salutations, my friends," and he would close the program by wishing his listeners "pleasant dreeeams." When Benny presented the idea of organizing an orchestra to the Music Corporation of America, the agency felt Benny lacked "name" value to star in another Bernie-type radio show. Anxious about his future, the comedian went to Miami for a nightclub engagement. While in Florida he received a telegram from his agents, Sam and Arthur Lyons, two brothers who headed the Lyons Agency. Canada Dry wanted him to be the master of ceremonies on their new program.[12]

Canada Dry was one of several commercial firms eager to enter network radio in the early 1930's. Since 1926, Clicquot Club, Canada Dry's competitor, had sponsored the Clicquot Club Eskimos, one of the most popular early network musical programs. Douglas Coulter, advertising agency executive for Canada Dry, had liked Benny on the Sullivan broadcast and had convinced his client that the comedian would be an excellent master of ceremonies for their show. The thirty-minute *Canada Dry Ginger Ale Program* began over NBC on May 2, 1932. It was broadcast twice weekly at 9:30 p.m. and in January 1933 was heard once a week on CBS. On the first program Benny was introduced by the announcer as "that suave comedian, dry humorist and famous master of ceremonies—Jack Benny." Benny replied:

> Thank you, Mr. Thorgenson. That's pretty good from a man who doesn't even know me. Ladies and Gentlemen, this is Jack Benny talking, and making my first appearance on the air professionally. By that I mean, I am finally getting paid, which will of course be a great relief to my creditors.

Throughout the premier broadcast Benny made wry comments and introduced musical numbers by George Olsen's orchestra and songs by the vocalist Ethel Shutta.[13]

On the Canada Dry series Benny mainly kept to the witty style he had used in vaudeville and as a master of ceremonies at the Palace. He hired Boasberg, a former jewelry salesman and vaudeville gag writer for Burns and Allen, to write the show. The one-liners Boasberg wrote for Benny resembled vaudeville material. "A master of ceremonies is really a fellow who is unemployed and gets paid for it," Benny joked. When he introduced the singer Ethel Shutta the comedian jested: "Last week she had her nose lifted so she could be heard in Philadelphia." He exchanged witticisms with the orchestra leader, George Olsen, who also served as Benny's straight man. It was Olsen who was depicted as the skinflint on that series. "He [Olsen] paid the check with a five dollar bill that was in his pocket so long that Lincoln's eyes were bloodshot," Benny wisecracked.[14]

Although the Canada Dry series lasted less than a year, there were hints in the program of Benny's future radio style. On the fourth program Benny's opening lines were a spin-off from his Sullivan show:

> Hello somebody. This is Jack Benny talking. There will be a slight pause while you say "What of it." After all, I know your feelings, folks, I used to listen in myself.[15]

The catchy opening line, "Hello somebody. This is Jack Benny talking," was used during the 1930's with some variation ("Hello, again" or "Jello, again"). The self-disparaging remarks were also a clue to Benny's eventual role as radio's funniest fall guy.

In the middle of the programs Benny did an integrated commercial in which he sometimes told jokes about Canada Dry. Like Wynn, Benny was one of the first entertainers to kid the sponsor. The joke Benny cracked on the first program was a variation of an old vaudeville gag from Prohibition times: "Her father drank everything in the United States and then went up North to drink Canada Dry." After doing the commercial the comedian jested: "Gee, I thought I did that pretty well for a new salesman. I suppose nobody will drink it now." Spoofing the sponsor was such an innovation that Canada Dry was upset about Benny's jokes, which was probably one of the reasons why the company dropped the program.[16]

The broadcasts in total were not very innovative due to the number of revised vaudeville jokes. The shows sound dated today because of the slow pace of the broadcasts and corny gags. After a few months Benny realized that his routine was growing stale and that the vaudeville material he relied on to entertain different audiences every night was quickly dissipated in weekly radio. He thought of hiring more writers. David Freedman, Eddie Cantor's radio writer, was asked to develop a new format. He prepared a synoptic outline, comedy sequences, and a draft script for future Canada Dry programs that stressed developing Benny's personality and using Mary Benny and several character actors in skits. Freedman was aware that radio required new types of comic routines, but for some reason he was not employed by Benny.[17]

The comedian instead hired Harry Conn for $50 a week. Conn had written material for the Burns and Allen program and was considered to be one of the most talented writers in the field. The writer was difficult to work with, however, and once he wrote a line he insisted it remain in the script. On the show he worked alone, and for a time Benny tolerated his temperament. Conn concentrated on developing Benny's radio personality on the Chevrolet series in 1933–34. Canada Dry canceled the Benny program in late January 1933, and beginning on March 3 his weekly Friday night show was sponsored by General Motors on NBC at 10. The program was later switched to a Sunday night time slot.[18]

The aristocratic type Benny had portrayed on stage was expanded, emphasizing the comedian's persona of the braggart. On the Chevrolet program Benny described himself as a handsome young bon vivant:

> Hello again, this is Gentleman Jack talking. . . . America's representative youth. . . . And unless I am mistaken, the Beau Brummel of the air. And by my own concensus of opinion, a swell guy.

"I must say you're modest," commented announcer Alois Havrilla. "Oh, yes. I'm not a bit egotistical," retorted Benny, "In fact, I'm much nicer than you think I am." He also called himself the "Clark Gable of the Air" and complained that the announcer did not exalt his talent enough in the introduction. Conn used the cast to deflate Benny's ego. Instead of the jokes stemming exclusively from the star comedian, the cast—or the "gang," as they came to be known—got laughs by picking on Benny, who became the butt of innumerable jests. Stubbornly, and with an air of innocence, he clung to false beliefs about himself. The formula of self-delusion and mockery, a classic comedy format, could be reworked repeatedly.[19]

Insult jokes and hostile repartee had been comic stage devices for centuries. In Elizabethan times audiences enjoyed seeing the pompous court fool exposed, and in the eighteenth-century American theater the rustic uncouth Yankee character debunked the pretentious city slicker. A major comedy routine in nineteenth-century minstrel shows was the cross fire dialogue exchange between the smug interlocutor who spoke correct English and the ignorant endmen who talked in exaggerated Negro dialect. Two-man vaudeville routines contrasted the silly, eccentric comedian, dressed in a zany outfit, and the literate and dapper straight man. In those stage acts the show-off was often made the laughing stock. Comic deflation of vanity in the American comic theater allowed audiences to feel superior. Thus the humor on the Benny shows can be traced back to earlier theatrical forms.

A regular routine on the Chevrolet series was the verbal duel between Benny and his cast. Frank Black, the orchestra leader, ridiculed the comedian's boasting. "I think I'm good, and I have the courage of my convictions," bragged Benny. "That's only one punk's opinion," said Black. Another member of the "gang" was tenor Frank Parker, who sang, joked, and played in skits. The singer took the role of an insulting employee who complained of Benny's stinginess. The comedian's continual borrowing of money from his cast became a running gag on the Chevrolet series. The success of those jokes led Benny's writers to use more stingy gags and to increasingly characterize the comedian as a pennypincher.[20]

Benny once asserted that his character as a skinflint started accidentally and "happened because on one show I did some jokes about my being stingy." Benny's statement is only half true. As mentioned earlier, he had used stingy jokes in vaudeville and knew how effective they could be. He began to apply those jokes to himself on his radio shows in the early 1930's and found that they enhanced his personality. In real life Benny was a generous person who donated considerable sums to charity, volunteered his time for benefits, and gave his wife a present on his own birthday. By contrast, he was the most notorious cheapskate on radio. By the mid-1930's Benny's writers had developed a number of running gags and comic situations around that characteristic. He gave small tips to porters and waiters, a minimal salary to his cast, and fined them for being late. His inexpensive gifts to the "gang" became a running gag on the annual Christmas shows.[21]

A permanent cast member in the Chevrolet series was Benny's wife, Mary Livingstone. The daughter of a wealthy businessman, Sadie Marks was born in 1908 in Vancouver, British Columbia. Her parents often entertained vaudevillians playing at the local theater. She first met her husband at a dinner party attended by the comedian and Zeppo Marx. At that time she was thirteen years old, and Benny hardly noticed her and left early. Mary felt he was impolite, so she and some school friends heckled the comedian during a performance. She next saw Benny in Los Angeles in 1926 when he was appearing at the Orpheum Theater. She accompanied her sister Babe, who was married to the vaudevillian and violinist Al Bernivici, Benny, and several other people to dinner. Although Mary still did not think much of the comedian, Benny was impressed by her attractiveness and sense of humor. He visited her at the May Company department store, where she was employed as a saleslady, and pretended to be interested in the hosiery items she was selling. He dated her again, and when he left Los Angeles he telephoned her during stopovers on tour. Mary was about to marry another boy friend when Benny changed her mind by proposing to her. They were married on January 14, 1927. She soon joined Benny's vaudeville act as a singer and foil. Despite having had no previous stage experience, Mary enhanced the act. Known as Marie Marsh, she played an innocent "dumb dame" type who got the last laugh by putting Benny down for his conceit.[22]

She first appeared on radio on the Canada Dry program of August 3, 1932. She played a young girl from Plainfield, New Jersey, named Mary Livingstone, a fan of Jack Benny who had come over to see him at the studio. Mary was so nervous she laughed during her lines. She made sporadic appearances on the Canada Dry shows and appeared regularly playing a smart-aleck girl. Mary had an excellent voice for radio and was given her own laugh lines. Although Mary was a shy person in real life, and constantly suffered from mike fright, her wit and contagious laughter added spark to the program. She read funny poems and related amusing stories about her family, especially her mother, who disliked Benny's show and wrote letters poking fun at the comedian. Jokes revolving around her family, including her "ugly duckling" sister Babe, continued over the years. Mary also became known for her jokes, which mocked Benny's vanity. Whenever the radio entertainer flaunted his looks or lied about his generosity she made a cutting remark.

Other supporting character actors also added to the broadcasts' humor. Benny was the first comedian to have stooges knock on a door and make funny statements. The first important supporting actor on the Benny show was Sam Hearn, who played an ethnic Jewish character. Jewish comics with exaggerated dialects and awkward mannerisms had been popular in vaudeville. Their monologue often included amusing comments or stories concerning the problem of the immigrant Jew's adjustment to the American city. At the time those routines were not criticized, and they have been interpreted as a means of making the immigrant's habits and life more understandable to the public. Immigrants enjoyed laughing at the stock figures that represented themselves, and as a result many ethnic comedians specialized in self-mockery. Hearn first impersonated a Jewish character at the Friars Club annual dinner show in New York City in 1933. Benny was in the audience, and he liked Hearn's high-pitched Jewish accent so much that he asked Conn to write Hearn into the next program. Hearn's role as "Dr. Vatson" in a Sherlock Holmes skit was so funny that he appeared in other programs. Benny believed in first testing a character for listener reaction, and if it was successful the part was repeated. By August 3, 1934, Hearn was playing a character called Schlepperman, a gregarious fellow who loved to tell stories. Benny kept running into Schlepperman wherever he went. "Hullo, *stranzer*," was his perennial greeting to the comedian.[23]

Other innovations made the Chevrolet programs more entertaining than the Canada Dry series. Skits satirizing movies, plays, and novels climaxed the program. Although sketches had been broadcast on the Canada Dry program, on the Chevrolet programs they became a regular feature. Benny and the cast took roles spoofing such novels as *Little Women* and *Uncle Tom's Cabin* and Western films. Those parodies were a major innovation in comedy programming and appealed to listeners. The program had a C.A.B. rating of 25.3 in 1934, and that year Benny was voted the best comedian in a New York *World-Telegram* poll. Compared with Wynn and Penner, Benny was pioneering in a new form of radio comedy built around his personality and repartee with his cast. The novel format nonetheless seemed too unorthodox to General Motors executives, who decided that a music program would sell more automobiles.[24]

The comedian's next series, in 1934, sponsored by the General Tire Company, showed a growing maturity. Skits on movies and plays were continued, but many also dealt with everyday situations, including Benny's home life. Some portrayed him preparing for the broadcast; others depicted his activities during the week. That realistic background gave his character more authenticity and was another important innovation in comedy programming. Benny's vanity and cheapness became increasingly accented on the General Tire series. Mary Livingstone was especially used to deflate the comedian's braggadocio:

> MARY   Gee, Jack, I think you'll be just swell in pictures.
> JACK   Do you really think so, Mary?
> MARY   Sure, there's always room for another Boris Karloff.
> JACK   But I'm not a Karloff, Mary.
> MARY   No, but you certainly bore us.[25]

The General Tire program featured an important new cast member, Don Wilson, the announcer. Once a football star at the University of Colorado, Wilson weighed over 200 pounds and was 6 feet 3 inches tall. Wilson had worked as a salesman for a pharmaceutical company and as a singer in a trio before entering radio in 1923 on Denver's KFEL. He had done an early morning wake-up program called "The Early Birds" with Martin Dougherty; it was heard locally over Los Angeles' KHJ. He then became a staff singer at the station. Wilson next joined rival KFI, an NBC affiliate, and, as "Big Brother Don," he broadcast a children's program. Wilson became better known to the public as a sports announcer of regional football games and the Rose Bowl contest. In 1933 he joined the New York division of NBC as a sports announcer. The following year he and other network staff men and free-lancers auditioned for the job as announcer on the General Tire program. After reading a few lines from a script Wilson was selected for the opening. "I just happened to laugh in the right places," he recalled.[26]

His jovial personality and sense of humor added zest to the shows. The announcer, who had a powerful resonant voice, got the programs off to a rousing start by introducing Benny. Wilson's forte was the integrated commercial, and his habit of sneaking in an advertisement became a popular running gag. He also ridiculed Benny's pennypinching and violin playing. The two enjoyed sparring with one another in the program's opening spot. "Say, Jack, I don't want to appear fresh, but what are you talking about?" Wilson asked. "I don't know, Wilson, what is there to talk about? There's nothing new," the comedian replied. "So your jokes tell me," the announcer said. Benny had a store of "fat" jokes, poking fun at Wilson's obesity. "I'm afraid the show isn't big enough for both of us," he wisecracked. Wilson played an important role as announcer and comic foil during Benny's reign on the airwaves.[27]

The first three years of *The Jell-O Program* completed the formative phase of the comedian's radio career. In the fall of 1934 Benny signed with General Foods to do the Sunday broadcast on NBC at seven. The Sunday evening family hours between seven and nine o'clock attracted a wide listening audience. Listening to Jack Benny at seven became a Sunday night ritual, for his humor was clean and appealed to the entire family. Benny was a Sunday night radio favorite for twenty-one years.

During the first year the Jell-O shows were written by Harry

Conn, who was the highest paid gag writer in radio comedy in 1935, earning $1500 a week. He liked to brag he was solely responsible for Benny's fame and told the comedian's father that his son owed his success to him. Once Conn's wife saw Mary Livingstone wearing a fur coat and mentioned to Mary that if it was not for her husband she would not have owned the coat. When Benny refused Conn's demand for a half-share in the revenue from *The Jell-O Program*, the writer refused to prepare a script for the next broadcast. Benny borrowed Sam Perrin and Arthur Phillips, two writers from Phil Baker's staff, to write the show. The program was so well written that the comedian realized he no longer needed Conn's services. Conn was fired in 1935, and thereafter he wrote scripts for Joe Penner and Eddie Cantor. He also tried his own situation comedy show for a year, but it was unsuccessful. Conn's writing career ended in failure. He occasionally sold a script or a few gags to Benny, but the comedian rarely used his material. Bitter about his old boss, Conn liked to create the false impression that Benny "couldn't ad-lib a belch after a hungarian dinner." The comedian last saw Conn in the late 1950's working as a doorman backstage at a Broadway theater.[28]

Instead of relying exclusively on one writer, Benny hired a team to collaborate on the Jell-O shows, including Ed Beloin, Bill Morrow, Al Boasberg, Hugh Wedlock, Jr., and Howard Snyder. The Jell-O scripts featured a series of spots between Benny and his "gang" and a concluding skit. Benny regularly opened the show with the line "Jello again. This is Jack Benny talking." In the opening spot Benny and Wilson usually got into a brawl. Mary joined them, and she was followed by Phil Harris and the singer Kenny Baker. In the middle of the program Wilson inevitably sneaked in a plug for Jello's six delicious flavors: "I shopped around until I found half a dozen neckties, each one corresponding in color to a different flavor of Jello. . . . You know, Strawberry, Raspberry, Cherry, Orange, Lemon, and Lime." Benny started doing the famous "Buck Benny" sketch, parodying Western movies, around 1936. Andy Devine played the deputy, and the comedian played Buck Benny, the sheriff of Cactus County—"as tough an hombre as ever held up a pair of socks

with a garter snake." The skit was so successful that Benny
starred in the Paramount movie, *Buck Benny Rides Again*
(1940).[29]

Two new regulars on *The Jell-O Program* were Kenny Baker
and Phil Harris. Baker, a relatively unknown singer, joined the
program on November 3, 1935, playing a credulous young man.
Like the other characters, he teased the comedian about his violin talent and stinginess. The tall, attractive tenor also played
in the skits, and his singing was so popular that the show made
him a national celebrity and teenage idol. Phil Harris replaced
Johnny Green as orchestra leader for the 1936–37 season. The
son of a musician, Harris had grown up in Nashville, Tennessee.
His father had taught him to play various instruments, and he
had started playing with him in vaudeville and carnival orchestras. He then formed his own group, the Dixie Syncopators, a
popular band in the South. At the time he joined Benny, Harris
was a well-known band leader playing at Hollywood nightclubs
and ballrooms. Benny saw him in an RKO film short, *So This is
Harris*, and liked him so much he signed him for *The Jell-O
Program*.[30]

The altercations between the brash bandleader and the vain
comedian highlighted the Jello shows. Harris played a conceited
Southern playboy who loved flashy cars, hard liquor, and fancy
clothes. The two taunted and teased one another in several ways.
Benny once interrupted Harris's orchestra during a musical
number:

> JACK   I said I was sorry . . . I apologize, isn't that enough?
> PHIL   No, I wanna punch you in the nose.
> JACK   Hh! . . . Phil, I've expressed my regrets, now let me
>   go and tell some jokes, will you?
> PHIL   Well, don't expect my orchestra to laugh.

Harris, in turn, needled Benny about his violin playing and age.
The bandleader especially liked to poke fun at the comedian's
stinginess. "All I meant was your wallet doesn't know the sit-
down strike is over," Harris said. "It's lucky you insulted my
wallet, not me," retorted Benny. Harris bellowed his lines. "Hiya, Jackson!" he exclaimed when meeting Benny. His lively

Jack Benny began on radio as a suave dry humorist, and he had a low-key style less dependent on sight gags than Wynn's. This photograph was taken in 1937.
(Courtesy, Margaret Herrick Library, Academy of Motion Picture Arts and Sciences, Beverly Hills, California.)

Jack Benny and others broadcasting *The Jell-O Program* in the mid-1930's. The show changed the nature of radio comedy. Benny and Mary Livingstone appear on the right, while Don Wilson and Sam Hearn are standing in front of the microphone on the left.
(Copyright, Frank Bresee.)

renditions of songs, including his famous "That's What I Like About the South," added zest to the broadcasts.[31]

Another important newcomer on *The Jell-O Program* was Eddie "Rochester" Anderson. His ancestors had been runaway slaves smuggled North by abolitionists on the Underground Railroad. Anderson was raised in a show business family. His father, Ed Mae, had performed in minstrel shows, and his mother, Ella Mae, had been a circus tightrope walker. Born in Oakland, California, on September 18, 1905, Anderson started singing and dancing at age thirteen, when he and his brother Lloyd entertained servicemen in San Francisco's Presidio. In 1923 he performed in the vaudeville song-and-dance act "Three Black Aces" with his brother Cornelius and another partner. Then he did a single in carnivals and vaudeville and eventually became a popular nightclub entertainer in Los Angeles and at Harlem's Cotton Club. Anderson got bit parts in the films *What Price Hollywood* (1932) and *Three Men on a Horse* (1936), and a leading role in *The Green Pastures* (1936), playing a rural preacher and the biblical figure Noah. Benny did not discover Anderson, who was already a fairly successful black entertainer, but he did give him a unique opportunity to enter radio.[32]

Before he hired Anderson Benny had occasionally used black actors to play minor parts on his radio show. Because of racial taboos it was extremely difficult for blacks to enter the radio industry and obtain regular acting jobs. White impersonators were often used in their place, and if blacks did get roles it was usually playing small stereotyped parts as servants and porters. Anderson won the audition for the role of an ignorant, happy-go-lucky railroad porter on the March 28, 1937, broadcast. In the skit Benny asked Anderson what time the train arrived in Albuquerque:

EDDY   Who?

JACK   Albuquerque?

EDDY   I dunno, do we stop there.

JACK   Certainly we stop there.

EDDY   My my!

JACK   Hm!

EDDY   I better go up and tell the engineer about that.

152   THE NEW RADIO COMEDY

    JACK   Yeah, do that.
    EDDY   What's the name of that town again?
    JACK   Albuquerque.
    EDDY   (Laughs) Albuquerque, what they gonna think up next.

A little later the "lazy" porter reappeared and the Albuquerque
gag was repeated:

    JACK   Hey Porter!
    EDDY   Yas-suh?
    JACK   When I got on the train yesterday I gave you a suit to
           press, where is it?
    EDDY   Gee I'm lazy, don't I remind you of Stepin Fetchit?
    JACK   Yeah. And what did you find out about Albuquerque?
    EDDY   He can't press it any better than I can.
    JACK   Albuquerque is a town.
    EDDY   You better check on that.[33]

During the next few months Anderson played small parts in
other broadcasts, including a waiter in a Buck Benny sketch on
May 21, 1937. The comedian and the writers discovered that his
shrill, grating voice and infectious laugh added considerably to
the program's humor. Anderson had acquired his hoarse voice
from hawking newspapers in San Francisco as a youth: "We
thought that the loudest voice sold the papers, which wasn't true,
of course," he recalled. "Anyway I ruptured my vocal chords
from straining them." Because Anderson also had a remarkable
sense of timing and delivery and was a talented actor, the writers
believed he would be an asset to the program. On June 20, 1937,
Anderson was written permanently into the show. He became
the first regular black performer on radio.[34]
    Although he was given a large speaking role as Benny's valet
and chauffeur, Anderson's part as a servant still reflected type
casting. Known as Rochester, the black actor was the only member of Benny's "gang" without a last name, a practice common
during the period of slavery, when slaves were given single
names. During his initial years on the program Rochester spoke
in an exaggerated Negro dialect and was characterized as an
uneducated, happy-go-lucky, lazy, and comically inefficient
servant:

JACK   Hmm! . . . Oh Rochester! . . . Rochester!
EDDY   Yessah, Boss.
JACK   Did you lay out my full dress suit?
EDDY   You mean de one with da red stripes?
JACK   Stripes? No, the black one with the tails. You've been pressing the pants for an hour. Are they done yet?
EDDY   Yessah, dey is done to a crisp.[35]

Rochester's drinking, dice playing, and girl chasing during his days off were also the subject of many jokes. One particularly offensive script suggested that Rochester carried a razor as a weapon:

JACK   Wait a minute, wait a minute. Do you mean to say you lost my bicycle shooting *craps?*
ROCHESTER   Well I was lucky for the first three passes.
JACK   Lucky? . . . And *then* what happened?
ROCHESTER   My dice went into a minuet. . . . And my opponent became suspicious.
JACK   Oh. . . . Well I don't care *what* happened. . . . I want you to go to that garage, and tell your friend to give you back my bicycle.
ROCHESTER   Without payin' for it?
JACK   Yes, without payin' for it. . . . Just *grab* it.
ROCHESTER   Now wait a minute, boss. . . . That boy's got a razor that does everything but run out and get the mail.
JACK   Well Rochester, what are you scared of? . . . *You* carry a razor yourself.
ROCHESTER   Yeah, but it's only a *Gillette* and I'm outta blades.[36]

The character Anderson portrayed nonetheless had many redeeming features. Rochester was not an obsequious servant, but a man who stood up to his boss and spoke his own mind:

JACK   Hey, Rochester, have you got my shoes?
EDDY   Here they are, Boss.
JACK   *Those are my sports shoes.* Where did you ever see sports shoes with a full dress suit?
EDDY   In the Harlem Esquire.
JACK   Well run over to my dressing room and get my plain *black* ones and hurry.
EDDY   Black coat, black shoes, black pants . . . you is de most *monotonous* man I ever worked for.

JACK   H'm, I'd fire him if he didn't have an iron-bound contract.[37]

Anderson's role as a sassy servant became a prototype for new
black radio parts, like Beulah the maid. Rochester also needled
Benny regarding his age, cheapness, and violin playing in put-
down gags. Rochester and Benny had a friendly relationship beyond one of servant to employer.

Members of the black community protested the character of
Rochester in the mid-1940's. White Southern listeners found the
portrayal offensive for different reasons. The 1946–47 *Negro
Handbook*, a historical reference book, described the role as
"good-natured . . . quick-witted and wise, yet it is stereotyped
on all the usual counts—addiction to drink, dice, wenching and
razor-cutting." Anderson disagreed with the criticisms; he felt
the protests were never a problem for him while he was playing
Rochester. Southern whites, by contrast, complained that Benny's servant was too uppity. On one broadcast Benny was training for a boxing match against Fred Allen and asked Rochester
to help him by throwing a punch. Rochester hit his "boss" so
hard the punch knocked him out. Thousands of letters were written by Southerners denouncing the broadcast in which a "colored" man had hit a white man. The incident is supposed to have
caused the largest deluge of mail in the program's history. In the
1940's Benny's new team of writers attempted to phase out the
stereotyped characteristics, and some of Rochester's offensive
habits were dropped.[38]

Nonetheless, black citizens and organizations became increasingly resentful of Sambo caricatures. For example, the program
of February 5, 1950, which actually was a replay of a show that
had been broadcast ten years earlier, produced considerable
criticism of the Rochester character. Several writers had been
unable to write a new script because of illness and an old show
was selected—one that portrayed Rochester chasing girls and
shooting craps in Harlem. It could not have been a worse choice.
The *Los Angeles Sentinel* editorialized:

> Jack Benny certainly laid an egg, to use theatre par-
> lance, with his recent broadcast about Rochester's ad-

> ventures in Harlem. Most of us are sufficiently accustomed to Jack's show to forgive its lapses into corny buffoonery now and then. But the Harlem experience dished up cliches and horse play that we had supposed had died a quiet and unmourned death a generation ago. . . . Negroes have been cast in a bad and unwarranted light by the Benny show.

The network received many telephone calls protesting the crude misrepresentation of black people, and the NAACP and other civic groups launched a nationwide campaign urging people to write letters of complaint. Stunned by the criticism, Benny apologized for the broadcast.[39]

The character of Rochester thus had some positive and negative features. Anderson's role represented a transition between cardboard Negro stage caricatures and the less stereotyped depictions of blacks in the media. Anderson's regular appearance on the Benny show also led to the employment of more black performers on radio.

Benny's family of characters was only one of several reasons why *The Jell-O Program* was so successful. Equally important was Benny's radio personality as an egotist, skinflint, and fall guy. He portrayed a sympathetic lovable character easily identifiable in everyday life. What made this character so universally funny were two major traits—his vanity and his refusal to admit his faults. The "gang" made fun of his obtuseness. "Basically our show is built on a foundation of real people," Benny said.

> We try to have things happen to us that would happen to anyone. Things that will be interesting and, above all, funny. I'd be willing to bet that there are very few who don't know people like Mary Livingstone, Phil Harris, and Rochester. Therefore, we feel that we represent, to a certain extent, the audience. They see in us, themselves, and they get a laugh out of the jokes that fit them.[40]

Because of the use of familiar characters listeners knew what to expect when they tuned into a Benny broadcast. The show's humor revolved around the predictability of Benny's personality and the believable comic situations arising from his character. Because of its sure-fire formula appealing to listener expectancy *The Jell-O Program* was the top-rated comedy show in 1935. During the late 1930's it was generally rated the number one or number two comedy program. The broadcasts were so successful that other entertainers began imitating Benny's format. He also proved that a thirty-minute broadcast could be as entertaining as an hour-long variety program and that summer layoffs did not hurt a comedian's popularity. Largely due to Benny's success, character comedy replaced vaudeville buffoonery as the dominant comedic form on the airwaves by 1937.[41]

8

Town Hall Tonight

Fred Allen was another entertainer who created a novel form of radio comedy. Realizing that radio was an entirely different entertainment medium than vaudeville, the comedian spoofed the news and developed skits using a variety of humorous characters. His *Town Hall Tonight* program was one of the most entertaining comedy shows in the 1930's. A stinging social satirist, he had the sharpest wit on radio and was able to lampoon various sacrosanct subjects. A master of verbal slapstick, Allen threw words around like custard pies over the airwaves.

The story of Allen's rise in show business is fascinating. Like many other comedians, Allen grew up in a poor immigrant neighborhood. He once jested about his start in life:

> Allen, Fred. Born in Boston. And at my birth a strange thing happened. The doctor slapped me after I started crying. My first brush with a critic. My parents immediately started me in show business by taking an ad in *Variety* announcing my arrival: "Fred Allen has diaper—will travel." I traveled to the three corners of the earth. Since then there have been many changes. I'm not referring to the diaper.

Allen did not actually become an itinerant vaudevillian until he was a teenager. The son of an Irish bookbinder, James Henry

Sullivan, Allen was born in Cambridge, Massachusetts, on May 31, 1894, and christened John Florence Sullivan. His father earned only $20 a week at his trade, and the Sullivans were relatively poor. Allen claimed he inherited a sense of humor from his father, who had a reputation as a storyteller. Allen's quick wit, jocoseness, and sense of irony may have come from his ancestry, for they are qualities found in Irish humor, particularly in the plays of Bernard Shaw and Sean O'Casey.[1]

Allen liked playing pranks as a boy and was known as the school jester. He once demonstrated an equation in algebra class: "let x stand for my father's signature." His mother died when he was three years old, and he was raised by his Aunt Lizzie, Elizabeth Herlihy, in a rough Irish neighborhood in Boston, where he picked up many of the attitudes of the city's Irish. He never did like Boston's upper-class snobs or Harvard intellectuals, who were often a target of his radio jokes. The occasional tone of cynicism in Allen's humor and writings could possibly stem from the scars of having to struggle to reach the top.[2]

Because Aunt Lizzie wanted her nephew to be a respectable businessman, he was sent to the Boston High School of Commerce to learn a practical vocation. During the evenings he worked as a stockboy and runner in the Boston Public Library for 20¢ an hour. Years later he jokingly commented on his library job on the radio:

> I guess if I had any sense years ago I'd have stayed home and kept my job in the library. Who knows, today I might be in full charge of the Encyclopedia Britannica. Volume six Coleb to Damasci.[3]

One night he discovered a book on the history of humor in the stacks, and after he read it he presented a five-minute talk on comedy in the school's salesmanship course. He also found a book on juggling and, unbeknown to his aunt, began practicing at home for one or two hours. He juggled tennis balls, tin plates, and cigar boxes, and tried balancing broomsticks on his chin. At afternoon vaudeville shows the boy attentively watched juggling acts and copied down the jokes the jugglers told during their routines. Allen first performed his juggling act mixed with a few jokes at an amateur show staged by the library employees. He received an ovation, and after the performance a spectator urged him to enter show business.

The eighteen-year-old youngster began appearing in vaude-ville amateur nights in the Boston area. Theater managers often booked amateur performers to stimulate business because customers enjoyed seeing local talent perform. It also gave novices an opportunity to break in their routine. Sometimes the amateurs won prize money for the best act or received a token payment of a few dollars. Sam Cohen, an agent for amateur nights in New England, booked Johnny Sullivan, as Allen was then called, into small theaters. He was so terrified during his debut at the Hub Theatre that he almost missed his cue. After a few minutes he became less nervous and managed to do his act successfully. Because he was not a deft juggler the manager recommended that he talk louder and add more jokes to his routine. One night at Boston's Bowdoin Square Theatre four plates broke on the stage. Spectators liked to boo the amateur performers and throw rotten eggs and tomatoes. Allen learned to come back with a witty gag whenever the audience heckled him for his poor juggling. Jokes eventually became more important in his repertoire than juggling.

Allen entered small-time professional vaudeville in 1914. He got a chance to substitute for another juggler in an audition and was booked into the Keith vaudeville circuit in New England. After the tour he was unable to obtain regular bookings and had to settle for occasional dates in second- and third-rate theaters and one-night stands entertaining at fraternal lodges. Between engagements he worked as a stockroom boy for a paper company and as a shipping room clerk in a hardware store. Once he went unemployed for three months and lived off doughnuts and coffee. Traveling from one town to another was tiring. He slept in railroad stations and flea-ridden hotel rooms and rooming houses. "I had a room that was so small it had removable door knobs," Allen recalled:

> If you wanted to bend over in your room you could take off the door knob just in case. At Mrs. Brown's when

you took a bath you had to keep singing. There was no
lock on the bathroom door.[4]

His first few years as an entertainer were precarious, but afterward he got better bookings. He played theaters in New York
City, joined the Poli and Loews circuits, and went to Australia
for a sixteen-week tour.

Allen was known in the vaudeville trade as a juggler monologuist. He used various stage names: Paul Huckle, European
Entertainer; Fred St. James; Freddy James, The World's Worst
Juggler; and Freddy James and His Misses. Vaudevillian Benny
Drone remembered the young juggler looking like an under-
nourished, thin, pimply-faced kid. Allen had chestnut-brown
hair, blue eyes, high cheek bones, and an upturned nose. He
modeled his routine on a British comic juggler named Griff,
whom he had seen perform in Boston. Dressed in a little derby
hat, oversized shoes, and wearing white-face makeup, he performed what was called a twelve-minute "act in one" in front
of a curtain. Allen got laughs from intentionally breaking plates
and other objects. The performer did a stock comic monologue
with hackneyed puns deriving from gags he had collected and
filed in a book:

> Did you hear about the guy who was run over by a
> brewery wagon? It was the first time the *drinks* were on
> him. . . . A gentleman is a man who wouldn't think of
> hitting his wife with his hat on. . . . She used to be a
> schoolteacher but she has no *class* now. . . . I had sore
> feet and I tried some corn syrup. It was nasty to have in
> my shoes during the hot weather. And it didn't do my
> corns a bit of good.[5]

Allen later varied his routine by doing unusual "nutty" stunts
on stage. He played comic tunes on the banjo and clarinet and
did a burlesque ventriloquist number using a dummy named
Jake. Theater ushers and stagehands were employed to imitate
the dummy's voice off stage. The dummy pretended to sing like
John McCormack, whose voice came from a hidden phonograph.
As the song reached its conclusion Jake came apart piece by
piece. Allen loved to startle the audience by walking off in the

middle of his act. He would sit at the stage's edge and read his press notices to the audience with dead-pan seriousness. The comic juggler tried to catch a turnip with a fork in his mouth and instead let it splinter on top of his head. Allen had a clever way of stimulating applause at the end—he took his curtain calls as pictures of Abraham Lincoln, George Washington, and the American flag were flashed on a screen.[6]

During the 1920's Allen moved into big-time vaudeville and Broadway musical comedy. In order to present a fresh face to the public he changed his name to Fred Allen, using the last name of his agent, Edgar Allen.[7] A successful engagement at the Palace in 1919 led to bookings on the Pantages, Keith-Albee, and Schubert circuits. Jake Schubert liked his act so much he signed him for *The Passing Show of 1922*, a musical comedy revue at the Winter Garden. Allen eventually became a well-known Broadway entertainer, starring in the 1924 *Greenwich Village Follies*. In the fall of 1926 he teamed with the comedian Bert Yorke in a double act at the Palace in a comic routine called Mr. Fink and Mr. Smith. The pair split within a year, Yorke claiming that he was tired of playing straight man.

While appearing in *The Passing Show of 1922* Allen met his wife, Portland Hoffa, a chorus girl in the production. She was the daughter of Frederick Hoffa, the optometrist, and was named after the city of her birth, Portland, Oregon. A talented dancer with a slender figure, short brown hair, and an engaging personality, Hoffa had been a chorus girl in *George White's Scandals* before she met Allen. After their marriage on May 4, 1927, she joined his act doing bit parts, "dumb dame" jokes, and dancing. Vaudevillians often included their wives into their routines because a double act received additional money, which paid for clothes, hotels, and train fare. Allen and Hoffa later played in the popular musical revue *Three's a Crowd* (1930), starring Clifton Webb and Libby Holman.

When that production closed in 1932 the comedian was faced with an impasse in his career. Because of the Great Depression ticket sales on Broadway were declining, and a production he was scheduled to do in the fall of 1932 was canceled. Like other stage comedians, Allen began to think of entering radio. "Many of the big-name comedians were appearing on regular programs," Allen wrote:

> In the theater the actor had uncertainty, broken promises, constant travel and a gypsy existence. In radio, if you were successful, there was an assured season of work. The show could not close if there was nobody in the balcony. There was no travel and the actor could enjoy a permanent home. There may have been other advantages but I didn't need to know them.[8]

Allen regarded radio as an exciting new form of aural entertainment, and different from the live stage, where the visual elements in comedy were accented. In the early 1930's he was aware that radio comedy was dominated by Broadway showmen such as Eddie Cantor, Jack Pearl, Ed Wynn, and Joe Penner, who overused timeworn vaudeville gags and slapstick routines. Allen criticized them for playing to the studio audience rather than the home listener:

> The bewildered set owner in Galesburg, Illinois, suddenly realized that he no longer had to be able to understand radio comedy. As he sat in his Galesburg living room he knew that he had proxy audiences sitting in radio studios in New York, Chicago and Hollywood watching the comedians, laughing and shrieking "Vass you dere, Charlie" and "Wanna buy a duck" for him.

The Broadway comics' weekly scripts containing a hodgepodge of stale jokes "would soon drive listeners to other diversions."[9]

Radio required a special type of humor that stimulated the listener's imagination. The living room console was a theater of the mind, said Allen:

> Radio is meant for people at home. Give 'em the right sound effects and music, and their imaginations will work for you. A man in his armchair can picture all kinds of fantastic scenes: a fly crawling up the Empire State Building, scenes in outer space or under the sea. These are things radio can do best—better than the movies.

He aimed to create a variety comedy program emphasizing dialogue and skits playing on the listener's imagination:

> Since the radio comedian really had to depend on the
> ears of the home audience for his purpose, I thought
> that a complete story told each week or a series of episodes and comedy situations might be a welcome change.
> It would enable the listener to flex his imagination, and
> perhaps make him want to follow the experiences of the
> characters involved. This, if it worked, would insure the
> radio comedian a longer life. Hoping for longevity in
> the new medium, I planned a series of programs using
> a different business background each week—a newspaper office, a department store, a bank, a detective
> agency, etc. The comedy would involve the characters
> employed in, or indigenous to, the assorted locales.[10]

Allen wrote an audition script and selected actors and actresses to play supporting roles. A phonograph record was made of a trial broadcast and submitted to the president of Corn Products, manufacturers of Linit Bath Oil. The executive could hardly hear the recording, which had been badly damaged in the subway, but he liked Allen's nasal twang. "That's enough," he shouted. "Never mind the show. Get me that man with the flat voice!" Allen's first broadcast, *The Linit Bath Club Revue*, occurred on October 23, 1932, on the CBS network.[11]

The thirty-minute Sunday night program featuring comedy skits and musical entertainment had certain problems. Allen felt there was too much music, and the transitions between spots were not always smooth. A Wurlitzer organ solo was played in the middle of the show to please the sponsor's wife. It was "like planting a pickle in the center of a charlotte russe," commented Allen. The sponsor was worried that the show might bore the studio audience and told the comedian to dress as a Keystone Cop for the premiere. Allen refused, but on opening night he discovered thirty boys from an orphan asylum seated in the front row. They had been ordered by the sponsor to laugh at the announcer's signal.[12]

The Linit Bath Club Revue was highlighted by innovative comedy vignettes called little revues, which were written by

164

Allen and an assistant. "We want you to forget your troubles for the next half hour . . . while our little revue is on the stage," said Allen on one broadcast. "You can bring your worries and troubles to us at nine o'clock and we'll try to iron them out and return them to you at nine thirty." Allen played many different roles in these clever sketches, including a hotel manager, a judge, a marriage counselor, and a circus barker. As the owner of the Mammoth Department Store the comedian got into altercations with disgruntled buyers and employees. An assortment of oddball stooges appeared in the sketch: a pompous floorwalker, a fast-talking efficiency expert, a "cheap" Scotsman, a stuttering professor, and a melancholy Santa Claus. As a court judge, Allen heard cases involving a number of types—an insulting gas station attendant, a shoplifter, a drunk. The dialogue between Allen and the supporting cast was fast-paced and witty.[13]

Portland Hoffa also played various scatterbrain parts in the Linit revues. What made Portland funny was her high-pitched falsetto. Her husband wrote that her voice sounded like "two slate pencils mating or a clarinet reed calling for help." On the first Linit program she appeared as a giddy young girl from Schenectady, New York, who had run away from home. Allen, the court judge, quizzed her:

ALLEN   How did you come to get lost in New York?
PORTLAND   I didn't come to get lost. . . . I came to go on the radio.
ALLEN   Who told you . . . you could go on the radio.
PORTLAND   I won a contest and ran away from home.
ALLEN   Didn't your Mother say anything before you left?
PORTLAND   No. . . . Ma can't talk. . . . She just had her face lifted.
ALLEN   Really?
PORTLAND   Yes. . . . The Doctor lifted her face too high. . . . it's awful.
ALLEN   What's awful.
PORTLAND   Ma's skin is so tight. . . . Every time she sits down her mouth flies open.[14]

On the Linit program Allen also began commentaries on American politics and society. The scripts contained gems of political and social satire. On the repeal of the Prohibition Amendment: "You perhaps noticed that the Senate has approved the repeal of the 18th Amendment. It looks as though the Lame Ducks want to make the country wet enough for them to waddle out of office." On government programs to relieve the Great Depression: "The nearest we've come to Farm Relief recently was when one politician called another Old Potato." On President Roosevelt's inauguration: "Things are looking up. Real estate has certainly turned the corner. I see where a family named Roosevelt just took a four year lease on a house in Washington. Good work—Franklin!" On justice: "Everything else is Cut-Rate and I'm running a Cut-Rate Court . . . No case too small for me to handle. . . . I want to put crime within the reach of every man and you'll get justice as cheap as you'll get it anyplace."[15]

Although the 1932–33 Linit show sparkled with new ideas, it was not without its faults. The dialogue sometimes resembled vaudeville patter and punning, and the humor sounded trite in spots. Nonetheless, considering the early dates of the broadcasts, the series was an important stepping stone in the evolution of Allen's radio career. After six or seven weeks on the air radio critics realized that Allen was offering listeners a program that was different from the Wynn–Penner type of comedy. Although Allen never matched Wynn's popularity in 1932–33, he drew a sizable audience during that year. The Linit show gave Allen a chance to experiment with different vignettes, using many character types. Its relative success led to future NBC programs, *The Salad Bowl Revue* (1933), *The Sal Hepatica Revue* (1933–34), *The Hour of Smiles* (1934–35), and *Town Hall Tonight* (1935–40).[16]

Allen changed the name of his program to *Town Hall Tonight* when the advertising agency handling the broadcasts felt his programs lacked appeal to small-town listeners. They also believed he did not have a friendly enough personality on the air. There was a belief in the industry that comedians should sound affable and that comedy programs should have a convivial background. Sponsors aimed to reach as large a market as possible. "Radio shows get results mostly in smaller towns," Allen wrote. "To give them some appeal the content of the program should be as simple as possible and exploit a few likeable people who won't wear a person out over the long pull." During the 1934–35 season *The Hour of Smiles* had been partly organized around a small town (named Bedlam). Allen would read a local news bulletin and follow it with a vignette spoofing the news story. He himself had played in New England town halls as a vaudeville juggler, and it was he who suggested the title *Town Hall Tonight*. So the name of his program was changed in 1935 to give his show a broader appeal.[17]

Every week Allen read numerous newspapers and magazines for topics to jest about in the Town Hall News. He scanned reviews of movies, books, and plays that could be satirized on his skits. Wherever he went, the comedian had his nose in a newspaper, magazine, or book. Allen read in subways and taxicabs and while walking on the street, clipping articles and stuffing them in his pockets. "As the day wore on my pockets seemed to be herringbone goiters," he remembered, "and I looked as though I was a walking wastebasket." He selected local news items on topics such as weather, food, clothing, housing, and money. Allen also got his material from a large gag file and from joke books that he kept. An avid reader, Allen enjoyed the writings of Charles Dickens and Mark Twain and literary humorists Sydney Smith, Artemus Ward, William Nye, and Josh Billings. He also perused the English humor magazines, *Punch*, *Tid-bits*, *London Opinion*, and *Pearson's Weekly*. His knowledge and appreciation of comedy aided him in writing his own broadcasts.[18]

Preparing the Wednesday night *Town Hall Tonight* show took an entire week. Allen did two live evening broadcasts, one at nine o'clock and the other at midnight, the latter for listeners in the Far West. That was a common practice, since recorded transcriptions were not permitted on NBC and CBS until the late 1940's. After the second broadcast, Allen went to a Sixth Avenue delicatessen with his director and two writing assistants, Arnold Auerbach and Herman Wouk (later author of *The Caine Mutiny*). His assistants had prepared a tentative comedy sketch for the Mighty Allen Art Players spot, which was discussed at the late-night meeting. They selected the individual to be interviewed on the "People You Didn't Expect to Meet" routine. Allen suggested comic subjects that might be discussed with the upcoming guest celebrity. The conference ended at about three o'clock in the morning, when the comedian went to bed. After resting all day Thursday he returned to work on Friday, answering fan mail and writing letters to acquaintances and friends. He often typed fifty to sixty letters a week, habitually using all lower case letters. During the week Allen worked on the script in his suite at the Hotel Dorset in midtown Manhattan and later in a large apartment on 58 Street and Seventh Avenue. Auerbach described him as sitting "in a straight-backed chair at the rickety card table, bespectacled, frowning, intent, wearing an old-fashioned green eyeshade, elastic bands around his sleeves, a bulge of tobacco wadded into his cheek, toiling hour after silent hour, scrawling tiny, almost illegible hen tracks with a stubby pencil across neat piles of paper."[19]

During the winter the Allens lived modestly in New York City, and they had a summer cottage in Maine. He disliked the Hollywood atmosphere, and was the only major comedian still broadcasting from New York in the 1940's. "California," he wisecracked, "is a wonderful place to live if you happen to be an orange." The comedian shunned publicity and enjoyed simple pleasures. He played handball and boxed regularly at the local YMCA, ate at his favorite Chinese and Italian restaurants, and took nightly strolls with Portland.[20]

A generous man, Allen was known as the easiest touch on Broadway. He was often approached for handouts by panhandlers, unemployed actors, and former vaudevillians. Remembering his own difficult early life, he gave generously to those people and paid extra money to newsboys. A few needy people actually lived off him. One, nicknamed The Whistler, always waited in front of a Broadway theater for Allen to pass. On one occasion The Whistler was absent, and Allen was worried he might be ill. "Where is he?" he asked the theater manager. "It's his birthday," the manager replied. "Here's two dollars for The Whistler," Allen said, "and extra money because I'm going on vacation."[21]

The comedian usually devoted each day of the week to some aspect of the script. On Saturday he sorted numerous news clip-

Fred Allen and Portland Hoffa on
radio in the 1930's.
(Courtesy, Frank Bresee Collection.)

Fred Allen shows his disdain of timeworn Joe Miller jokes told by vaudevillians on radio.

pings and picked the best subjects for the Town Hall News. He met again with his assistants, who gave him a draft for the "People You Didn't Expect to Meet Sketch." Since Allen always edited their material, they were lucky if they had three unedited lines in the entire broadcast. After attending Sunday morning mass at St. Malachy's Roman Catholic Church, Allen worked on the script. Sylvester "Pat" Weaver, the show's producer from 1935 to 1937 (and later head of NBC television programming in the 1950's), came to Allen's hotel with the "continuity" part of the program that he had written—the introduction, lead-ins, commercials, and ending. From this basic structure and the various routines Allen had written the comedian pieced together the weekly program. Then he gave a draft to his sister-in-law for typing. The typescript was mimeographed and copies sent to NBC, the sponsor, and the advertising agency for clearance.

An executive in NBC's Continuity Acceptance Department, convinced that Allen's scripts contained risqué material and double entendres, scrupulously combed every line. Possible libelous references to living people, celebrities, and organizations were censored, as well as the mention of rival products. Although Allen was not a "blue" comic, that lady always managed to discover ambiguous words or language she felt offensive. Pat Weaver persuaded her to change her mind on most points, but there were generally a few words or sentences that the department ordered deleted or rewritten. Allen "would climb up the wall and scream and yell," Weaver recalled, whenever the department wanted the comedian's lines cut.[22]

There were further changes during the cast readings and rehearsals. On Monday afternoon the performers gathered to read the script. Allen, the writers, and the producer took notes during the two readings on the effectiveness of the dialogue. They met afterward to improve the script, deleting dull material and strengthening the weak parts. A perfectionist, Allen went over the script again on Monday night. On Wednesday the entire crew worked from 10 a.m. until one in the morning. The cast rehearsed the script several times, then held a final dress rehearsal, which was attended by representatives of the network, advertising agency, and sponsor. During that rehearsal the script

was timed, with seven minutes set aside for laughter and applause and fifty-three minutes for entertainment and commercials. A talented ad-libber, Allen had considerable difficulty finishing his program, particularly the second broadcast, in which
the performers were more relaxed. After the dress rehearsal last
minute cuts were made, and the show was ready to go on the air.
Countless hours had gone into preparing one hour of radio comedy entertainment.

After the broadcast this tedious procedure was repeated and a
new program written for the following week. Commercial pressure required comedians to give listeners something new to laugh
at every week. This process, which Allen called "a treadmill to
oblivion," devoured the talents of comics and gag writers. The
comedian claimed he had written "three feet more than Shakespeare." Allen had initially enjoyed writing the show, but preparing a new script thirty-nine times a year eventually became
a chore. "The work involved in writing and assembling a weekly
radio show began to seem like a recipe for a nervous breakdown,"
he later recollected.[23]

The *Town Hall Tonight* program was broadcast from NBC's
lavish Studio 8-H, located in the RCA Radio City skyscraper at
Rockefeller Center in midtown Manhattan. The sixty-eight-story
building was the network's new headquarters, and it contained
impressive offices and modern facilities. Twelve hundred people jammed into the studio for each Allen broadcast. Tickets
were difficult to obtain, and often the audience stood outside in
the rain or snow waiting to enter. Allen sometimes told warm-up
jokes before the broadcast for about ten minutes. At other times
he ignored the audience and was even known to scowl at them.
This was part of his act as a hard-boiled comedian who felt that
his program was mainly for home listeners. Comedians found
the nighttime audience slow to respond to jokes. Lured by free
tickets, radio fans went from one show to another during the day
and ended up at the evening comedy programs tired and fam-
ished. Allen had a slightly condescending attitude toward the
audience. On one occasion he telephoned Pat Weaver in the control room during the broadcast. "Where are they giving the tickets out for this show?" he asked. "I can reach down in my toilet

and pull up a better class of people than we get coming to our audience."[24]

At the broadcast's beginning listeners heard people arriving to attend the weekly show in the old town hall. After Lennie Hayton's orchestra played some bars from the program's theme song, "Smile, Darn Yer, Smile," the announcer gave a rousing welcome: "An Hour of Smiles in the Town Hall Tonight, folks. . . . Sixty minutes of fun and music. . . ." A lively band number was then heard, followed by the announcer shouting like a circus barker:

> Here they come . . . up the street . . . Fred Allen and his whole cast, marching to the Town Hall. Lennie's right behind him, leading the Ipana Troubadours . . . and there's a big crowd following. Portland's waving from an old rig that's pulled by the Mighty Allen Art Players . . . everybody's laughing and ready for a big time. Let's join the parade! The whole town's going!

Cheers and crowd noises were heard as Allen greeted the citizens entering the old town hall:

ALLEN   You don't have to eat and drink to be merry, folks. Just try the Town Hall for the same results.

MAN   Where d'yer get yer tickets, Mr. Allen.

ALLEN   Admission's free, friend. You're the guest of Ipana and Sal Hepatica tonight.

MAN   Good. I'll remember them two names Ipana and Sal Hepatica.

ALLEN   That's right. Step right in. Plenty of good seats down front.

WOMAN   Are ya goin to be funny tonight, Mr. Allen.

ALLEN   I hope so, Mrs. White. I always try to tickle the ladies.[25]

On the opening spot, the Town Hall News, Allen broadcast witty news bulletins about the town's citizens. The comedian often mentioned the unique items Hodge White had for sale in his general store:

> Hodge White, the first grocer to put bi-focal cellophane on apple pie so that nearsighted customers could see what the lower crust looks like, has a special announce-

ment. Hodge is calling your attention to his Little
Dandy soda syphon, folks. Hodge says people are using
soda syphons to make everything but soda these days
but his Little Dandy's got them all beat. If you want
whipped cream just pour your cream into the syphon,
put in a cartridge, press the lever and you've got a mess
of whipped cream that'll flood a bathtub. Hodge says
you can put two pounds of rump steak in a little Dandy
and it'll spray out six helpings of the finest beef stew
you've ever tasted. Or break three eggs into your little
Dandy, squirt into a frying pan and in a jiffy you've
got an omelet with a head on it.[26]

Hodge White was actually a grocery store proprietor the comedian had known in Dorchester, Massachusetts. He became such
a celebrity tourists drove to his store to get his autograph. The
news of the odd happenings in the town was one of the program's
funniest parts.

Allen also broadcast news flashes about current events, celebrities, and topics of special interest. The bulletins were generally
followed by a short skit illustrating the item. The comedian also
interviewed people in the town about their reaction to the news,
a forerunner of *Allen's Alley*. Various talented character actors
were employed in the news skits, and they rarely played the
same role twice. In the 1930's Allen created hundreds of bizarre
parts, but, unlike Benny, he did not use regular characters. Minerva Pious, for example, played different Jewish characters on
Town Hall Tonight before she became famous for her role as
Mrs. Nussbaum on *Allen's Alley*.

A running gag on the Town Hall News was the "outstanding
sound of the week." The routine depended on the sound effects
man illustrating a word in a news bulletin. An alarm clock
sounded after Allen's statement, "Fear that President Roosevelt
will veto Patman Bonus Bill causes *alarm* in political circles."
The sound effects man, Agnew Horine, was one of the best in radio. He could imitate any type of noise by using such equipment
as guns, plates, glass, tire chains, clunkers, and whooshers. He
dropped heavy sandbags to imitate a falling corpse and opened
and closed doors in different ways to simulate entrances and
exits.[27]

Allen lampooned all sorts of people on the Town Hall News, including lawyers, politicians, gangsters, professors, and network and advertising agency executives. His skits parodied such topics as real estate fraud, marriage, divorce, Mother's Day, unions, and income taxes. The humor in those sketches was often based on comic exaggeration, as this vignette poking fun at plastic surgery demonstrates:

ALLEN   Washington, D.C. Federal Bureau of Investigation threatens prosecution for plastic surgeons altering fingerprints or features of hunted criminals. Town Hall News gets statements from parties involved—Joe Nab . . . secret service man . . . says.

NAB   A crook with any other face is just as dangerous. Scarface McGee had his face lifted and was using the scar for a part in his hair. How did I catch him. His mouth was so high he hadda take off his hat to cough. I seen him raisin his derby to pick his teeth—so I grabbed him.

ALLEN   Dodo Twirl . . . dance hall hostess favors plastic surgery.

DODO   All public enemies should be operated on from the neck up. I danced with a guy last night—his ears was so full of cauliflowers—he was gettin farm relief.[28]

Another skit satirizing speculation on Wall Street and public relations illustrates the tongue-in-cheek tone of the Town Hall News:

ALLEN   New York City, New York. The New York Stock Exchange plans to present radio programs to further its educational and good will campaign. Town Hall News presents types of program brokers will probably favor— be prepared for this—(Fanfare)

ANNOUNCER   High—Low—Everybody—This is the Voice of Wall Street—Folks and the program tonight opens with a few words from our guest star . . . Mr. Lester Fidget. (Applause)

FIDGET   Thank you, folks. I'm the guest star. I hope you won't mind me comin' into the studio in my union suit. . . . I lost me shirt in the market. . . .

ANNOUNCER   Thank you, Mr. Fidget. . . . Thousands of satisfied investors say the same thing. Folks. . . . And you, too, can make a million dollars playing the stock market.

Ask your broker about Margin . . . spelled M A R G I N
—Earn while you learn to play . . . this is the Voice
of Wall Street signing off. . . .[29]

Allen especially enjoyed jesting about politicians on the Town
Hall News:

ALLEN Washington, D.C. New Deal officials plan to put 1,000
beavers on the Federal Payroll to provide $300,000
worth of range improvement and conservation work in
Idaho. Town Hall News invites little known politicians
to explain reason for government's sudden decision to
subsidize beavers. Presenting, then, that authority on
wind and beavers, Congressman Trundle Scat. Mr. Scat.

HARRY The workingman will have a beaver in every pot. Two
beavers in every garage. Beavers to the right of us,
beavers to the left of us, into the valley of beavers. . . .
beavers. . . . beavers.

ALLEN But how will these beavers lift America's morale?

HARRY The beaver will give a dam for his Country. . . . I
won't be surprised by 1948 to find a beaver has gnawed
his way into the White House![30]

Despite Allen's reputation as the intellectual's comedian he
also liked to make fun of college professors and Harvard students:

ALLEN You *are* a Harvard man, Mr. Higginbottom.

JOHN Yes. At Harvard we speak Latin practically all of the
time. Pro bono publicum.

ALLEN Pro bono.

JOHN Publicum. It means don't pick your bones in public.

ALLEN I rarely do. But thank you for this little etiquette hint.
Now, Mr. Higginbottom you were voted the smartest
student in the class of '38.

JOHN Yes. My name is going to look like a prologue to the
alphabet.

ALLEN You have so many degrees?

JOHN Yes. I've got a B.A., an A.B., a Ph.D., an M.A., and
L.L.D., an M.D.

ALLEN What are you going to do now that you're out of Harvard?

JOHN I'm going right home, the town is giving me another
degree.

ALLEN Another degree?

JOHN Yes, it's a W.P.A. [Works Progress Administration] Whatever that is.

ALLEN You wouldn't know at Harvard, naturally. . . .[31]

Because Allen often jested about sensitive issues he often found himself in an embarrassing situation. One particular comment about an old actors' hotel in Philadelphia caused a furor. The rooms, said Allen, were so tiny "even the mice were humpbacked." Believing that the comedian had slandered the city's hotels and fearing loss of an upcoming Republican party convention, Philadelphia civic leaders called for an apology. The Chamber of Commerce and tourist organizations joined in the criticism, and an editorial in Philadelphia's *Public Ledger* criticized Allen's remarks. The comedian wrote back to the newspaper that he had only jested about one old hotel and that other hotels in the city had spacious rooms. Allen's letter presumably quieted the controversy.[32]

On another occasion Allen told a cheap Scotsman joke and received a protest letter signed by two hundred Scottish-Americans pledging not to buy Sal Hepatica as long as he was on radio. When Allen made fun of the fact that the American Meat Institute had hired the poet Edgar Guest to write public relations poems for the meat industry, Swift & Company boycotted Texaco gasoline (Allen's sponsor) for their trucks. The comedian also received letters from individuals or their lawyers threatening to sue him for using their names in skits. He consequently began using more unusual names for his characters: Doberman Drizzle, weatherman; Titicomb Frond, gardener; Wilda Fang, society debutante; Mrs. Fester Rake, farmwife; Kindle Rocket, fireworks authority; Montaigne Fink, Hollywood producer; Falstaff Ramsbottom, professor; and Tina Wind, city clock cleaner.

Inventing comical names was only one example of Allen's talent to coin clever phrases and quips that sounded funny over the air. He excelled in using language in novel ways. A statue cleaner in the city park was called a "statue valet" who scrubs "granite varicose veins." The American eagle was nicknamed "patriotic poultry." Allen had a large vocabulary and liked to get laughs by uttering such long-winded statements as the fol-

lowing: "The eternal class struggle confirms mid-Victorian prog-
nostication that unionization advocates are usually bombastic
theoreticians suffering from cerebral infantilism." As these ex-
cerpts suggest, Allen was a master at playing with words:

> There's an old saying—If all of the politicians in the
> world were laid end to end they would still be lying.

> In a few years the automobile will be obsolete. Every-
> body will be traveling by plane. . . . All the clouds
> will have Burma-Shave signs on them. Instead of bill-
> boards, skywriters will be spelling out Pepsi-Cola. The
> air will be full of Sunday drivers. If Superman travels
> at night he'll have to wear a tail-light.

> They planted the trees right over the subway. It took
> them three weeks to get the roots out of the Bronx Ex-
> press. People going to work were sitting in bird's nests.
> Squirrels were hiding nuts under the third rail. An ad
> for White Owl cigars came to life. Fortunately the air
> down in the subway killed everything off.

> The only time a native Californian will admit it's rain-
> ing is when he steps out the front door and goes down
> for the third time.

> I heard it rained so hard in Hollywood the Brown Derby
> shrunk three sizes. They say the water got so deep you
> couldn't tell Veronica Lake from any side street. It
> rained so long Walter Pigeon started looking like Don-
> ald Duck.[33]

The second spot on *Town Hall Tonight* was called "People
You Didn't Expect to Meet." Allen conducted interviews with
men and women engaged in unusual occupations. Guests were
chosen for their comic potential and included "A Lady Black-
smith, A Goldfish Doctor, A Sausage Stuffer, A Worm Salesman,
A Canary Specialist, The Last Hurdy-Gurdy Player in Manhattan, A Smoke Watcher, [and] A Tea Taster." One evening Allen
interviewed a trainer who owned a dog that barked answers to
questions:

ALLEN   When I was in vaudeville all of the dogs in dog acts knew me. I was always billed so low that dogs kept bumping their noses into my name as they passed the front of the theatre. . . . How about a couple of more questions?

LEW   Go right ahead, Fred. Get ready, King.

ALLEN   Fine. I think I'll try him out on politics this time. King, how many states voted Republican in the last presidential election? (Dog barks twice) Right. I don't want to ask him how many voted Democratic, Mr. Miller. He'll be here barking for the rest of the night.

LEW   It's all right, Fred. When there are two digits in the answer he'll bark the first digit and stop. Then bark the second.

ALLEN   A lightning calculator, eh? All right, King. . . . How many states voted Democratic in 1936? (Dog barks four times . . . then six) Forty-six.[34]

One night Allen had as his guest Captain Knight, the "World's Foremost Authority on Eagles," who brought his pet eagle, Mr. Ramshaw, to the studio. "All I know about an eagle is enough to keep away from one," the comedian said. "I am a man who hears no eagle, sees no eagle and speaks no eagle." Allen noticed the large talons on Mr. Ramshaw, who was sitting on Knight's wrist. "I'd like to have his clause in my contract," he joked. Knight mentioned that his escaped eagle was once found perched on a taxicab on Madison Avenue. "Probably looking for a taxidermist to give himself up," Allen wisecracked. During the interview Captain Knight ordered the bird to fly around the stage and return to the bandstand. Mr. Ramshaw had several times successfully performed the stunt in rehearsal. The uncooperative eagle instead obstinately circled the studio and refused to return to its owner. The audience shrieked hysterically as the eagle flew around. "I think as long as the eagle is a bird of prey that we have just better discontinue the question and start praying," Allen ad-libbed. "We have a loose eagle in the studio here. Mr. Rockefeller is hurriedly building a lot of ad-lib exits here."[35]

Allen proceeded with the program, occasionally making jests about the escaped eagle. Captain Knight offered a chickenhead to the bird, but it was too busy enjoying its freedom to notice. Mr. Ramshaw finally lighted on a beam and had a bowel movement, the feces narrowly missing a spectator. After the broadcast the owner got the eagle to descend by promising it a steak dinner. *L'affaire eagle*, as the incident was called, was one of radio's most hilarious moments. When unhappy NBC officials accused the comic of staging the event, Allen wrote a network executive that

> when Radio City is being torn down, to make way for another parking lot, the one movement that will be recalled will be the eagle's movement on Wednesday last. If you have never seen a ghost's beret you could have viewed one on Mr. Rockefeller's carpet during our sterling performance.
>
> I know that you await with trepidation the announcement that I am going to interview Sabu with his elephant some week.
>
> Yours for a wet broom in 8-H on Wednesday nights.[36]

An equally amusing incident concerned a retired fireman who owned a talking mynah bird that answered various questions. "What does Mae West say?" the owner asked the bird. "Come up and see me sometime, come up and see me sometime," it replied. At rehearsal the bird answered questions cooperatively, but during the broadcast the embarrassed owner could not coax his pet to speak. The studio audience laughed loudly at the situation, and the silent mynah bird was such a success Allen asked the owner to return the following week. The bird again refused to talk on this and subsequent programs. Listeners wrote letters offering advice: to darken the studio and to "soak its birdseed in hot milk." The regular appearance of the bird turned out to be a good publicity gimmick. Allen's ratings increased as listeners tuned in to hear when the bird would finally talk. The sponsors were unhappy because they suspected Allen and the owner had contrived to substitute a non-talking bird. They urged the comedian to discontinue the act, but Allen insisted it was not a stunt. On the last appearance the owner finally got his pet to speak. Whether or not the incident was contrived is still a mystery.[37]

Another funny segment on *Town Hall Tonight* was Allen's

repartee with Portland Hoffa. She played a friend who dropped in on the comedian during the broadcast. Her opening line became one of the show's trademarks. "Mr. A-a-a-allen . . . Mr. A-a-a-allen," she called shrilly. Allen was always ready with a clever retort:

> Well, sir. As I live and shave every morning so the fuzz on my lip won't look as though I've just finished eating a peach . . . if it isn't Portland.

> Well, sir. As I live and walk around bent over so the tongue in my shoe can get at the water on my knee when it's thirsty . . . if it isn't Portland.

> Well, sir. As I live and walk around bent over not knowing whether I've got lumbago or whether my suspenders are pulled up too tight . . . if it isn't Portland.

Portland got many laughs playing a daffy, illogical character:

PORT   I've brought you a present.
ALLEN   Oh! For little old wrinkled me?
PORT   Yes. These two packages are for you.
ALLEN   Well, thanks. What's in them?
PORT   This one has the last ten pages of *Gone With The Wind*.
ALLEN   The last ten pages?
PORT   Yes. And this is the last twenty pages of *Anthony Adverse*.
ALLEN   The last twenty—
PORT   Yes. Last week, you said you'd like some book-ends. So I tore the ends out of two books.[38]

Like Mary Livingstone, Portland told ludicrous stories about her relatives:

PORT   Mama's farsighted. She has to stand in the middle of the street to see what's in the windows.
ALLEN   Why doesn't she just get a telescope and shop out of the attic window.
PORT   Well, it's all right. She only wanted some tweezers and I bought them.
ALLEN   Tweezers, eh? Are you saving the price of an Easter rabbit plucking your own hares.

PORT   No, Smarty. Papa sat down on a rose bush yesterday and some of the thorns are missing.

ALLEN   It'll take more than tweezers to get anything out of Papa.

PORT   I wish you'd quit picking on him.

ALLEN   Somebody's got to pick on him if you expect to get those thorns back.

PORT   Papa has the worst luck—Hasn't he?

ALLEN   He can't even go by a chiropodist's office without putting his foot into it . . . can he?

PORT   Oh—well—He expects to make a lot of money this Summer.

ALLEN   How? Using three different names on relief?

PORT   No. Papa's making a list of every hot dog stand in the country.

ALLEN   What is he going to do . . . bootleg mustard?

PORT   No. He's going to open stands half a mile past the hot dog places and sell Bi-carbonate.[39]

The last spot on *Town Hall Tonight* featured a comic skit performed by the Mighty Allen Art Players. Allen and Portland were assisted by such versatile character actors as Minerva Pious, Charlie Cantor, and John Brown. They could imitate many different voices and dialects, and sometimes they took eight to ten roles in a single skit. In one hillbilly sketch Allen played a country yokel, and in another a judge who presided over a court that was a mockery of justice. His portrayal of the famous Chinese detective One Long Pan was a riot:

ALLEN   Fleetings and salutations, Kiddies. Detective One Long Pan on job. Make things hum plonto. (Sings) Heigh-Ho! Heigh-Ho! I love a Minsky show.

DOUG   Who is this person, Metcalf?

JOHN   I shall try to ascertain as I'm tossing him out. Hop it, Celestial!

ALLEN   Ho! Ho! Sissy lough stuff—Not flighten One Long Pan. Boo. Yo see. Long Pan not flighten One Long Pan.

DOUG   Speak to this person, Metcalf.

JOHN   Rawther. I say! If you're leaving samples of egg foo yong.

ALLEN   Foo yung, you, Misser Flunky.[40]

Allen's famous radio feud with Jack Benny supposedly began accidentally. "My feud with Fred Allen was an accident," Benny declared:

> Fred said something one night, I answered him—he answered me—I answered him, and it went on and on. We never got together and said, "Let's have a feud." If we did, the feud would have flopped, because it would have been contrived. We would have worked so hard at it it would have been lousy.[41]

True, the feud was never officially planned, but as professional comedians and former vaudevillians they must have been aware of the success of that type of comedy. Their comic ridicule of one another largely revolved around insult jokes that had been common in vaudeville routines between stooges and comedians. Nor were they the first to have a radio feud. Nils T. Granlund, a Broadway producer, and Harry Richman, the entertainer, had a running quarrel on radio in 1927.

Ben Bernie and Walter Winchell had been exchanging innuendos on the air a number of years before the Benny–Allen feud. On his *Jergens Journal* news program, Winchell needled Bernie by making sarcastic comments about the maestro's music and phony accent. In retort, Bernie lambasted Winchell on his program. Sometimes the two appeared on the same show and insulted one another. On one such occasion Bernie quipped: "I don't know why all them oil companies have to go to Ethiopia for gas when it would be just so easy to lay a pipeline direct to Winchell!" Because of the feud their ratings increased, and they made a movie together called *Wake Up and Live*. Listeners liked their harmless fun, and the audience appeal might have unconsciously spurred Benny and Allen to begin their feud.[42]

In fact, the two comedians had been good friends since vaudeville times. Benny remarked that if it had not been for their friendship the feud would have never taken place: "Fred Allen was probably the only comedian I could have had a successful feud with," said Benny. Before starting their radio squabble the two comedians had been guests on each other's programs and had exchanged cutting remarks, but those jokes were mild compared to their later programs, which were considered to be among the most hilarious comedy broadcasts.[43]

Fred Allen triggered the feud on his *Town Hall Tonight* broadcast of December 30, 1936. That evening the child violinist, Stewart Canin, a ten-year-old *wunderkind*, played Rimsky-Korsakov's "Flight of the Bumblebee." Knowing that Benny liked to listen to his program, Allen ad-libbed a cutting remark comparing the comedian's atrocious violin playing with Canin's virtuoso performance. There are two different versions of what Allen said. According to Benny, Allen quipped: "To think that a boy ten years old can play a violin like that—Jack Benny ought to be ashamed of himself." In his autobiography, Allen wrote that his remarks had more bite: "If Mr. Benny had heard this tyke's rendition of 'The Bee' he should hang his head in symphonic shame and pluck the horsehairs out of his bow and return them to the tail of the stallion from which they had been taken." Allen might have made that comment to see if Benny might reply on his broadcast.[44]

On Benny's next program, Sunday, January 3, 1937, the comedian asked Mary to send the following telegram to Allen:

> Dear Fred: I am *not* ashamed of myself. When I was ten years old I could play "Flight of the Bumble Bee" on my violin too. Aegh. You know how to spell Aegh. Signed Jack Benny.

The "Battle of the Century" between the two popular comedians was on. "Before we knew it we were into the darnest feud you have ever seen which was very funny," recalled Benny. "And the strange part of it is I can safely say [it was] from six to eight months with this feud before we even called each other on the phone about it."[45]

During the weeks which followed the two traded insults on their respective programs. When Allen lampooned Benny's violin talent on another broadcast, Benny complained to Don Wilson:

JACK   Did you hear Allen make those innuendos . . . you know, those slurring remarks about my violin playing?

WILSON   Yes, yes I did.

JACK   Pretty catty, wasn't it.

WILSON Oh, I don't know . . . he was just kidding and you're taking it seriously.

JACK Well, so would Heifetz or any other musician. . . . Why didn't Fred make those cracks when we were both in New York instead of waiting till I'm four thousand miles away. . . . It ain't cricket, you know.

Benny liked imitating Allen's nasal twang and jested that he stuck a clothespin on his nose to do the impersonation. Benny rarely got any sympathy from his cast, because they sided with Allen:

JACK The way he talked about my violin playing I ought to sue him.

MARY You ought to sue your teacher too.

JACK Is that so. Well I expected that from you. . . . Anyway, for your information, young lady, I took violin lessons before Allen was born.

MARY You did a lot of things before Allen was born.

JACK Well then let him respect his elders. . . . Hm, imagine saying that I couldn't play "Flight of the Bumble Bee" at the age of ten! Why I played "Flight of the Bumble Bee" so often I got the hives.

MARY (Giggles) I'll bet you stung-up the whole town with it.[46]

During January 1937 the two comedians hired stooges to play parts in the funny fracas. A renowned violin teacher insisted that Benny could have never been a child prodigy. When Benny produced a picture of himself playing "The Bee" at age ten, Allen responded on his next program that "l'affaire Benny" had become "a new low in composite photographic skulduggery." To prove his point, Allen interviewed the photographer, who confessed that the photograph had been taken in a pawnshop using a brownie camera. Benny had posed with a hocked fiddle and held the violin backward with the thin end under his chin! Benny spoke to Phil Harris about the accusation: "Oh, I suppose you didn't hear him say that when I was ten years old I had my violin in a pawn shop." "Well, didn't you?" said the bandleader. "That's not the point . . . it was years later."[47]

Benny's announcement that he would play "The Bee" on his February 7 broadcast intensified the feud. "I'll have a big sym-

phony orchestra and show that guy up," he boasted. Allen sniped
at Benny's violin playing on his next program:

> Now, before presenting our next guest I would like to
> react to some verbal mayhem shunted at me, from
> Hollywood on Sunday last, by an itinerant vendor of
> desserts. I won't mention this gelatine hawker's name at
> the moment. Suffice it should be to say he has a sideline,
> called by some a radio program. . . . Reeking of men-
> thol he swore that he would play "The Bee" on his pro-
> gram next week. This dire news has seeped into every
> nook and cranny of the country. What effect will this
> solo have on contemporary life in America. Mr. Kut
> Priceler, the eminent violinist says:

JOHN   If Jack Benny plays the Bee next Sunday, it will set the
violin back 200 years.

ALLEN   Mr. Lemuel Randyphone . . . Southern Planter . . .
Says.

CHAS   If Benny plays the violin next Sunday the cotton crop is
saved. The South will be all ears. And the ears will be
stuffed with cotton.

Allen invited Stewart Canin back to play a violin solo and challenged the comedian to give a better performance. The following
Sunday, Benny retorted:

> I do not entertain any hard feelings toward that certain
> New England boiled comedian . . . in fact I could al-
> most forgive him for keeping that ten-year-old boy up
> till all hours of the night in an attempt to belittle a man
> once called . . . friend. . . . I did not come here to
> praise Allen or to bury him. But what I am going to do
> tonight, I am doing in the name of justice.

Benny never played "The Bee" on his program, because he was
unable to find his violin.[48]

The missing violin added zest to the feud. Allen offered a reward to anyone finding the instrument and returning it to Benny,
while the latter hired a detective to search for his violin. Allen
continued to poke fun at Benny's stingy habits: "If he ever gets
his hands on all the nickels in the country the buffalo will be-

come extinct." He also accused Benny of being anemic: "Any guy who goes out to a night club and has to get a transfusion before he goes to bed so that his eyes will be bloodshot in the morning is anemic." The sudden discovery of the violin prompted Benny to play "The Bee" on his February 28 broadcast. "Do you know, that solo did more for the aspirin industry than the last flu epidemic," Allen remarked about the performance. "I have never heard such wailing and squalling since the time two ghosts got their toes caught in my ouija board. Of all the foul collections of discord foisted on a radio loving public under the guise of music, that herd of cat calls took the cake. . . . I haven't recovered yet."[49]

On Benny's next broadcast, originating from New York's Waldorf-Astoria, his guest was Stewart Canin. "What did you want to see me about, Mr. Benny?" the young boy asked. "If it's about the violin I don't give lessons." Benny questioned him about his background and accused him of lying about his age. On his next broadcast Allen called Benny a "bully" for picking on the boy:

> Why doesn't he pick on somebody his size? He's the kind of a guy who'd give Shirley Temple a hot foot. Of all the cowards. The last time he got into an argument with the Dionne Quintuplets he invited them outside one by one.

Allen warned Benny he was going to visit him on his next program and settle the feud.[50]

Their famous face-to-face encounter occurred on the March 14 Jell-O show, broadcast from New York's Hotel Pierre. Their previous programs had drawn considerable publicity, and this broadcast had one of the largest listening audiences in radio history:

> JACK Well, as I live and regret there are no locks on studio doors, if it isn't Boo Allen. Now listen, Allen, what's the idea of breaking in here in the middle of my singing.
>
> FRED Singing? Well, I didn't mind when you scraped that bow over my suit case and called it "The Bee," but when you set that croup to music and call it singing . . . Benny, you've gone too far.

JACK   Now, look here, Allen. I don't care what you say about
        my violin playing on your program but when you
        come up here, be careful. After all, I've got listeners.
FRED   Keep your family out of this.
JACK   Well, my family likes my singing and my violin play-
        ing too.
FRED   Your violin playing? Why, I just heard that a horse
        committed suicide when he found your violin bow was
        made from his tail.
JACK   Hm. Well, listen to me, you Wednesday night hawk,
        another crack like that and Town Hall will be looking
        for a new janitor.

After trading other innuendos the two decided to go into the
hallway and box, but, instead of fighting, they returned as the
best of friends reminiscing about vaudeville days. Their truce
did not last long, because they were soon back on the air ribbing
one another.[51]

"The Punch and Benny Show" continued on the airwaves in
the 1940's. In March 1942, Allen's program began to be heard
on Sunday night, which gave him a chance to ad-lib impromptu
retorts right after Benny's wisecracks. At one time they decided
to fight in a boxing ring. Allen was photographed with his sparring partner and Benny posed in boxing gloves with his right arm
extended in a victory salute. Allen sniped at Benny's boxing
ability:

> If Benny ever gets in a ring with me I'll have him
> bouncing around the ropes so much he'll think he's
> Omar, the Tentmaker. . . . Benny's told his last lie
> about me. When I get through making Benny eat his
> words he'll think he's been on a diet of dry alphabet
> soup.

When the match of the century was canceled, Allen called Benny
a coward: "He's got a yellow streak so big if he had a tail-light
you couldn't tell him from a taxicab."[52]

The feud's humor largely depended on the comedians' throwing exaggerated insults at one another and deflating one another's braggadocio. The word duels between Allen and Benny
resembled the quarrels between bragging frontiersmen. In one

heated exchange Benny called Allen "a weatherbeaten gargoyle" and a "Town Hall Buddha" and Allen dubbed Benny a "Waukegan Whippersnapper." He accused Benny of stealing restaurant silverware and hotel furniture to decorate his house: "All of the hotels in New York are ready for Benny," Allen jested. "It's the first time they nailed down the furniture since the American Legion was in town." Allen's clever wisecracks about Benny's stinginess kept the feud at boiling point: "Benny, you're so tight you not only got the first dollar you ever earned, you've got the guy's right arm that handed it to you."

> Why Benny's so cheap he braids his toes to get a rate from his chiropodist. Going into the racetrack on a sunny day, Benny tries to make his shadow pay half the admission. Don't tell me about Benny, the first man to ever demand 26 letters in his alphabet soup. I've seen better heels on secondhand shoes.

Benny retorted by poking fun at the bags under Allen's eyes:

> He just happened to sneeze so hard that the bags under his eyes kept banging together for thirty minutes.

> With those bags under his eyes his face looks like an old pair of pants with the pockets inside out.[53]

Allen's sharpest barbs were aimed at Benny's broadcasts and movies. "They waited till they put the lights out on Broadway, then they sneaked it [Benny's film] into town. . . . I've seen more entertaining pictures tattooed on a sailor's arm." Both comedians did skits parodying the other's program, and each claimed they had more listeners. "You couldn't draw a crowd as big as this if you were a gutter on New Year's Eve," Allen boasted about his large audience. "You've got less listeners than the Siamese Twins with one of 'em out of town," Benny joked.[54] Allen ribbed Benny about his hesitance to ad-lib on the radio. "Benny without his writers couldn't say anything if he was sitting on Edgar Bergen's knee," Allen jested. Benny was actually a good ad-libber, although he preferred reading from the script. Benny's writers had a difficult time matching Allen's imagina-

tive extemporaneous rejoinders. To get even they planned a practical joke. During one broadcast with Allen, Benny suddenly
dropped his pants on stage. Labeled on the shorts were the large
printed letters LSMFT—"Lucky Strike means fine tobacco," the
slogan of the cigarette company that sponsored him. "I don't
need writers," Benny roared. "My underwear can out ad-lib
you."[55]

The adversaries played preposterous tricks on one another.
Once they parodied the giveaway program *Queen for a Day*. As
the winning contestant on "King for a Day," Benny won a free
pants-pressing and Allen had his trousers removed on stage.
"Give me back my pants," Benny screamed. "For fifteen years
I've been waiting to catch you like this," Allen yelled in delight.
"You haven't seen the end of me," said Benny. The Benny–Allen
feud was successful because it pitted two major comedians with
colorful radio personalities against one another. Their insult
jokes kept listeners laughing for years.[56]

Allen's *Town Hall Tonight* was one of the most popular comedy programs during the 1930's. Pat Weaver claimed that at the
height of its popularity three out of four American homes were
listening to the show. *Town Hall Tonight*, like Benny's *Jell-O
Program*, was an important groundbreaking series in the new radio comedy. Allen had pioneered in writing an innovative format that was entertaining to the ear. The Town Hall News and
the other sketches were highlights of American humor. Allen
earned his reputation as a great satiric wit on *Town Hall Tonight*
and continued that success later on *Allen's Alley*.[57]

9

Scatterbrains

Easy Aces and Burns and Allen were two other significant programs in the new radio comedy. Both programs starred a married couple, Jane and Goodman Ace and George Burns and Gracie Allen. Husband-and-wife teams had been popular in vaudeville. As mentioned earlier, vaudevillians often added their spouse for economic reasons because mixed acts, as they were called, received higher salaries. The girl or wife normally played a "dumb dame" foil, or straight part, while the man or husband delivered the jokes. The woman partner occasionally danced and sang. If the wife was a great laugh-getter, the roles were reversed. She usually gave ridiculous answers to questions posed by her husband. Over the air Goodman Ace and George Burns played light-comedy straight men and Jane Ace and Gracie Allen portrayed "dizzy dames" or scatterbrains, an old comic stage type very common in radio. The humor derived from character comedy—the foolish personalities of the wives and the preposterous situations they got themselves and their husbands into.[1]

Known as "radio's distinctive laugh novelty," *Easy Aces* was created and written by Goodman Ace. Born in Kansas City on January 15, 1899, Ace (whose real name was Aiskowitz) was the son of immigrant Latvian parents. He displayed writing talent at an early age. In high school Ace edited the student paper during his senior year and won a writing prize. He majored in

journalism at Kansas City Polytechnic Institute, where he wrote
a column for the college newspaper, making terse, tongue-in-
cheek comments on campus life. Ace was drawn instinctively to
comedy writing. He liked reading the short stories of Ring Lardner and was an ardent fan of Charlie Chaplin's slapstick. The
young man yearned to be a journalist but because of his father's
early death was forced to support his mother and two sisters. He
was employed at the post office and as a salesman at the Wormser
Hat Store at $50.00 a week. Selling haberdashery, however, was
not Ace's forte.[2]

His cousin Hy White, a press agent, helped him obtain a position as a drama, movie, and vaudeville critic on the Kansas City
Post in 1919. He had to take a cut in pay—$25.00 a week—but it
was well worth the opportunity. The city's most respected drama
critic was E. B. Garnett of the rival Kansas City Star. Ace admired Garnett's writing, but the young reporter concentrated on
developing an original style. His critiques were humorous and
pointed, and sometimes his razor sharp comments angered readers. After reading Ace's criticism of a film playing in his theater,
the owner canceled his movie ads in the Post. Harry Tammen,
the Post's co-owner, came to his employee's defense. I will send
"a boy with smallpox . . . through all your theatres" Tammen
threatened the owner, who immediately renewed his advertisements. Ace once panned a road company musical that had advertised the great number of its magnificent stage scenes. "The
sets were beautiful—both of them," Ace curtly reported. The
theater manager complained to the paper about sending a novice
reporter to review the production. Ace expected to be fired, but
instead Tammen gave him a $5.00 raise.[3]

Ace watched many vaudeville comics at work, including
Groucho Marx, Burns and Allen, Fred Allen, and Jack Benny.
He interviewed the entertainers for a gossip column he wrote
about the theater entitled "Lobbying." He met Benny, who later
asked Ace to send him jokes for his routine at the Palace Theatre
in 1927. Benny was the number two act on the bill, following a
Chinese magician. The comedian took one of Ace's jokes for his
opening line: "My, how vaudeville's changed—it used to take
Japs or better to open." Benny asked Ace for more gags and sent

him a check for $50.00. Ace returned the check, writing: "Your check got lots of laughs. If you have any more, send them along." A prolific jokesmith, Ace supplied Benny with free gags for years.[4]

Ace became interested in radio in the late 1920's. He won an Atwater Kent set in a lottery and started avidly listening to programs, including *Amos 'n' Andy*. He watched Gosden and Correll perform in blackface on a stage in Kansas City. The vogue of *Amos 'n' Andy* convinced him that radio was going to be a significant entertainment form. A colleague of Ace's at the *Post* read the midday news over a direct line to Kansas City's station KMBC. Ace also wanted to enter radio and needed the extra money. The ambitious newspaperman approached Arthur Church, KMBC's co-owner and manager, and convinced him to schedule two fifteen-minute weekly programs. On Sunday morning he read the comics to children, and on Friday night he was the host of *Ace Goes to the Movies*. He chatted about current films in town and related the latest Hollywood gossip. His initial salary was only $20.00 a week, but it was the start of a new career that led to another opportunity on radio.

Goodman and Jane Ace became a comedy team by accident. An attractive woman with blue eyes and blond hair, Jane Ace was the daughter of Jacob Epstein, a Kansas City clothing salesman. Epstein would have preferred to have his daughter marry a businessman, but he reluctantly consented to Jane marrying Ace in 1922. Jane had a witty sense of humor and a talent for acting. One evening in 1929 she was in the studio waiting for her husband to finish his program when the station engineer failed to pick up a CBS broadcast scheduled after Ace's show. Ace was quickly signaled to continue broadcasting and began talking extemporaneously. He called his wife over to the microphone and introduced her to the listeners. For fifteen minutes they exchanged sallies on various matters, including their recent auction bridge game. The couple made ad-lib comments about a wife who had recently murdered her husband over a dispute in bridge. "Would you care to shoot a game of bridge, dear?" Jane asked. The poor husband "had been buried with simple honors," quipped Goodman.[5]

After the broadcast the Aces received many fan letters congratulating them on their program. Don Davis, a Kansas City advertising executive, heard them on the air and felt they would
make a good team. He made a contract with a drugstore chain to
sponsor the couple in a domestic situation comedy for thirteen
weeks over KMBC. Listeners in Kansas City began to like their
flippant style.

The Aces were too good to remain on local radio. John Rich, an
advertising executive with Blackett, Sample, & Hummert, made
an agreement with Lavoris to sponsor the show over CBS on a
thirteen-week trial basis during 1931–32. The fifteen-minute
evening broadcast originated from Chicago three times a week
at 10:15. Fearing that the show lacked a large audience, the
sponsor hesitated to renew the contract. The Aces decided to test
the program's appeal by a mail campaign and asked their listeners to write in their approval. When over twenty thousand letters arrived, Lavoris renewed the contract and sponsored the
domestic comedy again during 1932–33. The Aces drew a respectable 12.1 C.A.B. rating but were unable to find a sponsor
for the next season.[6]

During summer 1933 the couple went to New York City,
hoping to find backing for their program. They visited the New
York office of Blackett, Sample, & Hummert, then headed by
Frank Hummert. One of radio's most creative producers, Hummert presided over the agency's radio department, which employed a large staff to develop shows for their clients. The Hummert agency was to become the leading factory for soap operas
in the 1940's, but in the early 1930's it was already a beehive of
activity. Hummert liked the Aces brand of slick sophisticated
humor and felt they would especially appeal to urban audiences.
Since Goodman Ace wrote, directed, and performed in the show,
the series had a low overhead, so Hummert put them on CBS
four times a week as a daytime feature for the 1933–34 and
1934–35 seasons. In fall 1935 they switched to a seven o'clock
slot for Anacin. That fifteen-minute program, broadcast three
times a week, competed against *Amos 'n' Andy*. Although this
competition led to low ratings, their show was a domestic comedy classic considered by loyal fans to be the most humorous program on the air.[7]

The locale and characters on *Easy Aces* contrasted with *Amos 'n' Andy*. The Aces were a prosperous white couple who lived in an upper-class neighborhood in Manhattan. Mr. Ace was a successful New York advertising executive and Jane a housewife whose sole worries concerned getting her friends into the country club, finding a suitable husband for a girl friend, tricking her husband into buying her a mink coat, and keeping her maid happy. Serious social issues were nonexistent in *Easy Aces*. The programs instead focused mainly on exposing human foibles in a humorous manner. Ace created strong supporting character roles, like Jane's best friend Marge (Mary Hunter), the program's "laugh track." Other regular characters included the Aces' twenty-one-year-old adopted son Cokey (Ken Roberts), the uppity maid (Helene Dumas), and Ace's troublesome secretary (Ann Thomas).

Easy Aces was broadcast without a studio audience. The cast sat around a card table hiding a concealed microphone so that the players would be less conscious they were on the air. The dialogue sounded more conversational that way. "We just did our stuff," said Ace. "I just had to depend on what I thought was good for the characters."[8]

Ace generally wrote the scripts one week in advance of the broadcast. He liked writing *Easy Aces* but sometimes found it difficult to produce three shows a week. Ace could measure a difficult script by the number of cigars he smoked while writing it. A diligent craftsman, he painstakingly selected each word to fit the characters. "Everybody has his own idea of how a joke will get a laugh," the writer remarked. "The basic rule is that it should be phrased correctly. A word out of place will spoil the whole joke." Ace did not aim for belly laughs, but for consistent character humor: "A lot of times, on the air, I've noticed comics in a sketch do a joke that destroys the character because it gets a big laugh."[9] Thus *Easy Aces* was a departure from the raucous humor of Ed Wynn and Jack Pearl.

The comedy on *Easy Aces* stemmed largely from the scatterbrain radio personality of Jane Ace. Today the role might well be considered demeaning to women, but at the time the many "dumb dame" and scatterbrain comic characters on stage and radio were never questioned. The basic plot structure of *Easy*

Aces was simple. Jane would get herself foolishly involved in some incident or problem and manage to extricate herself by the program's conclusion. Jane's nonsensical ways were played off against Mr. Ace, the voice of logic and sanity.

Jane generally got the best of her husband, who was often dragged into the turmoils created by his wife. On one program the maid refused to work because Jane's mother was coming to visit and she did not want to clean up after an extra person. In order to pacify her maid Jane made an agreement to let her sleep in the guest room. Jane's mother slept with her daughter, while Ace was assigned the couch. Another typical broadcast dealt with Jane's jury duty. She disturbed the judge by arriving late, disappeared during the trial, and obtained a substitute without permission. When her brother appeared as a witness, the judge declared a mistrial, stating that Mrs. Ace "should never be allowed in a jury box again." The incidents resulting from Jane's wacky character and the frustrations of her husband entertained listeners for years.[10]

Jane became especially noted for malapropisms and misquotes. "Making up these things was easy," said Ace, "because wherever we went we heard people saying weird things." Her funny verbal blunders, called Janeaceisms, always made a point: "We're insufferable friends" . . . "Familiarity breeds attempt" . . . "Time wounds all heels" . . . "He's a rugged individualist" . . . "I was down on the Lower East Side today and saw those old testament houses" . . . and "We're all cremated equal." The malapropisms, a device well suited to radio, highlighted *Easy Aces*.[11]

Beginning in 1943, the Aces broadcast a thirty-minute CBS Wednesday night program at 7:30 for two years. They returned to the air in February 1948 in a new thirty-minute version called *mr. ace and* JANE performed before a live audience with musical entertainment. That program was not as successful as their earlier shows, and it went off the air in May 1949. The Aces were better in a fifteen-minute format than on a variety program. Jane Ace retired in 1949 and died in 1974. Goodman Ace became a leading television comedy writer for Milton Berle, Perry Como, and Sid Caesar, and a columnist for *Saturday Review*. Radio fans still remember their marvelous characterizations and clever dialogue on *Easy Aces*.

Gracie Allen also played an illogical scatterbrain whose constant chatter and inane statements befuddled her husband-partner George Burns. One of several children in an Irish Catholic family, Ethel Cecile Rosalia Allen was born in San Francisco on July 26, 1905. Gracie grew up in a show business environment. Her father, Edward Allen, performed as a song-and-dance man in vaudeville and musical revues. She made her stage debut at the age of three, dancing in her father's act. At fourteen she and three older sisters formed a song-and-dance act which toured vaudeville houses on the West Coast. A little over five feet tall, with hazel eyes and curly black hair, Gracie was a nimble dancer who could do a lively jig. She also could do Irish dialect and got bit parts playing colleens on stage. In the early 1920's she toured as a dancer with the vaudeville act Larry Reilly and Company. Gracie left the act over a billing dispute in Hoboken, New Jersey, and settled in New York City, where she hoped to find acting jobs. She lived at the Coolidge Hotel with two show girls. One was Renee Arnold. The other was Mary Kelley, Jack Benny's girl friend, who later introduced Benny to Burns. Because she had trouble obtaining parts Gracie thought of becoming a secretary and enrolled in a secretarial school. Then, in 1922, Gracie went to see her roommate, Renee Arnold, in a vaudeville show in New Jersey, and there she met the vaudevillian George Burns, who was appearing on the same bill.[12]

George, who had grown up in New York City's Jewish ghetto, came from an entirely different background from Gracie's. Burns's real name was Nathan Birnbaum, and he had been born on January 20, 1896, at 95 Pitt Street on the Lower East Side. He came from a large family—seven girls and five boys. They were very poor, and they lived in a crowded three-room apartment in a tenement house on Rivington Street. There was no inside bathroom, so Burns bathed in the kitchen tub. The comedian's mother was a seamstress, and after his father died she worked hard to keep the family fed and sheltered. The young boy had to help out, earning money hawking newspapers and shining shoes.

The Jewish street life, with its bustling activity of pushcart peddlers and clothing merchants, was Burns's education. He liked roaming the streets rather than going to school at P.S. 22. The five-year-old followed the organ-grinder around the area and started dancing on the street to the music. "The people clapped for me," Burns said, "and I got my first feel of an audience." He loved to show off and sing as a child. The youngster earned pocket change by singing on streetcorners and in a saloon on a ferryboat. He watched the children tap dance at Hamilton Fish Park and learned a few steps to entertain his audience. When Burns was seven he formed the Pee Wee Quartette with three neighborhood children. They sang in back yards and saloons and performed at smokers and stags. Their audience often consisted of gangsters and neighborhood ruffians. At one saloon that had unlicensed boxing matches they were hired to sing during police raids. After the performances the children passed the hat, earning about fifty cents each. They also sang at amateur nights in a local theater and at a Coney Island political dinner. Burns also worked as a dance instructor and in a dress factory, but he was fired from the factory job for entertaining the seamstresses with songs and dances during lunch breaks.[13]

Burns's main ambition was to become a vaudeville star. For a young budding entertainer from the Jewish ghetto, show business appeared to be an exciting, adventurous, and financially lucrative career. Burns, however, had to begin in a small-time vaudeville, and it was a long road to the top. As a teenager he did anything on stage to make money and promote his name. In one act he put on roller skates and got laughs by taking pratfalls. He sang in a "kid act" with five boys and four girls called "The Fourth of July Kids." At one time Burns starred in a seal act, "Flipper and Friend." "The seal smelled better than I did," Burns confessed. He advertised himself as a dancer and appeared in several dancing acts, including Burns and Garry and José and Burns. The latter was highlighted by a lively Spanish tango with an attractive woman partner. For a time he used the stage name Harry Pierce. "That was a lucky name for me," Burns joked. "I once got a job to play a Sunday concert in Ronkonkoma with it." He changed his name to Willie Delight, that of a retired vaudevillian, because he bought for $2.00 nearly two thousand printed cards reading "Willie Delight, Songs, Dances and Syncopated Chatter." He began inserting patter in his song-and-dance routine. As "Nat Burns, Monologuist," a stand-up comic "working in one," he did three or four exhausting shows daily in small-time vaudeville theaters.[14]

When he met Gracie, Burns and Billy Lorraine had a song-and-dance and comedy patter act. She saw them perform at the Union Hill Theater in New Jersey. By then the team had decided to split, so Burns was looking for a new partner. Gracie also wanted to find a partner, and her friend Renee Arnold told her to talk to Lorraine. He was not interested, so she asked Burns. Gracie impressed him as someone who might make a good foil in a mixed act, so he decided to try her out.

They opened in 1923 at Newark's Hill Street Theater, with George as the comedian and Gracie playing the straight part. They got paid $5.00 daily for a three-day engagement. To highlight his role as laugh-getter, Burns dressed in a flashy gold jacket, large red bow tie, baggy pants, and turned-up hat. The act did not click as planned. Every time Gracie said a word the audience howled, while George's one-liners "laid eggs." Burns quickly changed their routine by reversing their roles and changing into a pinstripe suit. He recalled that

> when we first started, I had all the funny jokes and Gracie had the straight stuff, but even her straight lines got laughs. She had a funny delivery. Very sharp and quick and cute, and they laughed at her straight lines— and they didn't laugh at *my* jokes. If she asked me a question, they would laugh and I didn't expect a laugh there. While I was answering her, I talked in on her laugh so nobody heard what I had to say. I knew right away that there was a feeling of something between the audience and Gracie. They loved her, and so, not being a fool and wanting to smoke cigars for the rest of my life, I gave her the jokes.[15]

On the vaudeville stage and radio Gracie played a nonsensical young girl who made ludicrous statements that she believed to be true. Gracie was a very talented actress and character comedienne who convinced the audience of the credibility of her personality. "Gracie could do the wildest kinds of jokes and make people believe them," her husband commented. At first Burns wrote their own stage act because they could not afford gag writers. He selected material from *Whizbang* and *College Humor* magazines and changed the jokes to fit his partner's character. "No matter how mad the jokes were," said Burns, "when Gracie told them you would believe they were true." The key to Gracie's personality was what Burns called "illogical logic."

> When Gracie would take pepper and put it in the salt shaker and salt in the pepper shaker, she would look at you like you had two heads. Her reasoning was people always get mixed up and know when they do they are right. She knew what she was doing. We called that illogical logic. It makes sense but it only made sense to Gracie.[16]

The pair initially played dates in dingy theaters in small towns on what was called vaudeville's "death trail." The couple had a difficult time obtaining bookings and were known as a "disappointment act" that replaced ill performers. Burns and Allen, however, were too talented to remain in small-time vaudeville. One day they received a call to substitute for an act at Brooklyn's Bushwick Theater, a leading vaudeville house. The partners were excited by the chance to break into the "big time." Burns and Allen were a hit and soon were booked into other New York theaters. They toured the Loew's circuit for nineteen weeks in a routine called "Dizzy," which was highlighted by Gracie's daffy stage personality. By the mid-1920's they were touring the country on the Keith-Orpheum circuit playing the number three and four spots.

Burns and Allen usually performed a boy-and-girl-friend act with considerable comic patter. Once the curtain opened with Gracie annoyed at George for keeping her waiting on a street corner. Late for his date, George arrived calmly smoking a cigar and asked his girl friend for a loan:

GEORGE Now listen, I liked you the first minute I saw you but I'll never trouble you again. I'm going to kill myself.
GRACIE Kill yourself. Why?
GEORGE I haven't got a dime. I owe friends fifty dollars. I need

twenty dollars to start life anew. Seventy dollars would save my life. . . . Have you any money?

GRACIE No, I haven't got a dime.

GEORGE Where's that gun—Where's that gun.

GRACIE Oh don't shoot, I was only fooling.

Another time they opened their act with Gracie waving to someone in the wings and a man walked out and kissed her. "Who was that?" Gracie asked. Then they went into a comic he-she routine with Gracie getting the funny lines:

GRACIE On my way in, a man stopped me at the stage door and said, "Hiya, cutie, how about a bite tonight after the show?"

GEORGE And you said?

GRACIE I said, "I'll be busy after the show but I'm not doing anything now," so I bit him.

GEORGE Gracie, let me ask you something. Did the nurse ever happen to drop you on your head when you were a baby?

GRACIE Oh, no, we couldn't afford a nurse, my mother had to do it.

GEORGE You had a smart mother.

GRACIE Smartness runs in my family. When I went to school I was so smart my teacher was in my class for five years.[17]

On the Gus Sun circuit the pair introduced a new act called "Lamb Chops," which was a sensation at New York's Jefferson Theater. Burns played a young man who spent his money on taking his girl friend, Gracie, to restaurants. The routine featured eating jokes, then the rage in vaudeville:

GEORGE Do you like to love?

GRACIE No.

GEORGE Do you like to kiss?

GRACIE No.

GEORGE What do you like?

GRACIE Lamb chops.

GEORGE A little girl your size, can you eat two big lamb chops alone?

GRACIE No, but with potatoes I could.[18]

While on tour George courted Gracie by taking her to expensive restaurants and nightclubs. They especially enjoyed dancing

in elaborate hotel ballrooms. George, however, had to compete
with Gracie's boy friend, Benny Ryan, a dancer and songwriter,
for his partner's affections. In 1925, Gracie suddenly underwent
an emergency appendectomy operation in San Francisco, and
she asked Burns to wire Ryan that she was ill. Burns obligingly
sent the telegram, but Ryan forgot to send flowers. With money
Gracie had lent him (he was short of cash because their performance had been canceled) Burns bought all the flowers he could to
fill her hospital room. George's thoughtfulness impressed Gracie,
and her partner became her favorite suitor. Around Christmas
time he delivered an ultimatum. Gracie should let him know
within ten days if she would marry him. Nine days later she
consented, and the two were married on January 7, 1926.[19]

After their marriage Burns and Allen continued their career
as vaudeville headliners. They played the Palace Theatre several
times, including a nine-week engagement in 1931 with Eddie
Cantor and George Jessel. The star-studded attraction was vaudeville's last major effort to survive the competition of talking pictures and radio. In the red for several years, the Palace had attempted to draw large audiences by engaging several headliners
on the same program. Burns realized that vaudeville was a dying
institution and that radio offered an opportunity to further their
career. They had tried radio during their stage engagements in
London, where they broadcast over the British Broadcasting
Corporation (BBC). "This was our first radio experience," Burns
remembered, "and I was grateful for it because I recognized then
that if we were ever given a chance at it back home, radio was a
good medium for us."[20]

While appearing at the Palace, Gracie accepted Eddie Cantor's
invitation to be a guest on *The Chase and Sanborn Hour* on
November 15, 1931. Gracie had found talking into a microphone
without an audience over the BBC disconcerting. She felt more
self-assured in her five-minute spot with Cantor before a live
studio audience. Gracie played a screwball reporter who interviewed the singer:

> GRACIE   Mr. Cantor, what do you intend to do when you are
> elected Sheriff?

CANTOR   What Sheriff? President of the United States!

GRACIE   You can't be president of the United States. My father told me this morning that *he* is going to be the President of the United States.

CANTOR   Your father?

GRACIE   Yes. My father said, "Gracie, if you can get on the Chase and Sanborn Hour, then I'll be President of the United States."

CANTOR   Well, that's fine.

GRACIE   And he will make a good president. He will be as good as Calvin Coolidge, the Rough Rider.

CANTOR   Calvin Coolidge, the Rough Rider. You remember George Washington, the fellow who freed the slaves?

GRACIE   Anybody knows that, and my father said that if Washington was elected, he would have made a great president.

CANTOR   How do you like Abraham Lincoln?

GRACIE   I read the "Life of Lincoln" four times.

CANTOR   And had trouble each time. Do you remember the Gettysburg Address?

GRACIE   I think they live in Buffalo now.

CANTOR   In Buffalo?

GRACIE   Maybe they moved.[21]

Gracie's high-toned voice sounded very funny over the air. After the Cantor guest spot, Burns and Allen made appearances on Rudy Vallee's *Fleischmann Hour* and on Guy Lombardo's radio show.

Their first regularly scheduled broadcast, *The Robert Burns Panatela Program*, began in February 1932 on CBS. They shared top billing with Guy Lombardo and the Royal Canadians. The thirty-minute program is considered to have been the first major show to use joint remotes. Burns and Allen and Guy Lombardo often broadcast from separate cities where they were making stage appearances.

The thirty-minute music and comedy program was prepared by a writing staff. Carroll Carroll and the temperamental Harry Conn wrote the early scripts. Conn wanted Burns to appreciate his writing talent, so he gave the comedian one joke at a time, which infuriated Burns. The egotistical Conn did not like work-

ing with Carroll or any other writer. When Burns disapproved
of one gag Conn got angry, and the comedian fired him. A more
loyal assistant who wrote Burns's radio material for years was
John P. Medbury, a newspaper columnist and humorist. Willy
Burns, George's brother, served as idea man and business manager. "Willy wasn't the kind of a writer who put a piece of paper
in a typewriter and knocked out a scene," George wrote, "but he
was great in a room where everybody would sit around and
pitch funny lines." A few days before the broadcast Burns met
with his writers in a script conference. Like his close friend Jack
Benny, he selected and edited his writers' material and had an
uncanny sense of knowing what was funny.[22]

The first Burns and Allen broadcasts resembled their vaudeville act, with Gracie playing a scatterbrain and George her befuddled partner. They did comic he-she routines at the program's
beginning and a concluding skit. Gracie's giddy personality and
naïveté was the key to the broadcast's success. Once when their
rating slipped because Gracie was getting out of character, Burns
told his writers:

> Last night I was going over some of the routines we've
> been doing in the last few months and I have an idea
> what's wrong. We're making Gracie try to be funny
> instead of unconsciously funny. We've had her seem-
> ing to be purposely telling jokes instead of being un-
> aware that she is. It's not that we have to do any differ-
> ent jokes, it's just that we've loused up our formula for
> Gracie.[23]

Her routine was highlighted by many language jokes. If Jane
Ace was noted for her malapropisms, Gracie was known for her
mixed-up vocabulary:

GEORGE   You're absolutely brilliant. I'm beginning to think you
         are a wizard.
GRACIE   I'm a wizard?
GEORGE   Yes. You know what a wizard is.
GRACIE   Yes, a snowstorm.
GEORGE   Well, if that's a snowstorm, then what's a blizzard?
GRACIE   A blizzard is the inside of a chicken. Anybody knows
         that.

GEORGE   Then if that's a blizzard, what's a lizard?
GRACIE   A lizard is a man that's smart . . . a genius.
GEORGE   Did something happen to you when you were a baby?
GRACIE   When I was born, I was so surprised I couldn't talk for a year and a half.

Gracie was one of the best in radio when it came to playing with words:

GEORGE   Did you ever hear silence is golden?
GRACIE   No, what station are they on?
GEORGE   It's an adage, you know what an adage is.
GRACIE   Oh sure, that's where you keep your old trunks.[24]

Gracie's inane conversation left Burns flabbergasted. "Somewhere, someplace there must be someone who can stop this chatter that goes on for days," he jested. The show's humor partially stemmed from Burns's frustration. On one broadcast he wanted to be the comedian and have Gracie play the straight part:

GEORGE   . . . this time I've got an idea. I'm going to ask you something, then you ask me the same thing. In other words, I am going to be the comedian.
GRACIE   I know what you mean. You're going to be the funny fellow.
GEORGE   That's the idea.
GRACIE   Well, go ahead, be funny.
GEORGE   Well, I might have a little trouble, but this is what I want. If I should say to you: "Why are apples green?" All you have to do is just repeat the same thing. You say: "I don't know. Why are apples green?" Whatever I say, you say.
GRACIE   I get the idea. I repeat what you say, and then you tell the answer.
GEORGE   That's it. Well, here we go. What fellow in the army wears the biggest hat?
GRACIE   I don't know. Why are apples green?
GEORGE   Now don't be silly, when I say what fellow in the army wears the biggest hat, you must say: "I don't know. What fellow in the army wears the biggest hat."

> GRACIE Oh, I got it. Yeah, you're the comedian.
> GEORGE Alright now, what fellow in the army wears the biggest hat?
> GRACIE The fellow with the biggest head.
> GEORGE I certainly am the comedian.
> GRACIE I think so. Try another one.
> GEORGE Alright, here's another one. What is it that sings and has four legs?
> GRACIE Two canaries.
> GEORGE I picked out a good game.[25]

Gracie specialized in the comic comeback and topping her partner's innuendos. "You ought to live in the home for the feeble-minded," said George. "Oh, I'd love to be your house guest sometime," replied Gracie. She was a master at the comic put-down. "Gracie, all I have to do is hear you talk and the blood rushes to my head." "That's because it's empty," retorted Gracie. She sometimes pretended to take Burns's criticisms as a compliment by saying, "Oh, George, I'll bet you tell that to all the girls." After Burns cracked a joke Gracie occasionally paused and said calmly, "I don't get it."[26]

Burns and Allen kept bound joke books containing thousands of one-liners and routines. The jokes were listed in an accompanying index according to subject matter, from Absentminded to Zoo. It was easy for them or their writers to look under the appropriate heading and find a number of gags about any subject. Under the topic Department Stores are listed ten routines. One was used almost verbatim on their program of March 28, 1932:

> GRACIE I'm going into the department store business. I made up my mind.
> GEORGE What mind?
> GRACIE Somebody told you to say that. I'm going to open up about five or six department stores, of course, that's only for a start.
> GEORGE No doubt in a few months, you will have several hundred department stores.
> GRACIE Well, I don't want to count my chickens before they're department stores.[27]

George Burns and Gracie Allen. "Somewhere, some place there must be someone who can stop this chatter that goes on for days," Burns jested.

Goodman and Jane Ace rehearsing *Easy Aces*, April 13, 1939. (Courtesy, Frank Bresee Collection.)

Burns and Allen also employed Depression gags in their radio routines in the early 1930's. Under the heading Depression in the joke book indexes are listed references to thirty jokes on the economic crisis. The first joke, dealing with the Marx Brothers, was employed on their broadcast of March 7, 1932:

GEORGE   How do you like the Lombardo Brothers?
GRACIE   How many are there?
GEORGE   There are four of them.
GRACIE   Four of them? . . . just like the Three Marx Brothers.
GEORGE   Three Marx Brothers? There are Four Marx Brothers.
GRACIE   Well, I thought with the depression and everything . . . you know.

The banking crisis of March 1933 is the subject of another gag in their joke book. "Things are getting very bad in our house," exclaimed Gracie, "the baby's bank failed." The Depression gags gave listeners a chance to laugh at their troubles:

GRACIE   George, I've got the most marvelous idea for settling this unemployment situation.
GEORGE   Do you mean to say you have an idea . . . that's good? It isn't possible.
GRACIE   Well, I've decided to put all the men in the world on an island in the middle of the ocean. Then soon everybody will be working.
GEORGE   You don't mind if I get this straight. (Repeats speech)
GRACIE   That's right.
GEORGE   In the same ocean? . . . and they will all be working? What would they be doing?
GRACIE   Boat building.[28]

Like other radio comedy stars, Burns and Allen tried to boost the country's morale during the Great Depression. They made guest appearances on special government-sponsored radio programs, including a 1933 broadcast publicizing the National Industrial Recovery Act, establishing fair competition codes on an industry-wide basis:

GEORGE   We're here to talk about the N.R.A.
GRACIE   Well, N.R.A.—C.B.S.—N.B.C. One radio station is as good as another, don't you think so?

GEORGE   I think so but Gracie, the N.R.A. is an industrial code.

GRACIE   Oh, code! My nephew went to prison on account of a code. You see, he had a code in his nose and my nephew went to a doctor and the doctor told him to take something warm as quickly as possible, so my nephew took the doctor's overcoat . . . so you see, all on account of a code.

GEORGE   Gracie, not a cold! A code!

GRACIE   Oh you mean a code and a vest and two pairs of pants.

GEORGE   If that's a code, then what's a coat?

GRACIE   A coat is a small horse.

GEORGE   Skip it! Skip it! You see the N.R.A. . . . . it stands for national recovery.

GRACIE   National recovery!! Oh, George, could they recover my missing brother?

GEORGE   Yes and while they are looking for your missing brother, they can also look for your missing brain.[29]

The most publicized running gag on their early radio programs concerned Gracie's missing brother. She had earlier told imaginary stories about her brother on stage. Gracie could ramble on incessantly about her relative, recalled Burns:

> Gracie and I were in the middle of a broadcast one night when the lights in the studio went out so naturally we couldn't see the script. So we decided to do an old vaudeville act. I said to Gracie how is your brother and she kept on talking until the lights went on.

The missing brother radio routine was a stunt concocted by Bob Taplinger, a CBS publicity executive, to improve their ratings. Burns liked the idea and related it to his writers. "What we've been looking for is right in our laps and we've been too dumb to recognize it," said the comedian. "The thing to do is to send Gracie on a hunt for her missing brother."[30]

The publicity gimmick began on the January 4, 1933, program and continued for months on the broadcasts. She barged into other programs, including the Rudy Vallee, Eddie Cantor, and Jack Benny shows, seeking the whereabouts of her lost brother. Newspapers publicized the search, and magazines printed photographs showing her looking on top of the Empire

State building and at Coney Island. Many fans wrote letters offering help and some even included photographs of people pre-
sumed to be the missing brother. A newspaper reporter discovered Gracie's real brother, George, a San Francisco accountant,
and his picture was printed in newspapers across the country.
He went into hiding until the stunt wore out after a few months.
The publicity increased the comedians' rating. Like the well-
publicized breach-of-promise trial on *Amos 'n' Andy*, this running gag offered amusing diversion for a fun-hungry public during the Great Depression, and illustrated radio's power to involve
listeners.

During the 1930's Burns and Allen were usually listed among
the top five comedy programs, but around 1939 their rating
started to decline, reaching a low of 14.9 in 1941. As the years
passed their comic he-she jokes had grown stale and become
unbelievable. They had outgrown their smart-aleck roles as a
boy and girl friend. Part of Gracie's act had been to flirt with
the announcer, Bill Goodwin, and the handsome movie stars that
were guests on the program. In real life they had children and
were approaching middle age. Burns became aware of the
problem:

> What happened was that our jokes were too young for
> us. You see, Gracie and I had two children then, but we
> were still doing a street-corner act . . . and you can't
> do that. You've got to be your age in show business. You
> can't be any younger than you are supposed to be, nor
> any older. We told a lot of jokes that were all right for a
> young boy and girl, but not good for a married woman.
> Like Bill Goodwin coming out and making love to Gracie
> . . . well, the audience knew we were married and they
> wouldn't accept it. For instance, Gracie once said to me
> when she was about thirty-five, "I can't continue to play
> this character." I asked her why and she said, "Because
> I'm thirty-five!!" . . . When you are thirty-five you
> tell jokes about cooking, about roast beef in the oven.[31]

Beginning with the 1941–42 season, Burns and Allen switched
to a domestic situation comedy format that took place in the
Burns's home in Beverly Hills. It was a successful change that

allowed them to play essentially the same character types, but in a new framework. Gracie impersonated a scatterbrained housewife who invariably got herself and her husband into difficulties. George portrayed the frustrated husband driven to despair by his wife's idiocy. The new formula was similar to *Easy Aces*. Gracie's illogical logic always got the better of her seemingly more rational husband. A talented supporting cast (Mel Blanc, Elvia Allman, Gale Gordon, and Hans Conried) made *Maxwell House Coffee Time* a popular series in the 1940's.

Burns and Allen were on radio for eighteen years doing jokes and routines deriving from Gracie's scatterbrained personality. Like Jack Benny, they excelled in acting character comedy and creating comic situations arising from their roles. Gracie retired in 1958 and died on August 28, 1964. Her husband recently made a comeback in movies, winning an Academy Award in 1976 for his role as an old-time vaudevillian in *The Sunshine Boys*. Although they had a successful television series beginning in 1950, Burns and Allen are still remembered most for their radio broadcasts.

PART FOUR

Midwestern Small-town America

10

Wistful Vista's Comic Bungler

Radio had two major situation comedy programs that depicted life in Midwestern small-town America—*Fibber McGee and Molly* and *Vic and Sade*. Both programs originated from Chicago in the 1930's over NBC. They were written not by a team of writers, but by gifted comedy writers, Don Quinn and Paul Rhymer. The shows focused on households in small towns and recreated life in Midwestern America. The programs also accented the idiosyncrasies of odd character types.

The *Fibber McGee and Molly* program starred a husband-and-wife team, Jim and Marian Jordan, two excellent situation comedy performers. They were born in Peoria, Illinois, which in vaudeville days had a reputation as a bad show town. Entertainers had joked about "laying eggs" in Peoria for years. James (Jim) Jordan was born in 1896 on a farm five miles west of the city, and Marian Driscoll, a coal miner's daughter, was born and raised three miles from Jim's farm. Peoria was then a typical Midwestern town of small businesses catering to farmers in the surrounding area. Because of its size the Jordans got to know their neighbors well, and the experience of living in a small town later proved useful for their roles in *Fibber McGee and Molly*. On the broadcasts the Jordans often referred to their early days in Peoria, and Wistful Vista, where the McGees lived, resembled a town in the Midwest.[1]

How the Jordans met, married, and worked their way up in show business resembled the plot of a soap opera. Jim, who was attending a boys' parochial school in Peoria, first met Marian at a church choir rehearsal. Since Marian was enrolled in a near-by girls' parochial school and his older sister was dating Marian's elder brother, Jim already knew about her and had seen his future wife play the piano at a school function. They had much in common, including aspirations for careers in music. Jim wanted to be a singer and Marian a professional piano player. Her parents at first objected to her romance with a young tenor who offered little financial security. After graduation, Marian gave piano lessons, while Jim obtained a position as a clerk in a wholesale drug house at $8.00 a week. In September 1917 Jim joined the vaudeville quartet in an act called A Night with the Poets, but, unaccustomed to one-night stands and lonesome for Marian, he returned to Peoria in May 1918. He acquired a job as a mailman, and finally, on August 31, 1918, married his high school sweetheart.

The first years of marriage were difficult for the Jordans. Five days after the ceremony, Jim was drafted into the Army to fight in World War I. He was dispatched to France, but he missed participating in the trench warfare because of influenza, which caused him to be hospitalized. By the time he recovered the war was over. Assigned to a show-business brigade as a singer, he entertained troops waiting to come home. In July 1919 he was discharged and returned to Peoria. Jim and his wife decided to form a singing and piano team. They entertained at local clubs and church halls, but the pay was so meager that Jim was forced to find other employment. He tried several jobs, including selling insurance, washing machines, and vacuum cleaners, and working as a day laborer in a machine shop. Marian had to give up performing temporarily when their daughter, Kathryn, was born. The bills started to mount up after they purchased a four-room house, and for a time it looked as if they would never leave Peoria.

Then, unexpectedly, around 1922, the Jordans were offered their first important show business opportunity. Ralph Miller, a theatrical agent, saw their act and felt the Jordans had enough

talent to go on a professional tour. Needing $1000 for suitable
apparel, travel expenses, and props, they mortgaged their home,
sold their automobile, and borrowed $500 from Jim's Aunt Kate.
For approximately a year they traveled daily from one Midwest
town to another by train, playing one-night stands in opera
houses, theaters, and school halls. Dressed in tux and tails, Jim
sang classical and popular numbers to Marian's piano accom-
paniment. Although the concert tour life was fatiguing, they
gained considerable experience in show business by having to
face different audiences nightly.

The Jordans toured as a team until shortly before the birth of
their son, James, Jr., in the summer of 1923. Jim decided to do
a single while Marian was recovering. He went to Chicago,
where he was hired for occasional café and club dates but was
unable to obtain any permanent bookings. He finally obtained
a job singing between picture shows in a movie theater, but,
realizing he was a flop without Marian, he returned to Peoria.
The Jordans rejoined the tour circuit, but this time they were
not as successful, and they ran out of money in Lincoln, Illinois,
fifty miles from Peoria. Back home they did club dates while
Jim supplemented their income by working as a drygoods store
clerk. For a brief time he formed a vaudeville singing team with
Egbert Van Alstyne, but that act never clicked. By 1925 the "big
time" was still an allusive goal for the Jordans.

If it had not been for radio the pair might have remained
small-town vaudeville performers or unknown local citizens of
Peoria. Luckily, the fledgling years of radio were a time of ex-
perimentation open to all budding entertainers with a degree of
talent. Stations could not afford to hire well-paid professionals.
Jordan recalls radio's early days:

> In those days the radio announcers and engineers and
> everybody went out on the street and dragged people in
> to get them to go on this thing. Because nobody would
> go on. Professional people didn't fool around with this
> kind of business. They didn't pay anybody.[2]

In 1925, the Jordans were visiting Jim's brother in a Chicago
suburb and heard some mediocre singing on the home crystal

set. Jim bet his brother $10.00 that they could sing better than that. The couple went to station WIBO on Chicago's North Side, and after a successful audition they were hired at $10.00 a week. For five months the Jordans broadcast daily the singing and piano routines they had done on stage. The show increased their popularity as vaudeville entertainers. On the radio they mentioned their theater performances in the Chicago area, and then more people came to see them.

Two years later, in 1927, the Jordans moved to Chicago station WENR, where they were heard in a variety of programs. They then began to deviate from their standard musical routine by doing some comedy patter on the air. The couple was paid $60.00 weekly to act in a children's program called the *Air Scouts*. Jim was also hired to play several bit characters on WENR's programs, including an old man. This character became the basis for Luke on the Jordans' *Luke and Mirandi* farm program, written by Harry Lawrence. A farmer who liked to tell tall tales and white lies, Luke was the forerunner of Fibber McGee. Mirandi, played by Marian, was a character much like Mrs. Wearybottom on the *Fibber McGee and Molly* program. The Jordans also acted in *The Smith Family*, a domestic comedy serial written by Lawrence and considered to be one of radio's first soap operas. Broadcast once a week with a repeat on Sunday, *The Smith Family* concerned a policeman (Jim), his Irish wife (Marian), and their two marriageable daughters. The character of Molly was later based on Marian's portrayal of the Irish wife. The change to situation comedy over WENR was an important stepping stone to *Fibber McGee and Molly*.[3]

In 1931 the Jordans signed a contract for $200 a week to do the comedy show *Smackout* over Chicago station WMAQ. The daily fifteen-minute comedy skit program was aired over the NBC Blue network for two years and was heard locally over WMAQ until 1935. The character Luke (Jim) reappeared on this program in the guise of a country grocery store owner who was always "smack out" of every item. Like Fibber McGee, Luke Gray was a folksy neighborhood type who enjoyed spinning yarns. Marian also played the little girl, Teeny, a character she later enacted on *Fibber McGee and Molly*. *Smackout* was written by Don Quinn, a former illustrator and cartoonist from Grand Rapids, Michigan. He had a natural writing talent for depicting small-town Midwestern characters and had started in radio as a writer for the comedy team Olsen and Johnson. The Jordans met him at station WENR and later collaborated with him to do *Smackout*, a partnership that proved invaluable.

The origin of *Fibber McGee and Molly* derived from *Smackout*'s appeal. John J. Lewis, an advertising executive with Needham, Lewis, & Brorby, handled the Johnson Wax Company's account. In 1935, he was searching for a new network program to advertise the company's products. His wife, Henrietta Johnson of the Johnson Wax Company family, listened avidly to *Smackout*, and she told her husband about the performers. Henry Selinger, who had been influential in putting *Sam 'n' Henry* on the air, also recommended the Jordans to the advertising executive. Lewis asked Quinn to write some initial scripts, and after a successful audition the company hired the Jordans at $250 a week.

Fortunately, the couple had a twenty-six week contract, because their half-hour weekly program, which premiered on April 16, 1935, got off to a slow start. "If we had been on for thirteen weeks I'm sure we would have been off by the end of thirteen weeks," Jim Jordan recollected. The initial programs, broadcast on Monday night, were only occasionally funny. The program also had to compete against the popular *Lux Radio Theatre*. In early January 1936, *Fibber McGee and Molly*'s rating was only 6.6, but then it began to capture a larger audience and to lure listeners away from the Lux program. By January 1937 its rating was up to 13. A more favorable broadcasting time—9:30 Tuesday night over the NBC Red network—contributed to its growing popularity during the late 1930's.[4]

Listening to *Fibber McGee and Molly* on Tuesday nights became a household ritual during the 1940's, when it was among the top four comedy shows on the air, rivaling Bob Hope, Jack Benny, and Bergen and McCarthy for the top spot. By the early 1940's Quinn had introduced amusing character types into the plot and perfected a sure-fire format. In early January 1944 *Fibber McGee and Molly* led the list of comedy programs with an audience rating of 31.9. During that decade approximately one-quarter to one-third of American households which had radios were listening to the series. The Jordans were so popular that they signed with RKO Radio Pictures to make several movies. The couple were earning $3500 a week on radio, and the starvation wages of their vaudeville days were now a memory.[5]

Don Quinn was largely responsible for making *Fibber McGee and Molly* superb, well-written entertainment. Long-term radio comedy success depended on writers creating a polished, humorous script every week, and often large writing staffs were hired for that purpose. By contrast, Quinn worked alone and was solely responsible for the writing until later, when he was aided by Phil Leslie. The writer met with the cast on Friday afternoon to consider the upcoming broadcast. The next day he outlined the plot, and on Sunday he did the actual writing, often typing until dawn. After the first rehearsal on Monday, Quinn revised the script, cutting lines that failed to get a laugh. By Tuesday evening the script was ready to be broadcast.[6]

Quinn partially modeled Fibber McGee (a name conceived by John Lewis) on Jordan's earlier portrayal of Luke Gray, but he made his central character more of a colossal "fibber" and braggart in a small-town setting. The early broadcasts were especially highlighted by Fibber's preposterous tall tales. On the first program he boasted about riding in the English steeplechase on a "hoss" named Dover that leaped over a hedge eleven feet high and galloped riderless across the finish line. The next week Fibber bragged about his courage as a construction worker on a ninety-six-story building:

> Jest imagine them narrow girders sticking up 1835 foot in the air and think o' me, walking along nonchalant-like onto a beam six inches wide with the wind whistlin' 'round my ears like a tornado. Shucks, that was work for a MAN . . . the higher the better fer me.[7]

At the conclusion of these episodes Fibber's inflated bravado was punctured by an event exposing his exaggerated tall talk. After listening to Fibber flaunt his feat as a daredevil skyscraper construction worker, a gas station attendant raised McGee's car on the rack with Fibber inside. McGee nervously exclaimed:

> Ye don't git me way up on one o' them things. Leggo,
> Molly, leggo. Lemme outa here. . . . Hey, don't raise it
> yet, boy. . . . Lemme outa here. . . . Lemme out. . . .

In another broadcast Fibber boasted about his agility as the fast-
est football runner in the nation—"Touchdown McGee, the
Tuckapooka Tornado." He joined the neighborhood children in
a game to show them his swiftness, was tackled by two children,
and was knocked unconscious. Fibber McGee represented radio's
version of the foolish show-off, a venerable comedy type.[8]

Although Fibber went through a ritual humiliation in the
programs, he still emerged as a lovable radio comedy hero. A
major character in radio comedy was the vain egotist or pompous
braggart (Benny, Hope, Fibber McGee, and Andy) who retained
his self-image despite being the victim of countless jests. Ego deflation is an old comedic device, but the formula had special
significance for the Great Depression. During that time of widespread bankruptcy, unemployment, and poverty many Americans bore a feeling of personal inadequacy and internal shame
for failure. A listener whose self-image was low readily identified
with the egotist, who, despite constant ridicule, maintained his
vain traits and delusions. The great radio comedy hero was the
lovable fall guy or fool whose affectations derived from traits common to us all.

Fibber pretended to be a superhuman jack-of-all-trades: the
greatest broncho-buster in the West, the daring pilot of a strato-
sphere balloon, the wrestler Mad Mauler of Muncie, the boxer
Murder McGee, and the deep sea diver Mudbank McGee. One
whopper described his daring hand-to-hand fight with an Alas-
kan big bear, and another magnified a three-hour fishing duel
with a swordfish. His wild imagination often ran to extreme
lengths:

> I'll never forget the time I rid acrosst Africa on a
> huntin' trip on a bicycle. Yes sir, Toots, that was in
> 1897. Capetown to Tripoli. Made it in twenty-two days
> exactly. Would of made it in fifteen and a half if it
> hadn't been for bein' captured by cannibals up in the
> Belgian Congo. . . . Well, sir, on them cannibals
> came, with a hungry look in their eyes, while I jest

stood there in the kettle of boiling water real calm and collected.[9]

Fibber was Wistful Vista's most monstrous liar and windbag. He once wanted to legally change his first name, but his request was denied when the judge heard him describe how he caught a gigantic salmon with a piece of roquefort cheese. Another time Fibber sent a note to a committee running a tall-story contest: "Gentlemen: I'm sorry but I just don't seem to be able to sit down and deliberately tell a falsehood." Fibber was later informed over the radio that he had won first prize: "To anyone who knows Mr. McGee, this will be recognized as the most fantastic whopper of all time! Congratulations, Mr. McGee!"[10]

A device employed to highlight Fibber's braggadocio was the tongue-twister. The studio audience delighted in watching Jordan read his lines. A few seconds before reading the tongue-twister he rocked back and forth on his heels and suddenly uttered an avalanche of words that caused the audience to roar with laughter. Fibber's grand feats and numerous occupations were described in rambling, alliterative sentences:

> Punch bowl McGee, pronounced by press and public the pugilistic pixie of the pedigreed paperweight pugs, pummelling pudgy palooka, pulverizing proboscuses and paralyzing plug-uglies. Pounding poor preliminary pork and beaners to a pulp with a peppy pip of a pop—positively a peach of a punch that plunks the punks on their piazzas. Ping-pong pappa of the pineapple punch, a peculiar poke that petrifies the pit of the paunch of the pillow-pushers who plop to the platform, too popeyed to protest. Prancin and posin' and full of ambition.

The tongue-twister was a clever device, well suited to aural comedy. Used throughout the history of the program, it eventually became a permanent trademark associated with the show.[11]

Fibber McGee was descended from a long line of yarn spinners. The tall tale was an early vernacular form of American humor dating back to the opening of the Western frontier, where backwoodsmen and river boatmen gathered around camp fires to tell farfetched stories. Eventually the tall tales appeared in almanacs, magazines, newspapers, and books. Supernatural feats were emphasized in these exaggerated frontier stories in which the braggart was a major comic character. Often the protagonists became American folk heroes, as did Davy Crockett and Mike Fink. Nor had the tall tale disappeared in the 1930's, for Americans still enjoyed reading about the lumberjack Paul Bunyan and the itinerant sower Johnny Appleseed. Fibber McGee's yarns were as inventive as the oral frontier tales and his feats as grandiose as Paul Bunyan's. The early campfire stories and Fibber's radio whoppers were a hundred years apart, but both were aural forms of humorous entertainment.[12]

Fibber talked like a folksy Midwestern character, and his speech was punctuated with slang and colloquialisms. Some of his favorite expressions were "what's cooking," "take a gander," "doggone it," "hot dog," "aw pshaw," and "kiddo." On one broadcast he employed several currently popular idioms when he described his talent for dancing:

> I meant we were gonna paint the town red. We're goin' out and toss a torrid two-step or two. . . . I'm a hep cat tonight. I got a brain full of boogie and a jumper full of jive. I'm a wild-eyed wampus from the wavin' woogie and this is my night to sock the maracas.

He also used many contractions in his conversations—kiddin', beatin', crackin'. Since swear words were not allowed on radio, Fibber's pet expression was "dad-rat the dad-ratted"—one of the show's numerous catch phrases. Whenever he had an accident he exclaimed: "Dat-rat the dad-ratted thing anyway . . . the dad-ratted. . . . Of all the dirty breaks!!" Molly believed Fibber could "get more real profanity into a 'dad-rat' than the average mule skinner has in his whole vocabulary." Fibber's lingo gave him a degree of authenticity as a quaint small-town character.[13]

Fibber's dialogue sparkled with clever witticisms and amusing definitions:

> That material fits the davenport like the skin on a weenie.

> Them springs are tighter than a forty-dollar girdle after
> a spaghetti dinner.
>
> A committee is a small group of unqualified appointed
> by the unthinking to undertake the utterly unnecessary.
>
> Nostalgia is a longing for something you couldn't stand
> anymore.[14]

In the early broadcasts Fibber was also characterized as Wistful Vista's ne'er-do-well. He lacked a permanent job and moved
from one position to another, as a jewelry store manager, bank
officer, insurance salesman, newspaper reporter, court judge, and
temporary town mayor. He was fired when he botched his job
assignments. As an encyclopaedia salesman, he lacked the correct sales pitch and was talked into buying an entire set by the
publisher. Fibber had not bought his home by savings and hard
work, but had won it in a raffle conducted by the Hagglemeyer
Wistful Vista Realty Development Company. An unemployed
daydreamer and blunderer, he was the antithesis of the American breadwinner.[15]

During the 1940's Fibber became even more of a foolish bungler. The bungler was a clownish figure adopted from American
variety theater, the circus, and silent movies. The accident-prone
Fibber somewhat resembled Charlie Chaplin's clumsy tramp.
During the 1930's several comic strips dealt with the bungling
husband, among them Dagwood Bumstead, Andy Gump, Pa
Bungle, and Rudy Nebb.[16] Quinn updated the comic prototype
by turning Fibber into a modern American tinkerer who botched
his household projects. Listeners could easily relate to this ineffectual do-it-yourselfer. Most people knew a bungler in real
life and had a bit of "Fibber McGee" inside himself.

Fibber's household tasks led to inevitable accidents. While
repairing the water pipes, he forgot to turn off the main valve
and flooded the basement. He lit the furnace with gasoline, hung
wallpaper backwards, and while repairing the window shades
fell off the stepladder and broke his leg. Fibber was often unable
to do anything right:

> It's been one of them days! Everything's gone wrong.
> Couldn't get my pajamas off this morning. Cord was in

a hard knot. Busted my shoelace. Fell off the porch
gettin' the morning paper! Stuck my fork in my eye
eating my waffle.[17]

The chaotic scenes at 79 Wistful Vista resembled a slapstick
movie comedy. After attempting to fix a squeaky floor Fibber
discovered that it was his shoes that squeaked. A newly ordered
washing machine turned out to be a concrete mixer that tore his
clothes to shreds. Whenever he helped Molly in the kitchen or
did the cooking, the kitchen became littered with food, dirty
dishes, and broken glass. His home-made recipes, such as tuna
fish mixed with waffle batter, caused indigestion.

As the town fool Fibber was the laughingstock of Wistful
Vista. When he delivered a speech inaugurating the new court-
house his words were drowned out by the noise of a band. Another time he got stuck in the fresh cement in front of his house.
An air hammer was employed to chop McGee loose, and he returned home with two hunks of cement on his feet. An amateur
magician, Fibber performed his famous escape act in front of a
large audience, but by mistake he locked himself in a large milk
can. Unable to unlock the can, he asked the audience to give him
some corn flakes if he was not out by morning. When Molly
used Fibber as a model to hem a dress, his neighbors teased him
about his feminine appearance, and more embarrassment occurred when he went to the dressmakers in a taxi. The buffoon
formula was reworked repeatedly in an endless number of
situations.

A major device used to augment the format was the surprise
ending. In several programs Fibber supposedly captured wanted
criminals, but usually they were innocent, and sometimes they
were prominent citizens of Wistful Vista. Fibber once informed
the FBI that he was being followed; at the broadcast's end, however, he learned that the man was a journalist writing a story
about Fibber called "How a Small Town Busybody Spends His
Time!" The trick ending often exposed Fibber's absentmindedness. On election day McGee attempted to achieve a 100 per
cent turn-out in his precinct in order to collect $250 from the
Good Government Club. That seemed especially easy since 79
Wistful Vista was the polling place, and by the time the polls

closed everyone had voted—that is, everyone except Fibber. On another program he decided to make a home-made slapstick movie. He broke a mirror and a floor lamp and tripped over the kitchen chair, getting skinned elbows and a sore neck. When he picked up the film from the developers it was blank. Wistful Vista's star clown had forgotten to take the rubber cap off the lens. When done subtly without obvious contrivance, the surprise ending based on the reversal of audience expectations was a clever comic device.

Running gags were also employed on *Fibber McGee and Molly*. The repetition of sure-fire jokes were important to the long-term success of that and other comedy programs. The running gags took several forms: amusing situations, comic character bits, and funny sound effects. The most successful ones played on listener expectations in which the anticipation of the joke became as important as the joke itself. Writers regularly wrote such gags into the script so that they became an expected part of the format—aural trademarks listeners associated with a particular program.

The most famous running gag on *Fibber McGee and Molly* was the hall closet at 79 Wistful Vista. Inside was the best-known junk pile in American entertainment, a gigantic heap of assorted objects the McGees had collected over the years. Among the articles the closet contained were relics from Fibber's youth—his old mandolin, chemistry set, stamp collection, fish poles, dumbbells, and skates. Molly also stashed unneeded kitchenware in the closet, including tin cans, pie pans, coffee pots, and trays. Items were thrown in helter-skelter so that nothing was properly stored. The mess was so unmanageable that the only way to keep the junk from falling off the shelves was to keep the door closed. Whenever Fibber or a neighbor opened the closet out tumbled all the odds and ends, often on top of the unsuspecting person who had opened the door. "By George, one of these days I gotta straighten out that closet!" Fibber exclaimed. The gag poked fun at our gadget-loving society and our unwillingness to part with useless possessions. The routine was so effective that storage areas in houses became known as Fibber McGee closets, an example of radio's influence on everyday speech.

Jim and Marian Jordan as they appeared on early radio in *Fibber Mc-Gee and Molly*.
(Courtesy, Frank Bresee Collection.)

The routine also played on radio's strength as a sound medium. Frank Pittman, the program's sound effects engineer, simulated the noise of falling objects over the air. An initial click of the door latch was followed by a thump of several boxes descending on the floor. Then the clatter increased until a crescendo of falling bric-a-brac was heard, ending with the tinkling of a little bell. Listeners could visualize the falling clutter in their minds, and the routine made audiences laugh every time.

When the gag was first broadcast on March 5, 1940, the program was climbing in the ratings but needed new material to sustain its popularity. During that broadcast Fibber searched for a dictionary to look up the meaning of a word:

FIBBER   Where's the dictionary?

MOLLY   Probably in the closet with the rest of your stuff. Give me your key and I'll get it for you.

FIBBER   Oh, no ye don't . . . You lay off the stuff in that closet. I got all my stuff arranged in there just the way I want it. . . .

MOLLY   Maybe we better see if the closet is locked. Let me look.

FIBBER   Oh, it's locked all right. You don't think I'd leave all my personal stuff layin' around for any prowler to . . .

SOUND   *Doorlatch*

MOLLY   McGee. . . . It isn't locked. It's

SOUND   *Thump of a box falling . . . Repeat*

MOLLY   Better give me a hand, McGee—this stuff is all falling out.

SOUND   *More thuds and clatter. Building up to a terrific avalanche*

MOLLY   McGee . . . help . . . I'm buried alive! Get this junk off of me.

At the show's end Fibber dutifully packed every object back into the closet, including the dictionary:

FIBBER   I forgot to leave it out. I packed it back in there.

MOLLY   Heavenly days . . . what

FIBBER   Hey. . . . Stay away from there. I know exactly where I put it.

SOUND   *Door latch*

FIBBER   I can get it out without disturbin' a single . . .

SOUND	*Thump of box falling . . . repeat*
FIBBER	Hey Molly !!!! . . . Help! . . . Grab a hold of the . . .
SOUND	*More thuds and clatter . . . Build up to same avalanche*
FIBBER	(Smothered) Hey Molly . . . Molly!
MOLLY	Yes?
FIBBER	I found the dictionary . . . How do you spell annahiliated?

A form of radio comedy slapstick, the closet routine became funnier the more frequently it was used.[18]

The running gag rarely grew stale, for Quinn employed the routine in varying ways. Visitors to the McGee home often mistook the closet for the front door. When someone opened the closet and nothing fell out, the silence received as much laughter as the noise. It also figured as an important element in the plot. One amusing broadcast concerned two burglars who entered the McGee home and tied Fibber up. Informed by Fibber that the family valuables are in the closet, the robbers opened the door and were smothered by the falling objects. Several shows depicted Fibber's futile attempt to clean the closet. "Isn't it terrible how this stuff piles up, McGee?," said Molly. "We just cleaned this closet out four months ago." "I think the pixies do it," replied Fibber. "I think the pixies go around at midnight and steal stuff outa junkyards and attics to put in this closet." In another broadcast Molly decided to reward Fibber with a special dinner for cleaning the closet. Opening the linen closet to set the table, she discovered her husband's priceless goods that he had promised to throw out. Caught in a white lie, he ran out of the house.[19]

Fibber's bungling and daydreaming contrasted with Molly's realism and practicality. As a voice of sanity in the turmoil at 79 Wistful Vista, she refereed the quarrels between her husband and the neighbors and often saved Fibber from difficult situations. Her relationship with her husband was one of warmhearted affection and toleration. "I could tell you any number of things but the reason we stayed married is because I didn't," she remarked. Although Molly was capable of loosing her temper, she had learned to live with Fibber's white lies:

> FIBBER There ain't a more honest, upright, straightforward, guy in the world than me. You know that.

MOLLY   Yes, I know it. But I seem to be unique.

FIBBER But why? Why? What'd I ever do to make people doubt
        me?

MOLLY   Well, you're always so . . . so imaginative, dearie.
        Your memory is too good. You remember things that
        never happened.[20]

Molly was used regularly as a foil in the plots. In one broadcast Fibber wanted to sell their house to a professor who needed
a quiet place to write, but Molly prevented the sale by hiring
the neighborhood children to make noise when the potential customer arrived. She often made fun of her husband's vanity,
especially his movie-acting ability:

MOLLY   Oh McGee . . . I almost forgot . . . RKO called this
        morning and they want you to come back!

FIBBER Hot Dog. . . . To make another picture?

MOLLY   No, you left your Correspondence Course in "How to
        Act" in the dressing room.[21]

Molly had her own brand of subtle humor, punch lines, and
catch phrases. One—"tain't funny, McGee!"—lampooned Fibber's stale jokes:

FIBBER Now, Molly, I need a cigar darn sight worse than I
        need a glass of Guernsey Gruel. (Laughs) Don't ja get
        it, Molly. Instead of using the word 'milk,' I called it
        'Guernsey.'

MOLLY   Tain't funny, McGee![22]

Another of her favorite expressions was "heavenly days!" The
character of Molly, played by Marian Jordan, was indispensable
to the program's success. Marian conveyed a warm, friendly personality on the radio and concluded the broadcasts by saying
"goodnight, all" to the listeners. When she was off the program
during the 1938–39 season because of illness, the series dropped
in the ratings. She helped make the program a popular favorite
for years.

A talented voice imitator, Marian also played various bit parts:
Teeny, Mrs. Wearybottom, Lady Vere-de-Vere, and Old Lady
Wheedledeck. Mrs. Wearybottom spoke in a monotone without
stopping for punctuation, while Teeny, the precocious little girl

across the street, supposedly modeled on the Jordans's daughter Kathryn, spoke in a shrill nasal voice that drove Fibber crazy.

Since the McGees were childless, Teeny, a young neighborhood nuisance and mischief-maker, was added to the plot to torment Fibber. "Hi, mister," she would say to Fibber at the front door. "Hello, sis. Go away, will you? I got worries enough without your juvenile jabber. Go wan, go away. Go home. Go anywhere." Teeny knew Fibber was a habitual fabricator and enjoyed teasing McGee about his tall tales:

TEENY   My mamma. She says to take everything you handed out with a grain of salt.

FIBBER   Oh, she did, eh?

TEENY   Sure . . . she says you can pull more wild yarns than a puppy with a sweater.

FIBBER   Is that so. Well. . . .

TEENY   Fibber is a Fiberrrrr. . . . (*Door opens*). . . . Fibber is a Fibber. . . . (*Door closes*). . . . Fibber is a Fibber.

Fibber was pestered by Teeny's endless questions—"whatcha doin', huh, mister, whatcha?"—and repeated remarks—"I betcha . . . I betcha." Her favorite game of What? Where? When? Why? exasperated him:

TEENY   . . . got a hundred in history for doing our home work right.

FIBBER   You did, hey?

TEENY   And our teacher . . . uh?

FIBBER   I said you did, hey?

TEENY   Who did?

FIBBER   You and Willie Toopes.

TEENY   Did what?

FIBBER   Got a hundred.

TEENY   Where?

FIBBER   In history.

TEENY   When?

FIBBER   Today.

TEENY   Why?

FIBBER   For doing your home work right. (Yells)

TEENY   I know it.[23]

Fibber McGee and Molly depicted neighborly life in a quaint Midwestern town. The plots usually took place at 79 Wistful Vista, the McGees' home. The town's center was 14th and Oak, where the drugstore, bakery, and dry goods shop were located. Listeners learned of the Wistful Vista *Gazette*, Dugan's Lake, where Fibber went canoeing and fishing, the soda fountain at Kremer's drugstore, and the local Elks Club. *Fibber McGee and Molly* presented a generally positive and nostalgic picture of small-town America. The program's tone corresponded to the favorable reassessment of small-town life in American culture during the 1930's. The Great Depression caused many Americans to question the impersonality of urban life. Writers in the 1930's began to rediscover the value of community living. Thornton Wilder's *Our Town* (1938) stressed the importance of neighborliness and a shared sense of community. *Fibber McGee and Molly* seemed to satisfy a yearning for "the good old days" at the very time American society was becoming heavily urbanized.

Quinn created a range of different characters representing a cross section of small-town types. They included the local doctor, the mayor, the old-timer, the weatherman. He gave minor characters amusing names: Gilda Gorgeous, the movie actress; Edward Uppercase, the newspaper editor; Mrs. Fordelia Blakewell Butler, the society lady; and Mr. Burpwhistle, the radio repairman. Fibber and Molly talked about several characters who never appeared on the program, including Fibber's pals, Fred Nitny and Egghead Vanderween. The most important off-mike character was Myrt, the local telephone operator. When McGee picked up the telephone, Myrt was sure to be on the other end of the line. Fibber would usually ask Myrt about her family and then make a remark to Molly implying that something tragic had happened to one of Myrt's relatives. One time he told Molly that Myrt's uncle had smashed his face and broken one of his hands. "What happened, McGee, did he fall down the stairs?" "Naw, he dropped his watch," said Fibber.[24]

The series featured a cast of small-town oddities with strong personality quirks who contrasted with Fibber. The altercations between the common-man McGee and his highfalutin' neighbors could be reworked every week. "All these people were about ten levels above McGee when it came to intellect and everything else," Jim Jordan remarked. "This McGee he never worked. He didn't do anything. That was the strange part about it. These people . . . got a boot out of this guy because he was such a braggart."[25]

Excellent character actors appeared on the series, and the roles they enacted contributed enormously to the show's long-term success. The producers hired performers who could imitate unusual voices. The talented impersonator Bill Thompson played Nick Depopolous and Horatio K. Boomer during the broadcast's early years. Nick was a Greek immigrant restaurant owner who called McGee "Fizzer" and talked in garbled English:

> FIBBER Whatcha readin' now, Nick? The Encyclopaedia Britannica?
>
> NICK No—the Velocipedia Britannenbaum is being a little ponderpuss for me, Fizzer. . . . I am rather lending myself some friction from the Public Strawberry.
>
> FIBBER Library . . .
>
> NICK Sure . . . this book story I am reading to me now is entitled to be calling itself by the name of Little Red Robin Hood.
>
> FIBBER Whatcha mean? Little Red Riding Hood or Robin Hood—that's two different books.
>
> NICK No, Fizzer, it is only being one book—but I am making an allowances for you being an ignoramipuss about literacy—I am being an awful booksnake myself.

With his malapropisms and thick dialect, Nick was an ethnic stereotype, a stock figure borrowed from vaudeville and popular theater. Thompson adopted a W. C. Fields accent to play Horatio K. Boomer, the professional confidence man who proudly showed the McGees his stolen goods and burglary tools. He was probably the first character who got laughs by insulting Fibber. Some of the names he called McGee included "monkeyface," "prunepit," "zipperlip," and "pretzelpuss." Boomer and Nick were really cardboard characters, and when their repertoires grew stale after a few years they were dropped from the program.[26]

The well-known characters that made *Fibber McGee and Molly* a popular program were not introduced until the late

1930's. Thompson then became noted for his famous characterization, The Old Timer, a half-deaf codger who liked to visit the
McGees. "What say, Johnny?" he asked whenever Fibber made
a remark he could not understand. To do The Old Timer's seedy
voice Thompson distorted his jaw and spoke as if he had no teeth.
His corny stories were as farfetched as Fibber's tall tales. Whenever Fibber or Molly cracked a joke, The Old Timer tried to top
them with a yarn. He began by saying:

> Hey, hey, hey . . . that's pretty good, daughter. In fact
> that's very good. But it still ain't the way I heered it.
> The way I heered it, one feller, says to the other feller,
> "sayyyyyyy," he says. . . .

The Old Timer lived in the past. On one broadcast he decided to
enlist in the Navy in order to fight in World War II:

> FIBBER   They won't take you in the Navy. You're too old. You'd
>   lay an egg in the crow's nest.
> OLD TIMER   Is that so! *Well by John Paul Jones, Johnny, I can*
>   *spread a sail with the best of them young whipper*
>   *snappers.*
> MOLLY   But they don't use sails on our warships any more.
> OLD TIMER   Well, I can shovel coal, too.
> FIBBER   They don't use coal. They burn oil.

A quaint, neighborly type who reminded listeners of the "good
old days," Thompson's Old Timer was one of radio comedy's
most memorable characters.[27]

Thompson also did another unforgettable impersonation, the
henpecked husband Wallace Wimple. The actor first did the
character on the *Breakfast Club* program and later introduced
Wimple on the *Fibber McGee and Molly* show of April 15, 1941.
The next week Fibber encountered Wimple at the Elks Club,
where he had escaped from his "big old wife" Sweetyface:

> I talked back to her. That's why I'm here. I'm a wife-
> ugee. She's awful mean to me, Mr. McGee. Sometimes
> I think I can't stand it another year! You know how it is.

Wimple spoke in an effeminate whimper and his favorite word
was "peachy."[28]

The more Wimple complained about his marriage to Sweetyface, the funnier the repertoire became:

WIMPLE   I asked Sweetyface if I could go downtown and watch
         the parade and she said yes, if I got my work done in
         time.

MOLLY   What work, Mr. Wimple?

WIMPLE   Oh, she has me washing the windows today, Mrs.
         McGee.

FIBBER   Well, that shouldn't oughtta take long, Wimp.

WIMPLE   It does when I do it her way. With a piece of wet cotton
         on a toothpick.

MOLLY   Heavenly days . . . what on earth is the idea of that?

WIMPLE   Punishment, Mrs. McGee . . . just punishment. I was
         naughty this morning.

FIBBER   Were you really, Wimp? What'd you do—sneak out
         and inhale a dubeb?

WIMPLE   No, Mr. McGee . . . at breakfast this morning, she
         told me to eat all the crust off my toast or I wouldn't
         have curly hair and when she turned her back, I made
         a face at her.

MOLLY   That was safe enough, wasn't it?

WIMPLE   (Laughs) That's what I thought, Mrs. McGee . . . but
         she saw my face in the coffee pot.

FIBBER   And then what?

WIMPLE   And then I saw the coffee pot in my face!

MOLLY   Oh, you poor boy! Was the coffee hot?

WIMPLE   That's what Sweetyface asked me afterwards and I said
         I didn't think it was so hot this morning and that started
         it all over again.

FIBBER   This goes on day after day, doesn't it, Wimp? Why
         don't you hop a freight outta town and start life all over
         again some place else?

WIMPLE   Oh, I tried that once, Mr. McGee . . . I got clear to
         Minneapolis once before she caught me.

MOLLY   You mean she followed you all that way?

WIMPLE   No . . . I'd forgotten my toothbrush and she caught
         me when I sneaked home to get it.[29]

Another character was the snobbish society lady, Abigail Uppington, played by Isabel Randolph. A member of Wistful
Vista's upper-class, Uppy, as Fibber called her, chatted about

her afternoon teas, dinner parties, theater engagements, and club activities. When shocked by Fibber's uncouth manners, she would utter in a shrill affected voice, "well, reahlly, Mr. Mc-Gee," or "how teddible." Uppy pronounced words ending in "er" with a drawn out "ah": "Well, my deah, I am going to the decoratahs to select wallpapah." Fibber enjoyed teasing Abigail about her snobbery and old age: "Old Uppy may belong to the upper crust, but she's beginning to crumble."[30]

The difference between Abigail's social circle and the middle-class McGees supplied the basis for a good deal of humor. Uppy was perturbed when she heard that Fibber was contemplating joining the Wistful Vista Country Club:

> UPPY   Well, there would have to be some inquiry as to your social background. Tell me, Mr. McGee, have you any Mayflower stock in your family?
>
> FIBBER   I did have, Uppy, but I swapped it for A. T. & T.
>
> UPPY   I mean, Mr. McGee . . . Were any of your ancestors Pilgrims?
>
> FIBBER   Pilgrims! Why shucks, Uppy, my folks was here long before the Pilgrims landed. I'll never forget what my great great great great Uncle said when he seen them Puritans splashin' ashore at Plymouth. "Hey, folks," he says, with a sneer on his face. "Get aload of the immigrants."
>
> UPPY   Indeed.
>
> FIBBER   Oh yes. Us McGees has always been definitely upper crust, I always says.

When Fibber got stuck in the fresh cement outside his house, Uppy complained that McGee was "lowering the tone of the whole neighborhood." Molly, who knew how to put Uppy in her place, came to her husband's rescue: "Don't give me that Vassar vaseline, dearie! Next thing you'll get so exclusive you'll want our fire department to have an unlisted phone number!" The clash between the stuck-up Abigail Uppington and the common-man Fibber McGee entertained listeners for many radio seasons.[31]

An equally popular characterization was Gale Gordon's masterful portrayal of the haughty Mayor La Trivia, introduced as a character in 1941. The conceited mayor, whose name was a takeoff on New York's Mayor La Guardia, acted as the perfect foil for the windbag McGee. La Trivia felt he was slumming with hoi polloi when he visited 79 Wistful Vista. Sometimes he offered Fibber a job as temporary garbage collector or street cleaner. The mayor detested Fibber's white lies, while Fibber disliked La Trivia's pomposity. They often misconstrued each other's remarks and argued heatedly. Fibber got the temperamental La Trivia so angry the mayor mixed up his words:

> (Roars) I don't want to balk a stossum? Squawk a blossom! Look—when I said I was playing posse—possum, I merely meant I was lowing lye! Er, lying low . . . I never said I was—you're the one that always misconwords my strues . . . strue remarks my words! . . . Every time I stake a simple matement—make a staple mintment—stinkel satement—minkel statement. . . . You were the one . . . I . . . You. . . .

After his tirade the mayor would curb his temper and utter frustratingly, "McGeeeeee." "Ooooooo, good day," he would remark angrily, and slam the door.[32]

Fibber and the pseudo-intellectual Doctor Gamble, played by Arthur Q. Bryan, also engaged in arguments rife with insult humor. Gamble called McGee "Neanderthal," "gruesome," and "marblehead," while Fibber nicknamed the doctor "butcher boy," "epidemic chaser," and a "barrel-bottom cowtown Kildare." Fibber needled Gamble about his ability as a physician: "He must have studied sewing under Omar the tentmaker," and, "Is it true you lost your satchel last week and three patients got well before you could find it?" The doctor, in turn, scoffed at Fibber's pretensions. He once mocked McGee's ambition to become a great poet:

> Don't drool that Greenwich Village nonsense at me, you little faker! Poetry, my peritoneum! You couldn't rhyme moon and June if you collaborated forty years with Ira Gershwin. You haven't got a sonnet in your bonnet that would bring twelve cents at a literary rummage sale!

The comic altercations between Fibber and the town's leading citizens highlighted the program during the 1940's.[33]

Fibber's loudest adversary was his next-door neighbor, Throck-morton P. Gildersleeve, played by the comedy star Hal Peary. He had entered radio in 1928 in San Francisco as a singer on *The Spanish Serenader* program. In 1935 he moved to Chicago, where he obtained parts playing a variety of character roles in a children's show, soap operas, serials, and plays. Because of his training as a singer Peary could imitate various voice ranges, and he would play as many as six characters on a single pro-gram. Around 1937 he began doing bit parts on *Fibber McGee and Molly*, including a Chinese laundryman, Wu Fu, and Perry, the Portuguese Picolo Player. He created for the program a boisterous stuffed-shirt individual initially called George Gilder-sleeve. Peary defined the character as "the familiar blow-hard, an earnest, sincere man who fumbles a great deal in his enthu-siasm to get ahead." An important trademark of the role was a "he-he-he-he" laugh, which derived from a singer's scale Peary had used when he had been a vocalist.[34]

Around 1939 Gildersleeve was permanently written into the script as the McGee's bothersome next-door neighbor. His first name stemmed from the street Peary lived on, Throckmorton Place. It was difficult to tell which had the biggest ego, Fibber or Gildersleeve. The two engaged in back-fence quarrels and played tricks on one another. Fibber once stole Gildersleeve's dress suit hanging in his neighbor's back yard. He used his telephone to make long distance calls and always forgot to return Gilder-sleeve's lawn mower. Another time the two fought a duel with water hoses. Whenever McGee outwitted his tempera-mental neighbor, Gildersleeve remarked despairingly, "You're a haaarrrd man, McGee."

Ludicrous insult jokes marked their routine, in which each at-tempted to outdo the other in verbal abuse:

> FIBBER You got no more gratitude than a collector of Internal Revenue!
>
> HAL Is that so!
>
> FIBBER Yes, that's so!
>
> HAL McGee . . . One of these days, I'm going to tangle with you and you'll wind up in a bigger cast than they had in the Wizard of Oz!

FIBBER Gildersleeve, if you even twitch a label toward me, I'll hand a couple of socks on your chin that Santa Claus couldn't fill in eight centuries.

HAL Oh, is that so!

FIBBER Yes, that's so!

Molly would attempt to intervene:

MOLLY Please, gentlemen . . . *Please.* . . . This is no way for good neighbors to talk.

FIBBER We ain't good neighbors . . . we're enemies.

HAL Yes we are . . . the *best* of enemies. You think I'm a stuffed shirt and I think you're a gabby little good for nothing runt.

FIBBER There . . . ye see, Molly? You don't find me and Gildersleeve indulgin' in no sentimental, hands-across-the fence drivel.[35]

During summer 1941 Peary left the show to form his own program, *The Great Gildersleeve*, radio's first successful spin-off from another broadcast. Playing the same character in a new situation comedy, Peary impersonated the water commissioner of Summerfield—an eligible bachelor who cares for his orphaned niece, Marjorie (Marylee Robb), and nephew, "Lee-ee-ee-ee-roy" (Walter Tetley). The plot mainly revolved around Gildersleeve's troubles rearing the children, and around his girl friend, the Southern belle Leila Ransom (Shirley Mitchell). Like *Fibber McGee and Molly*, *The Great Gildersleeve*'s success partially derived from the use of off-beat characters played by talented performers: Birdie the maid (Lillian Randolph), Floyd the barber (Arthur Q. Bryan), Peavey the druggist (Richard Legrand and Forrest Lewis), and Judge Hooker (Earle Ross). A popular situation comedy during the 1940's, the broadcast made Peary a radio comedy star. Although he later did several guest spots on *Fibber McGee and Molly*, Peary's last regular appearance on that show occurred on September 30, 1941:

FIBBER Gildy, old man . . . I . . . I hardly know what to say.

HAL Let's just say this isn't goodbye . . . it's . . . aurevoir . . .

FIBBER I . . . I can't say that . . . Gildy . . .

HAL   Why not?

FIBBER   I can't pronounce it. . . .

Marian Jordan was more sentimental: "We'll miss him on Tuesday nights, but we're proud that our association was a stepping stone toward his own show." Peary left *The Great Gildersleeve* in 1950, but the series continued until 1958. It was one of radio's most durable programs.[36]

Another successful spin-off from *Fibber McGee and Molly* was the *Beulah* show. The McGee's black maid, Beulah, first appeared as a character on January 25, 1944. (She was actually the program's second black character. The first was Silly Watson, a stereotyped, ignorant, and foolish handyman, played by Hugh Studebaker, a white man.) A happy-go-lucky maid and mammy type, the Beulah character had stereotyped traits, although she had more depth as a personality than Silly Watson. She was unafraid to talk back to the McGees. "Somebody bawl fo' Beulah?" she shouted from the kitchen. She also had her own ironic form of humor: "I been bendin' over a stove for fifteen years now. (Laughs) The job is new, but the position ain't." She laughed hysterically at Fibber's jokes and between giggles would utter, "love dat man!"[37]

Beulah was first played by a white man, Marlin Hurt, a former singer who had entered radio in 1929. Hurt specialized in imitating Negro voices during the time when racial impersonations were still acceptable and it was difficult for black performers to break into radio. Quinn heard Hurt do the Beulah routine on *The Fred Brady Show* in Los Angeles, and he wrote the character into the script. Few in the live audience attending the *Fibber McGee and Molly* broadcast knew that Beulah was played by a white man. His back to the audience, Hurt would suddenly turn around and shout his opening line. The audience, caught by surprise, would scream. In 1945 Hurt formed his own program using the Beulah character, but he died the following year, and the show temporarily went off the air. It was revived in April 1947 with another white man, Bob Corley, in the lead. In fall 1947 the show became a fifteen-minute serial over CBS, starring the black screen actress Hattie McDaniel. Louise Beavers, Lillian

Randolph, and Amanda Randolph also played the Henderson's maid on the series, which remained on radio until 1954. Ethel Waters portrayed the part on television. Because of its stereotyping, *Beulah* seems contrived and artificial today, but the series did help black performers enter radio.

Fibber McGee and Molly was sponsored for fifteen years by the Johnson Wax Company, one of radio's longest sponsorships. The use of the integrated commercial created strong sponsor identification. In the middle of the broadcast Harlow Wilcox, the announcer, visited the McGees and bragged about the beautiful shine Glocoat and Carnu gave floors and automobiles. The McGees ribbed him about his infatuation with Johnson Wax. Wilcox "thinks the Seven Wonders of the World are the pyramids, the Hanging Gardens of Babylon, and five cans of Glocoat," joked Fibber. The announcer's sales pitch was often a mixture of pure corn and poetry:

> My friends, you're familiar with Omar Khayyam
> Probably even more than I am.
> So listen to this, the Johnson version
> of "No-Mar, the perfectly polished Persian."
> A book of verse, a Glocoat can, and thou—
> Besides me in our little kitchen, toots
> Why worry now, about the milkman's muddy boots?[38]

Fibber McGee and Molly was more than a classic comedy program—it was an institution that upheld national morale during two critical events, the Great Depression and World War II. Jim Jordan believed that the show helped relieve people "from the cares of the day." For a half-hour on Tuesday night listeners habitually tuned in *Fibber McGee and Molly*. In 1939 Jim Jordan remarked at the end of a broadcast:

> We are not unconscious of the fact that these are serious days. In bringing you a few smiles . . . we hope we are helping to lift your spirits a little bit. The only members of the animal kingdom who are able to laugh are human beings so let's stay human as long as we can.[39]

Because of low ratings Johnson Wax dropped the program in 1950, but the series continued until June 30, 1953, as a weekly half-hour show sponsored by Pet Milk and Reynolds Aluminum. Between 1953 and 1957 the Jordans did a fifteen-minute weekday program and during the late 1950's five-minute spots on the NBC weekend *Monitor* show. Their act broke up when Marian Jordan got cancer in the late 1950's. She died in 1961.

In retrospect, the heyday of *Fibber McGee and Molly* was in the late 1930's and 1940's. American comedy became more sophisticated in the 1960's, and its subject matter often concerned the city and its social problems. Television's *All in the Family* signaled the new trend, and *Fibber McGee and Molly*, with its depiction of small-town America, now appears dated. *Fibber McGee and Molly* belonged to an age more conducive to small-town comedy featuring bizarre characters and a lovable comic bungler.

11

Radio's Home Folks

The origins of *Vic and Sade* can also be traced back to the heartland of the Middle West in the early twentieth century. Like Jim Jordan, Paul Rhymer, the creator of *Vic and Sade*, grew up in a small Illinois town. He was born in Fulton, Illinois, in 1905, and shortly thereafter his family moved to near-by Bloomington, where Rhymer spent his youth and college years, an experience that had a major influence on the radio program. Although it was never directly mentioned, Bloomington was the model for the locale of *Vic and Sade*, and many characters were based on people he and his family knew.[1]

From this personal knowledge of small-town life Rhymer created a classic of American humor. According to William Idelson, who played Rush Gook on the program, "Paul Rhymer was the funniest man that ever wrote." The poet Edgar Lee Masters called *Vic and Sade* "the best American humor of its day," while the author Hendrik Willem Van Loon viewed the show as "great folk writing." *Vic and Sade*, which received high ratings among daytime serials in the 1930's and early 1940's, claimed to have seven million loyal listeners. It was voted the most outstanding written radio program in 1936, and in 1940 the *Motion Picture Daily* named the show the best daytime serial.[2]

Rhymer's talent for writing was evident in his school years. At Bloomington High School he won the Merwin Cup award for short story writing and was president of the Short Story Club. He also wrote humorous pieces for *Aegis*, the high school yearbook. At Illinois Wesleyan University he was a member of the Sigma Chi fraternity and several literary clubs. During his sophomore year he published his first short story, "Hen," in *College Humor*. At this time he acquired a liking for literary realism, and admired the novels of Charles Dickens. A few commentators have noticed a resemblance between Dickens's figures and the characters in *Vic and Sade*.[3] He also enjoyed reading Ring Lardner and Booth Tarkington. Because of his father's death Rhymer had to withdraw from college after his junior year and go to work. He held a series of jobs, including those of a magazine salesman and a taxi driver. He once tried newspaper reporting but was fired for writing fictitious news stories and interviews.

In 1929, on the eve of the stock market crash, Rhymer received his first break, an opportunity to enter radio. A college classmate helped him obtain a position as a staff writer with NBC's Continuity Department in Chicago. Seated at a desk in a glass cubicle, Rhymer wrote copy for hundreds of broadcasts. His duties included writing lead-ins which announced musical numbers on orchestral programs and preparing sketches for the *Farm and Home Hour*. He was also assigned a Saturday morning children's program sponsored by the fire prevention bureau and featuring the fireman-clown Smokey Rogers. A practical joker with a keen sense of the ridiculous, Rhymer enjoyed inserting amusing circumlocutions and inane statements in his copy. He once gave a ludicrous line to an ex-Shakespearean actor, who, in a burst of outrage during the rehearsal, refused to read the sentence. Rhymer's inclination toward absurdity later marked *Vic and Sade*.

His most important assignment for the Continuity Department was the creation of a weekly program, *Keystone Chronicle*, which concerned the life of a small-town newspaper editor and his family. One of the first serials based on a prepared script, *Keystone Chronicle* was on the air from 1929 to 1931. The series gave Rhymer radio writing experience in handling a story line. The dialogue revealed his remarkable faculty for recreating small-town life and for capturing Midwestern speech.

Rhymer's affiliation with NBC led directly to the creation of *Vic and Sade*. In 1932 the network's program manager, Clarence

Menser, asked the writer to create a family show for Proctor and Gamble, which was interested in selling its household products to the large daytime market. Rhymer wrote an audition script dealing with a small-town couple called Vic and Sade, but Proctor and Gamble bought another series. Menser liked Rhymer's pilot program so much he put it on the air on a sustaining basis (that is, without a sponsor). *Vic and Sade* premiered on June 29, 1932, over the NBC Blue network as an early morning program six days a week.

During the next two years the series slowly developed appeal. Because of its popularity Proctor and Gamble then sponsored the serial beginning on November 3, 1934, and their affiliation lasted until 1945. The firm sent the cast three pounds of Crisco every week. "We did not know what to do with it," remembered William Idelson.[4] During the 1930's the fifteen-minute daytime program was heard on NBC five times a week. In the early 1940's the show was so popular that the cast did repeats for the CBS and Mutual networks.

During the fourteen years *Vic and Sade* was on the air Rhymer wrote more than 3500 scripts. The author rose early in the morning, entered his study in his robe and pajamas, and wrote the next day's script on an old rented Royal typewriter. Although a disciplined writer, Rhymer found it difficult work. Each script was an episode in itself—there was no carry-over plot from the previous program. "When they come easy and I don't have to work on 'em, I'll know I'm finished with the show," Rhymer said.[5] He generally completed a script within two and one-half hours, but if he was still writing after three hours he tore the pages up and began again. After finishing the script, Rhymer dressed and hurried to the studio, where network assistants retyped the original and made copies for the cast. He then attended the live broadcast and afterward met with the performers for a cast-reading of the next day's script. Parts that did not read smoothly were cut or changed; a second reading was then held one hour before the broadcast. Rhymer sometimes did not have enough material to fill an entire fifteen-minute show, so he would hastily type some extra lines in the studio. By broadcast time the script was ready to be aired.

Rhymer had the freedom to write whatever he wanted and

was rarely censored by the network and sponsor. Not only was he considered a reliable writer; his script was usually prepared too close to broadcast time for editing by NBC and Proctor and Gamble. Rhymer actually got away with satirizing sensitive subjects because of his tongue-in-cheek style. Some characters in *Vic and Sade* were named after NBC executives, and he once wrote a script about local ne'er-do-wells who had been jailed. In that he used the names of network vice presidents. Known for his insights into life's absurdities, he also enjoyed writing letters and postcards to his friends. They contained off-color stories and anecdotes.[6]

On one occasion Rhymer did encounter pressure from NBC. He wrote a script depicting Vic and Rush opening some canned food for dinner. After observing the contents of the can, Vic recommended that they eat out because the food had spoiled. The American Canned Foods Association protested that the program suggested canned products were inedible. NBC ordered Rhymer to write a show in which the Gooks ate a canned food dinner. After that incident NBC asked to read his scripts before broadcast time, but the request probably went unheeded.[7]

Vic and Sade was first broadcast in NBC's Studio B on the nineteenth floor of Chicago's Merchandise Mart. The large studio was used mainly for music programs, but for dramatic shows engineers installed a cloth tent open on one side to avoid booming sounds. *Vic and Sade* came on the air after a morning serenade program. The orchestra stayed on to play the opening theme, "Oh, You Beautiful Doll," and then the musicians went out for a smoke and returned for the closing theme. Later, a new theme song, "Chason Bohemienne," was played on an organ. Two mikes were employed in the studio, one shared by Art Van Harvey (Vic) and Bernardine Flynn (Sade) and a smaller one for teenage William Idelson (Rush). The show later moved into the studio Gosden and Correll used to broadcast *Amos 'n' Andy*. It contained more lavish facilities, including comfortable couches and a fireplace.

The script was so funny that the cast had a difficult time keeping from laughing. "The hardest thing was to keep a straight face," Bernardine Flynn recalled. During one broadcast the performers began giggling so hard the script was never finished. Rhymer himself often burst out laughing and fell off his chair in the control room. The director once asked the cast to position themselves so that they could not see the faces in the control room.[8]

Listening to *Vic and Sade* was like eavesdropping on friendly next-door neighbors. At the beginning of each program the announcer (Ralph Edwards, Ed Herlihy, Bob Brown, and others) set the tone:

> And now, folks, get ready to smile again with radio's home folks, Vic and Sade, written by Paul Rhymer. . . . Once again we present your friends Vic and Sade—at whose small house half-way up in the next block you are invited to spend a little while at this time.

The episodes took place in the Gooks' home on Virginia Avenue. The announcer described the homelike setting:

> Well, sir, it's early evening as we enter the small house half-way up in the next block now, and here in the living room we discover Mr. and Mrs. Victor Gook and their son Mr. Rush Gook. Mr. Victor Gook occupies his customary chair under the floor lamp; Mrs. Victor Gook sews quietly on the davenport, and Mr. Rush Gook sits at the library table, his school books before him. There has been silence for some little time, but now the head of the family says. . . .

At other times scenes took place in the kitchen or the front porch. The broadcast consisted entirely of conversations among the family members, called "radio's home folks." At the broadcast's conclusion the announcer said "this concludes another brief interlude at the small house half-way up in the next block."[9]

While *Fibber McGee and Molly* relied on comic incidents, *Vic and Sade* derived its humor from what the characters said rather than what they did. The program had four spoken parts: Vic, Sade, Rush, and Uncle Fletcher. The family discussed the daily happenings in their lives. Rhymer created entire episodes around such ordinary events as Vic bringing work home from the office or buying a hat. Sade might describe the sales at Yamelton's store or relate the town's gossip. Rush might tell his parents about his first day at high school and the tricks his friends played. Uncle Fletcher chatted about his landlady's love affair and cronies. The broadcasts did not have one-liners or punch lines. The humor instead came from Rhymer's ability to make small talk amusing. The writer made the most trivial incidents funny by subtly underplaying the comedy. From the inconsequentials of daily living and the banalities of small-town life Rhymer created a radio comedy masterpiece.

The author peopled *Vic and Sade* with hundreds of off-mike characters. These were neighbors and acquaintances the Gooks talked about. Rhymer liked giving them ludicrous names: H. K. Fleeber, O. X. Bellyman, Y. Y. Flirch, J. J. J. J. Stunbolt, I. Edison Box, Harry Fie, V. V. Jibe, Gus Plink, Cora Bucksaddle, Yorick Qnix, Dr. Bonebreaker, Reverend Kidneyslide, Hamilton W. Hunkermanlystoverdelmagintoshfer. Listeners heard about their idiosyncrasies. Godfrey Dimlock had invented a bicycle that said "mama"; the identical twins Robert and Slobbert Hink had ridden a power lawnmower from Moline to Decatur; and Mr. Buller, Vic's business colleague, had pulled his own teeth.

Rhymer was a master at writing dialogue that caught the rhythm of everyday speech. Slang and colloquialisms made the Gook family sound like authentic small-town types:

> SADE I told you at supper-time you weren't gonna scrunge any twenty-five cents outa me. I give you twenty-five cents just last Monday. I'm not *made* of twenty-five centses, ya know. Twenty-five centses don't grow on trees.
>
> VIC Sade, you'll kindly not mention that name to me *again*. I've *finished* with Fred Stembottom. I brush no more *elbows* with Fred Stembottom. Fred Stembottom an' I are *quits*.
>
> RUSH If *you* win an' get to be fire-chief of the world with your pockets fulla diamonds, you'll *still* be an ol' dirty banana peel with all your insides scooped out.
>
> FLETCHER Never bet your money on *me*, Sadie, when it comes to *postal* cards. I'll mislay a postal card quicker'n you can say Glenn Webster.

The four performers took the author's lines and made them convincing. Rhymer acknowledged that "they could read from the telephone directory and sound entertaining."[10]

Art Van Harvey played Victor R. Gook during the duration of the series. A former grain broker and advertising executive, Van Harvey had performed in vaudeville before becoming a radio actor. He was a Wallace Beery type—a heavy-set individual—whose Indiana Hoosier accent was perfect for the role. He played the mild-mannered Vic in a quiet low-key style with a twist of cynicism that made the small-town Midwestern character unforgettable.

Rhymer used Vic to poke fun at bureaucracy, fraud, and humbug in society. The character was supposedly modeled on the writer's father, but Vic was also a spokesman for Rhymer's own view of small-town life. Vic was chief accountant of the bookkeeping department of Plant #14 of the Consolidated Kitchenware Company. A typical nine-to-five organization man, Vic subscribed to the *Kitchenware Dealer's Quarterly*. The major event in his life was a business trip to Chicago or entertaining out-of-town kitchenware executives at the local restaurant. Vic proudly proclaimed his title as an honored Sky-Brother and Grand Exalted Big Dipper in the Drowsy Venus Chapter of the Sacred Stars of the Milky Way.

Rhymer, who liked to parody the elaborate ritual of fraternal clubs and lodges, created entire programs around the Sacred Stars. Vic once took offense at the garbage man, Mr. Gumpox, who was not a Sky-Brother, for wearing lodge regalia. Sade loaned Vic's lodge outfit to a friend for Christmas decorations and the pants for a Santa Claus costume. One of Rhymer's funniest off-mike characters was Hank Gutstop, Vic's best friend, who always forgot to pay his lodge dues. He was stripped of his membership in an elaborate ceremony in Latin in which Vic ripped the buttons off Gutstop's coat, vest, and underwear.

Sade once received an advertisement to buy a manual for wives of Sky-Brothers in the Sacred Stars of the Milky Way. The book was written by Homer U. McDancy, "a distinguished author residing in East Brain, Oregon." The volume, which cost $3.75, was bound in exquisite red leather and inscribed in gold.

Copies autographed by the famous Mr. McDancy were $4.25, while special limited editions with the author's photograph "in full regalia serving as a frontpiece" were advertised at $5.10. The manual listed rules of proper behavior for wives of Sky-Brothers: "To be a true an' loyal wife of a Sky-Brother in the Sacred Stars of the Milky Way, madame will take pains with the neatness of her person. She will never appear in her husband's presence with soiled hands or dirty face." Another read: "To be a true an' loyal wife of a Sky-Brother in The Sacred Stars of the Milky Way, madame will refrain from stealing property belonging to others, using coarse language, an' engaging in rough street brawls." The proper way to ask for the butter at the dining table was in Latin: "Yop voomer in pluribus hunk. In hoc signo veni vidi webster stockdale horse. Ip extra-curricular feep."[11]

Vic, who loved flattery, was a sucker for the most obvious swindle. One day he received a letter from the Board of Advisers of the Congress of Distinguished Americans congratulating him on his election to membership in the society:

> Henceforth you will be privileged to wear the badge of our order and append to your name the letters P. C.— Public Commander. Your engraved certificate will follow shortly. New York, Chicago, and Los Angeles newspapers have been notified. Yours very truly. Hamilton T. Looperman, Royal Chieftan.

A small fee was charged for the title:

> Public Commanders are assessed a small fee of seventy-five cents which is used to maintain the records. The engraved membership certificate is one dollar and is sent to you C.O.D. Another charge of one dollar is made to cover cost of having member's name printed on the Royal Roster in the Garfield Room of our National Capitol in Washington, D.C.

Vic believed he had received an exceptional honor until he learned that his friend Fred Stembottom had bought his own membership for twenty-five cents. He became incensed when he discovered that the garbage man was also a Public Commander and that his own son Rush had obtained a badge by sending in twenty chewing-gum wrappers.[12]

On another program Vic paged through a catalogue offering titles for sale. For thirty-five cents he could become a "Member of the Board of Directors of the Salt Lake City, Southwestern, Montana, and Pacific Deadline Railroad," while for $1.20 he could receive the title of "Life-time honorary President of the Town Beshaw Fine Arts College for Young Women, Dismal Seepage, Ohio." The ten-cent title was a real bargain:

> Member of the High Board of Executive Regents Inactive Pro Tempor Two Crosses Approved and a Garter Without Portfolio for Collisioning Interstate Trusteeships between Maine and Nebraska, Kentucky and Minnesota, Indiana, and Texas Without Recourse to Recall and Unconditioned Veto Not Withstanding.

In *Vic and Sade*, Rhymer satirized the money-making rackets that take advantage of people's desire for status.[13]

Vic's vanity was also the subject of several programs. When he boasted about the pictures of his mouth in a dental magazine Sade and Rush teased him about how dreadful the photographs were. In another program Sade heckled Vic when she learned an office secretary told her husband he had "piercing blue eyes." Because of a business trip to Chicago Vic was unable to be in charge of the town's Decoration Day parade. Believing that the parade could not go on without him, he phoned the mayor. To Vic's surprise, the mayor did not know who he was and told him that he, the mayor, would put instructions in the newspaper describing how to begin the parade. His pride shattered, Vic called the mayor a "fathead."[14]

One of Vic's irritating habits was falling asleep or giggling while Sade read a gossipy letter from her sister, Aunt Bess. Every letter told about the severe twinges in Uncle Walter's kneecap. "They . . . most always have the same stuff in 'em," Vic complained. When Sade suggested that they visit their relatives in near-by Carberry for a week, Vic declined, recalling the boring holiday he had last time. "By bedtime of the first day we've talked over everything we've got to talk about," said Vic. He proceeded to tell Sade how the vacation would be:

> All right take the *next* day—Tuesday. I get up an' have breakfast. Walter goes to work. I sit around the kitchen

watchin' you and Bess do the dishes. I go sit in the yard
an' read the Chicago paper. I play a couple records on
the phonograph. I turn on the radio. I don't know what
to do with myself. You an' Bess notice this an' say why
don't I go over an' see my old friend Whitey Kuhn. I go
chew the rag with Whitey a little while. I come back
an' sit in the yard. Walter comes home for dinner. We
eat an' talk a while. Walter invites me to come down an'
see the shop. I go see the shop, stall around till I catch
on. I'm takin' up too much of his time, stroll back to
Bess's an' sit in the yard. I try to take a nap. I sit in the
yard some more. I'm gradually going crazy. I know that
Wednesday's going to be the same as Tuesday, an'
Thursday's gonna be the same as Wednesday, an' Friday's. . . .

After that Sade decided to visit her relatives by herself.[15]

An easygoing, folksy character, Vic called his wife "kiddo"
and used such words as "shucks" and "I don't give a hoot." His
favorite pastime, in addition to belonging to the lodge, was playing gin rummy with Sade and Rush and five hundred with the
Stembottoms. He sometimes wandered over to Ike Kneesuffer's
house to play horseshoes in the basement. "I got eight ringers
and fourteen leaners in my system and I want to get them out,"
he said. Vic had an ironic, almost cynical, sense of humor.
"That's the *way* with love," declared Vic. "You may wear it on
your head like a gauntlet glove: you may throw it to the four
winds like canned salmon; or you may rub it in your hair like
potato peelings. In the end it always narrows down to the same
thing—vanilla."[16]

Another marvelous character was Sade, played brilliantly by
Bernardine Flynn. A native of Madison, Wisconsin, Flynn had
studied drama at the University of Wisconsin, where she had
acted in plays at the college theater and had once played opposite Don Ameche, who was also a student at the university. After
college she went to New York City and performed in several
Broadway hits, including a role as a French maid in *Seven Year
Love* and a part in Eugene O'Neill's *Strange Interlude*. Told by
Ameche of new opportunities in radio drama in Chicago, Flynn
moved there, where she did roles on the Great Northern Drama

series and the *Rin-Tin-Tin* adventure program. The major break
in her career occurred when she joined *Vic and Sade* in 1932. An
attractive woman with short black hair and an infectious smile,
she had the perfect crisp voice to play Sade, a character modeled
on Rhymer's mother.

Sade was a busy, chatty housewife, much involved in daily
domestic activities. She prepared such culinary delicacies as
"beef punckles," which became so popular that NBC received
hundreds of requests for beef punkle ice cream and beef punkle
pie. Rhymer enjoyed inventing other strange dishes, such as
"stingeberry jam" and "limberschwartz cheese." Between household chores Sade gossiped on the telephone with her best friend,
Ruthie Stembottom. A major topic of conversation was the wash-
rag sale at Yamilton's store. She also liked meeting her friends
for lunch at the Little Tiny Petite Pheasant Tea Shoppe. Sade
belonged to the Thimble Club, a sewing circle composed of the
town's best ladies.

Although Sade was presented as a typical small-town housewife, she had unique traits. Sade was strong-willed, temperamental, and often nagged Vic. She felt her husband was incapa-
ble of buying a hat without her help. Vic insisted that "since
organized society credits me with sufficient intelligence to permit me to walk the public streets without a strait jacket it might
be assumed that I'm smart enough to purchase an article of
wearing apparel without guardianship or supervision." Sade pestered him to write Uncle Walter and to be especially polite to
her Thimble Club ladies. Whenever she visited her sister she
worried if Vic and Rush could take care of themselves. One time
during her absence Rush invited so many friends to sleep at his
house Vic had to share his bed with a stranger:

> VIC Your mother prophesized we'd get ourselves tied in
> knots if we had to get along by ourselves a week. Well,
> apparently she was right.
> RUSH Yeah, it takes mom to keep the wheels on the track.
> Wouldn't be anything like this if she was on deck.

Sade was generally the victor in the family's minor altercations.
Vic had to admit that "generally, kiddo, you're a pretty shrewd
girl."[17]

Bill Idelson (Rush), Bernardine Flynn (Sade), and Art Van Harvey (Vic) broadcasting *Vic and Sade* in the mid-1930's.
(Frank Bresee Collection.)

Vic and Sade were close, and Rhymer sometimes wrote intimate scenes between the couple. One program depicted the pair sitting on the front porch and conversing about a threatening rainstorm. Another show, entitled "Vic Confides in Rush about Mothers," illuminated Vic's love and concern for his wife. He urged Rush to stop teasing his mother:

> The whole thing in a nut-shell, Box-top, is that a lad oughta rally around his mother an' do the big thing every chance he gets. Excuse the wishy-washy phrase, but a lad don't *have* a mother *forever* . . . an' when she's gone he's apt to start kickin' himself all over the place.[18]

The couple's adopted son, Rush, was played by William Idelson. Before joining the cast he had played the role of Skeezix on the *Gasoline Alley* comic strip program. Idelson's father, a friend of Art Van Harvey's, suggested to the actor that his son take the role. The young boy did not like working, and when his mother told him that they had accepted the job for him at approximately $27.00 a week, he refused. Idelson agreed after his mother told him that NBC wanted to test the part for only four days. The actor enjoyed playing the role so much he was on the program for over ten years.[19]

Vic and Sade had actually started as a husband-and-wife series in which the couple did not have any children, but the scripts were too narrow in scope. In order to correct the situation it was decided that a new character, perhaps a son, should be introduced. Inserting the boy into the plot was difficult, because the Gooks could not suddenly have an eleven-year-old son. The problem was solved by having the couple adopt a child. Sade's sister had a large family, and because of the Great Depression she could not afford to care for all of them. The Gooks decided to adopt one of the children. Rush was partly based on a boyfriend of a neighborhood girl Rhymer had known in Bloomington, partly on the author's own boyhood, and partly on the experiences of his own son, Parke.

Rush was a typical teenager growing up in a Midwestern

small town. He enjoyed playing baseball in Tatman's vacant lot and seeing the fat men play handball at the local YMCA. Listeners heard Rush talk about the adventures of his school friends: Blue-tooth Johnson, Orville Wheanie, Rooster Davis, Smelly Clark, LeRoy Snow, Leland Richards, Fat Vogel, and Nicer Scott. Rush told of how Rooster Davis opened a restaurant serving only bacon sandwiches and how Smelly Clark gave him, Rush, a haircut called a "Feather-Flo-Sheep-Deck." Other programs described Rush informing his parents about Smelly's ability to show off with his girl friend and about the time Smelly sent two hundred Christmas cards to strangers so he could get presents in return.

Attending the movies at the downtown Bijou theater was Rush's favorite pastime. He once asked his father for a year's allowance in advance so he could buy a lifetime pass to the Bijou. Rush's screen idols were the sultry movie queen Gloria Golden and the adventure hero, Four-fisted Frank Fuddleman. They were featured in every picture at the Bijou. Only the gushy titles changed: "Gazing into Your Eyes Like This Is Heaven, Minor-league Assistant Umpire Drake," "Our Friend, the Diamond-Baked Rattler, or the Serpent Who Will Submit to Your Sweetest Caresses," and "Yours Is a Magnificent Love, Petty-Officer Griswold." Vic, who disliked going to the movies, called the last "absolutely the rottenest movie that ever was given out to a suffering people."[20]

Rush's paragon was the courageous dashing hero of juvenile books, Third Lieutenant Clinton Stanley (named after Clint Stanley, the program director). Stanley was a shining example of virtue for every boy to follow. Rush read sections from the books on the broadcasts. One story, entitled "Third Lieutenant Clinton Stanley on the Campus" or "Winning Laurels for Old Alma Mater," described how Stanley scored touchdowns for both Harvard and Yale in the same football game. In "Third-Lieutenant Clinton Stanley's Big Love Affair" the hero "picked up a camel by the hind feet an' used him like a club an' gave that sheik such a bash in the head he expired on the spot." Rhymer enjoyed parodying the sentimentality of romance-adventure stories:

Third Lieutenant Stanley gave the villainous crew of counterfeiting smugglers one supercilious glance. Then his eyes softened as he turned and gazed at the oval face of Lady Margaret. The beautiful woman smiled bravely, revealing twin rows of perfect teeth the rich color of ivory. Her hand trembled slightly as she twirled her dainty pink parasol and her small foot in its fashionable French spat tapped nervously. Third Lieutenant Stanley touched her arm. "Let us share a hug an' kiss before we fight these miserable wretches," he grunted. Nothing loath, the beautiful woman lifted her veil an' thrust her lovely head forward.[21]

On several broadcasts Rush talked about his experiences at high school. He once recounted how Rooster Davis appeared at school wearing glasses attached to a six-foot black ribbon. It ran "down the side of Rooster's face an' ended up 'way down at the bottom button of his coat where it was attached to a brooch of his mother's about twice the size of a silver dollar." The glasses, said Rush, were a "bomb-shell that hit civilization." Listeners learned about Rush's instructors, including Miss Lorah Monroe, the algebra teacher, Miss Shade, the Physical Geography instructor, and Ole Chinbunny, the principal, who lived across the street from the Gooks. The family liked to spy on Chinbunny from the front porch and laughed over the funny way he ate ice cream. Rush urged his father to teach Chinbunny how to smoke cigars so he would look older and more dignified as a school principal.[22]

The broadcast in which Rush described his first hurried day at high school was a *Vic and Sade* classic:

In high school, by George, ya have *seven* different rooms an' seven different seats. An' in every room there's a different bunch of kids. . . . Ya dash into whatever classroom you're due at, chew the rag a moment, the bell rings, ya shut up, ya recite an' listen to the teacher for forty minutes or so, the bell rings again, ya bounce outa there like a fire engine, an' go whippin' down the corridor to wherever your *next* classroom is. Oh, it's the life.

At the end of the broadcast Rush declared that he must return to school: "Hafta switch lockers with a guy, reserve a book outa the library, notify the office about the changes in my schedule, put in an application for Assembly monitor, an' get my name on the Voluntary Usher list."[23]

Rush differed from the teenage brats that dominated radio in the 1940's. Although he teased his mother and was sometimes reluctant to do household chores, he generally had a good relationship with his parents. He attended the movies with his mother and played rummy with Vic. Rush and his father were good pals. He called his father "gov," while Vic jokingly nicknamed Rush Box-top, Dishwater, Felix, Stovepoker, and Monkeywrench.

The fourth member of the family was Uncle Fletcher, a half-deaf codger who spoke like The Old Timer on *Fibber McGee and Molly*. Uncle Fletcher was first an off-mike character known for writing cryptic letters to his niece Sade and sending the Gooks unusual presents—such as three fierce bulldogs and ten barrels of oysters. Rhymer was faced with a problem when Art Van Harvey temporarily left the program in 1940 because of a heart attack. The author thought of inventing an entirely new character to keep the program versatile but decided instead to use Uncle Fletcher. The well-known character actor Sidney Ellstrom was favored for the role, but Clarence Hartzell was hired because he was so convincing at the audition. "There was Uncle Fletcher in the flesh," said William Idelson.[24]

Born in Huntington, West Virginia, Hartzell had started in radio doing a harmony act with his brother on a home-town station and as an announcer in Chicago. He took up acting and first played the part of an old man with a local stock company. "I never did study acting," Hartzell said. "I guess I just kinda fell into it." He began to specialize in playing elderly characters. A major turning point in his career occurred when he was hired to do Uncle Bud on the *Uncle Ezra* show and Pappy Yokum on the *Li'l Abner* program. Later, he enacted the role of Doc Withers on *Lum and Abner*. Hartzell's interpretation of the eccentric self-centered Uncle Fletcher gave the program added dimension.[25]

Uncle Fletcher was a perpetual chatterbox who reminisced about his old pals in his home town, Dixon, Illinois, and his

friends in Dismal Seepage, Ohio, and Sweet Esther, Wisconsin.
He often concluded his stories with the curt phrase, "later died."
The half-deaf Uncle Fletcher absentmindedly replied "fine,
fine" to any question. He once brought his easy chair over to
the Gooks and chatted during the entire program about all the
people who had ever sat in the chair. A favorite topic of conversation was the upcoming marriage between his landlady, Mrs.
Keller, and Harry Feedburn. Uncle Fletcher complained regularly about his landlady treating him like a child. One time
when Mrs. Keller went on vacation she prepared his meals five
days in advance, putting them in different places. "Saturday's
breakfast sits on the library table in the living room," Uncle
Fletcher grumbled:

> Saturday's dinner is on the numbskull sideboard. Sun-
> day's breakfast is laid out on the top of the buffet. And
> Sunday's dinner is on a tray in the lame-brain nit-wit
> *pantry!* Monday's breakfast sits on my dresser up in
> my bedroom. And Monday's dinner is perched like a
> numbskull parrot on the doggone fat-head *piano* stool![26]

The old codger had several idiosyncrasies. He liked to carry
many keys on a chain and collected washrags and watch fobs.
Uncle Fletcher enjoyed sitting in the Gooks' living room watching the flies buzz around on the ceiling. When they came near
he would futilely try to swat them. The Gooks rarely got anything done when he visited, for he always wanted someone to
talk to. He also spent his time at the venerable Bright Kentucky
Hotel, located by the railroad tracks. Every time the Chicago–
St. Louis went by the building shook. Guests complained that
hot ashes from the passing trains landed in their beds. Uncle
Fletcher liked to talk to the other old-timers at the hotel, particularly Smelly Clark's Uncle Strap, the night clerk, and Mr. Rishi-
gan Fishigan from Sishigan, Michigan, who was married to
Jane Bane from Payne, Maine. After his visit to the Bright Kentucky Hotel he would saunter over to the Chicago Northern Depot to watch the Kansas City meat train speed by. He also visited
the interurban railroad station, where he played with the peanut
machine. Sometimes he would gossip with cronies on the court-

house steps or listen to people talk politics in the lobby of the Butler House Hotel. If he got bored he sat on the wooden bench at Ed Kennedy's gas station on Route 66, counting out-of-state license plates.

Another one of his favorite diversions was riding on the garbage truck with Mr. Gumpox, one of the program's unique off-mike characters. Gumpox's truck was driven by a horse, Howard, which suffered from dizzy spells. Mr. Gumpox, the garbage man, was noted for never wearing socks and for losing his false teeth in the neighbors' garbage cans. Gumpox threw everything he saw on the street into his garbage wagon. Vic wanted to give him a present and leave it by his garbage box but was afraid Gumpox would think it was a piece of rubbish. Gumpox once obtained a wife from a matrimonial agency; he paraded her through town on his wagon.

Although there were moments of intimacy among the Gook family, each self-centered character lived in a separate world. They were involved in different activities. Vic had his lodge pals and business colleagues, Sade her Thimble Club ladies, Rush his high school pals, and Uncle Fletcher his cronies at the Bright Kentucky Hotel. One program, entitled "The Stillness of an Afternoon Is Broken," portrayed the four characters chatting about their own acquaintances and not listening to the others. Sade gossiped over the telephone with Ruthie Stembottom, Uncle Fletcher talked about his landlady and pals, Vic told of his experiences buying a new hat, and Rush described the special teachers' meeting at the high school. After meeting briefly at the Gooks' house the four characters departed and went their separate ways. As one commentator observed, *Vic and Sade* portrayed "the vast gulf that exists between *types* of people."[27]

The last regular fifteen-minute program, broadcast on September 29, 1944, was entitled "Goodbye." The program depicted the four conversing at the Gooks' house and then leaving for various destinations. Vic went to a lodge meeting, Sade to a picture show at the Bijou, Rush to see the fat men play handball at the YMCA, and Uncle Fletcher to meet his friend Harry Feedburn. At the program's end they discovered that each was going downtown, but in different directions:

SADE	Well, we're all going in different directions.
FLETCHER	Is that a fact.
RUSH	Mom's going North, I'm going East, gov's going South, and you're going West.
FLETCHER	All different directions, by george.
SADE	We're all going downtown, all going to the same place.
FLETCHER	Yes—we're all going to the same place. And we'll see each other again.
SADE	Sure, we'll see each other again.
VIC	No doubt about it.
RUSH	Well, let's go.
SADE	Yes, let's go.
VIC	Goodbye.
SADE	Goodbye.
RUSH	Goodbye.
FLETCHER	Goodbye.[28]

The series was revived in 1946 in a half-hour format and broadcast over the Mutual network. Played before a live audience, the program was expanded to include more characters and scene locations. The new *Vic and Sade*, which lasted approximately a year, was slick and commercial compared to the older version. The series had encountered cast problems before 1946. Idelson had joined the Navy Air Force in 1943. Two new actors, Johnny Coons and Sid Koss, were hired to play Rush and a new teen-age character Russell. Their shrill voices were not as effective as Idelson's, and with his departure the program lost part of its original style. After playing other roles on radio, Idelson became a television writer and producer of several programs, including *Love American Style* and *The Bob Newhart Show*. Rhymer died in 1964 and Bernardine Flynn in 1977. But *Vic and Sade* remains a remarkable radio portrait of everyday life in small-town America.

PART FIVE

The Slick Comedy of the 1940's

12

Hollywood and the Home Front

After 1940 most comedy programs originated from Hollywood in new network studios. The broadcasts reflected the glamour and glitter of Hollywood showmanship: large audiences applauded and laughed on cue; there were cinema guest stars, name bands and vocalists, and "personality" announcers. The scripts were generally written by a team of writers and, compared with the 1930's, the broadcasts were faster-paced, slick, and predictable. The radio comedians starred in Hollywood movies, and some films were based on story lines from their broadcasts.

Commercialism became an increasingly dominant force in the industry. Jack Benny and Gosden and Correll formed corporations and sold their holdings to CBS for huge tax-exempt profits. The comedy stars hired publicity agents, who published their clients' life stories and pictures in the many popular radio fan magazines. The biographies usually had a "rags to riches" theme and described how the comedian had developed from a struggling vaudevillian into a successful radio star. Because they were heard in the privacy of their living rooms, listeners viewed the favorite comedians as friends who visited regularly at the same hour. They often referred to them by their first names. Jack Benny was known as "Jack" and Mary Livingstone as "Mary." The comedy stars also became important in upholding national morale during the country's involvement in World War II. They broadcast from armed forces bases, toured the campaign areas, sold war bonds, and participated in special wartime broadcasts.

In the early 1930's it was expensive to broadcast from Hollywood, for line charges by the telephone company were high for programs originating from California. The main network circuit was housed in New York City and relayed programs westward. A separate channel had to be set up every time a show was broadcast from Hollywood to the East Coast. It cost Eddie Cantor $2100 in line charges to do a Hollywood broadcast. When Gosden and Correll were making RKO's *Check and Double Check* in 1931, it cost the film company $1000 daily to have *Amos 'n' Andy* originate from California. The extra toll charges were eliminated in 1937 when the telephone company constructed a permanent reversible channel which made network broadcasting from Hollywood economically feasible.[1]

Network executives realized that Hollywood, with its surplus of acting talent and movie guest stars, was an ideal location for broadcasting. NBC built its Hollywood studios, a large sprawling headquarters in the Art Moderne Style, on the corner of Sunset and Vine in the late 1930's. A few blocks away, on Sunset Boulevard, was the new CBS Radio Building, designed by the architect William Lescaze in the International Style in 1936–37. ABC also had a large headquarters in Hollywood. Those impressive structures, which had spacious studios accommodating large audiences, represented the presence of network radio in California.

In the early 1930's most major film studios feared the competition of radio and did not permit their stars under contract to appear on programs. Most studio heads eventually changed that policy when they discovered that radio could publicize their movies. In 1934 the Young & Rubicam advertising agency developed *Forty-five Minutes in Hollywood*, in which movie stars were interviewed about their current film. On Louella Parsons's *Hollywood Hotel* (1934), film actors and actresses performed sketches from their movies. Parsons's show gave films and their stars free publicity. Considered the first important broadcast originating from Hollywood, the gossip columnist's successful show started the trend of major broadcasting from the West

Coast. Thirty-five major network programs were broadcast from the movie capital during the 1935–36 radio season. Cecil B. De Mille's *Lux Radio Theatre* (1934), featuring dramas and film adaptations performed by Hollywood stars, originated from California in 1936. In the mid-1930's New York advertising agencies began opening Hollywood branch offices with radio departments.[2]

Realizing that Hollywood was becoming a significant radio center and an excellent base for a film career, comedians began broadcasting from California. *The Jack Benny Show* and *Amos 'n' Andy* originated from Hollywood during the 1936–37 season, as did *Fibber McGee and Molly* in 1939. Gosden and Correll often did *Amos 'n' Andy* from a tiny studio inside the tower of Palm Springs' plush El Mirador Hotel, a fashionable retreat for movie and radio stars. Most major comedians, with the exception of Fred Allen, a staunch New Yorker, were broadcasting from Hollywood by the early 1940's. The comedy shows took on the flavor of their new locale. Listeners heard many jokes about the California sun and rain, smudge pots, the auto dealer Mad Man Muntz, Pismo Beach, Anaheim, Azusa, and Cucamonga. The California–Hollywood gags popularized the area to people who had never been to the West Coast.

Many radio comedians had a side career in the movies. Burns and Allen, Jack Benny, and the Jordans were under contract to Paramount, a studio which had a large financial interest in CBS. Paramount had produced movies with radio themes since *The Big Broadcast of 1932*, an all-star spectacular featuring Burns and Allen, Bing Crosby, and other celebrities. In that movie Burns had played an harassed radio station owner and Gracie had impersonated his babbling receptionist. Burns and Allen also co-starred with Jack Benny in *The Big Broadcast* musical comedies of 1936 and 1937. *The Big Broadcast* motion pictures had trite plots and were chiefly vehicles which allowed the stars to perform their comedy and musical routines.

Radio films were a popular box office attraction because listeners enjoyed seeing their favorite comedian on the screen. Jack Benny made several comedy films, among them *Buck Benny Rides Again* (1940), deriving from the subject matter of his programs. He and Fred Allen starred in *Love Thy Neighbor*

(1940) and *It's in the Bag* (1945), takeoffs on their feud. Charlie McCarthy and W. C. Fields continued their radio squabble in *You Can't Cheat an Honest Man* (1938). The Jordans played Fibber and Molly McGee in *Heavenly Days* (1944). The radio films often suffered from inane stories, corny jokes, and miscasting because radio characters and materials did not transfer well to a visual medium. Gosden and Correll were more convincing on radio, which disguised their blackface. In *Check and Double Check* (1931), Amos and Andy become ridiculous caricatures in an unbelievable plot ridden with atrocious sight gags and overexaggerated dialogue. Jack Benny, by contrast, made some very entertaining movies, such as *To Be Or Not To Be* (1942) and *The Horn Blows at Midnight* (1945). Bob Hope's "Road" films with Bing Crosby are classics of their kind. Yet the majority of radio comedians' films are mediocre and best viewed as nostalgic pieces from the "Golden Age of Radio."[3]

The Hollywood-based comedy show often featured a weekly guest cinema star. The celebrity traded one-liners with the comic and played parts in skits. The guests ranged from popular stars like Marilyn Monroe to serious dramatic actors like Charles Laughton. Some performers became semi-regulars, such as Ronald Colman on *The Jack Benny Show* and W. C. Fields on Bergen and McCarthy. The movie celebrities added glamour to the comedy shows.

In the 1940's the comedy program became a thoroughly commercial product packaged by advertising agencies for their client sponsor. Radio comedy had been big business in the 1930's, but now the sponsor completely dominated programming. Network advertising revenue increased throughout the decade. Top comedy shows cost from $700,000 to $1,000,000 to produce in the mid-1940's. Comedians were paid as much as $25,000 weekly. Sponsors carefully watched the Hooper charts and canceled shows when ratings fell below 20. They were not willing to gamble on unknowns, but competed instead for established entertainers. That policy largely prevented new comics from entering the medium and stifled creativity. To keep the sponsors happy, writers stayed with sure-fire, predictable formulas.

Advertising copywriters invented ingenious, entertaining commercials. Products were glorified in jingles, slogans, and catch phrases. The American Tobacco Company tried every type of sales pitch on *The Jack Benny Show:* a slogan ("L.S.M.F.T., L.S.M.F.T., Lucky Strike means fine tobacco"), songs about Luckies by The Sportsmen Quartet, and a tobacco auctioneer ("Sold American"). Sponsors continued to strive for a close association between comedian and product: "This is Bob 'Pepsodent' Hope." Certain products were particularly linked with entertainers: Lucky Strike (Jack Benny), Johnson Wax (the Jordans), Pepsodent (Bob Hope), Chase and Sanborn (Bergen and McCarthy), and Maxwell House (Burns and Allen). The "personality" announcer who could sell a product and play a role in the script became fashionable: Ken Carpenter and Bill Baldwin (Bergen and McCarthy), Don Wilson (Jack Benny), Harlow Wilcox *(Fibber McGee and Molly)*, Bill Goodwin (Burns and Allen).

The sponsors also dressed up the comedy broadcasts with big-name bands: Phil Harris (Benny), Robert Ambruster and Ray Noble (Bergen and McCarthy), Billy Mills *(Fibber McGee and Molly)*, Al Goodman (Fred Allen), Ozzie Nelson and David Rose (Red Skelton), Skinnay Ennis and Les Brown (Bob Hope), and Paul Whiteman and Meredith Willson (Burns and Allen). The big bands played popular melodies between the comedy parts of the program. As before, the orchestra leaders sometimes took straight or character roles. Most comedy programs also had a vocalist or a singing group: Dennis Day (Jack Benny); Judy Garland, Doris Day, and Frances Langford (Bob Hope); The King's Men *(Fibber McGee and Molly)*; the De Marco Sisters (Fred Allen); and Harriet Hilliard and Anita Ellis (Red Skelton). Some of those young singers went on to become stars.

Hundreds of actors and actresses were available to play bit character and dialect roles on the comedy shows. Most performers were listed in *The National Radio Artists Directory*, a periodical which contained advertisements of their specialties and indexes of character types and dialects. A radio producer who needed a character or an actress to play a particular part needed only to find the proper heading. The February 1941 issue listed performers under Baby Cries, Little Boys and Girls, Adolescents (male and female), Ingenues, Juveniles, Matrons, Old Women, Old Men, Molls, Neurotics (male and female), Animal Imitators, Heavies (male and female), Impersonators, Fast Talkers (male and female), Screams (male and female), and Barkers. The Dialect Directory included four major classifications, American, British Isles, European, and Oriental. Those categories were divided into subheadings. The American section included Canuck, Brooklyn, Hillbilly, Indian, Mexican, Midwestern, Negro, Rural, New England, Southern, and Tough Western dialects. The names of versatile impersonators (Mel Blanc, Hans Conried, etc.) were cross-listed under several headings.

Every seat in the studio was taken for the top-rated comedy shows. A tourist's trip to Hollywood was not complete without seeing a broadcast. Tourists stood for hours in long lines waiting to attend the comedy programs. Tickets were printed on thin, pastel-colored cardboard and distributed to the public. A ticket did not necessarily guarantee admittance, for more were issued than there were seats. Some programs had two audiences—one for the preview or dress rehearsal and another for the regular broadcast. Advertising agencies gave tickets to favorite clients who wanted to see a live broadcast from Hollywood. There was much fanfare before air time. The comedian often "warmed up" the audience by telling jokes and anecdotes. The remainder of the cast was introduced, including the announcer, who cued the audience when to laugh or applaud during the broadcast. Hand signals, printed signs, and flashing lights were used to prod the spectators.

Amos 'n' Andy, a weekly thirty-minute variety comedy program in the 1940's, illustrates how the nature of radio comedy had changed. The series' rating began declining in 1938 and dipped steadily over the next few years, reaching a low of 9.4 in January 1943.[4] Gosden and Correll consequently decided to change their format in order to compete with Jack Benny, Fred Allen, Bob Hope, and Edgar Bergen. They broadcast their last fifteen-minute show on February 19, 1943, and then, after a long vacation, they returned to the air on October 8, 1943, with a half-hour show on NBC. Instead of having a continuous story line, each broadcast revolved around a single comic situation. Many

episodes depicted the Kingfish duping Andy. The major characters were still played by Gosden and Correll, but new parts were
created, including Lou Lubin as the stuttering Shorty, the Barber, and Ernestine Wade as Sapphire Stevens, the Kingfish's
domineering wife.

Although the broadcasts were often hilarious, the new *Amos
'n' Andy* had a commercial look compared with the older series.
Instead of an opening and closing organ theme, Jeff Alexander's
large orchestra and chorus supplied the music. Rinso soap was
the show's new sponsor. A whistle was heard at the opening followed by Amos's voice: "Andy, did you hear that? Come on
. . . that's the Rinso White whistle." Harlow Wilcox was hired
to make the commercial announcements brisk and entertaining.
Broadcast from Hollywood, the new *Amos 'n' Andy* also featured
many cinema and theater guest stars playing roles in the episodes. Unlike the earlier broadcasts, the show was performed
before a live audience. The two comedians did "warm-ups" for
the spectators. They impersonated the characters; Correll sometimes played the piano and Gosden the banjo. Boxes of Rinso
were passed out to the audience. The new show displayed the
influence of Hollywood showmanship and Madison Avenue
salesmanship.

The two comedians no longer wrote the script by themselves;
they were aided by a team of writers. Gosden and Correll had
often written the show just before broadcast time, but now it took
a full week to produce a program from a series of story conferences, a cast reading, and a dress rehearsal. The script was rewritten several times by the writers and the two comedians.
"Every line [was] carefully scrutinized for humor and sharp-
ness," remarked Correll. The new show had a "mass-produced"
slick quality compared with the programs of the 1930's. The
embellished format helped boost the show's rating to 17.1 in
January 1944. The series had a large audience until it left the
air in 1954, but the new *Amos 'n' Andy* never became a rage.[5]

During America's involvement in World War II the radio comedians helped boost national morale. The jokers had kept listeners laughing during the Great Depression; now the war
against Japan and Germany was another critical time. Because

In the mid-1940's Gosden and Correll were still popular radio comedy entertainers.
(Courtesy, Frank Bresee Collection.)

of blackouts, gas rationing, and general wartime constriction, Americans began spending more time at home between 1942 and 1945. Radio listening increased 20 per cent in 1942 and was up every year until the war's end. The news broadcast, epitomized by the dramatic reporting of Edward R. Murrow, kept Americans informed of the conflict. The comedy programs, however, drew the largest audiences, for Americans needed to keep laughing during the war.

As national celebrities, the comedians felt a patriotic obligation to entertain the troops at home and abroad. Most radio comedians were exempt from the draft because of that service and their importance to home front morale. Many broadcasts took place at armed service bases in the United States, and the comedians toured the campaign areas of Europe and the South Pacific, where they staged camp shows providing live entertainment for the war-weary troops. At home they performed at benefits for the Red Cross and USO. The entertainers helped the government sell the war. Over the air they urged listeners to contribute to wartime charities, buy war bonds, and obey government rationing programs. The comedians made "curtain speeches" at the broadcasts' conclusion, praising the courage of the fighting men. Sometimes they delivered urgent messages prepared by the Office of War Information, whose policy it was to inform citizens of the aims of the Roosevelt administration.[6]

Treasury Department officials eagerly enlisted show business celebrities to convince Americans to buy bonds. Advertising agency executives trained in the techniques of mass persuasion were brought in to direct the sales campaigns. Citizens were told to purchase bonds as a sacrifice to help win the war and save American democracy. Over three hundred actors and actresses went on tours across the United States during the first bond drive in September 1942. Greer Garson, Bette Davis, and Rita Hayworth worked so hard that they suffered from exhaustion. All types of stunts were used to raise money, including the auctioning of Betty Grable's stockings and Jack Benny's violin. Hedy Lamarr offered to kiss anyone who bought a $25,000 bond. Popular radio stars made excellent salespeople because they were known to millions of Americans as friendly voices in their living rooms. Kate Smith, who had an honest and patriotic image, was selected to be the host of the CBS War Bond Day broadcast on September 21, 1943. During the eighteen-hour marathon Smith raised close to forty million dollars by stressing the theme of self-sacrifice.[7]

The Treasury's Defense Saving Section had a radio department. One of its first war bond programs before Pearl Harbor was *Millions for Defense*, which began on July 2, 1941, as a summer replacement for Fred Allen's *Texaco Star Theatre*. Allen and other comedians appeared on the sixty-minute variety show. During the war the Treasury Department also sponsored *Treasury Star Parade*, a fifteen-minute weekly program. The format varied each week and included drama, music, and comedy. On one program Yehudi Menuhin played the Mendelssohn violin concerto, while another featured Fanny Brice as Baby Snooks. *Treasury Star Parade* illustrates the government's belief that radio entertainment could help sell the war.

Servicemen overseas enjoyed listening to the comedy programs, which were rebroadcast over the Armed Forces Radio Service (AFRS) stations. Believing that radio was crucial to maintaining troop morale, officials in the United States Army Morale Service Division (later called the Special Service Division) established the AFRS in 1942 for the purpose of informing, educating, and entertaining military personnel. Later, the AFRS was under the aegis of the War Department's Troop Information and Education Division. The AFRS constructed stations with low-powered transmitters at overseas bases and campaign areas and broadcast programs over foreign government and privately owned stations on leased time and via short wave from the United States. By the end of 1943 the AFRS had 306 outlets in 47 countries; two years later they had 869 outlets.[8]

The major networks gave the AFRS their programs free of charge. The recordings were shipped by plane and boat and traveled on a circuit from one station to another. Over 92,000 discs were shipped in 1943, and 1.33 million in 1945. Recordings of all the major comedy shows were sent abroad. The programs were heard over public address systems on ships and submarines, in hospitals, mess halls, and base recreation buildings. Listening to their favorite program reminded the GIs of home. The Armed Forces Network in England followed the schedule in the United States by broadcasting shows such as *Fibber McGee and Molly* at their regular time.

Besides serving as a distributing agency, the AFRS produced their own programs at their headquarters in Hollywood. The organization was headed by Colonel Thomas H. A. Lewis, former vice president of Young & Rubicam, and Pat Weaver, another Young & Rubicam executive, managed programming. The Program Production Section produced between thirteen and seventeen hours of broadcasts a week. The Talent Subsection obtained actors and actresses from the Hollywood Victory Committee, a clearance agency that scheduled performers on AFRS programs, wartime benefits, and tours of military bases. Among the AFRS programs were *G.I. Jive*, featuring "Jill," an attractive female disc jockey; *Yarns for Yanks*, human interest stories; *Jubilee*, a musical variety broadcast starring black entertainers; and *Are You a Genius?* a comedy quiz hosted by Mel Blanc. Two popular musical comedy programs were *G.I. Journal* and *Mail Call*. The first *Mail Call*, recorded on August 11, 1942, starred Loretta Young, Bob Hope, Jerry Colonna, and Frances Langford.

The most prestigious broadcast produced by the AFRS was *Command Performance*, a spectacular variety show. The program was initiated by three officials in the radio division of the War Department's Bureau of Public Relations (BPR)—Glenn Wheaton, Louis Cowan, and Robert Coleson—who believed very much in the value of radio entertainment for troop morale. They thought up the idea of a weekly show in which the servicemen could request the entertainers they wanted to hear. The stars had to voluntarily appear on "command." The BPR produced *Command Performance* between March 1 and December 15, 1942, and then it was taken over by the AFRS. *Command Performance* was AFRS's showcase broadcast. Many singers appeared on the program, including Judy Garland, Frank Sinatra, Dinah Shore, Ginny Simms, and Bing Crosby. There were also big-name bands, such as Kay Kyser, Spike Jones, and Harry James, and the special AFRS military orchestra conducted by Meredith Willson. Servicemen also requested familiar sounds from back home. Programs featured the noise of Las Vegas slot machines, San Francisco foghorns, and the New Year's Eve celebration from Times Square. One hospitalized GI was granted his request—one long, sensual sigh by Carole Landis.[9]

Radio comedians made frequent appearances on *Command Performance* because the servicemen and women wanted to hear their favorite funnymen. Bob Hope appeared twenty-six times and was the master of ceremonies of the special Christmas show of 1942, broadcast short-wave to Europe and on the major networks at home. That broadcast and a special V-J Day program in September 1945 were the only two *Command Performances* heard in the United States. On the Christmas show Hope traded insult jokes with Bing Crosby. The all-star program also included Edgar Bergen and Charlie McCarthy, Red Skelton, Fred Allen, and Jack Benny. Benny appeared on *Command Performance* twelve times, often with his entire cast. On one program he taught the renowned violinist Jascha Heifetz how to play the violin. "How'm I doin', Mr. Benny?" asked Heifetz, during an exquisite violin solo. Another program dramatized the wedding of Dick Tracy, the comic-strip detective. Bing Crosby played Tracy; Bob Hope, Flat Top; Dinah Shore, Tess Trueheart; Jimmy Durante, the Mole; and Frank Sinatra, Shakey. Others in the cast included Harry Von Zell, Jerry Colonna, Judy Garland, the Andrew Sisters, Frank Morgan, and Cass Daley. The broadcast, considered the best series on the AFRS network, entertained servicemen and servicewomen all over the world.[10]

Command Performance was recorded live, and in its entirety it ran approximately fifty minutes. From this the best sequences were selected and assembled into a thirty-minute program by rerecording the show. Long comic monologues were often cut and the best material pieced together. The AFRS programs were also among the first to use laugh tracks. Because the comedians felt they were playing primarily to a GI audience they sometimes told risqué jokes, but since the AFRS had high standards even those off-color gags were often deleted. The policy of the AFRS editorial subsection was not to broadcast anything offensive. Because the broadcasts were heard months after the original recording, topical jokes were also eliminated. Network shows shipped overseas were denatured by removing commercials, dates, and material judged helpful to the enemy.[11]

The use of transcribed and edited programs by the AFRS differed from the policies of NBC and CBS. Except for sound effect tracks those networks did not permit recorded material on their stations. Network executives believed that listeners preferred live broadcasts to the "canned" material heard on independent stations. They also criticized the sound quality of recordings. Live broadcasts nonetheless placed an undue hardship on entertainers, who often had to perform two shows for different time zones. Even though the cast held script readings and rehearsals there were often fluffs and overtime problems in live programming.[12]

Bing Crosby, who appeared on *Command Performance* twenty-nine times, was impressed by the transcribed assembling process on the AFRS program. That was the only way to do a radio show, Crosby concluded. He could make a number of transcribed programs at one long session and record at a time when his voice was at its best. In 1946 Crosby wanted to make edited transcriptions for his *Kraft Music Hall* program on NBC. When the network refused, the crooner negotiated with the new American Broadcasting Company, an offshoot of the old NBC Blue network. (In 1941 the FCC had ruled that no license could be issued to a station affiliated with a company owning more than one network. Thus NBC was forced to sell its Blue network in 1943 to Edward J. Noble, manufacturer of Life Savers.) Because ABC had no official policy against recorded programming and were eager to compete with NBC and CBS, they accepted Crosby's proposal. Murdo McKenzie, the director-engineer on Crosby's *Philco Radio Time* on ABC, recorded and edited the singer's broadcasts. Crosby's programs were the first to be recorded on an Ampex tape machine in 1948.[13]

ABC's policy prompted other entertainers to sign with the network, including Abbott and Costello and Groucho Marx. Marx recorded *You Bet Your Life* for ABC beginning in 1947. Fearing that their stars would desert to the new network, NBC and CBS began relaxing their policy on recorded shows. They decided to use transcribed broadcasts for the western time zone so that performers would not have to do two live shows. By 1950 most major programs on NBC and CBS were transcribed. Jack Benny, Edgar Bergen, Red Skelton, and Burns and Allen then recorded their programs before a live studio audience. Producers of comedy shows could edit the material and eliminate fluffs. That process contributed to an even slicker end product.

The radio comedians also aided the war effort by broadcasting from Army, Navy, and Marine bases and making overseas tours of the campaign areas. They were part of a massive effort to keep the servicemen and servicewomen entertained. Besides Bob Hope, other comedians volunteered for "entertainment duty." Jack Benny broadcast frequently from stateside armed service bases and military hospitals in 1943–44. He and his cast also put on live stage shows for military personnel at home and abroad. During the summer of 1943 Benny entertained fighting troops in Africa, Italy, Sicily, and Iran; the next year he toured Australia and the South Pacific. He received citations from the War and Navy Departments for bringing merriment to the war-weary GIs.

Another comedian cited by the government for his service was Edgar Bergen, who with his dummy Charlie McCarthy entertained troops in the Aleutians, Alaska, and Greenland. Charlie McCarthy was so popular that he was made an honorary master sergeant in the Army Air Corps. (When he also accepted a commission in the Marines the Air Corps accused him of duplicity. A court-martial was broadcast from an Army base at Stockton, California, with Jimmy Stewart as Charlie's defense attorney.) Bergen and Charlie were once asked to do a routine for a soldier in an Aleutian hospital who was suffering from amnesia and battle fatigue. The GI, who had sat staring into space, suddenly smiled when Charlie spoke. The soldier remembered Charlie's voice from home, and he recovered after Bergen's visit.[14]

The comedians also appeared as guests on special radio programs devoted to the war effort. Burns and Allen, for example, performed on a China Relief program, a War Bond Campaign show, and a special Navy Enlistment broadcast. The pair generally did a short routine and urged listeners to support the cause associated with the broadcast. During the Navy Enlistment program Gracie made a short speech:

I have something to say to all the young men of the
Navy. You have set an example to all America. From
every walk of life you have come to take your place in
the defense of our beloved country. You are an inspira-
tion to the thousands of others, who like yourselves, are
Americans, and who will come from homes like your
own to be shipmates with you. Yours is that shining
courage which is needed to bring our country through
her ordeal victoriously. I salute you all . . . and may
God bless you.[15]

Like Kate Smith on the War Bond broadcast, Burns and Allen
stressed the values of sacrifice, patriotism, and courage in their
wartime appeals.

The comedians also made spot announcements near the end
of their own programs. These ranged from making listeners
aware of critical gas, meat, and rubber shortages to urging
Americans to remain on the job. Benny reminded listeners to buy
war bonds and to follow the government rationing programs.
He often stressed the idea that citizens at home could also help
win the war. The comedian also delivered special urgent messages from the Office of War Information (OWI), including a
plea for more nurses to join the Army Nurse Corps. The OWI
put a large amount of emphasis on entertainment in selling the
war to the American public through the media. The OWI's Domestic Radio Bureau, under Donald Stauffer, a former advertising agency executive, dressed their war messages "in six
delicious flavors," and encouraged radio stars to sugarcoat the unpleasant reminders of war. Government representatives also appeared on the comedy programs. Eleanor Roosevelt gave a short
talk asking for contributions to the Red Cross on the Fred Allen
program.[16]

The *Amos 'n' Andy* scripts contained many references to the
war and to the courage of the fighting men. Amos read a poem
written by a Marine in the Pacific asking for more military sup-
plies and encouraging citizens to buy bonds. "The war would
lead to a more peaceful and better world," Amos said. In 1942
Amos 'n' Andy was cited by the government "as the perfect morale show during the wartime," and *Amos 'n' Andy* fan clubs
were established at armed service bases. As in the Great Depres-

Burns and Allen broadcasting a show for the recruiting drive at a naval training station, December 1940.

sion, *Amos 'n' Andy* helped boost the country's morale during the national crisis.[17]

The sponsors of *Fibber McGee and Molly* believed their program had a special mission during the war years. Two days after Pearl Harbor, Harlow Wilcox read a telegram from the president of the Johnson Wax Company: ". . . the makers of Johnson Wax believe it is in the public interest to continue a program as entertaining as *Fibber McGee and Molly*. They have a place in the national morale." On their broadcasts the Jordans repeatedly urged listeners to contribute to the Red Cross and to buy Defense Bonds and Stamps: "This is not an invitation to a tea party or a bingo game," said Jim Jordan nine days after Pearl Harbor:

> This is WAR and we've got to do something about it. It is going to cost a lot of money to win it, but it would cost a lot more than mere money to lose it. . . . This isn't the other fellow's fight. It's yours and mine. So . . . here it is again! . . . *Buy Defense Bonds and Defense Stamps.*

On D-Day, when the Allies invaded occupied France, the Jordans's regular program was suspended for news bulletins and comments by the couple. "Our men have a weapon which our enemies cannot have—the knowledge that God is on our side," said Marian Jordan. "To us—D-Day means Divine Help, and H-Hour the hopes of all of us for a speedy victory." The *Fibber McGee and Molly* story lines often dealt with such subjects as the draft, sugar rationing, gas and rubber conservation, and the black market. Public support of government rationing programs was urged in the plots.[18]

Comedy was an excellent way to subtly remind the public of wartime issues, because the government messages were often more palatable when inserted in humorous routines. This sketch on a mileage rationing program with Eddie Cantor, Jack Benny, and Gracie Allen illustrates the soft-sell entertainment approach:

CANTOR Gracie, haven't you heard that gasoline is being rationed?

GRACIE Well of course I know gasoline is being rationed! My goodness, what do you take me for, a dunce? I've read all about it. You're only allowed one cup a day.

CANTOR   Gracie, that's coffee.

GRACIE   Eddie, don't be silly. A car won't run on coffee.

BENNY   No, no, Gracie—I don't think you understand. You see, cars run on gasoline—so at this point gasoline has to be rationed.

GRACIE   But why? There's plenty of gasoline.

CANTOR   I know, but the real reason for cutting down on the amount of gasoline we use is to save rubber.

GRACIE   Really? That's very interesting. I had no idea gasoline was made from rubber.

CANTOR   It isn't. You see—

GRACIE   I had the impression that gasoline came out of wells in the ground.

CANTOR   That's right.

GRACIE   And I've often thought how convenient it was for the filling stations that those wells were always found under the busiest street corners.

CANTOR   Jack, you try it.

BENNY   Gracie, look—what they're really rationing is mileage. The less we drive our cars the more rubber we save. And the rubber we save is vital to essential industries— and to the army.

GRACIE   The army? Uses rubber?

BENNY   Sure.

GRACIE   Gee, wouldn't you think with all the modern weapons that soldiers wouldn't have to use sling shots?[19]

Skits on the Fred Allen program at times satirized how life in America had changed due to the war. The "comedy dialogue had to be written carefully," Allen wrote, "while trying to get laughs we had to be serious in the treatment of the matter discussed and stress its importance to all of us in the country." Rationing, food shortages, and blackouts were often the subject of the comic interviews the comedian conducted on *Allen's Alley*. On one broadcast he asked Mrs. Nussbaum (Minerva Pious) about the point system of rationing:

ALLEN   How does the point system work?

MINERVA   You are going into a store.

ALLEN   Yes.

MINERVA   You are wanting two pounds of coffee.

ALLEN   Yes.
MINERVA   You are pointing to the coffee grinder.
ALLEN   Yes.
MINERVA   The grocer is pointing to an empty shelf.
ALLEN   Yes.
MINERVA   You are pointing to your rationing book.
ALLEN   And?
MINERVA   The grocer is pointing to the door.
ALLEN   That is all there is to the point system.
MINERVA   You are getting the point. So lonk!

The government approved of the way Allen reminded listeners about rationing programs: "We received letters from Mayor La Guardia of New York City, Leon Henderson, head of the O.P.A., and many other government agency heads complimenting us for calling government drives and other information to the attention of the mass audience."[20]

Comedy broadcasts contained innumerable GI gags, particularly when the program originated from armed forces bases and the audience included thousands of servicemen. Gags about army life received considerable laughter and applause. On a short-wave broadcast from a naval hospital in New Caledonia Benny called the South Pacific island "Waukegan with Coconuts." Benny started using many wartime gags in his 1943–44 broadcasts and quickened his delivery for the GI audience. The comedian's shows consequently became more lively and his ratings increased. His writers even related Benny's stinginess to the war. "You donated a pint of blood, they gave it to a soldier, it made him so cheap he shot a Jap and he ran after him to get the bullet back," Mary joked. "They don't call me 'get the lead out' Benny for nothing," Jack replied.[21]

The comedians also lampooned the Axis and its leaders in jokes and routines. A loss of a battle by the Germans and Italians made good comic material:

ALLEN   Do you know why the Germans and Italians surren-
           dered at Tunisia this week?
JIMMY   Why, Fred?
ALLEN   They know the quickest way they can get back home to
           Germany and Italy is to follow the American and En-

glish armies. The Germans were yelling 'Heil Hitler' and leaving the I out of heil.

Mussolini and Hitler were characterized as stupid, ineffectual leaders. On the Benny show Mel Blanc played Hitler in a skit which depicted the German leader as a mad idiot who chewed up a rug like a dog. The comedy shows contained many jokes about the "Fuehrer's Face." Fred Allen composed a poem about one of Benny's broadcasts:

> I heard your program, Mr. Benny.
> By an open window was the place
> A show like you put on tonight
> You should do in Der Fuehrer's Face.

The McGees also poked fun at the Germans and Japanese. "I have a theory that anybody wearing pants can lick anybody wearing a kimono," said Molly. Comedians also caricatured the Japanese "slant-eyed" physical appearance and traits. Radio comedy gags depicted the "Japs" as devious, sly, and cruel, much as they were stereotyped in magazines and newspapers. "Jap" and Hitler jokes perpetuated the evil images of the Axis found in wartime propaganda movies made by the government and Hollywood.[22]

During the Great Depression radio comedy had reaffirmed the country's traditional values and institutions. In this second crisis entertainers likewise spoke out for democracy and patriotism. Most comedians had risen from relative poverty as small-time vaudevillians to financial success as famous radio stars. Many were sons of immigrant parents who had emigrated to the United States seeking religious and political freedom. They consequently believed very much in the American dream of success and democracy. The comedians felt an obligation to aid the country by bringing laughter to the soldier and by reminding listeners of important wartime government drives.

13

Smart-aleck Wisecracker

Bob Hope's Tuesday night Pepsodent broadcast was rated the most popular comedy program during World War II. The comedian's rapid-fire monologues and slick shows, written by a large staff of writers, symbolized the fast pace and predictability of radio comedy in the 1940's. During World War II Hope became a popular public figure through his broadcasts from Army and Navy bases and his extensive overseas tours in which he entertained the troops. At that time he gained a reputation as America's smart-aleck wisecracker and ambassador of laughter to military personnel around the world.

Leslie Townes Hope's "road" to stardom resembled a rags to riches story of a young immigrant boy. He was born on May 29, 1903, in Eltham, England, a London suburb. Hope was a member of a large family, the fifth of seven sons. His penchant for show business derived partly from his Welsh mother, Avis Townes Hope, a concert singer with an exquisite voice. His father, William Henry Hope, was a talented artisan, a stonemason noted for intricate carvings. William Hope's favorite pastimes were betting on horses and carousing at the local pub. In 1906, because of difficulties finding work in England, Hope's father decided to emigrate to the United States. He settled in Cleveland, where his two brothers lived, and his family joined him two years later, in March 1908. Bob was then nearly five years old.[1]

Life was difficult for the Hope family in their new surroundings. William obtained few commissions, because stone-cutting was being done primarily by machines. He actually lost money on one contract. He drank heavily during long periods of unemployment, and had bitter regrets about leaving England. To make ends meet Bob's mother rented rooms to lodgers in their house and kept the family spirits high through her resourcefulness and optimism. Avis Hope viewed America as the land of opportunity, and she wanted her sons to become successful. Religion and family values were also important to her. She insisted upon her sons going to Sunday school at the local Presbyterian church and attending public school. His mother instilled in young Bob a sense of moralism and piety, qualities that led to Hope's devout support of traditional American values and institutions.

A self-confident, ambitious youth, Hope showed an eagerness to succeed at an early age. He earned money working at different jobs after school. Hope was employed as a delivery boy in a butcher shop and bakery and as a soda jerk, shoe store clerk, and flower salesman. "I tried so many different ways of raising a dollar Horatio Alger could have used me for a technical expert," the comedian recalled. The Alger stories of poor boys becoming respectable middle-class citizens were popular during Hope's childhood. One advocate of the self-made man was the wealthy oil magnate, John D. Rockefeller. Every evening on his way home from work in a "chauffeur-driven brougham automobile" Rockefeller bought a newspaper from Hope, who sold papers on a Cleveland street corner. The youngster did not know the name of his customer. Hope once had to obtain change in a near-by grocery store for Rockefeller and during the absence missed some customers. "Young man, I'm going to give you some advice," Rockefeller instructed Hope:

> If you want to be a success in business, trust nobody. Never give credit and always keep change on hand. That way you won't miss any customers while you're going for it.

"Do you know who that was?" a streetcar inspector asked the youth. "He is only the richest man in the world. That's John D. Rockefeller, Senior."[2]

Hope was a clever and daring youngster. At the local pool hall he beat players at three-cushion billiards, and in the public parks he won footraces by knowing the starter's call beforehand and bumping other runners. At sixteen Hope fought as a lightweight in an amateur boxing contest under the name "Packy East." The state amateur champion knocked "Packy" out in the second round of the semifinals.

Singing was a means by which Hope earned pocket change. According to an older brother, Hope's grandfather put young Bob on a table to sing and dance and to play a melody on a comb wrapped with tissue. As a boy he enjoyed singing around the piano his mother had bought with her savings. At school Hope excelled in singing class and was the favorite pupil of his music teacher. He and a friend sang on neighborhood streetcorners, where passersby gave them money and residents of high-rise apartment houses threw coins down to them. They also collected pocket money by singing outside a local beer garden and on the streetcar to the Luna Park amusement center, where they spent their earnings on the rides. While working at night in the service department of the Chandler Motor Car Company he and three other employees formed a barbershop quartet. Hope was fired for recording the group's singing on the manager's dictating machine.

Hope's mother encouraged her son's interest in singing and the theater. She took him to see the comic monologuist Frank Fay perform at a Cleveland vaudeville house. "He's not half as good as you," she said to her son, who appreciated Fay's delivery and suave manner. Like most children his age, he enjoyed watching silent movies and mimicked Charlie Chaplin. Wearing his father's pants and derby, with oversized shoes and a moustache made of stove blacking, he sauntered down the street bowlegged, spinning a cane carved from a tree limb. He won a Charlie Chaplin imitation contest at Luna Park, because his brothers and friends shouted and applauded the loudest at his performance.[3]

Hope initially wanted to be a dancer. He took lessons from

two hoofers, King Rastus Brown and Johnny Root, and entered amateur dance contests. In 1921 he became a dance instructor and gave lessons on various steps from the soft-shoe to the Buck and Wing. The comedian broke into show business when he teamed up with a girl friend, Mildred Rosequist, in a dance act at local theaters. When Mildred's mother refused to permit her daughter to go on tour, Hope found another partner, Lloyd Durbin, a neighborhood friend. The two-man dance act was booked into a 1924 revue at Cleveland's Bandbox Theater, then starring Roscoe (Fatty) Arbuckle, the silent comedy film star. Arbuckle liked their act, and he introduced them to Fred Hurley, the producer of tabloid shows, who put them into his *Jolly Follies*.

Tab shows, as they were called, were short musical comedy revues consisting of singing, dancing, and comedy acts separated by blackouts and played by a repertory company. Considered a step above burlesque, tab shows were popular in the Midwest and in the Middle Atlantic states. Hope performed in second-rate theaters in small towns in Ohio, Indiana, Pennsylvania, and West Virginia for $40 a week, and slept in dingy hotels. The entertainer found it a rewarding experience because he was able to do so many routines. He tap-danced with his partner, sang in a quartet, played the saxophone, and performed juvenile character roles in sketches. The young performer learned how to play to different audiences and began to develop stage poise.

When Durbin died suddenly of food poisoning, Hope teamed with George Byrne, an excellent dancer. They appeared in a new tab show, *Hurley's Smiling Eyes*, performing lively routines. In *The Blackface Follies* the pair added comedy to their act. Hope applied black greasepaint instead of burnt cork to his face and had a difficult time removing the grease. They soon gave up blackface and settled for corny comedy gags. Byrne entered carrying a suitcase, put it down on the stage, and stepped over it. "How are you?" Hope asked. "Fine; just getting over the grippe," his partner replied. Hope also did some Italian dialect and Irish jokes.[4]

The song-and-dance-and-patter team spent two seasons with Hurley. Then, in 1927, they entered vaudeville. Known as "The Dancemedians, Two Diamonds in the Rough," the pair played small-time circuits. In New York City they wore formal attire, white spats, and high hats in their opening soft-shoe dance number. They did a comedy-dance routine with firemen's hats. Hope carried a small hose containing a water bulb. After dancing to "If You Knew Susie," he squirted the orchestra. Hope and Byrne took any engagement to make money, and they once did an act dancing with Siamese twins. They performed a short song-and-dance number with Ruby Keeler in the musical, *The Sidewalks of New York*. Hope also watched the show's star comedian, James Thornton, do his "preacher-type" monologue. Wearing a high hat, long coat, and glasses, and holding a newspaper in his hand, Thornton parodied a political orator and made ludicrous comments on the day's headlines. Hope then realized how amusing a topical monologue could be. After their appearance in *The Sidewalks of New York*, Hope and Byrne decided to use more comedy in their act.

A major turning point in Hope's career occurred in 1927, when the pair played a three-day engagement in New Castle, Pennsylvania. The theater manager asked Hope to announce the next week's attraction on the stage. Hope promoted the upcoming program with a Scottish joke:

> Ladies and gentlemen, next week Marshall Walker will be here with his "Big Time Revue." Marshall is a Scotchman. I know him. He got married in the backyard so the chickens could get the rice.[5]

The manager liked Hope's style and encouraged him to tell more jokes. By the third evening he was doing a five-minute monologue. An orchestra member told him he should become a comic.

Hope had been thinking of doing a single for some time, so he decided to try performing alone. Wearing a small derby, a red bow tie, and white gloves, and smoking a cigar, he did a blackface song-and-dance-and-patter routine in a rotary unit that toured various Cleveland theaters. The blackface lasted only a few performances: when he was once late to the theater and did not have time to apply his makeup his agent told him he was funnier without the burnt cork.

In 1928, Hope was engaged as master of ceremonies for two

weeks at Chicago's Stratford Theater, a popular vaudeville house. He was so sensational that he lasted six months and got the chance to try out different routines. He sang songs, told dialect jokes, and exchanged witticisms with the orchestra leader. Because the bill changed twice a week and the audience consisted of neighborhood people, Hope constantly had to vary his patter. "It was like working to your family because it was the same audience all the time," remembered the comedian. "They'd come back, they knew you, they liked you, so you had their sympathy."[6] The entertainer took jokes from *College Humor* magazine and changed them to fit his audience. He worked on his timing and delivery, learning how to pause and to make fun of a corny gag. At the Stratford Theater the comedian began to develop a stage personality as a smart-aleck wisecracker who told snappy jokes.

Hope gained additional experience by touring on various vaudeville circuits in 1929 and 1930. He added to his act an attractive woman foil, Louise Troxell, who cracked inane jokes and played a "dumb broad" type. By performing at different theaters throughout the country Hope learned to adjust his style to the various audiences. After a poor reception in Forth Worth, Texas—he had talked too rapidly—the comedian moderated his fast delivery so the spectators could understand him. He changed his first name to Bob because it sounded friendlier and "had more 'Hi ya fellas' in it." After making a sensational appearance at New York's Eighty-Sixth Street Theater in 1929, Hope signed a three-year contract with the B. F. Keith circuit and began to tour first-rate houses doing his song-and-patter act. He sang a song while occasionally looking at his watch and taking some medicine from a bottle in his coat. After the song his body started to quiver. "I forgot to shake the bottle," Hope quipped. He hired Al Boasberg to write jokes. The two met in a New York Chinese restaurant, where Hope jotted down Boasberg's gags on the back of the menu. One joke dealt with President Hoover's belief that the Great Depression would soon be over:

> I was just standing out in front watching the other acts when a lady walked up to me in the lobby and said,

"Pardon me, young man, could you tell me where I could find the rest room?" and I said, "it's just around the corner." "Don't give me that Hoover talk," she said. "I'm serious."[7]

In the early 1930's Hope obtained parts in Broadway stage shows. In *The Antics of 1931* he used two stooges sitting in box seats to ridicule his haughty stage personality and to make cutting remarks about his routine. The show was very funny, and it moved to the Palace Theatre. That successful engagement led to major roles in several Broadway musical comedies—*Ballyhoo of 1932, Roberta* (1933), *Say When* (1934), *Ziegfeld Follies* (1935–36), and *Red, Hot and Blue* (1936).

While performing in those musicals Hope began making guest appearances on variety radio programs. He appeared a few times on Rudy Vallee's *Fleischmann Hour*, earning $750 for a guest spot, and on the *RKO Theater of the Air*. Hope also made early radio appearances on Major Edward J. Bowes's *Capitol Family Hour* in connection with his stage engagement at the Capitol Theatre in 1932. Bowes was then the theater's manager and host of a Sunday morning variety program which was a forerunner of his *Amateur Hour*. On Hope's first appearance Bowes changed the script the comedian had prepared, taking the punch lines and making Hope play the straight man. The comedian's other guest spots with Bowes were more successful. "After that when I worked up a routine for the two of us, I secretly prepared punch lines on top of punch lines, and also ad-libbed a lot," wrote Hope. "We got a lot of laughs, and he enjoyed every minute of it."[8]

The comedian was at first very nervous on radio. He felt awkward on the Bowes program, which did not have a live audience. On the Vallee show the engineers heard a thumping sound; Hope was kicking the microphone after every gag. "Of course, like all beginners I suffered from 'Mike Fright,' " he confessed.

> When I approached the microphone I shivered a little and the microphone would shudder a bit too. . . . My first program was one for the books—the police books. I was so nervous, I put my hands on the mike to steady myself and got three messages from the Spirit World.

Hope admitted that he was initially not very good on radio. "The first program I did was so bad that I got an envelope from my sponsor," he stated. "But there wasn't any letter in it. Just a handful of his hair."[9]

The comedian had a difficult time signing for his own radio show. Hope was well known in New York in the early 1930's, but he was not a national celebrity, as Eddie Cantor and Ed Wynn were. Nor did his style impress sponsors:

> Once, I auditioned for Heinz Honey and Almond Cream in New York. For insurance, I invited my wife and Dolores's relatives down from the Bronx because I thought they'd be my greatest audience. They all came down and sat in this little narrow studio and just stared at me, while I rattled off jokes. They didn't even think about the jokes, or laugh or applaud or anything. They just sat there. And I could tell they were thinking, "How is he getting away with it?" Well, I didn't. I was so bad I didn't get the show.

Hope really wanted to break into radio because he realized the medium's potential, and its growing popularity. Listeners were staying home instead of going to the theater. "There wasn't a theater in the country that opened in the evening before 7:30," he recalled. "Because they knew nobody was going to leave the house until after *Amos 'n' Andy*." He viewed radio as a new entertainment form that could give him national prominence:

> Gradually people here and there would come up and say, "Hey! I heard you on that radio show the other day. Pretty good." A light went on and I said to myself, "Yeah. Maybe there's something to this radio thing."[10]

For the next few years Hope worked as a comedian on radio variety shows. He appeared regularly in 1935 on the Bromo Seltzer *Intimate Hour*, sharing the spotlight with Al Goodman's Orchestra and singers James Melton and Jane Froman. Hope teamed with a girl, Patricia (Honey Chile) Wilder, a stunning Southerner with a thick Georgia accent which got laughs every time she spoke. Wilder was later a regular on the Pepsodent show. After fifteen weeks the series was canceled due to poor

ratings. During the 1935–36 season Hope and Wilder were featured with Red Nichols and his band on the Saturday night CBS
White Flash program, sponsored by the Atlantic Oil Refining
Company. Hope did several skits entitled "the courtroom bit,"
"office routine," "Bob's birthday routine," "the Julius Caesar
bit," and "the doctor's office." Although that program also had
a low rating the comedian was gaining valuable experience in
the medium.[11]

A major turning point in his career occurred on NBC's Woodbury Soap program between May and September of 1937. Hope's
success on Broadway in *Red, Hot and Blue* led to a twenty-six-
week contract to appear Sunday night on the Woodbury show
with singer Frank Parker and Shep Fields's orchestra. Hope did
a five-minute topical monologue in the opening spot. He had
performed a topical monologue on stage as a master of ceremonies, but now it became a major part of his radio routine. On
the Woodbury show Hope commented on current events and
popular topics. He told snappy jokes on such subjects as politics,
women and beauty, and sports. A topical monologue had not
been heard on radio since Will Rogers's death in 1935. "I'd decided that if I wanted to compete with all the other shows on radio, I'd have to have something different and ear-catching,"
wrote Hope.[12]

Under contract to Paramount, the comedian went to Hollywood to film *The Big Broadcast of 1938.* He did his Woodbury
show monologue on September 3, 1937, by remote hookup from
the movie capital. John Swallow, NBC's local program director,
believed Hope did not need a studio audience and did not print
any tickets for his short broadcast. "I've got to have an audience
to bounce my comedy off of or I'm dead," Hope told him a few
nights before the program. The comedian arranged with the ushers to erect some ropes so that the crowd leaving the Edgar Bergen and Charlie McCarthy show, which preceded his broadcast
in an adjoining studio, could be led into his studio. Hope told
Bergen, a long-time friend, of his plan. When the audience arrived only a few recognized Hope, who had just arrived in Hollywood. He had to coax them to stay. "Come right in and sit
down," he said. "I'm Bob Hope and I'm going to do a show

for New York in a minute. It's a very funny show and I think you'll enjoy it." He entertained them with a series of short telegraphic one-liners describing his impressions of Hollywood and the day's news. Years later Bergen joked about the incident on a broadcast honoring Hope's sixtieth birthday:

> Well, back in radio days, Bob Hope used to borrow my audience. He had the studio right next to mine and followed me on the air. And sometimes he would blame me if his show didn't go because I ruined the audience. And there were a few shows where I think I did it too.[13]

Hope arrived in Hollywood when the city was becoming a broadcasting center, and some studio executives viewed radio as an influential publicity medium for their films. Realizing that exposure on radio could aid his movie career, the entertainer hired Jimmy Saphier to manage his broadcasting appearances. Saphier booked Hope on Lucky Strike's *Your Hollywood Parade*, one of the first variety programs broadcast live from California. Hope did a swift seven- to ten-minute topical monologue on *Your Hollywood Parade* from December 1937 to March 1938. Hope's brash, rapid delivery on the show resembled the breathless, staccato manner of Walter Winchell in broadcasting the news. The comedian also began giving his monologue a setting. Sometimes he told a series of jokes about an important Hollywood event, such as the Academy Awards ceremony, or gags about places in or near the movie capital. Listeners thus began to associate Hope with the glamour of Hollywood.

The comedian worked with the writer Wilkie Mahoney two or three nights a week on his monologue:

> Wilkie would drop in, we'd figure out what we were going to talk about, then we'd sit down and kick it back and forth, with Wilkie at the typewriter tapping out the parts we thought usable. We kept on chopping away at it until we'd hacked out ten minutes of serviceable stuff. I talked about anything current and hot in my monologues—mostly Hollywood news, but anything as long as it was topical.

By then Hope felt confident and comfortable in front of a microphone. For several reasons he found radio easier to do than vaudeville and the movies:

> Working in radio was wonderful. You could just stand
> there in front of a radio audience, tell a joke, get a
> laugh, and then kiss the joke and get another laugh.
> When the show was over, I'd just walk out, toss the
> script in a wastebasket, and go right to the golf course.
> I didn't have to worry about makeup, costumes, or any-
> thing like that. It was something.[14]

The comedian's role in *The Big Broadcast of 1938* helped him
get his own radio show. The film had a trivial plot, like the other
Big Broadcast movies. Hope played a radio announcer who covered a transcontinental race between two ocean liners. The film
starred W. C. Fields, but Hope stole part of the picture when he
sang the Academy Award hit song "Thanks for the Memory."
He received a rave notice from Damon Runyon in the journalist's
newspaper column. The publicity came at a time when The Pepsodent Company was searching for a new program to replace
Amos 'n' Andy, which they had stopped sponsoring in 1937 because of declining ratings. Pepsodent's advertising agency was
Lord & Thomas, headed by Albert Lasker, who had signed Hope
for the Lucky Strike program. Lasker believed a program starring Hope would be an excellent property for the toothpaste
company. Saphier got Lasker to agree to a contract giving Hope
exclusive control over production. The Tuesday night NBC program premiered on September 27, 1938.

Hope then had to live up to Pepsodent's successful sponsorship
of *Amos 'n' Andy*. He was invited to have dinner on a yacht
owned by Kenneth Smith, co-owner of The Pepsodent Company.
The Lord & Thomas executive accompanying Hope pointed to the
luxurious yacht anchored off Lake Michigan: "I want you to remember one thing: Amos and Andy built that boat." The comedian retorted confidently: "When I finish with Pepsodent, Mr.
Smith will be using the yacht for a dinghy."[15]

Hope assembled a large staff of young talented comedy writers to write the show. "This time I was determined to succeed," declared the comedian:

> I felt I hadn't paid enough attention to my material on the previous shows, and that's why I didn't last. I set about to find the best comedy writers, not just the vaudeville old-timers who were writing most of the other radio shows. I wanted fresh young talent, newcomers who were willing to submit wild and wacky comedy.[16]

At one time he had thirteen writers, jokingly known as "Hope's Army," working for him. Hope's writers over the years included Milt Josefsberg, Norman Panama, Melville Shavelson, Jack Douglas, Norman Sullivan, Jack Huston, Jack Rose, Howard Blake, Larry Marks, Fred S. Fox, Ted McKay, Melvin Frank, Sherwood and Al Schwartz, Les White, and Mort Lachman. The employment of a large staff reflected a change in the production of a comedy program. In the early years of radio, Fred Allen, Will Rogers, and Correll and Gosden had written their own material, while other comedians had employed only a few writers. The increased competitive pressure in the "ratings war," larger budgets, and the insatiable need for new jokes every week led comedians like Hope to hire large staffs. The writing had become a mechanical team effort.

The production of a weekly Pepsodent program by Hope's "gag factory" was an efficient, streamlined process. The comedian held a story conference with his staff on Thursday to generate ideas for the upcoming broadcast. Hope favored the method of competition writing. The writers divided into two teams, with each group completing a preliminary twenty-page script. The entertainer selected the best material from each draft at another conference in his home office. The writers read their scripts and discussed with the comedian their colleagues' submissions. Hope made the final selection, marking the best jokes and routines to be part of a new ninety-minute script. A cast reading was held on Saturday and the preliminary script previewed on Sunday night before a live audience. During that rehearsal the writers checked the best laugh lines. Hope and his staff listened on

Monday to the recording of the preview, noting the audience re-action to the jokes. The funniest material was then chosen for the thirty-minute Tuesday night show. "If you had five jokes in the final monologue you were the hero of the week," Jack Doug-las recalled. By eliminating the least effective lines and rou-tines, Hope broadcast only sure-fire tested material. The Pepso-dent program was a slick, assembly-line, mass-entertainment product.[17]

The broadcast was generally divided into three conventional sections separated by music and commercials: monologue; mid-dle spot featuring repartee between the comedian, cast, and guest star; and a closing sketch. The series featured many guest movie stars, who contributed to the program's Hollywood image. "Thanks for the Memory" was the opening and closing theme song, sung by Hope in a sentimental tone. The catchy tune gave the comedian a needed signature. The lyrics could be changed to fit the program's theme, to advertise Pepsodent, and to remind listeners to tune in next week. On the first Pepsodent show the comedian sang:

> Thanks for the memory
> Of this our opening spot
> Oh! I practically forgot—
> You'll *love* the show next Tuesday—
> There's a scene where I get shot. . . .
> You'll like that so much.
>
> Thanks for the memory,
> And, Connie, I feel blue
> To think that we are through—
> Just drop in any Tuesday when you've nothing else to boo,
> And thank you so much.
>
> And now we are sorry to leave you,
> It's just for a week we'll be missin'—
> To show Pepsodent that you listen,
> Mail in the doors
> From four drug stores.[18]

Hope was aided by a regular supporting cast whose functions were much like those of Jack Benny's "gang." Bill Goodwin, one of radio's new "personality" announcers, did the commercials; he was succeeded by Wendell Niles, Art Baker, and Hy Averback. Over the years the broadcasts were highlighted by musical entertainment, including the Six Hits and a Miss vocal group and outstanding singers—Judy Garland, Frances Langford, and Doris Day. The orchestra was led by Skinnay Ennis and later by Les Brown. The announcer, singer, and conductor often played straight or comic parts. Ennis acted as a foil for Hope's endless number of "Skinnay" insult jokes. He called the lean orchestra leader a "spaghetti in search of a meatball." "We had a hard time keeping track of Skinnay at the picnic; the ants carried him away three times," Hope jested on another show.[19]

The program's zaniest character actor was Jerry Colonna, a former orchestra trombonist with bulging round eyes and a black, walrus-type moustache. Colonna had an unforgettable resounding voice that blared out of the radio loudspeaker. A versatile performer, he impersonated many nitwit characters. His routine as the moronic "professor" was highlighted by a series of curt one-liners.

HOPE   Well, Professor Colonna . . . Bushey's father, how are you tonight?

COLONNA   Solid!!

HOPE   Solid?

COLONNA   Yes. . . . *Water on my brain froze!!*

HOPE   Professor, I understand you're a horse lover.

COLONNA   Yes, I am. Hope. . . . *Of course, we're not engaged yet!*

HOPE   Professor. . . . there's a place for you in the Idiot's Hall of Fame.

COLONNA   Fine . . . *Leave the door unlocked!* . . .

HOPE   Have you made any good bets recently, Professor?

COLONNA   Yes, yesterday. And ah . . . what a thrill it was to see the winner flash past . . . with all six legs driving him across the finish line!

HOPE   Six legs. . . . How come six legs were driving him across the line?

COLONNA   *Short horse . . . Long jockey!*

HOPE   Shred-head. . . . tell me . . . what makes you act this way?

COLONNA   It's that pounding at my temples. That pounding, pounding, pounding!

HOPE	The pounding at your temples? What causes it?
COLONNA	Okay. This is it . . . my favorite horse "Valdina Moonglow." I've been following him all my life but I never won a bet on him.
HOPE	Colonna, if you never won a bet on him, why do you keep following him?
COLONNA	Mustache got tangled in his tail!
HOPE	Colonna, tell me, do you *like* being you . . . or would you rather be a member of the human race?
COLONNA	Can't be a member, Hope. . . . Can't afford to pay my duin.
HOPE	What's duin?
COLONNA	Nothing much. . . . *What's duin with you?*[20]

Many of the show's catch phrases stemmed from Colonna's lines. Whenever Colonna saw Hope or anyone else he said, "Greetings, Gate." Listeners began using that expression as well as another catch phrase, "Who's Yehudi?" (after Yehudi Menuhin, the violinist). Nobody in the cast seemed to know who Yehudi was, including Colonna, who kept asking, "Who's Yehudi?" The search for the mythical Yehudi became a running gag and a popular song. Other catch phrases included "Okay, so I ain't neat!" "You and your education," "That's what I keep telling them down at the office," and "Give me a drag on that before you throw it away," a statement the cast employed to poke fun at anyone's bragging.[21]

Two other characters were unattractive man-chasers, Brenda and Cobina, played by Blanche Stewart and Elvia Allman. Both were veteran radio actresses when they joined Hope in 1939. Stewart had acted on the Benny program and Allman had played Cora Dithers on *Blondie*. The characters were named after two society debutantes, Brenda Frazier and Cobina Wright. Brenda and Cobina had shrill, funny-sounding voices, and they would chat about their frustrated love life. Their opening lines were "Hey, Brenda! . . . What is it, Cobina?"

ELVIA	Imagine us being at Palm Springs, Brenda!
BLANCHE	Yeah. Gee aren't you glad to be here—such a change from the cave!
ELVIA	Brenda, darling . . .
BLANCHE	What is it, Cobina? . . .

ELVIA	Brenda, I'm worried. . . . I'm losin' my hair. . . .
BLANCHE	So what . . . if your wrists show a little! . . . Gee, there's something funny-lookin' about you today, Cobina . . . oh, I know what it is . . . you got your teeth in sideways!
ELVIA	Gee . . . if we only had some men.
BLANCHE	Cobina . . . this morning . . . I gotta tell you . . . I looked out the window and I saw something . . . it looked like us only it had short hair and was wearing trousers.
ELVIA	Brenda . . . that was a MAN!
BLANCHE	Man. . . . Is that good?
ELVIA	It ain't bad.
BLANCHE	Why ain't I never met one?
ELVIA	Why you met Bill Goodwin and Bob Hope. . . . Oh, I see what you mean.
BLANCHE	Cobina . . . who would you like to be cast away on a desert island with?
ELVIA	Johnny *Wish*muller!
BLANCHE	That's Weiss—look at your script!
ELVIA	That's Wish . . . look at my face! . . . Gee, Brenda, I can't understand it . . . there were a lot of men around the swimming pool when we walked out here!
BLANCHE	I told you you shoulda walked out here backwards. . . .
ELVIA	I did walk out backwards!
BLANCHE	Then I guess you scare 'em both ways!
ELVIA	I been in the sun an hour Brenda . . . is my face red?
BLANCHE	I can't tell, Cobina. . . . I'll have to wait till you comb your eyebrows back!
ELVIA	Gee, Brenda, isn't it wonderful when fellers try to kiss us under water?
BLANCHE	I'll say . . . but we haven't had much luck since we drowned them last two.
ELVIA	Come on . . . let's dive down and *look at them* again![22]

Another bit character was Vera Vague, played by Barbara Jo Allen. The actress based the character on a woman lecturer at a PTA meeting. She called Vera Vague "sort of a frustrated female, dumb, always ambitious and over-zealous . . . a spouting Bureau of Misinformation." Allen had acted the flirtatious "old maid" on *NBC Matinee* in 1939; then she joined Hope's program in 1941. Allen appeared on the broadcast in costume wearing a zany hat, and whenever she had a funny line her lorgnette would pop up and down. Vera traded insult jokes with Hope and flirted with the male guest stars. She got one of the longest laughs during a broadcast from the Great Lakes Naval Training Base. Allen's line read, "Only recently a sailor tried to flirt with me and I reported him to the head of the Navy." When she got to the word "head" (meaning the toilet in Navy language) the audience burst out laughing. "What did you say?" Hope ad-libbed, to "milk" the fluff. "And I reported him to the head," Allen replied, and the Navy audience laughed hysterically again.[23]

The highlight of the Pepsodent program was Hope's "speed-comedy" monologue. Unlike other comedy shows that opened with a commercial or music, the broadcast started with the comedian's monologue. It gave him the advantage of immediately capturing the listening audience. He consistently began the monologue with a familiar greeting that became one of his trademarks: "How do you do, ladies and gentlemen. . . . This is Bob Hope." Hope varied the opening by often mentioning the broadcast's location and plugging Pepsodent: "How do you do, ladies and gentlemen, this is Bob 'deep in the heart of Texas' Hope telling you Texans to use Pepsodent and your mouth won't be a scandal." The comedian's opening line set the stage for a series of one-liners about the area he was visiting.[24]

On his first Pepsodent broadcast Hope used an old vaudeville gimmick. After his opening line a stooge in the audience laughed out loud. "Not yet, Charlie," Hope responded. "But don't leave." Then he raced into his monologue, which contained a barrage of one-liners about a recent American Legion convention, a football game, California weather, his Paramount movie, and women's fashions:

> My uncle just left town . . . he was here with the American Legion Convention. He was in the army and was one of the first men to go over the top . . . somebody pushed him. He's from Florida. He spent most of his time dropping ice cubes out of the hotel window to make people think it was hailing here in California. It

was a nice, quiet convention. The second night the boys
at the hotel gave the house detective 24 hours to leave
town. But I want to thank the American Legion for getting me a half day off, last week at Paramount. They
came over to the set I was working on and took the camera with them as a souvenir. Paramount didn't care, but
they'd be very thankful if the fellow from Texas would
please bring back Dorothy Lamour. While my uncle
was here I took him to see the football game between
Alabama and the University of Southern California. It's
perfect football weather . . . only 90 in the shade. In
the second quarter the Alabama quarterback broke in the
clear and went thirty yards to the ten-yard line. He
could have stretched it into a touchdown if he hadn't
tripped over the electric fan he was carrying. Alabama
was using the Rockne system. But California was
smart—they used the cooling system. Whenever there
was a pile-up all the players tried to get on the bottom
so they could be in the shade. . . . And have you seen
the new doll hats the girls are wearing? . . . Doll hats!
Nothing with a feather in it! And I hear they're going
to wear those hooped skirts again. You know what a
hooped skirt is . . . a parachute with legs. My girlfriend bought one yesterday and took it home with her.
She has the canary going crazy . . . he doesn't know
where he lives anymore. I don't know where she got the
hoops for her skirt, but everytime I take her out, her
skirt wraps itself around a barrel of beef. These hooped
skirts are gonna save a lot of taxi fares for the men. All
they have to do is get a stick and roll their girlfriend
home. . . . Good, eh, fellows. . . . No, huh? At least
the styles are different this year, and that's what we're
going to try and make this radio show—different.[25]

The topics Hope talked about on his first program—fashions,
sports, California weather, and Hollywood—were subjects he
spoofed over the years.

The brisk pace of this monologue, twenty-three jokes in seven
minutes, or over three gags a minute, typified his rapid-fire delivery. "My idea was to do it as fast as I could and still have the
listeners at home get it and let the live audience in the studio

laugh too," Hope wrote. "Unless the live audience took the play away from me with their laughter, I raced." The writers checked the number of laugh lines on their script, and sometimes he clocked up to six or seven jokes a minute. A Hope monologue was strung together by a succession of staccato one-liners and joke toppers. The formula of an initial joke, topper, and then a series of toppers worked like an avalanche, the laughter increasing after each gag. This monologue suggests the rhythm of his soliloquy:

> But I'm happy with my new car. They think of everything these days. They delivered it this morning and it already had three pedestrians on the bumper! [laughter]. The new cars have bumpers made out of rubber. It's really great. After you hit a guy it erases your license number off the back of his pants [laughter]. Everything is made out of rubber. . . . It has a hard rubber steering wheel . . . soft rubber cushions . . . and a rubber floor mat. . . . Just to be in keeping I paid for it by check . . . [laughter]. Everytime I drive past the bank, the car bounces . . . [laughter]. It's the new streamlined type. It's so futuristic that Skinnay looked through the car for twenty minutes trying to find Buck Rogers [laughter]. It has a private phone to the chauffeur, a private phone to the footman and a private phone to the mechanic still working on the motor. . . . I told them I wanted a super charger—so they threw in a waiter from the Trocadero [laughter]. It's so long and close to the ground that when it passes a daschsound [*sic*] it wags its rear bumper [laughter]. The car is so swanky this morning I held out my hand to turn a corner and a traffic cop kissed it [laughter]. And what a smooth motor! You should hear it purr! It purrs so smoothly!—Yesterday two dogs tried to chase it up a tree . . . [laughter]. In fact, it purrs so smoothly, I don't know whether to put in gasoline or *milk* . . . [laughter]. Maybe you like it better *that* way. . . . And everything in the new car is run by *buttons!* You push one button and an ash-tray comes out. You push another button and the cigarette lighter comes out. I pushed the third button and what do you think came

302 THE SLICK COMEDY OF THE 1940'S

out?!! The man from the finance company! . . .
[laughter] I pushed the *fourth* button and opened a
WPA bridge in Salt Lake City [much laughter].[26]

On stage Hope had learned how to time his delivery and command an audience, which contributed to the effectiveness of his radio monologue. "I know how to snap a line, then cover it, then speed on to the next," he wrote. He developed a give-and-take relationship with the audience and knew how to play on listeners' expectations:

> You have to get over to the audience that there's a game of wits going on and that if they don't stay awake, they'll miss something, like missing a baseball someone has lobbed to them. What I'm really doing is asking "Let's see if you can hit this one!" That's my whole comedy technique. I know how to telegraph to the audience the fact that this *is* a joke, and that if they don't laugh right now, they're not playing the game and nobody has any fun.

Listeners were almost conditioned to laugh after hearing the opening line in his radio monologue. He also enjoyed toying with the audience. Hope would set them up to expect a certain punch line and then would say the exact opposite. His series of toppers allowed him to disguise bad gags and to quickly insert a joke saver. "If nobody laughs perhaps you squeeze some humor out of apologizing for it," Hope remarked. "Or you can play it as if you think it's terribly funny and you can't understand why the audience doesn't follow you." The comedian was an expert at "throwing away" funny gags by pretending a joke had little laugh appeal and quickly continuing to the next line.[27]

The manner, technique, and subject matter of Hope's monologue partially resembled the radio talks of Will Rogers. Where the cowboy philosopher had posed as a wise innocent, Hope played a brash "wise guy." Both were national court jesters who joked about politicians and celebrities and lampooned current events. Both rambled from subject to subject using one-line quips and colloquial expressions that appealed to their listeners. If Rogers had appeared as an unaffected, friendly cowboy, Hope personified the regular American "guy."

The two entertainers, however, represented different eras of radio comedy. Rogers spoke in a slow drawl, while Hope talked rapidly, his crisp, snappy jokes reflecting the hurried pace of American life in the 1940's, an era of wartime activity and postwar economic expansion. Rogers's folksy style had appealed to grass-roots America during the Great Depression. Hope's urbane style, accented by his neatly pressed blue suit or tuxedo, reflected the taste of the new urban and suburban mass society that evolved in the 1940's. Hope's predictable radio program, written by a large staff, was a glossy package of mass entertainment. Rogers, who had done his own writing and research, had often gained information by talking personally with people. Hope's writers, on the other hand, obtained information about life in the armed forces camps from public relations officers. Compared to Rogers, Hope seemed mechanically detached from his material, a joke processor rather than a joke teller.

Rogers had exposed deceit and corruption in memorable quips, but Hope's superficial jokes were momentarily funny and then forgotten. His humor rarely penetrated the surface of important issues. Hope's jokes about the nation's Presidents dealt mainly with their personal habits, Truman's piano playing or Eisenhower's golf. Rarely, if ever, did he satirize the quality of their leadership. Hope's lighthearted style is evident in his remarks about Truman's surprising victory over Dewey in the 1948 presidential election:

> Dr. Gallup was amazed at the outcome but he won't admit he was wrong. Last night he was still peeking into the White House window and singing "Maybe you'll be there."

> Now Margaret Truman has to go back to the White House, and she had it all set to be the fourth Andrews sister.

> The three candidates have really changed their tune since the election. Truman's changed from the "Missouri Waltz" to "It's Magic." Dewey's humming "Say It Isn't So" and Wallace is humming "On a Slow Boat to China."[28]

Because he generally avoided jesting about significant political issues Hope's humor rarely stung. He blamed commercial pressures for his cautious approach. "There was only one Will Rogers," Hope admitted:

> I'm really on the spot when I do political jokes. I would never do a joke to hurt any campaign or party. I can't afford to go out and start knocking Democrats and knocking Republicans because I'm usually selling a product everybody buys and I don't want to alienate my audience. It's pretty hard to do a comedy show and stay in the middle and please everybody when you're kicking current subjects around all the time. Will Rogers used to get away with it. But he was supposed to be a cracker-barrel type. I've got a lot of crackers in my barrel but there was only one Will Rogers.

There were other reasons why the comedian never became a pungent political satirist. Hope had risen from "rags to riches," and he deeply believed in traditional American institutions and values. He aimed to be the nation's favorite court jester, beloved by the public. Hope also wanted to be friends with the country's most influential business, government, and military leaders—the comedian of the "Power Elite." He wanted, in short, to be invited back to the White House.[29]

The entertainer represented the successful, patriotic, charitable, and virtuous All-American to radio listeners in the 1940's. Hope's life was devoid of scandal. He was a family man with a long-standing marriage to singer Dolores Reade and the father of four adopted children. His exhaustive tours, entertaining military personnel during World War II, the Berlin crisis, and the Korean War, gave him a reputation as a patriotic humanitarian and "ambassador of good will." That distinction, however, was partially eclipsed by his overzealous support of the Nixon administration and the Vietnam War. A shrewd businessman, in fact, a millionaire, the comedian formed Hope Enterprises, Incorporated, in the mid-1940's to consolidate his financial earnings in radio, television, and films, and his investments in real estate, sports, and oil. Hope practiced Andrew Carnegie's "Gospel of Wealth" by giving millions of dollars to philanthropic causes, universities, cultural institutions, hospitals, and churches and performing without pay at charity benefits.[30]

The comedian also portrayed a venerable American comic type—the smart-aleck wisecracking braggart. Hope's style was descended from the hyperbolic oral tall-tale humor of the boasting backwoodsmen and swaggering frontiersmen. His cocky radio (and film) personality partially resembled Benny's vain character. Both flaunted their looks, sexual prowess, and courage, but in actuality they were cowardly braggarts. Hope was "all talk and no action"—a boaster who backed down when faced with having to prove his mettle. The character he portrayed allowed listeners to laugh both with and *at* Hope:

> I went to a party here New Year's Eve and I wore my tuxedo suit. But I guess the pants were a little tight for me this year. When I bent over, the seams started singing, "Praise the Lord and Pass Some Stronger Stitchin!" . . . Some soldier started flirting with my girl and I was about to let him have it when I saw how big he was. . . . So I let him have *her*, instead!

> I really love football. . . . I have the physique of a football player, and I guess I even resemble the Georgia star, Frank Sinkwich. . . . Because every place I go, people point to me and say, "There goes Sinky"! . . . That is, I thought they said "Sinky." . . . Till I noticed they'd added their own "t" formation! . . . When I used to play I was something like Sinkwich, the Georgia Fireball. . . . They called me Hope, the Cleveland meatball!. . . . I used to hold the ball while our fullback kicked off, and boy, was he near-sighted. At the start of our first game, the other team ran back forty yards with *my head!*

Like Benny, Hope was a lovable fall guy with common virtues and faults.[31]

Guest stars on the radio show were used as foils to deflate Hope's ego. Hope once bragged to Dizzy Dean, the famous baseball pitcher, that "you'd be pretty popular with the girls if you were as big and strong as I am!" The comedian challenged Dean

to shake hands to see who was the strongest. After a sound resembling a "loud crunch of macaroni" Hope painfully asked
Dean to put his hand "in my pocket for me." Many glamorous
women film stars like Jane Russell kidded him about his pretensions as a handsome male movie actor:

HOPE   But, Jane, after being my leading lady, tell me, how
        does it feel to have me take you in my arms, whisper
        tender words in your ear, kiss you, and make love to
        you?

JANE   . . . *Well . . . it's a living!*

HOPE   How can you say that, Jane? I'm a great lover—when I
        kiss a girl, she always remembers it.

JANE   *Do you think it'll help if I join the Foreign Legion?*[32]

Bing Crosby was Hope's most persistent heckler. The two met
in New York City in 1932, and a few months later Hope and
Crosby appeared on the same bill at the Capitol Theatre. Hope
recalled the joke routines they did together after Crosby finished
his songs:

> We did our impression of two orchestra leaders meeting
> in the street. Each of us pulled out a baton and led the
> other while we talked as if we were leading an orches-
> tra. Next we did our impression of two farmers meeting.
> One of us asked, "How are things down on the farm?"
> The other said, "It's pretty cold in the reading room."
> Real Noel Coward! Then we milked each other's
> thumbs. It was the beginning of a long, pleasant and
> profitable association.

Their comic feud was a clash of two opposite stage personalities:
the boisterous, boastful Hope versus the soft-spoken, debonair
Crosby.[33]
    Instead of throwing custard pies, they threw insult jokes at
one another:

HOPE   Haven't you heard? I'm on for Swan this year. They
        make soap, you know.

CROSBY Yeah, too bad it's not something you use.

HOPE   Hey, Lumplap, you have two chins. Would you like to
        try for one?

CROSBY   To think that when I first met this boy he had a job blowing out glove compartments at a car wash.

HOPE   Steady, Couchpouch!

CROSBY   Now look, Ratchethead.

Hope teased Crosby about his large ears, while the singer referred to the comedian as "good old trout snout" and "the Pepsodent Pinocchio." Whenever Crosby jokingly derided Hope's movie-acting, the comedian might needle the crooner about his singing. Hope especially enjoyed ribbing Crosby about his age:

HOPE   You know, Bing, I can't understand why Paramount always lets you win the girl from me. . . . I really can't understand why they give the romantic role to an elderly man like you . . . instead of a boy like me.

CROSBY   Elderly man! Hope, I'll have you know that I just missed being eligible for the draft by two months!

HOPE   Yeah . . . it must have been swell back in 1917!

Their radio routines were often extemporaneous. "We used to frame writers to find out what he was going to ad-lib," Hope said, "and then they'd give somebody else the answer and we'd throw in the ad-lib just ahead of the time he was going to do it or I was going to do it whatever the case may be. We used to break each other up this way both in pictures and on radio." On a broadcast celebrating Hope's birthday Crosby unexpectedly walked into the studio and threw a cake at the comedian. Hope picked up the cake and hurled it back at Crosby, who threw the remains into the audience. Their running feud, which carried over into the *Road* movies, was similar to the Benny–Allen routines.[34]

Hope's reputation as a beneficent, patriotic American developed largely because he entertained so many servicemen and servicewomen during World War II. Encouraged by his radio producer, Hope began broadcasting from stateside military camps in March 1941. His first show of that type originated from the March Field Army Air Force Base in California, and he continued to broadcast most of his programs from Army, Navy, and Marine bases until June 1948. During the few times the comedian broadcast from Hollywood his audience consisted largely of GIs, who were given preferential tickets. Hope often did the Sunday night preview at one base and then traveled to another camp for the live broadcast. He also put on stage shows three or four times a day at various bases and did additional programs for the Armed Forces Radio Service, including *Command Performance*, *Mail Call*, and *G. I. Journal.*[35]

The military-base broadcasts had a wartime flavor. The comedian sometimes began his monologue by mentioning the program's location: "This is Bob 'Camp Pendleton Marine Base' Hope." Hope once joked about not being permitted to disclose his whereabouts for security reasons:

> Well, here I am at an unidentified spot, who ever thought I'd be broadcasting from a place I can't mention on the air, except my sponsor who once told me to go to one. . . . To get to this unidentified camp, an unidentified soldier drove me over an unidentified road in an unidentified jeep, and now I feel sore in an unidentified spot.

He used military lingo to advertise Pepsodent: "How do you do, ladies and gentlemen, this is Bob Broadcasting from Camp Cooke Hope, telling all you soldiers to use Pepsodent and the girls will always give you eyes right because you'll always have teeth left." Part of his monologue was usually directed at the GI audience:

> Well, here I am at Camp Hood in Texas. . . . This is one of the biggest camps in America. I never saw so many soldiers. They got five buglers here just to wake up the buglers! . . . Boy, is this camp tremendous. . . . To give you an idea how big Camp Hood is. . . . It's the only camp in the world where a soldier can go A.W.O.L. for a month and still remain in camp. . . . Some of the soldiers here took me for a ride in a tank. . . . You know what a tank is. . . . That's a jeep with hardening of the arteries. . . . And these boys have to be experts at camouflage. They disguise themselves with leaves and branches until they look just like the bushes around here and nobody can tell where they are. It worked fine until one day the commanding officer hap-

pened to drive into Dallas and saw 2000 tumbleweeds following a blonde down Main Street!

The soldiers and sailors whistled and made wolf calls whenever attractive movie actresses performed on the broadcasts. Hope once jested about the eight thousand WAACS who whistled when he appeared on stage:

> Well, here I am on WAAC island. . . . There are 8000 beautiful WAACS here. . . . But you should see the reception those WAACS gave me. One of 'em kept yelling, "We love Bob Hope . . . We love Bob Hope." . . . Finally the Commanding Officer had to go over and tell my mother to shut up.[36]

Jokes about the home front highlighted his monologues during the war years. A week after Pearl Harbor Hope referred to the recent blackout in Los Angeles:

> Well, Los Angeles had its first blackout the other night. Every electric light in the city went out. . . . I saw one guy standing in the street and laughing like anything. . . . I said, "What are you so happy about?" . . . and he said, "At last I'm not alone. . . . Look. . . . This month nobody paid their bills."

On the same broadcast the comedian joked about how the Allies could easily defeat Japan: "There's nothing to worry about though. . . . California alone could beat Japan. . . . After all, how long could the rising sun hold out against the drifting fog." Hope also spoke in a serious tone about the war at the conclusion of his broadcasts. He urged listeners to buy war bonds and support the Red Cross. His theme song praised the courage of the GI and entreated citizens to contribute to wartime drives:

> Thanks for the memory
> Destroyers of Camp Hood;
> A battling brotherhood,
> When trouble brews, you and your crews
> Do Axis tanks no good. . . .
> Folks, the Red Cross can use your donation
> To back up these boys at their station
> So they ask every purse in this nation

To give and give
Let freedom live.[37]

He and his cast made worldwide overseas entertainment tours
for the United Service Organizations (USO). Hope, Frances
Langford, Jerry Colonna, and guitarist Tony Romano traveled
to Alaska and the Aleutians in 1942 to entertain GIs. In the summer of 1943 they completed an eleven-week USO tour of bases in
Great Britain, North Africa, and Sicily. The next year Hope
toured the South Pacific and Caribbean, and in 1945 he entertained in Europe. They had an exhaustive schedule and often
staged five to seven shows daily in different camps to huge audiences. The cast performed in makeshift auditoriums, airplane
hangars, drill fields, officers' clubs, supply depots, hospital wards,
and trucks. The arrival of the comedian was a major event at the
bases. There was usually standing room only, and sometimes the
GIs had to alternate in shifts. Six hundred soldiers once marched
ten miles to attend a show, only to find the performance filled to
capacity. Learning that, they had started to march back. Hope
and the other performers rode in a jeep until they found the
hikers. By the roadside they put on a special impromptu show
for the tired GIs. Because they had heard him on the radio before the war, Hope reminded the overseas troops of home. His
stage shows gave diversion and entertainment to the battle-
weary soldiers.[38]

Since the soldiers were risking their lives, the comedian felt
obligated to make their world less dreary. Hope particularly
thought he had a duty to entertain the wounded:

> Those guys aren't asking for tears or sympathy. They
> had a job to do, and they did it. It was a tough job. But
> they did do it. What right would I have coming in on a
> bunch of men who had successfully carried out their
> mission, to meet the enemy and hold him, and not be
> able to carry out mine—the job of passing out a few
> snickers.

He viewed his role as a missionary of humor and believed that
laughter eased the drudgery of GI life. "A tidal wave of American humor is sweeping the world," Hope wrote about his overseas tour. "Its impetus in our American boys, with that God-

Bob Hope performing at a USO show.
(Courtesy, Frank Bresee Collection.)

given talent to laugh at their troubles and to laugh with the person who laughs with them." Hope earnestly believed that humor could help end strife and bring people together:

> Maybe if we could all laugh alike, and laugh at the same things, this world of ours wouldn't be able to find so many things to squabble about. As our fighting men march across the face of this messed-up globe to sweep it clean their laughter will be an inspiration that will echo through the corridors of time.[39]

Hope's foxhole humor allowed the serviceman "to let off steam." "Our fighting man likes his humor aimed straight at him," Hope wrote. "He can take it. The more the joke's on him the better he likes it." His military jokes often dealt with the uncomfortable weather in campaign areas. In Africa he jested: "It's so hot around here I took one look at a pup tent and it was panting," and "it's wonderful being back in Africa, good old Africa. Yes. Texas with Arabs." His writers tailored his material for each branch of the armed forces. The comedian had a store of special Navy jokes:

> You know what a sailor is—that's a wolf in ship's clothing.
>
> You know what a Navy uniform is—it's a girdle with legs.
>
> A naval receiving station is a place where sailors come for assignment to other bases. It's like Reno is for women.

Hope gags also dealt with GI gripes, like long chow lines: "I won't say it's tough waiting in that chow line, but they've got a guy riding up and down on a bicycle offering plasma." Like Bill Mauldin's Willie and Joe newspaper cartoons, the comedian's military gags let the fighting man laugh at his own existence. Hope was popular with the troops because he seemed to understand the problems of the average GI. Like the war reporter Ernie Pyle, who wrote about the ordinary soldier, Hope's monologue dealt with the life of "G.I. Joe." He spoke our lingo, wrote one soldier, who saw the comedian perform on a soccer field in Palermo, Italy:

> Bob came on the grandstand dressed as a man on the
> street, baggy trousers, an ordinary coat, and an open-
> neck collar. Nothing fancy at all. His nose was really
> sunburned and caught the brunt of a lot of his own
> jokes. He started his patter and all of us laughed until
> tears were just streaming down and we couldn't see a
> darned thing. He has been playing Army camps a lot
> and has picked up the lingo. He can tell you all about
> lister bags, atabrine tablets, and armor artificers. That
> made his comments much funnier to us. He was speak-
> ing our language.[40]

His ability to direct his broadcasts to both the soldier and the
home-front civilian helped make Hope the most popular radio
comedian during the war years. His USO tours were well publicized, and cover stories in *Time* and *Life* magazines depicted
him as a dedicated ambassador of humor to overseas troops. *I
Never Left Home* (1944), Hope's account of his exhaustive 1943
tour, was a best seller and sold over a million copies. Listening to
his program at home during the war became a Tuesday night
ritual. The Pepsodent program's Hooper rating increased steadily
from 1938 to 1943. In January 1943 it reached a phenomenal
40.9, the top-rated show on the airwaves. Hope continued to be
a rage during the remainder of the war. More people were listening to his show than any other program in January 1945. He
was clearly America's wartime comedian, a humorist whose
machine-gun style of delivery and foxhole humor caught the
spirit of the times.[41]

During the late 1940's his broadcast was always listed among
the top six comedy shows, along with *Fibber McGee and Molly*,
Jack Benny, Red Skelton, Fred Allen, and Bergen and McCarthy.
Nonetheless, by 1947 some radio critics were complaining that
his program was becoming monotonous, and that it was overworking certain routines. In 1948 he tried altering his format in
a new series sponsored by Swan Soap, but despite respectable
ratings the broadcasts never matched the enormous popularity
of the wartime Pepsodent programs. The comedian continued on
radio until 1958, but by that time Hope was personifying the
same smart-aleck wisecracker on television.[42]

14
Running Gags and Talent Raids

Listeners increasingly came to love Jack Benny and his comic Everyman character in the 1940's. His Sunday night program remained an habitual pastime for the entire family. The comedy on the Benny shows derived from the predictability of his radio character. On the Lucky Strike broadcasts Benny basically continued with the same format, using personality related jokes stemming from the comedian's delusions of generosity, violin talent, and perpetual youth. The writers had perfected that comic formula by repeating successful running gags and routines that played on the listeners' expectations. The Benny broadcasts of the 1940's were faster paced and slicker, and the program's style reflected the general nature of radio comedy during the decade.

The scripts were written by four new talented writers, all hired in 1942–43: Sam Perrin, George Balzer, John Tackaberry, and Milt Josefsberg. Each had a special knack for writing comedy. Perrin had been on the staff of *The Phil Baker Show* and was known for his ability to write situation comedy. Balzer, his protégé, had started writing for Bob Burns on the *Kraft Music Hall* and had a talent for screwball humor. The team of Perrin and Balzer had written the Burns and Allen Swan Soap program and *Tommy Riggs and Betty Lou*. John Tackaberry excelled at comic characterizations and feed lines. Milt Josefsberg, a former press agent and public relations man, had started writing gags

314

as a hobby. He had sent some to Walter Winchell, who had published them in his newspaper column. Josefsberg, who had been on Bob Hope's staff for five years, was considered to be one of the most creative young radio comedy writers.[1]

Benny collaborated with his four writers in the preparation of the weekly script. After his broadcast went off the air, the comedian met with them in his dressing room to discuss the next week's show. A tentative story line was suggested, usually some real-life situation featuring Benny at home or in another locale. Such scenes lent a quality of realism to the program and made Benny a believable character. On Monday the comedian and his writers met again to work on ideas for the routines. The comedy part of the program actually took up only one-half of the show. Three minutes were allotted for the opening, middle, and closing commercials and seven minutes to "spread," the time set aside for studio-audience laughter and applause. Dennis Day's song took two and a half minutes; Jack's "tag," or closing remarks, one and a half minutes; and the public announcement and credits one minute. The remaining fourteen and a half minutes were divided into two sections. The "cast spot" consisted of exchanges between Benny and his "gang," and the second spot featured a skit or episode describing Benny in a comic situation. Despite the rigid timing, Benny's broadcast often ran overtime because of unexpected laughter and applause. NBC is supposed to have started using chimes during the station breaks to prevent Benny and other programs from running overtime.[2]

Balzer and Perrin wrote one section and Tackaberry and Josefsberg the other. Every second week they exchanged assignments to avoid monotony and to ensure a fresh approach. The writers met for several script conferences. Early in the week the sessions were relaxed. They would arrive around ten o'clock, talk for an hour, have lunch, take a nap, converse about the script, and leave at 3:30. Later in the week, as Sunday approached and the script was still unfinished, the meeting had a sense of urgency, sometimes panic. By Friday the writers had prepared a draft, which they took to Benny's house. There they worked with the comedian on the script, making cuts and additions.

Benny had an excellent relationship with his staff, and he

often credited his writers in public and on the broadcasts. "No one came between Jack and his writers," Balzer remembered. In the editing sessions the entertainer had only one vote, and, since decisions were made by a majority, he was sometimes overruled. The comedian was an excellent editor of comedy material. He had a sharp ear, and he could measure a joke's effectiveness. "I always knew . . . what I should say or what I shouldn't," Benny remarked. He knew instinctively where to make cuts and to improve the dialogue so that it *sounded* funnier. He compared his role to a newspaper or magazine editor. The comedian, Benny said, "has to assign writers to produce certain material and then he must have enough knowledge to order rewrites and to know what to expand and what to cut. At least sixty percent of a show's effectiveness depends on this."[3]

Benny was a perfectionist in matters pertaining to the preparation of his program. He sometimes would work an entire hour on a single line. A cast reading took place at Benny's home on Saturday morning, when the script was timed. On Sunday another reading and dress rehearsal were held at NBC's Studio B on Sunset and Vine. During these sessions Benny insisted on the correct voice inflection and timing from his cast. He also demanded proper sound effects in the comic routines. The comedian once had the sound engineer rumple a piece of paper nearly forty times to obtain the right sound. Benny's editing ability and high standards were a major reason why his programs in the 1940's represented the apex of radio comedy entertainment.

To attain a continued high level of excellence was not easy. There was always a danger of overworking gags and routines which belittled Benny. Sometimes luck was involved. One of the funniest lines in radio comedy was created by accident at a script session attended by Benny, Milt Josefsberg, John Tackaberry, and Hilliard Marks, the producer. They were writing a scene in which Benny was held up on the street by a robber while carrying Ronald Colman's Academy Award Oscar. The writers were unable to think of a concluding punch line to the following dialogue:

MARR Got a match?
JACK Match? Yes, I have one right here in my—

Jack Benny and his writers in the early 1940's. Left to right: Sam Perrin, Milt Josefsberg, Benny, George Balzer, John Tackaberry.

MARR   *Don't make a move, this is a stickup!*
JACK   *What?*
MARR   *You heard me.*
JACK   Mister . . . Mister, put down that gun.
MARR   *Shut up. . . . Now come on . . . your money or your*
       life . . . (long pause). . . . *Look bud, I said,* "Your
       money or your life."

Josefsberg suggested a number of possible comments Benny
could make. Tackaberry, lounging on a sofa, said nothing, his
face expressionless. Josefsberg angrily turned to his partner and
exclaimed:

> Dammit, if you don't like my lines, throw a couple of
> your own. Don't just lay there on your fat butt day-
> dreaming. There's got to be a great answer to "Your
> money or your life."

Tackaberry, who sat pondering, replied nonchalantly, "I'm
thinking it over." Everyone in the room laughed hysterically.
Benny suddenly realized that his writer had accidentally given
him the right punch line.[4]

"I'm thinking it over" became radio's most publicized and
quoted gag line and was reputed to have received the longest
laugh by a studio audience. The first time Benny used it on his
March 28, 1948, broadcast the laughter was actually not exces-
sive and lasted between six and seven seconds. Benny thought
he could have "milked" the line much longer, but he was afraid
his program was running overtime. Because it was such a perfect character gag that played on Benny's tightwad personality
it was repeated several times on other broadcasts. Benny and his
staff believed that if a joke or routine received a large number of
belly laughs it could be reenacted. If it still retained its "socko"
quality after it was used a number of times on the air, it became
a running gag. Running gags exploited the anticipations of regular listeners, who knew the contents of the routine beforehand
and were almost conditioned to laugh.

One of the funniest running gags evolved from Benny's perpetual lying about his age. A master at self-delusion, Benny pretended to be much younger than he actually was. In the mid-
1940's, Benny claimed to be thirty-six, and he remained at that
age for several years. Then he boasted he was thirty-seven,

thirty-eight, and then thirty-nine. On his annual birthday show on February 13, 1949 (the birthday programs became noted for their jokes about Benny's age), he was supposed to celebrate his fortieth birthday, but he and his writers decided to stop at thirty-nine. It was "a real funny number," Benny recalled. "When you get to be forty, little kids say, 'hey, that's old' . . . we stuck at thirty-nine." Elderly listeners could easily identify with Benny's delusions of eternal youth. He got hundreds of letters urging him never to celebrate his fortieth birthday. Newspaper editorials heralded Benny as a morale booster for the aging. Most broadcasts had a routine making fun of Benny's self-deception:

JACK   Now, Rochester, here's why I called you. . . . I don't know what to do. I thought tomorrow was going to be my fortieth birthday . . . but I just got a wire from my sister and she says I'm going to be thirty-nine.

ROCHESTER   *Well don't argue with her, Boss,* grab it.

JACK   Rochester, I've got to be honest with myself. Now I want you to look at my birth certificate and tell me the date on it.

ROCHESTER   *Your birth certificate?*

JACK   Yes, do you know where it is?

ROCHESTER   *It's right here on the desk.*

JACK   What's my birth certificate doing on the desk?

ROCHESTER   *You got it out the other day when you applied for your old age pension.*

JACK   Oh, I just did that for a gag.

ROCHESTER   *Well, they must be laughing, your first check came today.*

JACK   Rochester, stop making things up. . . . Now look at my birth certificate.

ROCHESTER   *I'm looking at it.*

JACK   Now in the place where it says "Date of Birth" . . . what's there?

ROCHESTER   *A hole.*

JACK   A hole in the paper?

ROCHESTER   *Yeah, we erased it* once too often.

JACK   Oh . . . well, then there's nothing I can do . . . and I'll have to take my sister's word for it.

ROCHESTER   *I guess so, Boss . . . your sister must be right.*

JACK   Yep . . . I'm thirty-nine. . . . Goodbye, Rochester.[5]

Another running gag related to Benny's radio character was the vault routine—a takeoff on the comedian's cheapness. That and two other running gags (the racetrack tout and the railroad-station announcer) were first used on January 7, 1945. Benny stashed his money in a dungeon several hundred feet below his house. A moat, a maze of tunnels, steel doors, and alarms protected the locked vault from robbers. Like Fibber McGee's closet, the vault routine depended on sound effects done by an engineer, Gene Twombly. Considered one of the best sound-effects men, he could simulate any type of footsteps over the air, using a special pair of walking shoes with wooden soles and heels. He stood on a wooden board and moved his feet up and down, adjusting the pace to fit the desired sound. Heavy iron chains draped around a huge metal brace were used to imitate the opening of the creaking steel doors. Attached to the apparatus were various gears that the engineer moved to obtain the correct noise. Listeners heard clicks as Benny rotated the safe's combination lock and then the sound of the comedian turning the handle of the vault. Suddenly a burglar alarm reverberated, steam whistles blew, bells rang, gunshots exploded, and a fog horn went BEEEE OHHHHH. The opening of the vault got a laugh every time it was heard on radio.

The vault was guarded by a character named Ed, played by the veteran radio actor Joe Kearns. "Who goes there, friend or foe?" Ed would ask Benny, in a faint monotone. Ed had been buried beneath Benny's house for so long he was unaware of current events. The dialogue between the guard and Benny was highlighted by jokes based on the watchman's ignorance of the present. When Benny informed the vault keeper that World War II had ended, Ed asked if the North or South had won. Ed had never heard of automobiles and wondered if they frightened buffalo. Benny once offered him a radio to make his time more pleasant while guarding the vault. "A radio?—what's that?" Ed inquired. "Well, send it down. If I like it, I'll eat it." The watchman was also unable to decipher the strange shape on the cover of a calendar Benny gave him:

BENNY   It's a girl.
   ED   Oh. And what's that thing she's holding?
BENNY   Oh, that's a telephone.

ED	Oh. That's a girl and that's a telephone.
BENNY	Yes, it was invented in 1876.
ED	The girl?
BENNY	No, no, no. The telephone.[6]

Another character was the racetrack tout. The role was first played by Benny Rubin, a well-known vaudeville and night-club comic, but later the part was taken by Sheldon Leonard. Using a gangster's accent and speaking in racetrack lingo, Leonard made the tout one of radio comedy's most unforgettable bit characters. The tout encountered Benny at various places and offered him tips on horse races. He appeared whenever Benny was trying to make a practical decision. The comedian, of course, was unaware that he was being given a tip. In this scene the tout met Benny at the railroad station, where the comedian was buying some chewing gum:

SHELDON	Hey bud . . . bud . . .
JACK	Huh?
SHELDON	Come here a minute.
JACK	Who, me?
SHELDON	Yeah.
JACK	Look, fellow—
SHELDON	Where you goin'?
JACK	I'm going to buy some chewing gun.
SHELDON	What kind?
JACK	Spearmint.
SHELDON	Uh uh.
JACK	What?
SHELDON	Get Bubble Gum.
JACK	Bubble Gum? Why?
SHELDON	It's great in the stretch.
JACK	Well, I don't know . . . what about Chiclets?
SHELDON	Chiclets haven't got a chance.
JACK	Why not?
SHELDON	They're boxed in.
JACK	But I like Chiclets.
SHELDON	Now be smart, bub, and take bubble gum . . . just look at the breeding.
JACK	The breeding?
SHELDON	Yeah . . . it's by Penny out of Slot Machine.

JACK   Oh. . . . Well, I don't care about that, I'm going to get Spearmint.

SHELDON   Okay, it's your dough.[7]

One of the most hilarious routines on the Benny show was the railroad-station sketch. The skit was often repeated with the same running gags and bit characters, like the temperamental ticket seller, played by Frank Nelson. The actor's condescending voice was perfect for the easily irritated clerk who liked to insult Benny:

JACK   Oh, pardon me, are you the ticket clerk?

NELSON   Well what do you think I am in this cage, a canary?

JACK   Well don't get huffy about it, all I want is a ticket on the Chief.

NELSON   Oh. . . . Would you like the sixty-dollar ticket or the hundred-and-forty-dollar ticket?

JACK   Well . . . uh . . . what's the difference?

NELSON   With the hundred-and-forty-dollar ticket you ride *inside.*

JACK   *Well naturally I want to ride on the inside. . . . After all, I'm not as young as I used to be.*

NELSON   You're not as young as *anybody* used to be.

JACK   *Now don't get fresh. . . .* All I want is a ticket to New York.

NELSON   Return trip?

JACK   No, one way.

NELSON   *Good!*

JACK   *Now cut that out. . . .*[8]

Nelson played other snobbish characters who heckled Benny, and he became known for the expressions "Yessssss?" and "Ooh, would I!"

The highlight of the sketch was the railroad-station announcer gag: "Train leaving on Track Five. For Anaheim, Azusa, and Cucamonga." It was created by George Balzer and first used on the January 7, 1945, broadcast. Except for local Californians, most Americans had never heard of the three communities. The announcer was played by Mel Blanc, who enunciated the words (including a long pause between Cuc . . . amonga) to make them sound funnier. He got increasingly angry and frustrated as passengers refused to board the train. "Does *anybody* wanna go to Anaheim, Azusa, or Cucamonga?" the announcer pleaded. "Aw, come on . . . somebody must wanna go to Anaheim, Azusa, or Cucamonga!" A minute later he sobbed: "Look, we're not asking much . . . two of you . . . or even one of you . . . just somebody to keep the engineer company." Finally he screamed:

> Look, look . . . there are five thousand people in this station. . . . Isn't there somebody . . . *Anybody* . . . Are there volunteers? . . . Please, please, please. . . . I got a job to do. . . . I'll get fired if I don't get *somebody* on the train for Anaheim, Azusa, and Cucamonga!

Blanc was in tears as he delivered the last announcement: "Train leaving on Track Five. . . . For Anaheim, Azusa, and Cucamonga has just been canceled." Regularly used over the years with variations, the public address system routine was a tremendously effective running gag.[9]

A talented voice imitator, Blanc contributed enormously to the success of the Benny show. He had started mimicking foreign dialects as a young boy in Portland, Oregon, where he imitated the accent of a Jewish couple who owned a neighborhood grocery store and learned to speak pidgin English from an Oriental produce clerk. On Portland station KGW Blanc and his brother Henry had starred in *The Hoot Owls*, a musical program featuring Mel playing the violin and his brother at the piano. In 1933 the twenty-five-year-old Blanc had his own local program, and two years later he moved to Hollywood, where he was heard on station KFWB. He was hired to do the voice of Joe Penner's duck on network radio, and his talent for imitating animals led to a contract in 1937 with Warner Brothers' Looney Tunes. He eventually became well known as the voice of Bugs Bunny, Daffy Duck, Porky Pig, and Tweety Pie.[10]

Blanc's success in cartoons brought him to the attention of Benny, who hired him in 1939 to do the growls of Carmichael, the polar bear which guarded the comedian's money and ate any intruder. Blanc later imitated a variety of animal sounds on the Benny broadcasts, including a mouse and the funny parrot,

Polly, which repeated gags. As a practical joke the writers wrote a script in which Blanc had to whinny like an English horse. They believed he could not imitate the sound, but Blanc's interpretation was so convincing in rehearsal that it was left in the broadcast.[11]

Blanc also did such sound effects as the noise of Benny's Maxwell. During a rehearsal he noticed that the sound-effects man did not have the equipment to play a phonograph record of an automobile motor. Blanc volunteered to do an imitation of Benny's old car coughing and sputtering. His rendition was so funny it became a regular feature. Benny's Maxwell was really not an expensive antique automobile, but a dilapidated car that was difficult to start and traveled at slow speeds. Like the vault, the Maxwell sketch accented Benny's cheapskate radio character.

> JACK   Now come on, Rochester, we've gotta get to the studio. . . . I don't want to be late.
>
> ROCHESTER   *Yes sir. . . . I'll start the car.*
> *(Sound: Starter . . . lousy motor goes through full routine . . . aided and abetted by that talented youngster Mel Blanc . . . and winds up with duck call, as it finally dies.)*
>
> JACK   Hmm, did the motor die again?
>
> ROCHESTER   *It died twenty years ago, you just won't bury it.*
>
> JACK   Well . . . I have been thinking of getting a new car . . . but I don't know what kind I'd like.
>
> ROCHESTER   *Why don't you get one of those new Hudsons. . . . They're so streamlined . . . honestly Boss . . . they're so low you step down into them.*
>
> JACK   Well, you step down into this car.
>
> ROCHESTER   *I know, but the Hudson has a floor.*[12]

After appearing on the broadcasts for approximately six months, Blanc told the comedian he could also do character roles. Over the years the actor played a baseball announcer ("Greenberg's on third") and a racetrack announcer who made funny comments. He also impersonated Professor André Le Blanc, Benny's French violin teacher, who spoke in a heavy Parisian accent. Le Blanc's disgust at the comedian's violin playing always received many laughs. The frustrated professor sang little ditties to Benny's finger exercises:

> Watch the notes that you are striking,
> Bend your thumb, you're not hitch-hiking.
>
> Mr. Benny, when you're playing,
> You sound like a jackass braying.

The routine between Le Blanc, who considered his pupil inept, and Benny, who considered himself a virtuoso, was sure-fire comedy:

JACK   Tell me . . . do you think you can make a great violinist out of me?

MEL   Well . . . I think I can do something for you . . . but it will take time. . . . How old are you?

JACK   Why?

MEL   *How much time have we got left?*

JACK   Now wait a minute, Professor. . . . I know you're a great teacher, but if you don't like the way I play the violin, why did you take the job?

MEL   I'm working for that Yankee dollah! . . . Twenty-four years and all he knows is (SINGS) da da da da da da da da da da da da da da da. . . . If I wasn't so hungry I wouldn't come back.[13]

Blanc also portrayed a Mexican character who gave curt replies to Benny's questions:

JACK   Excuse me . . . are you El Supremo's Prime Minister?

MEL   Si.

JACK   I understand that he holds his prisoners for ransom.

MEL   Si.

JACK   And the ransom is a thousand bushels of beans.

MEL   Si.

JACK   What kind of beans?

MEL   Soy.

JACK   Soy?

MEL   Si.

JACK   Where?

MEL   A few minutes ago I was the French Captain.

JACK   The French Captain?

MEL   Oui.

JACK   Oui?

MEL   Si.

In written form the dialogue is not very amusing because the sketch largely depended on Blanc's accent, timing, and repetition of "Si." On the Judy Canova show Blanc played Pedro, the Mexican, a similar character who made silly statements such as, "Pardon me for talking in your face, senorita." During the 1940's, his caricatures based on the lazy, ill-mannered, and ignorant Mexican got many laughs, but they do not hold up well today because of the racial stereotyping. Although he did not consciously mean to offend anyone, those roles are the least admirable of his imitations.[14]

Blanc starred in his own Tuesday night situation comedy program in 1946 on CBS, playing the bungling owner of a fix-it shop. He was supported by an excellent cast that included Hans Conried, Joe Kearns, Alan Reed, Jim Backus, Mary Jane Croft, and Bea Benaderet. Although some broadcasts were very funny, the programs were not consistently amusing, so the series lasted only one season.

Another talented actor on the Benny show was Artie Auerbach, a former newspaper photographer, who played Mr. Kitzel, a Jewish dialect character. Jewish comical figures largely disappeared from radio and other forms of popular culture during the war years because of the sensitivity to anti-Semitism. For example, comedian Lou Holtz, who told Jewish dialect story jokes, had a difficult time getting radio work at that time. Schlepperman was dropped as a character on the Benny show in the late 1930's. Kitzel first appeared on the January 6, 1946, program a few months after the end of World War II. The character was modeled on a singing hot dog vendor John Tackaberry had heard selling frankfurters at a sporting event in Houston. Kitzel had sold hot dogs to a tune that became a popular hit record:

> Pickle in the middle
> And the mustard on top,
> Just the way you like 'em
> And they're all red hot. . . .

"Why do you sell 'em [hot dogs] so cheap?" Benny asked. "They do look like pretty tough weenies." "Tough! . . . Two of 'em are playing in the Alabama backfield," Kitzel replied. Benny encountered Kitzel in various places, and the two always had a hilarious conversation. Auerbach got laughs by mispronouncing words and giving well-known personalities Jewish names such as Ed Solomon (Sullivan) and Nat King Cohen (Cole).[15]

Two other popular characters were the loquacious switchboard telephone operators Mabel Flapsaddle and Gertrude Gearshift, played by Bea Benaderet and Sara Berner. Benny would place a telephone call, and the program would switch to them for a few minutes. They had funny voices and became noted for their put-down wisecracks about Benny's personality and looks. "Say, Gertrude, I wonder what Mr. Benny puts on his lips," Mabel asked her friend. "I went out with him once . . . kissed him goodnight and couldn't open my mouth for three days." Other supporting actors and actresses included Sandra Gould, Benny Rubin, Veola Vonn, Elliot Lewis, and Verna Felton. The bit characters helped make the Benny show an entertaining program.[16]

The most amusing guest stars on the show were Ronald Colman and his wife, Benita Hume. The couple were actually regulars because they appeared so frequently on the program between December 1945 and 1949. The Colmans played Benny's haughty and sophisticated next-door neighbors—social snobs who snubbed the comedian. A serious British dramatic actor with a flair for comedy, the witty Colman received many laughs when he jested about Benny's uncouth manners and stinginess. The skinflint comedian regularly borrowed their possessions and sometimes he came as an uninvited guest to the couple's elegant parties. Their futile attempts to tactfully tell Benny to leave were hilarious. Imitating a scene in a Ronald Colman movie, Benny once threw an antique glass into the Colmans' fireplace. The Colmans' running feud with the comedian was one of the show's comic highlights in the late 1940's. The couple later starred in their own radio series, *The Halls of Ivy* (1950–52), an excellent situation comedy in which Ronald Colman played a college president.

When Kenny Baker left the Benny show in June 1939 to join the Fred Allen program, the staff began listening to audition records for a new singer. An unknown young Bronx Irish tenor named Owen P. "Eugene" McNulty, who had done local New York radio shows, especially appealed to Mary Benny. At the audition at NBC in New York, he sang for about twenty minutes. During the break Benny asked him a question, and he responded naïvely, "Yes, please." Benny later told him the remark clinched the job, although the young singer still had to go through the ordeal of a few more auditions before he finally convinced the staff of his comic and singing talent. McNulty joined Benny's "gang" on October 8, 1939, using the name Dennis Day. His routine at first primarily revolved around his protective mother (Verna Felton), who disliked Benny and defended her "little boy."[17]

Day eventually settled into the role of a silly, naïve kid who made ridiculous statements that drove Benny crazy:

DENNIS   Will it be all right if I miss rehearsal next Saturday?
JACK   I guess so. . . . Why?
DENNIS   I'm gonna commit suicide.
JACK   . . . Suicide?
DENNIS   I may miss the broadcast, too.
JACK   Dennis. . . . Dennis, look at me.
DENNIS   Huh?
JACK   Dennis. . . . How could you get such a crazy idea like —I mean, why would you want to commit suicide?
DENNIS   My girl friend told me she was through with me.
JACK   Oh . . . well, maybe she was just teasing you.
DENNIS   No, she meant it all right. . . . She returned my engagement ring, my fraternity pin, and my skate key.
JACK   Your *skate key?*
DENNIS   We've been going together for a long time.
JACK   Dennis—
DENNIS   Goodbye, Mr. Benny, it's been nice knowing you.
JACK   *Dennis, come back here.*
DENNIS   Huh?
JACK   That's enough of that silly talk . . . and you're not going to commit suicide.
DENNIS   I'm not?
JACK   Certainly not. You and your girl just had a little quarrel . . . you'll probably make up with her.
DENNIS   Yeah . . . I guess you're right. . . . Can I use your phone?
JACK   Sure. . . . Are you going to call your girl?
DENNIS   No, Forest Lawn, I want to cancel my reservation.[18]

Day got laughs about his meager salary ($35 a week) and his contract, which required him to mow Benny's lawn. He was also a talented mimic who did an excellent imitation of an old man and clever impersonations of Ronald Colman and Jerry Colonna.

Because of his success Day became a popular singer with a national reputation, which led in 1946 to his own NBC situation comedy, *A Day In The Life Of Dennis Day*. The singer-comedian played an underpaid, bungling soda jerk who worked at Willoughby's store in Weaverville. The comedy derived from Day's screwball antics and relationships with the harassed store owner (John Brown) and Day's girl friend, Mildred Anderson (Barbara Eiler). Two other characters were Mildred's domineering mother (Bea Benaderet) and henpecked father (Francis "Dink" Trout). The series offered listeners solid, fast-paced entertainment until 1951.[19]

Another spin-off from the Benny broadcast was *The Phil Harris–Alice Faye Show*. The bandleader and his wife, the actress-singer Alice Faye, moved to their own situation comedy program on *The Fitch Bandwagon* in September 1946. The program followed Benny's broadcast and often began with Harris leaving the comedian's weekly program. In the domestic situation comedy Harris played the same brash character he portrayed on the Benny show. The plot concerned his daily life with his wife, who had forsaken a movie career to raise two young daughters. The *Phil Harris–Alice Faye Show*, as it was called in 1948, also featured some excellent comedy character acting. Frank Remley, Harris's guitar player, was written into the script and played by Elliott Lewis. Remley, a trouble-maker, always got Harris into difficult situations. Julius, the grocery delivery boy (Walter Tetley), also loved to play tricks on Harris. Tetley made the Brooklyn-accented Julius one of radio's most unforgettable kids. The actor, who also played Leroy on *The Great Gildersleeve*, had a naturally high soprano voice and was an excellent child impersonator. Another fine performance was given by Gale Gordon: he played Mr. Scott, executive of the Rexall Drug Company (the show's sponsor). The writers, Ray Singer and Dick Chevillat, created some hilarious situation comedy. Because of the high quality of its scripts and acting, the series remained on the air until 1954.[20]

The Benny show was a commercial success under the sponsorship of the American Tobacco Company from 1944 to 1954. Cleverly integrated Lucky Strike commercials on the high audience-rated program boosted sales of the cigarette. The Sportsmen Quartet sang jingles about the cigarette's taste, and the tobacco auctioneer's "Sold American" became another successful sales gimmick. Another advertising device was the catchy slogan "L.S. M.F.T. L.S.M.F.T. Lucky Strike means fine tobacco"—delivered to the click of a telegraph key. The series created a strong association between the comedian and Lucky Strike, even though Benny never smoked cigarettes.

Benny was actually unhappy with his financial earnings from the Lucky Strike program because his salary was heavily taxed under the new income tax rates established after World War II. After earning over $70,000 a year, a taxpayer had to give the United States Treasury 91¢ of every dollar he earned. A star radio comedian was considered fortunate if he netted $40,000 after taxes. During the 1946–47 radio season Benny averaged approximately $2000 per show after paying the salaries of the performers, writers, and other staff. In 1947, in order to receive a higher percentage of earnings, he formed Amusement Enterprises, a corporation in which he controlled the majority of the stock. The production company produced the Benny broadcasts, the Jack Paar radio program (Benny's summer replacement), and films.[21]

In late 1948 Benny sold Amusement Enterprises to CBS in the most publicized capital gains deal in the "talent raids." Radio had become progressively more competitive in the late 1940's when the three major networks—NBC, CBS, and ABC—avidly competed for listeners. Although noted for the high quality of its news and drama programs, CBS had never been able to match NBC's comedy lineup. Unable to develop a strong list of comedy stars on its own, CBS decided to lure talent away from NBC by offering lucrative capital gains deals to the comedians. Business corporations had been reaping profits from capital gains sales for years, but the device had not been used by show business entertainers. Howard Meighan, a CBS executive, initiated the idea of radio stars forming properties from the assets of their programs and selling them to the network. The large profit would be taxed at a lower capital gains rate. In September 1948 CBS paid Gosden and Correll approximately $2,500,000 for the rights to *Amos 'n' Andy*. The two comedians consequently jumped to CBS, which received exclusive ownership rights to the program for twenty years. Gosden and Correll were also paid enormous annual salaries by the network.[22]

CBS was also anxious to obtain Jack Benny, who, with Bob Hope, was considered to be the most popular radio comedian of the 1940's. Benny had been with NBC for sixteen years and was loyal to the network, but he found the corporation impersonal in its handling of entertainers. He had never even met David Sarnoff, president of RCA, the parent company of NBC. Although some NBC executives favored offering capital gains deals similar to those of CBS, the dictatorial Sarnoff opposed them because he was against stars gaining such a powerful financial position in the industry. Benny's agency, the Music Corporation of America (MCA), did offer to sell Amusement Enterprises to NBC, but the network's officials refused the offer because they felt they would be buying a property whose major asset, *The Jack Benny Show*, they already had on the air. When MCA approached CBS, which had made earlier overtures to purchase the company, NBC decided to negotiate.

Benny was furious when he learned that one of the network's negotiators was John T. Cahill, the former United States District Attorney who had prosecuted the government's case against Benny and George Burns for smuggling in 1939. Benny had naïvely given Albert Chapereau, a professional confidence man, some jewelry in Europe to bring tax-free into the country. The court fined Benny, and he had to pay extra duty on the jewels. The entertainer felt that Cahill had "persecuted" him in the courtroom by his discourteous remarks and by making him stand up while the charges were read. Whether or not Cahill had informed NBC of his role in the smuggling case is still unknown. Nonetheless, the network made a strategic mistake in hiring the former District Attorney. The incident confirmed Benny's belief that NBC was insensitive to the needs of its stars, so he called off the negotiations.

Agreement with CBS was reached in a friendly telephone call between Benny and CBS President William Paley. The latter told Benny that radio entertainers were the key to his network's success and that he would be proud to have him. Paley's more tolerant attitude toward the star system and his manner of carrying on personal relations impressed the comedian. CBS offered to buy Amusement Enterprises for approximately $2,400,000, and so a capital gains deal was made.

Benny's financial problems were far from over. The Internal Revenue Service sued the comedian on the grounds that his corporation was a *personal* holding company and that profits on the sale to CBS should be taxed as earned income. The case went to the Supreme Court, where Benny's lawyers argued that entertainers, like businessmen, had the right to create corporations and sell them as capital gains. The comedian won the case, and the decision had a major influence on the radio, television, and film industry. Thereafter, performers could make large profits by creating companies that controlled production of their own films and programs.[23]

Despite the loss of Benny, NBC still did not change its official position on capital gains deals. Niles Trammell, president of NBC, stated that his network would "continue to refuse to purchase stock in so-called production corporations where the artists who control such corporations are performing on the NBC network." The network charged that such agreements discriminated between entertainers who paid higher personal income taxes and those who paid lower capital gains taxes. CBS defended its actions: "Mr. Trammell's statement is unwarranted and reflects unfairly on many creative artists who have done no more than abide by our tax laws like any businessman or corporation." Burns and Allen, Red Skelton, and Edgar Bergen were subsequently lured to CBS by capital gains deals. Except for Bob Hope and Fred Allen, who received salary increases, NBC lost most of its comedy stars. The talent raids virtually destroyed NBC's position as the leading network in comedy entertainment. Believing that he could make up for those losses by creating new programs,

Sarnoff stated at a stockholders' meeting: "Leadership built over the years on a foundation of solid service cannot be snatched overnight by buying a few high-priced comedians. Leadership is not a laughing matter." One NBC official later remarked privately that the "talent raids" were a major defeat for Sarnoff and the network:

> The General, I think, got himself involved emotionally in what was a problem in cold business. He resented the attitude of the performers whom, after all, we had helped build up into stars. He felt, I think, that they were being "disloyal," and that kind of thing. Some of us thought of talent as a marketable commodity, that's all. In the final analysis we have had to accept the star system and live with it anyhow.

The talent raids illustrated the overwhelming commercialism of radio comedy in the 1940's. Programs produced to appeal to as many listeners as possible were up for sale to the highest bidder. This process had begun in the early 1930's, but by the 1940's broadcasting had become completely dominated by commercial considerations.[24]

Although the move to CBS was an emotional one for Benny, the comedian and Rochester joked about the network change on his last NBC broadcast:

ROCHESTER   *I forgot to tell you. . . . There was quite a bit of excitement today. . . . An airplane flew over Hollywood and started skywriting.*
JACK   Skywriting? What did they write?
ROCHESTER   *Next week Jack Benny's program moves to.*
JACK   Moves to where, moves to where?
ROCHESTER   *I don't know, NBC's anti-aircraft shot him down.*

"I want to take this opportunity of thanking everyone connected with N.B.C. for a very pleasant association," Benny stated at the program's conclusion.[25]

CBS had gambled that Benny would continue to be a success on their network. In the agreement the network promised for the first eight weeks to pay the American Tobacco Company $3000 for every point Benny's rating fell below his closing figure on

NBC. In order to garner a large audience CBS staged a large publicity campaign and Benny did guest appearances on network programs. Although NBC offered the very popular Horace Heidt amateur talent program opposite Benny, the comedian's first show received a 27.8 Hooper rating—over three points higher than his closing figure on NBC. Benny's premiere on CBS depicted the comedian and Rochester driving in the Maxwell to CBS and trying to get free parking at the studio. The show got Benny's association with CBS off to a good start, and the network never did pay the American Tobacco Company a cent. Benny remained on CBS radio until May 22, 1955, when he did his last regularly scheduled broadcast. By that time his fans were watching him do his running gags on television.[26]

15

Allen's Alley

One of the funniest shows on radio in the 1940's was *Allen's Alley*, which premiered on Sunday, December 6, 1942. After eight years on the air Wednesday night, Allen had switched to a Sunday night time slot, on March 8, 1942. Listeners could then hear Jack Benny (7 p.m.), Bergen and McCarthy (8 p.m.), and Fred Allen (8:30 p.m.), three of the top comedy shows, on the same night. Listening to all those broadcasts became a Sunday evening pastime for families. Allen's last one-hour program was aired on June 28, 1942, and that fall he began broadcasting a thirty-minute show.

The half-hour comedy show was a standard time length in the 1940's. Benny had proved that a thirty-minute comedy program could be as entertaining as a one-hour variety show. Costs of broadcasting time had risen over the years, so that sponsors were paying enormous prices for prime time in the evening hours. The expenses involved in solely sponsoring an hour-long program were prohibitive. Companies could cut costs by concentrating on hard-sell advertising during half an hour. Shorter programs also allowed the network to sell more time to more customers. Many hour-long programs were cut in half in the 1940's and some thirty-minute programs shortened to fifteen minutes.[1]

Allen had found writing a one-hour show exhausting work, and so preferred the shorter format. Unlike the loose-structured hour-long *Town Hall Tonight*, the new thirty-minute show had to be tightly knit. "The relaxed type of dialogue of the longer routines had to be replaced by brisk, staccato lines," Allen recalled. "For the first few programs I felt like a man who for years had been writing on the *Encyclopaedia Britannica* and suddenly started to write for *Reader's Digest*." Allen still wrote the script in longhand in a small room in his Manhattan apartment, and was assisted by several new writers, including Nat Hiken and Larry Marks. After an informal script reading Allen conferred with his cast, writers, and director for general editing. They rehearsed the program several times on Sunday and made more changes before the evening's broadcast. The new show contained two major comedy sections: first, Portland's spot and the *Allen's Alley* section, and second, dialogue and a sketch with a guest star. Music by Al Goodman and the De Marco Sisters completed the program. Compared to *Town Hall Tonight*, the comedy dialogue on *Allen's Alley* was snappy and reflected the faster pace of radio comedy in the 1940's.[2]

Allen's Alley partly grew out of comic interviews the comedian had conducted on "Town Hall News." On *The Texaco Star Theatre* (1941–42) Allen had also broadcast a spot called "The March of Trivia," a parody on the newsreel *The March of Time*. The comedian had interviewed various characters about their reaction to the "weekly lowlight from the world of news." In December 1942 he decided to focus the comedy news around a central locale, a street inhabited by bizarre characters. The comedian was influenced by journalist O. O. McIntyre, who wrote a popular column called "Thoughts While Strolling." The newspaperman concocted stories about people he met on the streets of New York's Chinatown and Bowery. "I felt that something of this type which would permit me to stroll through a nondescript neighborhood and discuss current events with its denizens would be very amusing," Allen wrote. "I knew that with music and sound effects we could establish the locale and that it would come off well in radio."[3]

Unlike *Town Hall Tonight*, *Allen's Alley* featured a permanent cast of character actors and actresses playing the same role every week. The comedian had previously created hundreds of different minor characters for the news sketches, and the parts were performed by a versatile cast whose names were never mentioned on the air. Allen had enjoyed creating these new comedy roles every week, for he felt listeners easily tired of hearing the same characters. During the 1941–42 season there were signs that Allen's format was not attracting as many listeners. His program had been declining in listener appeal since 1939, and in January 1942 his Hooper rating slipped to 14. The entertainer realized that he had to change the show's structure. "I also knew that we had been on a long time and I suspected that anonymity could be monotonous, too," he stated. "It might be a novelty for the audience if we developed several characters they could associate with our show." One key to longevity on radio was creating a regular cast of characters around the comedian—funny and familiar personalities that got as many laughs as the comic. Listeners looked forward to hearing them every week. One month after *Allen's Alley* went on the air his Hooper rating had escalated to 21.6.[4]

Allen mainly played a stooge on this section of the program. He would knock on the door of the houses in the Alley and ask questions on a particular topic. "Whenever I want to know how America is reacting to an important issue of the day, I just drop around to Allen's Alley," the comedian remarked on the premiere.[5] The humor on *Allen's Alley* emanated from the exaggerated personalities of the characters and their unpredictable responses to Allen's questions.

The comedian initially used actors who had already performed roles on his broadcasts. Alan Reed played the pompous poet Falstaff Openshaw, a ham actor who recited rhyming lyrics. The name Falstaff came from Shakespeare's comic character, while Openshaw was the last name of a person Allen knew. Shakespeare couldn't sue us," Allen said. "Mr. Openshaw didn't. It was a happy arrangement." Reed was an experienced radio actor before he joined Allen's program. During his teens he had started acting on the legitimate stage, and in 1927 he began to play dramatic parts in radio plays using his real name, Teddy Bergman. His acting soon led him to roles on comedy shows playing straight men and imitating foreign dialects. Sometimes he performed in nearly thirty-five shows a week. On *The Eddie Cantor Show* the actor did the voice of the violinist Dave Rubinoff, who suffered from mike fright. Cantor bet Rubinoff $100 he could not say one word over the air. The singer lost the wager when the violinist gingerly approached the microphone during one broadcast and said "Eddie Cantor, you owe me a $100." A versatile radio character actor, Reed also played Joe Palooka, Daddy Higgins in the *Baby Snooks* skits, Pasquale in *Life with Luigi*, and Solomon Levy in *Abie's Irish Rose*. He later did the voice of Fred Flintstone, the cartoon character, on television.[6]

On *Allen's Alley* Reed wrote his own dialogue and composed couplets that brought gales of laughter. "Are those new poems you have there?" Allen asked Falstaff.

REED Yea, old Saggy-Eyes. Have you heard. The F.B.I. Just Caught a Traitor. He Was Putting Bananas In the Refrigerator.

ALLEN No.

REED Mr. Churchill Lisped As He Came To Town. His London Bridge Was Falling Down.

ALLEN No.

REED Or perhaps—Every Time My Mother Hears Perry Como. She Has To Lie Down And Send Out For A Bromo.

Reed's routine included a verse on the evening topic. On one broadcast Allen asked the Alley characters their opinion of the 1946 steel strike. Openshaw read his poem "A Miracle Happened in Pittsburgh."

A miracle happened in Pittsburgh
That, with ancient miracles ranked
When each steel plant closed its blast furnace
And each roaring fire was banked
. . .
The terrified citizens stampeded
And abandoned their homes on the run
For the first time since the city was founded
Pittsburgh had seen the sun!

The pompous manner in which Reed delivered his lines was as amusing as the poems. Once, when his voice became hoarse during a show, he quickly ad-libbed: "Pardon friends, a discordant note / Falstaff found a frog in throat."[7]

Other characters on the early *Allen's Alley* broadcasts included John Doe, Socrates Mulligan, and Senator Bloat. John Doe, the average American, was played by John Brown, who had been doing roles on Allen's programs for many years. "If horse meat catches on, do you think it will have any effect on the country?" the comedian asked Doe. "Well, eating horses will put a lot of bookmakers outta work," Doe replied. "It'll make a pedestrian outta Gene Autry [and] the Horse Show this year might win the Good Housekeeping Seal of Approval." A gifted actor, Brown later played Digger O'Dell, the friendly undertaker, on *The Life of Riley*. Socrates Mulligan, the ignoramus, was enacted by Charlie Cantor, who had earlier played roles on *Town Hall Tonight*. Socrates Mulligan's favorite words were "Duh-yeah?" His "report card showed that he flunked in recess and got a D in lunch." Senator Bloat, played by Jack Smart during 1943–44, was a conceited politician, a forerunner of Senator Claghorn. But these and other characters were not funny enough to be used over a long period. In 1945 Mrs. Nussbaum, Senator Beauregard Claghorn, Ajax Cassidy, and Titus Moody became the four major characters used consistently on the program. Each represented different ethnic and regional types in America. The performers who enacted these roles made *Allen's Alley* a comedy classic.[8]

Minerva Pious played Pansy Nussbaum during the entire time *Allen's Alley* was on the air. The daughter of a wholesale candy merchant, Pious had emigrated from Russia as a young girl and had grown up in Bridgeport, Connecticut, and New York City. Harry Tugend, a singer, once auditioned for Allen and asked Pious, a personal friend and an accomplished pianist, to accompany him. When Tugend informed Allen that Pious did dialect characterizations, the comedian asked her to perform a routine. The radio star liked her rendition so much that he asked her to join his program. She played Jewish immigrant types and other characters on *Town Hall Tonight*.[9]

Her portrayal of the busy Jewish housewife, Mrs. Nussbaum, who spoke with an exaggerated Bronx accent, highlighted *Allen's Alley*. Her dialogue overflowed with malapropisms and other funny speech patterns. "Ah, Mrs. Nussbaum," Allen greeted when she opened her door. "You are expecting maybe Ingrown Bergman?" or "You are expecting maybe Tokio Rose?" Mrs. Nussbaum might reply. She called crepe suzettes "Kreplach Suzette" and pronounced Mississippi "Matzos-Zippi" and Massachusetts "Matzos-chusetts." She liked such food as "herring du jour, chopped liver cacciatore, [and] pot roast à la king." Mrs. Nussbaum talked constantly about her French husband, Pierre. When Allen asked her about the housing shortage Mrs. Nussbaum replied that so many relatives had moved into her house her husband had left. "For two weeks I am a widow," she declared. One night Pierre knocked at her door anxious to return. "Ah, it was true love," said Allen, "Pierre couldn't live without you." "Love—Schmove, Pierre couldn't find a room," exclaimed Mrs. Nussbaum. Although she was an exaggerated comic caricature of a Jewish housewife, Mrs. Nussbaum rarely, if ever, offended listeners.[10]

The second permanent character on *Allen's Alley* was the Southern politician, Senator Beauregard Claghorn, played by Kenny Delmar, the program's announcer. Delmar modeled Claghorn on a jovial Texas rancher he had met. Minerva Pious told Allen about Delmar's impersonation. The announcer made the boasting, boisterous Senator one of the most memorable characters in radio comedy.[11]

Senator Claghorn was a parody on Southern pride and romanticism. After Allen knocked on his door, listeners waited for the Senator to brag about the South: "Somebody—say—somebody knocked. . . . Ah'm from the South. The Sunny South. The garden spot of all creation." A series of staccato one-liners about his love for the South and hatred of the North highlighted his routine. "I represent the South. I'm from Dixie. . . . I don't see a movie unless the star is Ann Sothern. . . . On the radio I never listen to Mr. and Mrs. North." Allen once commented that the Senator looked pale. "Ah've been in the house the last two days," Claghorn said. "Ah refuse to come out. The wind was blowin' from the North." Allen rarely finished a sentence without the garrulous Senator interrupting to boast about the South:

KENNY   Somebody—I say, somebody knocked.
ALLEN   Yes, I—

KENNY   Claghorn's the name—Senator Claghorn, that is.

ALLEN   I know. Don't give me that routine about Dixie.

KENNY   I won't go into a room unless it's got Southern exposure.

ALLEN   Well—

KENNY   The only train I ride is the Chattanooga Choo-Choo.

ALLEN   Just a—

KENNY   (SING) The sun shines bright in my old Kentucky home.—

ALLEN   Now wait—

KENNY   I'm singin' "My Old Kentucky Home," Son.

ALLEN   I know—

KENNY   Son, bend down, and kiss my Jefferson Davis button.[12]

The character was also used to lampoon government bureaucracy and corruption:

ALLEN   Well, Senator, about our question. Do you think advertising has any effect on our manners and customs?

KENNY   Ah don't trust advertisin', Son. Especially them ads politicians put in the papers around election time.

ALLEN   Uh-huh.

KENNY   Ah saw an ad last election, it said—Elect this honest fearless, hardworkin' enemy of graft and corruption. I busted out laughin'.

ALLEN   Who was the candidate?

KENNY   Me! So long, Son! So long, that is![13]

Senator Claghorn talked so fast that Allen often missed his jokes. "That's a joke, son," Claghorn would remind the comedian.

ALLEN   What about this telegraph strike?

KENNY   I brought the subject up in Congress. There was a speech by Senator Ball bearing on it.

ALLEN   Then—

KENNY   Ball bearing! That's a joke, Son!

ALLEN   I know—

KENNY   That was a Louisville Lalapaluza!

ALLEN   I—

KENNY   That was a San Antonio Super-duper. . . .[14]

Delmar's impersonation became an overnight sensation. Fans mimicked his voice and bought Claghorn shirts and compasses that always pointed South. Streets in Southern cities were named after the character. "That's a joke, son" became a popular saying

across the country and was the title of a record and a movie starring Delmar.

The third regular character on *Allen's Alley* was Ajax Cassidy,
a temperamental Irishman played by Peter Donald. Donald was
hired to act the part when Alan Reed left the program. An expert
dialectician, Donald was especially adept at doing an Irish
brogue. Irish-Americans had been the subject of American stage
comedy since the nineteenth century and had often been depicted
as indolent, quarrelsome drunkards. Ajax was also characterized
as a heavy drinker:

ALLEN   Ajax, I heard you were sick.
PETE   I was at death's door. Luckily I didn't have strength
         enough to knock.
ALLEN   You were bad, eh?
PETE   The doctor gave me a big bottle of Corduroy pills.
ALLEN   Uh-huh.
PETE   After every meal the doctor said to swallow one pill and
         drink a small glass of whiskey.
ALLEN   Swallow one pill and drink a small glass of whiskey.
PETE   After every meal.
ALLEN   How is the treatment coming along?
PETE   I'm a little behind with the pills.[15]

While Southern jokes marked Senator Claghorn's routine and
Jewish jokes Mrs. Nussbaum's repertoire, Irish jokes abounded
in Ajax Cassidy's dialogue:

ALLEN   What is tomorrow?
PETE   What is tomorrow? You heathen infidel—It's St. Pat-
         rick's Day.
ALLEN   Oh. Are you going to be in the parade?
PETE   In the parade, says he. I'm leadin' the parade.
ALLEN   Really?
PETE   Wearin' me emerald green silk hat, me flowin' green
         cape, me pea green sneakers and carryin' a gold harp
         seven feet high. . . .

Ajax became noted for his catchy opening line: "W-e-e-l-l-l,
how do ye do?" An Irish-American himself, Allen especially en-

joyed Donald's impersonation, and so did most listeners. He was puzzled when a small minority of Irishmen threatened "to march an entire chapter of the Ancient Order of Hibernians down from Albany, or some upstate New York community, to Radio City if Ajax was not evicted from the Alley and chased from the industry."[16]

The old New England hayseed, Titus Moody, played by Parker Fennelly, was the last of the regional-ethnic types who inhabited *Allen's Alley*. Like the Irishman, the Yankee country bumpkin was a venerable comic stage character; he had appeared as early as 1787 in Royall Tyler's *The Contrast*. Fennelly had impersonated New England rural characters in early radio in *The Stebbin Boys* and *Snow Village Sketches*. Known for his witty turn of phrase and tall tales, farmer Moody talked like The Old Timer on *Fibber McGee and Molly*. He would greet Allen with "howdy, bub." Cornball humor marked Fennelly's routine:

PARKER   Farms don't need men no more—machines does all the work.

ALLEN   Machinery, eh?

PARKER   'Bout all a man can do with his hands on a farm today—is scratch himself.

ALLEN   Do you use machinery?

PARKER   I bought a big machine—'twas called the Jumbo Hired Man.

ALLEN   It did all the work?

PARKER   It had four iron hands on it—for milkin' cows.

ALLEN   I see.

PARKER   It had a suction thing—for pickin' eggs up outta nests.

ALLEN   Uh-huh.

PARKER   It had two big arms—for thrashin' wheat.

ALLEN   Yes.

PARKER   On the side it had two big clippers—for clippin' sheep.

ALLEN   How is the Jumbo Hired Man working out?

PARKER   Fust day I turned it on everything went wrong.

ALLEN   The milking hands?

PARKER   The four hands started pickin' up eggs and puttin' 'em into the cows.

ALLEN   No kidding.

PARKER   The suction thing started trying to milk the chickens.

ALLEN   Gosh!
PARKER   The two big thrashin' arms started beating the cookies
          outta me.
ALLEN   Jeepers!
PARKER   The two big sheep clippers clipped off my wife's hair.
ALLEN   Your wife was completely bald?
PARKER   She left town with an eagle.
ALLEN   Are you still using the Jumbo Hired Man?
PARKER   No I threw out the cow, the chickens and the whole
          contraption.
ALLEN   I see.
PARKER   I bought an adding machine.
ALLEN   What can you raise on your farm with an adding
          machine?
PARKER   Rabbits. So long, Bub![17]

Titus Moody and the other regular characters on *Allen's Alley*
were like Benny's "gang." Listeners became familiar with their
voices and comic routines. Those four inhabitants of *Allen's
Alley* were masterpieces of radio character comedy.

A Fred Allen program in the 1940's also featured guest celebrities. "To try to insure [*sic*] each guest a successful appearance
we created jokes and situations to fit his individual talents,"
Allen recalled. The comedian also liked to use guests in entertaining ways. Baseball manager Leo Durocher acted in a takeoff
on Gilbert & Sullivan's *H.M.S. Pinafore*; opera star Helen Trau-
bel parodied a singing commercial; songwriters Richard Rodgers
and Oscar Hammerstein appeared in a courtroom skit; and news-
casters Lowell Thomas and H. V. Kaltenborn made comments
about the comedian's program in a news broadcast.[18]

Actress Tallulah Bankhead and Allen once did a takeoff on an
early morning husband-and-wife broadcast called "Tullu and
Freddy, that happy homey couple." The comedian and the actress lampooned the number of advertisements on a wake-up
show:

BANKHEAD   Good morning, Freddie dear.
ALLEN   Good morning, Tulu angel.
BANKHEAD   Sweetheart, I must say you look refreshingly well-rested
           this morning.

ALLEN   Yes, thanks to our wonderful Pasternak Factory-Tested
           Pussy-Willow Mattress. The mattress that takes the
           guess-work out of sleeping. So soft, so restful—

BANKHEAD   And just Seventeen-fifty at Bambergers.

ALLEN   Only the hearts of the tender pussy-willows are used.
           Breakfast ready, angel-face?

BANKHEAD   Yes, Sweetums. Here's your coffee.
           (*Tinkle of china*)

ALLEN   Thank you, doll. The time is now six-three. (*Sip*)
           Ahhhh! What coffee! What aromatic fragrance! It must
           be—

BANKHEAD   You're right, Lovey! It's McKeester's Vita-Fresh Coffee.
           The coffee with that locked-up goodness for everybody—
           Grind or Drip.

ALLEN   Quick, darling. Another cup. Ahhhhh!

BANKHEAD   Peach-Fuzz! You've spilled some on your vest.

ALLEN   Goody. Now I can try some of that Little Panther Spot
           Remover. No harsh rubbing. Just spray some Little
           Panther on your vest and watch it eat the spot out.

BANKHEAD   And imagine, a big two ounce bottle for only 35 cents.

ALLEN   Or, if you are a messy eater, you can get the handy eco-
           nomical forty gallon vat.

BANKHEAD   Angel-Eyes. I have so much juicy gossip to tell our
           listeners this morning.

ALLEN   Stop! Don't move, Tallu!

BANKHEAD   But, Darling—

ALLEN   What have you done to your hair? Your hair is breath-
           taking. That sheen! That brilliance!

BANKHEAD   I just did what so many society women are doing these
           days. I went to Madame Yvonne's Hair-do Heaven. 424
           Madison Avenue, in the Loft.

ALLEN   It's divine, darling bunny fluff!

BANKHEAD   Madame Yvonne uses a sensational hair-dressing. It
           contains that new mystery ingredient—chicken fat.

ALLEN   I hear it's on sale at all the better delicatessen stores.
           But go on, Sweets—
           (*Canary twittering*)

ALLEN   Ah, our canary, Little Jasha!

BANKHEAD   My, doesn't little Jasha sound glorious this morning?

ALLEN   I'll bet I know just what he's saying, too. He's saying
           (*corney kid*) Gee willikers, Mummy and Daddy, thanks

for feeding me that swell Dr. Groobers three-way bird
seed that comes in 15 and 25 cent packages.
(*Canary twitters*)

BANKHEAD   Ah, little Jasha is so happy, so carefree. And why
shouldn't he be happy.

ALLEN   Yes. He knows that the newspaper on the bottom of his
cage is New York's leading daily—the Morning Record
32 columnists, 18 pages of comics, and all the news no
other newspaper sees fit to print.[19]

Couples on early morning programs were notorious for their
cheerfulness. Allen and Bankhead pretended that both husband
and wife had wakened in an irritable mood:

BANKHEAD   (*Big yawn*) Hey, knuckle-head! Get out of that bed,
we've got a program to do!

ALLEN   Will you stop yappin! Six o'clock in the morning. Who's
up to listen to us—a couple of garbage collectors and
some burglers, maybe. What a racket.

BANKHEAD   If you want to go back to hustling gardenias in front of
Childs, go right ahead.

ALLEN   Yeah? What were you? Queen of the Powder Room at
Gimbels. My mouth tastes like a sandhog just pulled his
foot out of it. Gad, I'm sleepy.

BANKHEAD   Why don't you stay home some night and try sleeping?

ALLEN   Sleeping? On that Pasternak Pussy-Willow Mattress?
Pussy-Willow? It's stuffed with cat-hair. Every time I
lie down on that cat-hair my back arches.

BANKHEAD   Oh, Stop beefing! Here's your coffee!
(*China tinkle*)

ALLEN   It's about time. (*Sip*) Ptoo! (*Spit*) What are you trying
to do, poison me? Ptoo!

At the end of the skit Allen shot their pet canary and his wife.
"Tune in tomorrow, folks, for something new in radio programs," the comedian said. "One Man's Family—without the
family!"[20]

Allen's social satire often irritated the network and sponsor.
Censorship was a problem comedians faced in radio comedy.
Jokes had to be clean and the material supportive rather than
critical of American institutions and manners. The high degree

of commercialism in broadcasting also contributed to censorship. The sponsor and its advertising agency feared offending listeners because they aimed to sell their products to as many customers as possible. Allen openly denounced the commercial influences on radio progamming: he accused advertisers of lowering the quality of entertainment in order to attract huge audiences. Decisions in radio, said Allen, were made by "molehill men"— bureaucratic vice presidents in advertising agencies:

> A molehill man is a pseudo-busy executive who comes to work at 9 a.m. and finds a molehill on his desk. He has until 5 p.m. to make this molehill into a mountain. An accomplished molehill man will often have his mountain finished even before lunch.[21]

Sponsors prohibited the mentioning of competitive products over the air, and the network carefully censored scripts for libelous remarks. It had been said that one comedian was not permitted to have any jokes about roller skates because his sponsor, an automobile manufacturer, believed it was a competitive form of transportation. A gag dealing with ham in an Allen script was censored because NBC had a program sponsored by the Hormel Meat Company. Allen had to stop making comic references about prunes because of complaints by the prune packers of California. The comedian remembered a rehearsal in which the soundman reproduced the fizz of Sal Hepatica by dropping a teaspoon of the competitive Bromo Seltzer into a glass of water. He was told that Sal Hepatica did not fizz loud enough. Censorship infuriated Allen. "You ought to spend a few months in radio," he wrote a friend. "With the sponsor, agency, network and strange people roaming around the studios cutting out your jokes and telling you what is wrong with the program, you would be ready for a fitting for either a coffin or a straitjacket." Allen once joked about censorship on his show:

> Isn't it dangerous to mention air on the radio. . . . They hear that word "air" and they think how nice it might be to go out and get a breath of it. And then where is our audience? . . . You never hear anybody on the radio call a spade a spade, do you. If people get

thinking about spades the first thing you know they'll get a shovel and start burying their radios in the backyard.[22]

Before his show could be broadcast, Allen's script had to be cleared by NBC's program acceptance department. The staff judiciously red-penciled any suggestive dialogue, including double entendres as well as mild swear words like hell and damn, and certain slang expressions. The department also discouraged references to programs on competitive networks. Jokes mentioning living people and spoofing organizations had to be cleared. Allen's gag that the sturgeon at Lindy's Delicatessen "tasted tired" had to be approved by the restaurant. One script contained a joke about Lucrezia Borgia, the fifteenth-century Duchess of Ferrara. A department executive thought she was still alive and asked his secretary to telephone her. Unable to find the exact name in the Manhattan telephone directory, she thought her employer must have meant Lucrezia Bori, the Metropolitan Opera star. "Will you permit your name to be used on the Fred Allen show?" the secretary asked. "He's mentioning you as a chef." The Spanish soprano agreed to sign the clearance.[23]

NBC constantly sent memorandums to Allen's staff urging the deletion of material and sometimes threatened to fade the program if the dialogue was not cut. Comedians had to be careful when joking about public officials. The network censored the following reference to President Truman on Allen's program:

> Yes, Harry gave us too much. His old haberdashery training, you know. He always makes it bigger to allow for shrinkage.

The line, "Bea Lillie has switched to water because water is milder," was considered objectionable because it suggested that the actress drank liquor. NBC also ordered the line, "In a wigwam there are no facilities" cut. Even so, the censors sometimes failed to catch words that seemed passable in written form but sounded offensive over the air. One NBC memo read:

> On last night's Allen show, Titus Moody remarked that he used to receive so many injections as a young man that he was soon all shot to health. This wasn't

> questioned when we read the script, but on the air
> sounded so much like hell that I was sure, at the mo-
> ment, that hell was actually said.[24]

If the censor's request was too farfetched or if Allen felt a certain routine deserved to remain in the script the comedian often
refused to make the changes. Fearing Allen might offend animal
lovers, the sponsor ordered him to omit a joke about a man who
deliberately stepped on a cat. Allen angrily responded to the
person who informed him of the proposed cut:

> I want you to paddle into the slime of your censor's
> subconscious, lower your head into its fetid depths, and
> tell him I am *not* cutting that joke. . . . Tell him the
> joke has been personally approved by the head of the
> Society for the Preservation of Animal Sadism—me.
> Tell him there's only one other sound that resembles the
> squealing of bagpipes, and that's the noise the censor
> will emit when I commit intimate personal mayhem on
> him with his own shears. Tell him that, please.[25]

Allen had other problems with NBC because he was often
unable to finish his program on time and was cut off the air before the show was completed. Unplanned laughter by the studio
audience and Allen's ad-libbing frequently caused the broadcast
to run overtime. The sponsor was angry because the closing commercial was not broadcast and the network lost money on station-
break commercials. *Take It or Leave It*, the quiz program hosted
by Phil Baker, followed Allen's show. Baker felt that the comedian was cutting into his broadcast time, and he once barged into
the middle of Allen's program, claiming his show was now on
the air because of the number of minutes the comedian owed
him.[26]

Allen joked about the difficulties of timing his broadcasts. On
one show he jested about having to edit his script to fit the required time length:

> You know people don't realize how radio scripts have to
> be cut to get them on in the allotted time. I hear that
> last week "We The People" had to cut the people out.
> And tonight I heard Hobby Lobby had to be cut down
> to Hob Lob.

NBC would cut Allen off the air even if the show was not finished. On another broadcast Allen and Portland talked about the network's policy:

PORTLAND   Your program was cut off again last week.

ALLEN   I know. Was your mother listening?

PORTLAND   Yes. Mama says she'll never hear the end of your program.

ALLEN   People will get to like my program—no end.

PORTLAND   Why do they keep cutting your program off?

ALLEN   Who knows? The main thing in radio is to come out on time. If people laugh the program is longer. The thing to do is to get a nice dull half-hour to make sure that nobody laughs or applauds. Then you'll always be right on time and all the little radio executives can send each other memos and be very happy.

PORTLAND   Radio sure is funny.

ALLEN   All except the comedy programs. Our program has been cut off so many times the last page of the script is a Band-Aid.

PORTLAND   Why is everybody in radio always in such a hurry?

ALLEN   It's the network policy. A program is going along—the people are enjoying it—the program gets a little long—Zip—it's cut off the air. Then a voice says "This is the National Broadcasting Company." This is very entertaining. People all over the country have been sitting by their radios all night just waiting so that every half hour they can hear some announcer with mink tonsils say "This is The National Broadcasting Company." Then another voice says "The correct time is nine p.m." Now you know what time it is and to what network you are listening—but nothing is going on.

PORTLAND   Mama says radio is like a cuckoo clock.

ALLEN   Radio is like a cuckoo clock?

PORTLAND   Every hour, every day you hear the same thing.

ALLEN   Some day the whole side of Radio City will open up—a vice-president will fly out and say "Cuckoo"—and that will be the end of radio.[27]

Allen's jibes at NBC perturbed some network executives. His running debate with the network climaxed during clearance procedures on a script the comedian had written for an upcoming broadcast. NBC objected to Allen's remark about a network vice president who kept cutting him off the air:

PORTLAND What does the network do with all the time it saves cutting off the ends of programs?

ALLEN Well, there is a big executive here at the network. He is the vice-president in charge of "Ah! Ah! You're running too long!" He sits in a little glass closet with his mother-of-pearl gong. When your program runs overtime he thumps his gong with a marshmallow he has tied to the end of a xylophone stick. Bong! You're off the air. Then he marks down how much time he's saved.

PORTLAND What does he do with all this time?

ALLEN He adds it all up—ten seconds here, twenty there—and when he has saved up enough seconds, minutes, and hours to make two weeks, the network lets the vice-president use the two weeks of your time for his vacation.

NBC ordered Allen's producer either to not broadcast the lines or to edit the dialogue so that there was no mention of the network. If those changes were not carried out NBC threatened to fade the program at the appropriate spot.[28]

Allen, who resented authority of any kind, was furious at the network for repeatedly cutting him off the air. Allen consequently did the script in its original form, and the program was faded for twenty-five seconds during the comedian's remarks. The incident received much publicity in the newspapers. The public, feeling they had been cheated of some very funny comedy, sided with Allen. Niles Trammell, president of NBC, then issued a form letter apologizing for the incident:

When Fred Allen, in accordance with his usual practice, submitted his script for approval, it contained some derogatory but humorous references to an imaginary NBC vice president which could have been permitted to remain in the script and which he should have been permitted to broadcast. The mistake was in making an issue with Allen over this particular reference. We regret the incident very much but since it represents a single mistake, we trust you will agree with us that no harm has been caused to anyone and that lessons are learned from mistakes.

After that incident Allen never had any further problem with the network cutting him off the air.[29]

Allen's caustic lampooning of censorship and bureaucracy, and his satirical bite, especially appealed to intellectuals. Although he was admired by all types of listeners, Allen can be called the intellectuals' comedian. "You can count on the thumb of one hand the American who is at once a comedian, a humorist, a wit and a satirist, and his name is Fred Allen," James Thurber wrote. For seventeen years on the radio Allen delighted audiences with his unique brand of comic satire. Compared with him most radio comedians were pure entertainers whose escapist humor was quickly forgotten. When Allen died of a heart attack in 1956, his former assistant, novelist Herman Wouk, wrote:

> His knife-like comment on the passing show of the thirties and the forties came from sources no other comedian had access to. He was a self-educated man of wide reading; he was a tremendously talented writer; and he had the deep reticent love of life and of people which is the source of every true satirist's energy. Fred's wit lashed and stung. He could not suffer fools. In this he was like Swift and Twain.[30]

16
Radio Brats

The impudent brat became a favorite comedy character in the 1940's. Charlie McCarthy, Baby Snooks, and Junior, "the mean widdle kid," were among the most popular radio rascals. Charlie McCarthy was created by the ventriloquist Edgar Bergen. The son of immigrant Swedish parents, Bergen was born in Chicago on February 16, 1903. The ventriloquist's father had immigrated to the United States in the 1890's and had worked as a draftsman and dairyman in the Windy City. When Bergen was a young boy, the family moved to Decatur, Illinois, where at age eleven he obtained a job building furnace fires in the basement of a small silent movie theater. The ambitious youngster was eventually promoted to projectionist and pianist. On a player piano Bergen provided background music for the silent films. At the movie's end he played a lively tune called the "Midnight Fire Alarm." The small-town theater was Bergen's initiation into show business. He was also fascinated by the performances of occasional vaudeville troupes when they passed through town.[1]

At the time Bergen was growing up, ventriloquism was a popular form of vaudeville entertainment. Voice-throwing was "done by taking a deep breath and then letting it escape slowly, the voice sounds being modified by means of the upper part of the throat and the palate; the tighter the throat is closed, the further away the sound seems to be." "It's as much of a gift as a good singing voice," said Bergen. "It is pressure on the vocal cords that diffuses the voice, and the greater the pressure the greater is the illusion of distance." The ventriloquist dummy was introduced around 1750 by Baron Mengen, an Austrian, who built a wooden doll with moveable lips. There were many ventriloquists working with dummies in vaudeville. One of the first such acts starred Fred Russell, who played straight man to his comic dummy, "Coster Joe." While still in high school Bergen saw the popular Great Lester and his dummy, "Frank Byron," perform at Chicago's Lincoln Theater. He visited Lester's dressing room and tried out his ventriloquism before the master. Lester also showed Bergen his own technique and gave the apprentice two lessons. The comic character dummies in vaudeville ranged from laughing dolls to ethnic dialect types. There were even flippant, precocious children—precursors of Charlie McCarthy.[2]

Bergen started mimicking the voices of birds, animals, and people in the eighth grade, before he knew what the word ventriloquism meant. When someone told him "you must be a ventriloquist" he went home to look up the word in a dictionary. As a young boy he "fooled some people completely." The gifted youngster tricked his mother several times into believing an old man was at the door by knocking on the bottom of a chair and throwing his voice. "One day, standing on the front porch, I shouted a greeting to a friend who was passing by," said Bergen. "He imagined the voice had come from another direction, and he called back to another boy standing on a porch three houses away from ours." He learned more about ventriloquism, magic, and hypnotism by reading *Wizard's Manual*, a twenty-five-cent instruction booklet. The schoolboy began practicing all three forms on his classmates, who enjoyed his imitations. He built "a cocky little character" made of papier-mâché, and he used a halloween mask and moveable mouth for the face. "It wasn't any good at all," Bergen admitted.[3]

While a senior at Chicago's Lakeview High School in 1922 he had a new idea for a dummy. He made a sketch of an Irish ruffian newsboy named Charlie, who sold newspapers in front of the high school. Bergen gave the drawing to a local carpenter, Theodore Mack, who carved the dummy from a block of pine for about $27. He named his wooden urchin after the newsboy and the sculptor. "He [Mack] followed my specifications," said Bergen, "and out of gratitude for his whittling, I added a Celtic suffix to his name and called my new friend Charlie McCarthy."[4]

Shortly after his creation Charlie debuted at the high school's spring recital program dressed as a poor newsboy. A few weeks before the performance Bergen had learned from his history teacher, Miss Angel, that he was flunking her course and that he probably would not be graduated. She had caught him writing jokes in his textbook and drawing sketches of a dummy. Much to the delight of the students, Charlie heckled Miss Angel and Square Deal Brown, the school principal, during the recital:

BERGEN   Charlie, how are your teachers?
CHARLIE   I have Miss Angel for history.
BERGEN   Miss Angel—that's a pretty name.
CHARLIE   Don't let the name fool you. She grows horns at examination time.
BERGEN   I see. Do you ever get sent to the principal's office?
CHARLIE   I've been there so often I have my own desk there. Sometimes we close the door and play checkers. There's only one thing wrong. Square Deal Brown cheats.
BERGEN   I find it hard to believe that the principal is so friendly with you. And a lot of students here don't believe you.
CHARLIE   Oh, what do they know!
BERGEN   Well, you can prove that he's a friend of yours because he's sitting in the front row and you can say, "Hello, Square Deal."
CHARLIE   You're kidding.
BERGEN   No.
CHARLIE   I'm afraid to look. (He looks at the front row—pans from right to left. When he sees Square Deal, he goes "Yipe" and falls down in a faint.)

"I had nothing to lose," the ventriloquist recalled about the performance. Bergen then believed he would never be graduated, but the next day Miss Angel told him: "I didn't know you had this genius—the world needs laughter more than history teachers." She offered to tutor him in order to improve his grades. "That's how I got out of high school," said Bergen.[5]

After graduation Bergen attended Northwestern University. He worked his way through college by performing a ventriloquism and magic act at small-time Chicago vaudeville theaters during the weekend. There he earned from five to seven dollars a day, and he was grateful when one theater manager gave him an extra quarter for carfare. The theaters were small and dingy, and often he had to dress in the basement boiler room. The young performer dropped the magic part of his act when he was offered a job only as a ventriloquist. Bergen also paid for his tuition by entertaining at social clubs and parties. During summer vacations he joined the Chautauqua Circuit and toured small-town schools, churches, and town halls. Bergen then left the university for a time and performed on the Lyceum and Orpheum Circuits. He traveled with Charlie across the United States by train and learned how to amuse different audiences. During the 1920's the ventriloquist gradually moved into big-time vaudeville: he played the Palace Theatre in 1929.

When vaudeville declined in the early 1930's, Bergen turned to entertaining in expensive nightclubs. Because he believed nightclub audiences preferred a more sophisticated act, he thought of using another dummy rather than Charlie the newsboy. He thought of a debonair playboy type and asked *Esquire* magazine if he could use Esky, their symbol, for a dummy, but the publishers, who had initially agreed, recanted. "That was one of the nicest things that happened to me," Bergen jested. "I would have been paying royalties from then on."[6] The entertainer decided instead to dress Charlie in tuxedo, white tie and tails, black top hat, and monocle. He also changed Charlie's voice to an affected British accent. The ventriloquist's new act was a hit at New York's Helen Morgan Club, Hollywood's Casanova Club, and Chicago's Chez Paree, where he returned for long engagements.

A successful appearance in the fall of 1936 at Manhattan's Rainbow Room led to Bergen's first radio engagement. The ventriloquist was suddenly a rage among New York café society, and he was asked to entertain at a lavish party held by Elsa Maxwell for Noel Coward. Charlie ribbed the English actor and playwright, and Coward in turn praised the entertainer's comedy style. The publicity helped Bergen gain a guest spot on the Rudy Vallee program, handled by the J. Walter Thompson agency. When John Reber, head of the advertising agency's radio department, heard that Bergen was being considered for the Vallee show, he said, "A ventriloquist! Well, he damn better be funny." The idea of having a ventriloquist on radio was unusual, for voice-throwing was considered an art largely dependent on visual contact with the audience. Bergen had earlier auditioned at Chicago's NBC Studios and had been told his act would not be believable. "I'd been trying for a year to get on radio and nobody would give me a chance," the ventriloquist recalled.[7]

Bergen made his debut on Vallee's *Royal Gelatin Hour* on December 17, 1936. The crooner introduced him by stating that Bergen was an extremely talented ventriloquist who deserved to be heard by a large radio audience. Speaking like a British aristocrat, Charlie told Bergen he had just returned from a hunt. "First day out got three cocker spaniels," said Charlie. "Second day got a horse." The repartee between the soft-spoken Bergen and his loudmouthed dummy was hilarious. "Suddenly, I was a hot number," said Bergen. The debut was so successful that he appeared on the Vallee program for thirteen weeks, including one remote broadcast from the Chez Paree nightclub.[8]

On May 9, 1937, Bergen began starring on the NBC *Chase and Sanborn Hour* (later called *The Charlie McCarthy Show*), a Sunday evening variety program of music and comedy. Don Ameche served as the program's master of ceremonies in its early years. A fine actor, Ameche also sparred with Charlie and played roles in the sketches. Ray Noble, the Englishman who led the orchestra, also doubled as a foil for Charlie's wisecracks. Numerous vocalists entertained over the years, including Nelson Eddy, Donald Dixon, Anita Ellis, Dale Evans, and Anita Gordon. Several comic characters were featured on the program, including Vera Vague (Barbara Jo Allen), Professor Edwin Carp (Richard Haydn), and Ersel Twing (Pat Patrick), who spoke in a singsong voice. Guest stars from the movie industry also appeared, including Dorothy Lamour, W. C. Fields, Mae West, Jane Powell, Margaret O'Brien, and Marilyn Monroe.[9]

The program was written by Bergen and a writing staff. A

perfectionist, Bergen worked all week to prepare for the broad-cast, and sometimes arose at night to work on the upcoming show. In the script conferences with his writers he acted as chief editor and idea man. Good writing was the key to the show's longevity, said Bergen. It "was the only way to stay . . . popu-lar. And the ventriloquism was a way of delivering the comedy." Bergen had a fine sense of timing, and his fast-paced comic ex-changes with his dummies were masterful. On radio listeners could not observe the movements of his lips, which were per-ceptible on stage. He concentrated not so much on technique but on developing Charlie's lifelike character. In his routines Bergen, a shy man, let his dummy become the dominant personality. "In my case I kept thinking up new facets to Charlie's personality and submerging my own," said the ventriloquist. "The loss of identity was such that many times people have come up to me and said, 'Hi, McCarthy,' or 'Glad to meet you, Mr. McCarthy.' "[10]

Charlie received as much publicity as any radio star. Bergen drew up a will creating a $10,000 Charlie McCarthy Fund, to be used by the Actors' Fund of America to put on ventriloquist en-tertainment for deprived and handicapped children. Charlie was once kidnapped from Bergen's hotel room at the Waldorf-Astoria. An amusement editor of a New York afternoon newspaper had staged the kidnapping as a stunt. He sent a pageboy to Bergen's hotel to fetch the dummy. When the boy left the Waldorf-Astoria he was forced into a taxicab by two men, bound and gagged, and let out at a midtown street corner. The local police and F.B.I. were alerted, but the next day the journalist returned the famous dummy. The ventriloquist took the hoax as a good gag and decided not to prosecute.[11]

Charlie was made by Frank Marshall and his partner, Alex Camero, in their carpentry workshop in Chicago. The body frame and facial contours were carved out of basswood and the arms and legs stuffed with wood wool. The face was painted with four coats of special paint and a wig glued to the scalp. Rolling eyes, winking lids, and a moveable mouth were inserted into the face and moved by cords, a bulb, and a lever. His clothes and body frame had to be replaced frequently, and the face repainted. Charlie had a wardrobe worth $1000, including a cowboy suit and a Sherlock Holmes outfit, and wore a size 4 suit, 2AAA shoes, and a 33⅜ hat. Bergen carried his dummy, insured for $3000, in a specially designed piece of luggage.[12]

On the broadcasts Charlie had the punch lines and Bergen acted the straight man. The ventriloquist played a moralistic, fatherly type who vainly tried to teach Charlie the difference between right and wrong. Bergen's moralizing and scoldings were only fuel for Charlie's comebacks. The brash, precocious youngster enjoyed ribbing Bergen about his baldness, stinginess, and the movement of his lips. Often Charlie's routine consisted of one joke topper after another. Whenever Bergen threatened to punish him, Charlie used his favorite retort: "I'll clip you, Bergen. So help me, I'll mow you down."[13]

One of their best routines dealt with Charlie's bad grades. The youngster much preferred missing class and playing with his pal Skinny Dugan than going to school. Bergen lectured his "adopted son" on how important grades were to future success:

BERGEN   Charlie, going to school is the foundation for your future, which is built by learning something every day.
CHARLIE I do that. I learned something new Friday.
BERGEN   What?
CHARLIE A new place to hide from the truant officer.

In return, Charlie needled the ventriloquist about *his* schooling:

CHARLIE What kind of student were you, Bergen?
BERGEN   Well, I can answer that by saying I completed my course in three and a half years.
CHARLIE That's pretty good for a two year course.
BERGEN   Oh, so you've been checking up on me, have you?
CHARLIE Yes, I have. I was talking to Dean Dennis, and he said you sat around that campus so long that ivy started growing up your leg.
BERGEN   Remember this, young man—never belittle Education, because Knowledge is Power.
CHARLIE Yeah, and you're the guy who blew the fuse.

Listeners usually took Charlie's cutting rejoinders as good fun, although once, when he called his history teacher, Miss Krausshoffer, "Pickle Puss" teachers wrote letters complaining about the remark.[14]

The program's humor stemmed largely from Charlie's brash, cocky personality. The smart-aleck youngster swaggered and boasted as much as the other radio comedy characters. Charlie was also descended from a long line of mischievous children in other forms of popular culture. "Kid strips" had appeared in newspapers as early as the 1890's. *The Katzenjammer Kids* (1897) concerned Hans and Fritz, two destructive rascals who defied parental and educational authority. Richard Outcault's *The Yellow Kid* (1895) pictured a rebellious ragamuffin in a city slum, while the cartoonist's *Buster Brown* (1902) portrayed a little boy and his bulldog, Tyke. Hank Ketchum's current comic strip, Dennis the Menace, suggests that the mischiefmaker is still a popular feature in the funnies. The early silent film *Peck's Bad Boy* and the Little Rascals' movies featured the antics of rowdy children. "Kid strips" and films dealt with the inability of parents to control children and parodied parental permissiveness. Little rascals like Charlie had always been popular comedy figures.[15]

Child characters could say things adults could not, and because he was also a dummy Charlie often got away with suggestive remarks. One of his routines was flirting with the glamorous guest celebrities. In one typical scene Charlie tried to date Rita Hayworth:

CHARLIE   Whadya say, Miss Hayworth, is it all right if I come over to your house?
HAYWORTH   That would be wonderful, Charlie. I'd love to have you meet my mother.
CHARLIE   Oh, I don't think it would be worth her while to come over just for that.
HAYWORTH   I live with my mother, silly.
CHARLIE   Yes, isn't it. . . . How about Monday afternoon? Does you mother stay home all the time?
HAYWORTH   No, she goes to the bridge club on Wednesday.
CHARLIE   On second thought, I'll come Wednesday.

On one broadcast Charlie was engaged to Marilyn Monroe. A newscaster commented on their approaching marriage: "Some-

where, in an army camp a soldier is tearing up his calendar." A
voice that resembled Winston Churchill's said tearfully:

> This is America's darkest hour. The entire British Em-
> pire extends its sympathy. If Charles McCarthy insists
> upon going through with this marriage with Marilyn
> Monroe I have only one thing to say. "Never has any-
> one so little taken so much from so many."[16]

One of Charlie's favorite foils was stage and film comedian
W. C. Fields, who appeared frequently as a guest star from 1937
to 1943. Until these programs, Fields had been rather indifferent
to radio and had initially turned down a number of offers to star
in his own broadcast. In 1939 he did a series for Lucky Strike,
but it only lasted a season. His guest appearances with Bergen
and McCarthy were much more successful. In 1937 Fields was
recuperating in a sanitarium for acute nervous and internal dis-
orders caused by habitual drinking. In his typical tongue-in-
cheek manner the comedian joked that he had become addicted
to radio while confined in bed:

> So she [the nurse] set it down at my bedside and it
> looked me right in the eye, yes, yes, an eye that once
> looked upon better days—the good old days when they
> gave you a free lunch with a stein. Throwing all caution
> to the winds, I lunged at it boldly and seized it by the
> throat with one hand while tweaking its nose with the
> other. And what did the gadget do? Did it strike back at
> old W. C. with demoniacal fury? Ah, no indeed, perish
> the thought. It began filling my etherized abode with
> most soulful melodies, like a chord of heavenly harps
> they were. . . .
> Yes, indeed, my radio and I became so inseparable
> that I could tell the time of day by Lum and Abner. It
> wasn't long before Jack Benny and Bing Crosby meant
> more to me than my nearest and dearest kin, yes, I am
> ashamed to say, more than my dear old father.

The chubby entertainer spoke from the sanitarium on a tribute
broadcast honoring Adolph Zukor, the film producer. His voice
sounded so effective over the air that Bergen's sponsors asked
him to do a series of broadcasts at $6500 a week. Not only was

the money attractive but, considering his health, the comedian thought a weekly radio spot would be easier to do than a film.[17]

The producers of *The Chase and Sanborn Hour* were not prepared for Fields's idiosyncrasies. The writer Dick Mack was assigned to write Fields's dialogue. Early in the week Mack would visit the comedian at his home, and together they perused the script. An individualist, Fields either changed most of the lines or wrote his own material. He would tell the producers at the rehearsal that he had not made any cuts. "We won't show the damned thing to them—the hell with them," he whispered to his secretary. Nor did he bother filing his script with the advertising agency before broadcast time. The sponsor and the network were always worried whether Fields would tell an off-color gag. The producers complained he talked too slowly and dragged the program. "Well, you'd better get yourself another boy," Fields told them. He would drink a shaker of martinis during the Sunday rehearsal, although he never would become intoxicated. Bergen recalled that Fields improvised constantly during the broadcasts:

> Fields could write good jokes, but he would forget them. His memory was bad. He'd start reading a joke and he wouldn't know what the payoff was until he got to it. So he couldn't lean on it. He wrote some lovely jokes and we would put toppers on them, which were real good. But he'd try to cut them out because he didn't think they were funny. Well, if there were any jokes we thought were real funny, we'd say, "Bill, that was one of your own jokes." And he'd say, "Oh it is?" We never had an argument. We protected him, whatever condition he was in. Sure he'd ad-lib, but Bill never said anything too dirty.

Bergen and Fields worked well together because they had great respect for one another. Fields admired the ventriloquist's timing and delivery, and Bergen called the film star "the greatest I ever worked with" and "the last of the triple-threat comedians."[18]

Fields and Charlie hurled name-calling and insult jokes at one another. Like the Benny–Allen and Hope–Crosby feuds, each tried to top the other with a cutting rejoinder. Charlie's favorite

target was Fields's drinking and his red nose. "Why don't you
have your breezer tattooed blue for the duration of the dimouts,"
Charlie proposed. "Silence, you frustrated hitching post, or I'll
cut you down to a pair of shoe trees," Fields retorted. The comedian refused to be put down by a wooden dummy. He called
Charlie a "little squirrel's warehouse," a "termite's flophouse,"
and a "dead limb on the tree of knowledge."[19]

The running battle between Fields and Charlie produced some
of the funniest lines in radio.

> FIELDS   Tell me, Charlie, is it true that when you slide down a
> banister the banister gets more splinters than you do?
> CHARLIE   Why, bugle-beak, why don't you fill your nose with
> helium and rent it out as a barrage balloon?
> FIELDS   Listen, you animated hitching post, I'll sic a beaver on
> you.

"Tell me, Charles, is it true your father was a gate-leg table?"
Fields asked on another broadcast. "If it is—your father was
under it," Charlie replied. "Why, you stunted spruce—I'll throw
a Japanese beetle on you." "Why, you bar fly," said Charlie, "I'll
stick a wick in your mouth and use you for an alcohol lamp."
One evening Fields sawed the dummy in half in front of a studio
audience.[20]

Fields's movie partner, Mae West, made a guest appearance
on *The Chase and Sanborn Hour* on December 12, 1937, that received considerable notoriety. Don Ameche and West played
Adam and Eve in a sketch about the Garden of Eden written by
the veteran radio writer Arch Oboler. The eight-minute takeoff
on the biblical story would be judged innocuous by today's
standards, but in 1937 it infuriated religious groups.

The dialogue that caused the most reaction was Eve's (Mae
West's) conversation with the Snake in the Garden of Eden:

> SNAKE   That's the forbidden tree.
> EVE   Oh, don't be technical. Answer me this—my palpitatin'
> python—would you like to have this whole Paradise to
> yourself?
> SNAKE   Certainly.
> EVE   O.K., then pick me a handful of fruit—Adam and I'll

eat it—and the Garden of Eden is all yours. What do ya say?

SNAKE   Sssounds all right . . . but it's forbidden fruit.

EVE   Listen, what are you—my friend in the grass or a snake in the grass?

SNAKE   But forbidden fruit.

EVE   Are you a snake or are you a mouse?

SNAKE   I'll—I'll do it. (hissing laugh)

EVE   Oh—shake your hips. There, there now, you're through.

SNAKE   I shouldn't be doing this.

EVE   Yeh, but you're doing all right now. Get me a big one. . . . I feel like doin' a big apple.

SNAKE   Here you are, Missuss Eve.

EVE   Mm—oh, I see—huh—nice goin', swivel hips.

SNAKE   Wait a minute. It won't work. Adam'll never eat that forbidden apple.

EVE   Oh, yes, he will—when I'm through with it.

SNAKE   Nonsense. He won't.

EVE   He will if I feed it to him like women are gonna feed men for the rest of time.

SNAKE   What's that?

EVE   Applesauce.

"There was nothing offensive in the dialogue or it would never have got on the air in the first place," said West. The blond actress admitted, however, that her sultry voice "smouldered a bit" as she read her lines:

> I only gave the lines my characteristic delivery. What else could I do? I wasn't Aimee Semple McPherson. Or Lincoln at Gettysburg, or John Foster Dulles, or even Eleanor Roosevelt. I was Mae West. Sunday on radio doesn't alter one's personality.[21]

Offended listeners criticized the Adam and Eve skit as an assault on the decency of the American home and "an insolent caricature of religion and the Bible." The critics felt that West's performance violated moral standards on the airwaves. Only clean family entertainment should be permitted on radio, they declared. One newspaper editorial protested that

> the radio has brought to many a fuller life, carrying the culture of the world into the homes of America. The

> home is our last bulwark against the modern over-
> emphasis on sensuality, and we cannot see why Miss
> West and others of her ilk should be permitted to pollute
> its sacred precincts with shady stories, foul obscenity,
> smutty suggestiveness, and horrible blasphemy.

The publicity led the FCC to request a transcription and a copy
of the script. In a heated debate in Congress the Representatives
discussed the incident and the question of obscenity on the air.
One Congressman demanded the FCC take punitive action
against NBC for permitting "this foul and sensuous radio program" to enter American homes.[22]

NBC officials attempted to curb the protest by issuing a statement of apology on the next *Chase and Sanborn Hour*. The embarrassed network executives had actually approved the sketch
prior to the broadcast. Stanley Resor, president of the J. Walter
Thompson advertising agency, which handled the program, also
officially regretted the incident:

> Obviously, the whole purpose of these broadcasts is to
> afford wholesome entertainment. . . . The script of
> this feature of the broadcast was our responsibility. It
> was a mistake and we can assure the public at large that
> the same mistake will not be made again.

Congressional pressure forced FCC Chairman Frank McNinch
to issue a strong letter of warning to NBC: "The admittedly objectionable character of these features is, in our opinion, attrib-
utable to the lack of a proper conception of the high standards
required for a broadcast program . . . reaching in the aggregate
a much larger number of people daily than any other means of
communication and carrying its message to men, women and
children of all ages." McNinch reminded NBC of its responsi-
bility to prevent the broadcasting of obscene material. Although
the government commission did not take any punitive action,
the FCC warned the network that it would not renew licenses
when stations failed to conduct their programming in the public
interest.[23]

Mae West, who had already been attacked by censors for her
so-called lewd performances on stage and film, was barred by

NBC from further radio appearances. The network also ordered that her name could not be mentioned on the air. The actress felt that she was the scapegoat of an embarrassed industry:

> The radio people had egg on their faces and their copies of the King James version. To pacify some pious frauds among the radio audience, I was *persona non grata* on radio until the heat was off. I must have produced a lot of heat on that broadcast; it took several years to cool off.[24]

The Mae West incident illustrates the close association of radio comedy with morality and the family.

In the late 1930's Bergen created the country bumpkin Mortimer Snerd. "I wanted something that wouldn't conflict with Charlie's voice," Bergen recalled.

> He had to be stupid, but likeable; homely, but very kind. So Mortimer Snerd was born. He is scientifically stupid. He's a lowbrow. He had high arched eyebrows. He's a dreamer and has a low-bridged bulbous nose. He's not nosy or aggressive. He has a weak chin, buck teeth, and little or no determination. But he's likeable, and there's something very nice about him. He's bashful and afraid of girls, so he doesn't conflict with Charlie.

Snerd was dressed in a plaid jacket with a bow tie and wore a straw hat or a derby. "Clod" music introduced Mortimer's "dumb" routine with the ventriloquist. "Mortimer, how can you be so *awfully, awfully* stupid?" Bergen asked. "Wull, when us actor fellers play a part . . . we live it," Mortimer replied.[25]

The comedy between Bergen and Mortimer revolved around the dummy's absentmindedness:

BERGEN Tell the people your name.
MORTIMER Mortimer.
BERGEN Yes . . . Mortimer what?
MORTIMER Yup. Mortimer What . . . no, no, that isn't it.
BERGEN What is your last name?
MORTIMER Mortimer . . . um . . . gosh, . . . Mortimer . . .
BERGEN Your last name.

MORTIMER	Mortimer . . . um . . . I know it as well as I know my own name.
BERGEN	Well, what is it? Hurry up.
MORTIMER	Well, I'm workin' on it.
BERGEN	All right, Mortimer—concentrate.
MORTIMER	Uh—it's Mortimer Snerd.
BERGEN	That's right. Now, tell the people where you come from.
MORTIMER	Iowa.
BERGEN	And what part of Iowa?
MORTIMER	Snerdville.[26]

Bergen later added to the show the bachelor girl Effie Klinker, named after one of the program's writers, Zeno Klinker. Introduced in 1944, owl-faced Effie wore a flowerpot bonnet, pincenez, a long black skirt, and red, white, and blue striped stockings. Effie kept Bergen informed about the town gossip and described her futile attempts to snare a husband.

The Chase and Sanborn Hour, and its successor, The Charlie McCarthy Show, were among the most popular comedy broadcasts in the late 1930's and 1940's. They were often rated the number one comedy program on the air, and in other years were always among the top five comedy shows. The Charlie McCarthy Show, which was part of NBC's Sunday night comedy lineup, went on the air at eight o'clock, a half hour after Benny finished his program. Ministers changed the time of their evening services so listeners could hear the program. People became addicted to Charlie, who became so real that fans often referred to him as a living person. On Monday morning listeners often quoted what Charlie had said the night before. Fans bought Charlie McCarthy souvenirs, including dolls, mugs, and spoons. Bergen not only earned royalties from those items but received a weekly salary of $10,000 for his broadcast. The Charlie McCarthy rage led more ventriloquists to work on radio. A favorite show was Tommy Riggs and Betty Lou, which premiered on NBC in 1938. Riggs, who did not work with a dummy, was really a voice impersonator who played Betty Lou, an impish seven-year-old girl with a squeaky voice. Other ventriloquists included Shirley Dinsdale and her dummy "Judy Splinters" and Paul Winchell and "Jerry Mahoney." Although they were talented, those ventriloquists were never as popular as Bergen and McCarthy, who were radio stars until 1956. In September 1978 Bergen announced his retirement and the news that Charlie McCarthy would go to the Smithsonian Institution. A few weeks later the famous ventrilo- quist died suddenly of a heart attack.[27]

Another popular radio brat was Baby Snooks, played by the famous musical comedy star Fanny Brice. Brice, whose real name was Fannie Borach, was born in New York's Lower East Side on October 29, 1891. When Brice was twelve the family moved to south Brooklyn, where they lived in a tenement house on St. Mark's Avenue. She and her friends earned pocket money by singing on neighborhood street corners. Brice was a natural- born entertainer. In a backyard shed she put on penny admission stage shows and impersonated a poor, hungry, old woman.[28]

Brice broke into show business in 1904, when she won five dol- lars singing in an amateur night contest at Brooklyn's Keeney's Theatre. The novice was so nervous during her debut she closed her eyes and imagined that only her mother was in the audience. The crowd liked her performance and threw coins on the stage. Frank Keeney, the theater owner, suggested she enter other ama- teur nights. She won contests in Brooklyn and Manhattan and sometimes earned $60 to $70 a week. Brice had grown up in poverty, and the money and applause led her to believe she had found her future. She quit school and obtained a job as a singer of illustrated songs projected on a screen at a Manhattan stere- opticon parlor.

Brice was one of the few radio comedians to come from bur- lesque, which had been an important training ground for such entertainers as Bert Lahr, Red Buttons, Red Skelton, Bud Abbott and Lou Costello, and Phil Silvers. She became a chorus girl with the Hurtig and Seamon Translantic Burlesque Troupe, a clean variety show. While working with that troupe Brice received an opportunity to sing and dance alone. Those successful solo per- formances eventually led to her being employed as the troupe's soubrette, or leading lady. In Max Spiegel's *College Girls* (1910), put on at Manhattan's Columbia Burlesque Theatre, she was a popular hit, singing Irving Berlin's "Sadie Salome" with an ex- aggerated Jewish accent and accentuated body movements. Impressed by her unique style, Florenz Ziegfeld signed her for his 1910 *Follies*, in which she sang the show-stopping "coon song," "Lovey Joe." During the next fifteen years she starred in *Ziegfeld Follies* productions, vaudeville shows, and Broadway musical comedies. A gifted singer and comedian, Brice had a lively, charismatic personality that enthralled the audience. She became well known for her comic stage parodies and Jewish characterizations. The pathos she conveyed while singing such emotional songs as "My Man" and "Second Hand Rose" brought tears to the eyes of theatergoers.

Brice had portrayed a little girl on stage before enacting Baby Snooks on radio. Baby characters were a rage in vaudeville in the early 1900's, the musical comedy star recalled:

> At that time there was a child called Baby Peggy, and she was very popular. The hair was all curled and bleached, and she was always in pink or blue. She always looked like an ice-cream soda or something. Then I had talked to people about doing a baby—I thought I could be very funny with it.

At a party in Detroit she sang the song "Poor Pauline" in a high-pitched treble like a little girl. Her imitation was so well received that she decided to do the song on stage as an encore number. She revived the character again in 1932 on her first radio series. On the broadcasts she sang songs and did other character sketches, including her famous monologue about Mrs. Cohen, a Jewish mother who took her family to the beach. Brice remembered that Mrs. Cohen had limitations:

> You know the way they have to go over your script for censorship? I found out when I was doing Mrs. Cohen at the Beach. We'd be ready to rehearse, and they'd say: "You can't do this, you can't do that. This will offend, and that will not sound nice." And I knew this couldn't happen with a baby. Because what can you write about a child that has to be censored?

Baby Snooks allowed Brice freedom of expression. She also enjoyed portraying Snooks because the character reminded the performer of her childhood:

W. C. Fields threatening to saw Charlie McCarthy in half on *The
Chase and Sanborn Hour* in the late 1930's.
(Copyright, Frank Bresee.)

Fanny Brice impersonating
Baby Snooks.
(Courtesy, Frank Bresee Collection.)

Red Skelton performing his "Guzzler Gin" routine after a broadcast during World War II at Studio B, NBC headquarters, Hollywood.
(Copyright, Frank Bresee.)

Gus Bayz recreating radio sound effects on Frank Bresee's *The Golden Days of Radio Television Special.*
(Copyright 1977, Frank Bresee.)

Frank Bresee, master of ceremonies, and his guests Bergen and McCarthy appearing on *The Golden Days of Radio Television Special,* CBS, June 6, 1977.
(Copyright 1978, Frank Bresee.)

> Snooks is just the kid I used to be. She's my kind of youngster, the type I like. She has imagination. She's eager. She's alive. With all her deviltry, she still is a good kid, never vicious nor mean.

When the skilled actress played the part on the radio she became completely absorbed into the character and made Snooks as real as the neighborhood brat down the street. "I love Snooks, and when I play her I do it as seriously as if she were real," she said. "I am Snooks. For twenty minutes or so, Fanny Brice ceases to exist."[29]

The entertainer found reading from a prepared radio script easier to do than theater. Her copy of the script was printed in large capital letters on a piece of cardboard, because she did not want to wear reading glasses while performing before a studio audience. Brice had a nonchalant attitude toward radio. "It's stealing money," she said. The actress had to be coaxed to rehearse before the broadcast. One of her writers, Everett Freeman, recalled that she rarely performed well in rehearsal, but "she never disappointed me on the air."

> While she was on the air she *was* Baby Snooks. And after the show, for an hour after the show, she was still Baby Snooks. The Snooks voice disappeared, of course, but the Snooks temperament, thinking, actions, were all there.[30]

In 1936 Snooks became a regular character on the CBS *Ziegfeld Follies of the Air*, a sixty-minute variety show broadcast Saturday night from New York's Winter Garden Theatre. Two years earlier, in the *Ziegfeld Follies of 1934*, she had created a sensation on stage as Snooks dressed in a baby's dress and bib. On the opening broadcast Brice sang "My Man" and impersonated the mischievous, cunning brat who angers her father (Alan Reed):

FATHER   Snooks, look at the mess in this parlor. The vase is broken—ink on the carpet—the window is smashed. Did you do this?

BRICE   Nope.

FATHER   Don't look down at your feet, Snooks. Look into my face when you answer me. Who made this mess?

BRICE   Nursie done it, daddy.

FATHER   Why, Snooks, you know Nursie is off today.

BRICE   Yeah—but she came back and done it. I seen her, daddy.

FATHER   You did, huh? Well, why is your dress covered with ink?

BRICE   She spilled ink on me too, daddy.

FATHER   Snooks, you know that Nursie went out of town this morning to visit her sick sister. She couldn't possibly have come back.

BRICE   I forgot. She done it yesterday.

FATHER   Yesterday the room was in perfect shape. Now Snooks, tell me the truth. How did this mess happen? Why did you break that vase?

BRICE   I had to do it, daddy.

FATHER   You had to? Why?

BRICE   On account of the three rattlesnakes.

FATHER   What three rattlesnakes?

BRICE   What did you say, daddy?

FATHER   You said you had to break the vase on account of three rattlesnakes.

BRICE   Yeah, daddy, they came into the parlor and I killed them.

FATHER   Snooks, you know you're not telling the truth.

BRICE   Well, maybe it was only two rattlesnakes. . . .

FATHER   Now listen, Snooks, I've had enough of this. I want you to tell me the truth—you understand? The truth! The truth!

BRICE   What did you say, daddy?

FATHER   If you tell me the truth, I won't punish you. Now promise me you won't fib any more.

BRICE   Awight, daddy.

FATHER   Now what happened?

BRICE   I took out the ink bottle to write a letter—and a big lion jumped in through the window and scared me.

FATHER   A lion jumped in through the window?

BRICE   Yeah—that's how the window got broke.

FATHER   Even if a lion did jump through the window, why did the pieces of glass fall on the outside?

BRICE   Well, the lion jumped in backwards.

FATHER	Go on.
BRICE	So I ran into the other corner and there was four lions —and they all jumped on me, daddy.
FATHER	And then what happened?
BRICE	I got killed.
FATHER	Honest Snooks, I don't know what to do with you. Will you ever tell the truth?
BRICE	I'll tell you the truth, daddy.
FATHER	Do you promise?
BRICE	Cross my heart.
FATHER	All right. Now, how could you tell me such stories about lions? You know you never saw a lion.
BRICE	I did so, daddy.
FATHER	Where did you see a lion?
BRICE	Mrs. Smith has one next door and that's the one that come in.
FATHER	Mrs. Smith has a lion? You know very well that's nothing but a little yellow dog. Now I want you to kneel down and pray for forgiveness for telling so many fibs.
BRICE	Awight.
FATHER	That's it. Pray to the Lord to make you an honest child.
BRICE	Awight. I'm finished, daddy.
FATHER	Did you pray?
BRICE	Uh-huh—and the Lord said, "I forgive you, Miss Snooks. The first time I looked at that yellow dog, I thought he was a lion, too."[31]

The impish Snooks also knew how to get the best of her harassed father through her childlike innocence and loud wails:

FATHER	I have a good mind not to buy you an Easter bonnet.
BRICE	Awight. Buy me a bicycle.
FATHER	I won't buy you a bonnet and I won't buy you a bicycle.
BRICE	(*Cries*) Waah!
FATHER	Stop crying!
BRICE	(*Cries louder*) Waahhh!!
FATHER	Good heavens . . . everybody in the store is looking at us. Stop crying and I'll buy you a bonnet.
BRICE	(*Laughs*)
FATHER	What are you laughing about?
BRICE	I knew it would work![32]

In the late 1930's and 1940's Snooks became a popular radio favorite. Brice appeared on the *Good News* programs (1938–39) and *Maxwell House Coffee Time* (1940–44), sharing the spotlight with comic monologuist Frank Morgan. Her most successful broadcast was *The Baby Snooks Show* (1944–51), a family situation comedy featuring Hanley Stafford as Daddy Higgins, Arlene Harris as the mother, and Leone Ledoux as Snooks's brother, Robespierre. The mischievous Snooks played all types of tricks on her family: planting a bee's nest at her mother's club meeting, cutting her father's fishing line into little pieces, ripping the fur off her mother's coat, inserting marbles into her father's piano, and smearing glue on her baby brother. Snooks usually received a spanking for her misbehavior, and many programs ended with a loud "waaahhh!" Brice was still doing Baby Snooks on radio in 1951 when she died suddenly of a cerebral hemorrhage on May 29. She had been scheduled to do the program the night of her death. Instead of the regular show a musical tribute was broadcast, and Hanley Stafford delivered a short eulogy. "We have lost," he said, "a very real, a very warm, a very wonderful woman."[33]

Another skilled child impersonator and comedian on radio was Red Skelton. Richard Bernard Skelton was born in Vincennes, Indiana, on July 18, 1913, and he grew up in a show business environment. His father had been a well-known clown with the Hagenbeck & Wallace Circus in the 1890's. As a young boy Red liked watching the comedians at the local theater and decided to become a comic. He first worked as a circus clown and pitchman with a traveling medicine show. He later joined a minstrel troupe and performed on a showboat on the Ohio and Missouri rivers in the mid-1920's. Around 1928 the red-haired performer began entertaining as a stand-up burlesque comic doing imitations and pantomime. In 1931, he married Edna Stillwell, who became a stooge in his act and helped write his material. During the 1930's he performed as an emcee-comedian at Walkathons and entertained contestants with impersonations. By the late 1930's Skelton was a successful vaudeville comedian known for his pantomime routines. His mime impersonations included a character dunking doughnuts, and another who was a gin guzzler.[34]

Skelton entered radio in the late 1930's. He made his debut on the Rudy Vallee program, and he did several guest appearances on the singer's show. In 1939, he starred on *Avalon Time* and performed a topical monologue and a concluding sketch. On that short-lived, unimaginative series Skelton did not impersonate the amusing characters that later became famous on *The Raleigh Cigarette Program*. That popular, thirty-minute NBC Tuesday night show began on October 7, 1941, and it suddenly launched the comedian into the limelight. Skelton's program was always rated among the top six comedy broadcasts in the 1940's. His charismatic personality highlighted the show, and he specialized in wildly exaggerated jokes. "My electric toaster broke down," jested Skelton, "so I repaired it with parts from an airplane. . . . Now when the toast pops out it circles the table twice before coming in for a landing."[35]

The unique features of his act were his impersonations from the Skelton scrapbook of satire. Skelton's enormous talent for pantomime was obviously lost on radio. Still, he was an exceptional voice imitator who made the character *sound* funny. One of his most memorable portrayals was Junior, "the mean widdle kid," a character he had enacted earlier on stage. Junior was a mischiefmaker much like Baby Snooks and Charlie McCarthy, but he was much more rude and mischievous. "Oh, I wish I had left you at home," his "Mummie" scolded. "Oh, no you don't," Junior replied. "Because by now I coulda had three rooms *completely wrecked!*" Whenever Junior did a mischievous act, he exclaimed "I do'd it," an expression which became a popular catch phrase.[36]

Junior was really a farfetched parody of the radio brat. One of the funniest parts of Skelton's routine was Junior's monologue describing his conscience. In one episode the impish youngster contemplated throwing a bottle of ink into the electric fan in his father's office:

> . . . Look at that pretty machine . . . but I is afraid to go near it. . . . I is scared by machines. . . . I was bitten by a zipper once . . . what's this . . . ? A map of the United States and lots of little pins stuck in it all over . . . ain't it pretty . . . ? Look . . . somebody put a pin in Lake Erie . . . it's getting all rusty . . . I

could take it out, but that would only lead to bloodshed. . . . Gee . . . what a big pencil sharpener . . . it gives me an idea. . . . I think I'll stick my fingers in the sharpener and get a manicure. . . . No I won't either . . . (*pause*) . . . Gee I is bored! Here I am all alone in Papa's office . . . and . . . Oh look . . . there's the telephone . . . now let me see who do I know in *Moscow?* . . . Nope I've changed my mind. . . . I won't telephone . . . I'll just snoop around a bit. . . . Gee . . . here's a large bottle of ink . . . nice black ink . . . and there's the electric fan . . . (*pause*) . . . If I do . . . *I get a whippin'. . . . I do'd it!* . . . I will turn on the electric fan and then I will throw the bottle of ink into it. . . . Well . . . hold on to your hats, folks . . . here goes the ink into the electric fan![37]

Junior was spanked for his devilish tricks by his grandmother, played by Verna Felton. Yet he could even make her feel bad about the punishment:

RED   Oh . . . oh . . . oh . . . you hit me. You broke me widdle back.

VERNA   I'm sorry.

RED   You hit me with all your might . . . and I never even laid a hand on you. I can't believe me widdle eyes! Hit by me own namaw! It can't be true! It can't be true. I must be dreaming!

VERNA   You aren't dreaming, young man . . . that was a real spanking.

RED   Oh, no. . . . It couldn't be. I can't believe it! It was just a nightmare!

VERNA   No it wasn't! I really hit you.

RED   You did?

VERNA   Yes, I did.

RED   (*Pause*) Oh-oh-oh . . . you hit me! Aren't you ashamed! Are you . . . old enough to be me grandmother!

VERNA   But I *am* your grandmother!

RED   Me own namaw . . . slugging widdle kids!

VERNA   Junior, stop that screaming.

RED   Oh, me own Namaw that I love so much . . . turned out to be a child beater!

VERNA   I'm very sorry. . . .

> RED   *That ain't goin' to heal the hurt in me widdle heart.*
> VERNA   Did I hurt you that much, Junior?
> RED   *Well, the seat of me pants is still smoking!*[38]

In addition to Junior, Skelton portrayed other exaggerated characters. One of the funniest was Deadeye, a parody on a Western outlaw. Deadeye did everything wrong; he could not even ride a horse. "Whoa! Whoa! . . . Ah, come on, horse . . . Whoa!" the cowboy yelled, desperately trying to get his horse to halt. Deadeye had to shoot the horse to get him to stop. Another farcical character was Clem Kaddidlehopper, a moronic country bumpkin who greeted his girl friend, "W-e-e-e-l-l, Dai-sssssssyy Juuuuuuune!" Willy Lump-Lump, Bolivar Shagnasty, and J. Newton Numskull were other impersonations.[39]

Like Bergen and Brice, Skelton made his radio characters strong, dominant personalities. "I think when I do those things I actually become those people," the comedian said. "If I am the little boy I am the little boy . . . I'm the kid next door." Because Skelton imitated so many different individuals successfully, he can be considered the most versatile character comedian on radio. He also had a friendly personality over the air and developed a close rapport with the audience. Skelton wanted to leave his listeners with "something that they'll remember" at the program's end. He closed his show by saying "Goodnight . . . may God bless." "Everytime you say goodnight it goes through my mind . . . something flashes through my mind . . . suppose this is the last time," the comedian said.

> Here's a whole group of people. I've been going into their homes and we're not strangers because I've said things that they've accepted. . . . I must have communicated with them.

Skelton continued doing impersonations on radio until 1953. But by then the heyday of radio comedy was over, and the comedians were turning to television.[40]

17

The Impact of Television

During the 1948–49 season a general uneasiness settled over the radio industry. Executives worried about the advent of television and its effect on radio, and ratings fell as more people bought television sets and became addicted to the new gadget in their living rooms. There was also another serious problem. The programs on radio generally lacked originality. In 1950 there were 108 series broadcast which had been on the air for ten or more years. Listeners were tiring of the predictable formulas and overused running gags on most comedy programs. Critics heard such comments as, "I don't listen to Bob Hope any more. Sounds to me like he does the same show every week." "Is Benny kidding with those toupee jokes?" "Burns and Allen? Are they still on the air?" The veteran comedians had dominated the airwaves for years. Gosden and Correll had been on radio regularly since 1926, Allen and Benny since 1932, the Jordans since 1935, Bergen since 1937, and Hope since 1938. Sponsors refused to take chances with new talent and competed instead for the top-rated comedy shows. Summer programs sometimes gave newcomers like Jack Paar (who replaced Benny) an opportunity. Those shows, however, were rarely continued during the fall season. "Something was happening to radio comedy," wrote Steve Allen, who had a difficult time breaking into radio in the late 1940's. "People were listening to the old programs out of habit more than anything else. Many were no longer listening at all."[1]

Radio critics were the first to notice the staleness of the broadcasts. The steady barrage of insult jokes was criticized by Gilbert Seldes in *Esquire* in 1946:

> Next Sunday night, will you please listen to all your favorite comedians and note the percentage of cruel jokes. They may be self-directed, a bit of light masochism, or straight jabs to someone else's jaw.
>
> The saucy dummy in Bergen's hands turns out to be relatively mild compared to the snarling and smearing that goes on between comedians and stooges and band leaders and announcers. Fred Allen's trademark is the bags under his eyes; Benny gets it (and takes it) right and left from Rochester and Mary Livingston[e]. . . .
>
> Maybe a philosopher will discover some deep meaning in this mania for cruelty. All I say of it is that it begins to bore me. It's a translation into popular terms of the smart wisecrack, the insults that pass for wit in the comedies of Noel Coward; there's a speakeasy-age staleness over it and I feel that other sources of humor must exist beyond the physical deficiencies and imputed meanness of the comedians.[2]

As Seldes suggests, the comedians and their writers were overworking timeworn joke formulas.

Radio comedy, once the most popular form on the airwaves, competed against other types of programs in the late 1940's. Drama shows, such as *The Lux Radio Theatre*, often drew more listeners than comedy programs did. Quiz shows became a broadcasting fad, with the winners receiving substantial prize money and lucrative prizes on such popular broadcasts as *Break the Bank!* (1945), *The Bob Hawk Show* (1945), *Hit the Jackpot* (1948), *Go for the House* (1948), *Chance of a Lifetime* (1949), and *Shoot the Moon* (1950). The hosts of the quiz shows were often comedians looking for radio work. Phil Baker, Gary Moore, and Eddie Cantor took turns as master of ceremonies of *Take It or Leave It*, Groucho Marx was the host of *You Bet Your Life*, and Edgar Bergen starred on *Do You Trust Your Wife?*

During the 1948–49 season Fred Allen's program competed

against the popular musical giveaway quiz show, *Stop the Music*, on ABC. Many of Allen's former listeners now tuned their dials to *Stop the Music*, hoping they would be telephoned to identify the musical number on the program and win a fabulous prize. Before the competition Allen's Hooper rating had been 28.7. A year later, in January 1949, it was down to 11.2, a drop of over seventeen points. The comedian felt that giveaway quiz shows were inane, and he often satirized them on his program. Knowing that the odds of winning a prize on *Stop the Music* were over a million to one, he offered $5000 to any person who was phoned by the quiz show while listening to his program. Although he never had to pay a cent, Allen's offer did not improve his ratings.[3]

The incessant demands of creating a weekly radio comedy program had always perturbed Allen, but now he became increasingly bitter about the medium's insatiable appetite to devour talent. "When *Stop the Music* can give three iceboxes away instead of two and get listeners, it's a silly business to be in anyway," he said in December 1948. He later wrote in his autobiography that

> a medium that demands entertainment eighteen hours a day, seven days every week, has to exhaust the conscientious craftsman and performer. . . . For the first time in history the comedian has been compelled to supply himself with jokes and comedy material to compete with the machine.

The exhaustive process of broadcasting since 1932 had affected his health, for he suffered from high blood pressure. Ill health and poor ratings forced Allen to relinquish his program; his last regular show was aired on June 26, 1949. He made guest appearances on other radio broadcasts but never regained his earlier prominence. In his autobiography he believed, mistakenly, that his humor would be forgotten:

> Whether he knows it or not, the comedian is on a treadmill to oblivion. When a radio comedian's program is finally finished it slinks down Memory Lane into the limbo of yesteryear's happy hours. All that the come-

dian has to show for his years of work and aggravation is the echo of forgotten laughter.[4]

Comedy shows also competed against a wave of local and network disc jockey programs. Indeed, the combination of favorite recorded music and personality host was so popular even some old-time broadcasting pioneers turned to that form in the 1950's in order to remain on radio. Eddie Cantor was the host of a network disc jockey program in 1952. In 1953 Rexall canceled *Amos 'n' Andy* due to low ratings and the competition of television. Between 1954 and 1960 Gosden and Correll broadcast *The Amos 'n' Andy Music Hall*. The two comedians, who had been instrumental in radio comedy's evolution, ended their careers by playing popular records and telling *Amos 'n' Andy* jokes.

Between 1948 and 1952 television gradually began to replace radio as a major entertainment medium. In 1948 there were only 172,000 television receivers in the nation, but by 1952 Americans owned approximately seventeen million sets. In the late 1940's network executives adopted the policy of pouring radio profits into television development. A 1948 Young & Rubicam survey concluded that most advertisers preferred to sell their products via television rather than radio. When television and radio "slug it out there is little doubt who is the coming champ," said Young & Rubicam's research executive. So many sponsors wanted to advertise on evening television in the late 1940's that there was not enough time available. Despite a dwindling audience, many companies continued sponsoring their radio programs for several more seasons. As a result radio network sales remained relatively stable between 1948 and 1950.[5]

Television became the country's new pastime. Listening to Jack Benny was no longer a Sunday night ritual. The radio comedians' ratings plummeted between 1949 and 1953. Bob Hope's rating fell from 23.8 in 1949 to 12.7 in 1951. By 1953 it was down to 5.4. Television affected other leisure-time activities. In major American cities movie attendance dropped as much as 40 per cent, and many theaters closed because of lack of business. Book sales and library circulation also decreased. Restaurants and nightclubs were deserted during the hours of the most popular television shows.[6]

The nature of radio entertainment changed in the 1950's because of television. The automobile radio and the portable radio became fashionable. People listened to their car radios for
weather and traffic reports and instant news. Stations specialized
in playing rock-and-roll music or, like black stations, developed
their programming to attract a particular audience. Housewives
still depended on listening to the radio while they worked; consequently, soap operas tended to remain on the daily program
log. By contrast, the only major evening comedy show on the air
in January 1956 was *The Charlie McCarthy Show*, which was
sustained by CBS on Sunday night.

NBC attempted to revive radio variety programming with
The Big Show, which debuted on November 5, 1950. The network needed a spectacular broadcast to compete with the new
CBS comedy lineup on Sunday night which featured stars that
had been lost in the talent raids. NBC also wanted to attract advertising revenue back into radio and budgeted $50,000 for the
ninety-minute extravaganza. The hostess of *The Big Show* was
Tallulah Bankhead; Goodman Ace was the chief writer; Meredith Willson the orchestra leader; and Ed Herlihy the announcer.
Bankhead stole the broadcasts with her repartees with the guest
stars. "I've been dabbling in something which for want of a better name we shall call tee vee," Allen said. "Please, dahling—
people are eating!" Bankhead said. She addressed everyone as
"dahling" in an affected accent, and sang songs, including the
closing number, "May the Good Lord Bless and Keep You." Despite the appearance of many celebrities *The Big Show* lasted
only two seasons, and NBC lost a million dollars on the series. It
also did not attract enough listeners, because most Americans
preferred watching television.[7]

There were several reasons why the top radio comedians did
not turn to television immediately. Although they knew that radio entertainment was in trouble, the celebrities still had weekly
broadcasts earning profits. Some were also skeptical about how
they would appear visually and were not willing to take any
gambles. Then, too, television demanded more preparation than
radio. The entertainer could not read his lines from a prepared
script. A television production was much more time-consuming

than a radio broadcast. Long hours were devoted to costumes, scenery, and makeup. Instead of just standing to the side of a microphone, the television entertainer was surrounded by a maze of equipment which often blocked both his vision of the audience and the spectators' view. The hot, glaring lights caused perspiration. The comedian now worried about his image rather than the sound of his voice. On television the humor was largely visual and physical, while on radio it was aural and verbal. Radio humor relied on stimulating the listener's imagination through character exaggeration and sound effects. Television, a more literal medium, tended to take the imagination out of comedy.

Fred Allen's career in television illustrates the difficulty some radio comedians had adjusting to a visual medium. The entertainer was an outspoken critic of television. "I've decided why they call television a medium," Allen said. "It's because nothing in it is well done." Allen and Portland Hoffa often joked about television on their radio broadcasts. "Mama says since she got her television set she hasn't turned on her radio," Portland remarked. "Why?" asked Allen. "Mama says after looking at television her eyes are so blurred she can't find the radio to turn it on." Compared with radio, Allen viewed television as a mindless diversion:

> It's the poor average man who gets it in the end. As I said, up until now he could at least listen to the radio and use his imagination. Now they're even taking his imagination away from him. He has to grope his way around in a darkened living room while his 8-year-old kid has her supper served on a card table so she can watch the cowboys kill the Indians while she eats. You think we've got troubles? Imagine the digestive disorders in the next generation.

He also realized that television would devour comedians, writers, and comedy material at a much faster rate than radio had.[8]

Allen's experiences on television confirmed his suspicions. He was one of the rotating stars on *The Colgate Comedy Hour*, broadcast live from the Center Theater in New York City. The comedian was very nervous during his first program, presented in the fall of 1950, and he was bothered by the constant movement of cameras and microphone dollies. "I haven't been able to relax on a television stage with all those technicians wandering back and forth in front of me while I'm trying to tell a joke," he admitted. "They've been listening to me and the joke in rehearsals for two days, and by the time the performance rolls around, they're leaning on their cameras and staring at me with all the enthusiasm of a dead trout." The hot lights caused him to perspire profusely. *Life* magazine reviewed his debut:

> From the moment rehearsals began, he was struggling to do his best and was very nervous. He performed half apologetically, and too many of his jokes attempted to kid TV. His admirers harmed him by expecting too much and felt let down when his show was only so-so. Allen has one of the sharpest wits in show business, he can regain his prestige if he will simply relax, take TV for granted and be Fred Allen.

A television version of *Allen's Alley* on the *Comedy Hour* was not effective.[9]

There were several reasons why Allen was not a success on television. The bags under his eyes and his protruding jowls stood out. The lack of a handsome appearance was nonetheless not the main reason for his troubles. After his heart attack in 1952 he was unable to withstand the rigors of a weekly television show. The comedian's wit and social satire did not transfer well to television, while the characters of *Allen's Alley* were too exaggerated for the realism of TV. The television audience did not want to hear social commentary in the 1950's, an era symbolized by the "organization man" and the suburban "feminine mystique" housewife. The tired businessman much preferred watching Milton Berle's slapstick and pratfalls. Allen would have been excellent as the host of a late-night program similar to *The Tonight Show*, where he could have freely ad-libbed in an extemporaneous format. His talent instead was wasted as a panelist on *What's My Line* and as master of ceremonies on the quiz and interview shows, *Two for the Money* and *Judge for Yourself*. Mark Goodson, producer of those two programs, said Allen even lacked the friendly smooth personality for these productions:

Fred is a complex parodox. On the air he can't function unless he's holding something of life up by a tweezers and frowning at it. If we had a contestant on the show who had just lost a leg, saved somebody's life, beat out a fire with his bare hands and joinied the Marines, Fred would simply be constitutionally unable to say to the guy, "Gosh, we certainly are proud and happy to have you with us tonight." And yet, after the show, when some glad-handing emcee might be brushing the hero off, Fred would probably hand him a personal check for two hundred dollars and walk away fast.[10]

Allen remained bitter about television up to the time of his death on March 17, 1956.

Radio's "top bananas" entered television cautiously around 1950, doing a few specials a season rather than a complete series. That approach allowed them to test viewers' reactions and to adapt slowly to the new medium. By contrast, the first television comedians were not tied to radio and had both the freedom and desire to dedicate themselves fully to television. In television's formative years networks and sponsors were willing to take chances with newcomers, and as a result the burgeoning industry was open to innovation.

Many of the first television comedy stars were new entertainers who came from areas of show business other than radio. Sid Caesar and Imogene Coca were relative unknowns who had performed in nightclubs and off-Broadway theater. The talented pair started doing their impersonations and skits on *The Admiral Broadway Revue* in 1949 and later starred in *Your Show of Shows*. Jackie Gleason came from the Broadway theater and nightclub circuit. On *The Cavalcade of Stars* (1950), and, later, on *The Jackie Gleason Show*, he amused viewers with brilliant characterizations, ranging from the haughty millionnaire Reginald Van Gleason III to the bus driver Ralph Cramden. Dean Martin and Jerry Lewis, headliners on *The Colgate Comedy Hour*, had also been popular nightclub entertainers. They had a weekly radio show on NBC from 1949 to 1952, but Lewis's mugging and the duo's vaudeville-style slapstick were more effective on television. That medium also featured a host of other young talented comedians, including Dave Garroway, Jerry Lester, Sam Levenson, Jack Carter, Red Buttons, George Gobel, and Ernie Kovacs.

Some early television comedy stars, among them Milton Berle, had trouble in radio. A vaudeville headliner in the early 1930's, Berle had broken into radio by doing guest appearances on Rudy Vallee's show. He was master of ceremonies of *The Gillette Original Community Sing* (1936), was host of the panel joke show *Stop Me If You've Heard This One* (1939), and starred on *Let Yourself Go* (1943). On *The Milton Berle Show* (1947) and *The Texaco Star Theatre* (1948) the comedian did a typical comedy format of opening gags and closing sketches. None of those programs were very successful. The entertainer's brash manner and raucous style were not well suited to radio. Berle was primarily a visual comedian. "I didn't think I was too great on radio," he conceded. Berle admitted that he was best working in an extemporaneous format, and that a prepared script hampered his style:

> I got my biggest laughs when I did the warm-up before the show. Then I could work on the studio audience without a script, doing material I had tested out on stages and in nightclubs. But reading from a script didn't feel as good for me. I was too used to winging it in front of a live audience, feeling them out, working them. A script ties you down, and radio, being a medium for the ears, not the eyes, was not the best exposure for a visual comedian. I did okay, but I never felt I was getting across my best.[11]

In the fall of 1948 Texaco, Berle's radio sponsor, was searching for a comedian to be the host of their new television show. The oil company asked Berle and two other entertainers to do a pilot program. For the test he decided to do a show relying on the routines he had performed in vaudeville and nightclubs. Texaco executives liked the format and selected Berle to star in the television program. He was nonetheless uncertain about the new medium and did not want to give up his radio show. "As much as I thought my kind of comedy was right for television, it was still an unknown medium," he said. "Radio was here to stay, but was television?" Berle did his weekly radio program in 1948–49, but after the first year he concentrated solely on television.[12]

The Texaco Star Theatre, which premiered on September 21, 1948, was primarily a revival of the skits the comedian had performed in vaudeville. It "was the outcome of my vaudeville experience," said the comedian. "It was a vaudeville show." The program was described on circulars handed out to the studio audience as *The Texaco Star Theatre Vaudeville Show*. He hired one writer, "an old friend who helped me remember skits I'd done." Berle relied on standard slapstick sight gags, including pie-in-the-face routines and squirting stooges with seltzer bottles. He wore zany costumes and dressed as an Easter Bunny, a little kid with missing teeth and a large lollipop, and in drag. The live, hour-long program, which had a budget of only $15,000 a week, also had guest stars and regulars such as pitchman Sid Stone and ventriloquist Jimmy Nelson.[13]

Known to millions of fans as "Uncle Miltie" and "Mr. Television," Berle achieved the success there he had never received on radio. The Tuesday night eight o'clock program drew 75 per cent of the television audience in 1949. Thousands bought sets just to watch Berle's antics. When the series ended in 1954 twenty-six million homes had television receivers. His immensely popular program affected business in restaurants, nightclubs, and movie theaters. Apparently viewers even held off going to the bathroom to watch Berle. Water usage in Detroit increased dramatically as soon as the program went off the air. The phenomenal success of Berle's vaudeville-style show signaled the demise of radio comedy.[14]

Television gave new opportunity to certain other visual comedians whose style had been handicapped on radio. Ed Wynn had been off radio for a number of years when he starred on a television series during the 1949–50 season. *The Ed Wynn Show*, directed by Ralph Levy, was performed live in Hollywood and televised on the East Coast in dark gray kinescope. Like Berle, Wynn pulled out all his vaudeville sight gags. Viewers now could see his artful clowning, mugging, and bizarre costumes and hats. Wynn also proved that he was a great character actor.

In 1958–59, he played a grandfather in an amusing family situation comedy and gave an excellent dramatic performance in *Requiem for a Heavyweight* on *Playhouse 90*. Wynn also performed character roles in such films as *Mary Poppins*, *The Entertainer*, and *The Diary of Anne Frank*.[15]

Red Skelton's enormous talent for pantomime and clowning also suited a visual medium. Like the other big-name radio comedians, Skelton entered television a number of years after the first wave of television comics did. *The Red Skelton Show* premiered in September 1953 and quickly became a popular television series. Skelton brought to life his radio characters, including Junior, Sheriff Deadeye, Clem Kaddidlehopper, and Willy Lump-Lump. The comedian wore funny costumes in the vignettes. As Junior, "the mean widdle kid," he dressed in shorts, high socks, and wore a holster holding a cap pistol. Skelton enacted some of the pantomime skits he had done in vaudeville, but the ingenious comedian also created new routines. His programs always received high ratings, and he remained regularly on television until 1971. Skelton lasted much longer than the average television comic because of his large repertoire of impersonations.[16]

Another comedian who adapted successfully to television was Bob Hope. The comedian's debut occurred in 1947, when he appeared on the inaugural broadcast of KTLA, a local Los Angeles television station. Three years later he signed a five-year television contract with NBC. He did his first network program on Easter Sunday, 1950. He performed in a few yearly specials rather than a weekly series, a pattern Hope consistently followed. At first he was reluctant to leave radio and devote himself exclusively to television. In December 1952 he signed a two-million-dollar contract with the General Foods Corporation to do five weekly fifteen-minute morning shows and an evening program. On his morning radio broadcasts for housewives the comedian performed his usual short topical monologue and an ad-lib question-and-answer session with the audience. That daytime feature remained on the airwaves for two years, while his evening program lasted until 1955.

Hope found television more difficult than radio because he had to memorize lines and worry about his appearance. The format of his initial television programs, which were organized around an opening monologue and a sketch, was borrowed from the radio show. Hope, however, slowed down the pace of his monologue delivery and used facial expressions, particularly a deadpan stare, to stimulate laughter. He also relied on the techniques he had learned in vaudeville and films. The comedian was still doing television specials in the 1970's.[17]

Jack Benny's career on early television illustrates the tendency of radio comedians to either revive old vaudeville gags or to visualize comedy material from their broadcasts. Benny's debut took place on March 8, 1949, when he participated in the dedication of KTTV, which, like KTLA, was a local Los Angeles station. He performed a comic violin duet with the renowned violinist Isaac Stern and did a hillbilly musical skit. Benny, who had worried whether he would be a success, utilized sight gags from his vaudeville days. "Old Vaudevillian Benny found that the same visual gags that held old vaudeville audiences are making television grow, and as a result he was a hit . . . ," reported *Life* magazine. "But watchers who took a close look at him in moments when he was not being alert and vigorous thought he could change his line about being 'only 39' to 'only 49' and still get a laugh."[18]

Benny's television programs were partially a visual reenactment of his radio broadcasts. When Benny and his writers got together to discuss the show's transference to the new medium one of the ideas considered was televising the radio program. They decided instead to use some of the same characters and running gags. Benny's first CBS television special was shown live on the East Coast from New York's Lincoln Square Theater on October 28, 1950. For the premiere the cameras were placed in the center of the theater to give the effect of a vaudeville show. He began the program with a short monologue, which he had not done since vaudeville. "I'd give a million dollars to know how I look," he said in his opening remarks:

> Ladies and gentlemen, I must tell you why I decided to go into television at this time. You see, last year it got to be a bit embarrassing. . . . So many of my fans kept asking me why I didn't get into this particular medium. They wanted to know if I was afraid, it was my sponsor who didn't have the nerve.

Appearing with Benny were several members of his radio "gang," including Eddie Anderson, Don Wilson, Mel Blanc, and Artie Auerbach (Mr. Kitzel). Benny and his cast played the same characters they had on radio. A sketch with Dinah Shore, the singer, also highlighted the forty-five minute show. The program concluded with Benny playing his theme song, "Love in Bloom," on the violin as the disgusted audience exited on cue. The reviews were mostly favorable, although one critic felt there was too much dialogue describing the action. This was not a radio program, the reviewer reminded Benny's writers. In 1955 Benny decided to give up his radio show, which had received a rating of 5.8 in January of that year. His last regularly scheduled broadcast was on May 22, 1955. During the next nineteen years Benny appeared in many specials and a weekly TV series using many comic characters and situations from his radio program.[19]

Whether these routines were funnier on television than radio is a matter of personal preference. Certainly, the sound-effect gags (the parrot, Maxwell, and vault) did not transfer as well as other material. On television the Maxwell looked like an expensive antique collector's car. Viewers could now see the moat, crocodiles, and quicksand that surrounded Benny's vault, but the realism of television no longer allowed listeners to imagine the scene themselves. This is not to deny Benny's originality and success on the visual medium. Like Hope, Benny used facial expressions and physical gestures to gain laughter: a deadpan stare, the familiar hand-on-cheek, a forlorn expression, and a prancing walk. The humor on his television programs still depended on the fall-guy character he had created on radio. His ability to create an endearing Everyman comedy personality with universal flaws and virtues enabled him to survive on television long after Berle and the first television comics had vanished from the screen. The great American entertainer was working on a television special when he died on December 26, 1974. Benny has left the nation a treasury of unforgettable humor.[20]

Radio comedy had other influences on early television programming. Some of the first television "sitcoms" (situation comedies) were derived from radio shows. The adjustment of Italian immigrants to American life was the subject of the dialect comedy *Life with Luigi* (1948), starring Alan Reed and J. Carrol Naish. The television version of *The Goldbergs* (1949), starring Gertrude Berg, presented a sentimental portrait of Jewish family life. Family situation comedies emphasizing home, love, and family togetherness were popular television favorites in the 1950's. *Father Knows Best* (1954), *Ozzie and Harriet* (1952), *The Aldrich Family* (1949), and *The Life of Riley* (1949) were radio spinoffs. In October 1950 Burns and Allen began a family situation television comedy that resembled their radio program, and it was a popular show until 1958. Lucille Ball's *I Love Lucy* (1951), an early television comedy classic, was partly derived from the radio series, *My Favorite Husband* (1948–51), in which she had also portrayed a scatterbrained housewife who got into domestic squabbles with her husband. The two-man situation comedy format—a form perfected by Gosden and Correll—was also carried over into television. Two examples are Jackie Gleason (Ralph Cramden) and Art Carney (Ed Norton), in *The Honeymooners*, and the television version of the Neil Simon play and film *The Odd Couple.*[21]

Amos 'n' Andy made its debut on television on June 28, 1951, with an all-black cast. Gosden and Correll had performed in blackface in an experimental RCA telecast on February 26, 1939, from the New York's World Fair, but the pair felt they were now too old for the television roles. Blackface had been increasingly resented by the black community, and on television their impersonations would look unbelievable. The talented black actors and actresses chosen for the parts included Alvin Childress (Amos), Spencer Williams, Jr. (Andy), Lillian Randolph (Madame Queen), Amanda Randolph (Sapphire's mother), Ernestine Wade (Sapphire), and Tim Moore (Kingfish). Despite strong performances, the characters, dialogue, and situations still contained stereotyped features inherited from the radio series. The 1951 NAACP convention declared the television program an insult to the Negro race. The civil rights movement was beginning to agitate for black equality, so continual protests forced *Amos 'n' Andy* off the air in 1953. Although the series was withdrawn from syndication in 1966, the debate over the significance of *Amos 'n' Andy* continues. "What its detractors failed to mention is that it was the very first time that we saw blacks playing professionals—judges, lawyers, and doctors," said Alvin Childress. "It was a happy experience," Ernestine Wade told an interviewer. "I know there were those who felt offended by it, but I still have people stop me on the street to tell me how much they enjoyed it. And many of those people are black members of the N.A.A.C.P." *Amos 'n' Andy*, like *The Birth of a Nation*, remains one of the great paradoxes of show business.[22]

Other television versions of radio situation comedies failed because they did not transfer well to television. *Easy Aces* (1949), a comedy depending on witty dialogue, lasted only one season. *Fibber McGee and Molly* was televised on NBC in 1959, with Bob Sweeney and Cathy Lewis in the title roles and Hal Peary as Mayor La Trivia. The exaggerated characters of Wistful Vista lacked credibility in a medium which demanded a certain amount of realism. *The Great Gildersleeve* (1955), with Willard Waterman, also flopped for a similar reason. *Fibber McGee and Molly*, however, remained a radio favorite in the 1950's. Although Bergen and McCarthy performed in specials and did frequent guest appearances, they did not have a successful television series.

A small-scale revival of radio comedy did occur in the 1950's. The competition of television caused radio executives to experiment with new program innovations to hold listeners. That led to a more creative environment in the industry and less censorship. "Vice presidents interfered less," wrote Erik Barnouw, the broadcasting historian.

> Ad-libbing was permitted, even encouraged. Taboos fell. Venereal disease, long a forbidden subject, was suddenly discussed on scores of programs. Comedy was also liberated.

Radio now opened its doors to several freewheeling comedians whose style resembled the zanies of the early 1930's. Stan Freberg amused listeners on CBS in 1957 with his parodies of popular songs and musicians. Bob Elliott and Ray Goulding, known as Bob and Ray, created satirical skits that resembled the routines of Stoopnagle and Bud. Bob and Ray had started doing their routines after the hourly news on Boston's WHDH in 1946. Listeners liked their style so much they were soon hosts of a local program, *Matinee with Bob and Ray*. In the 1950's the two comedians appeared in various shows on network radio and local New York stations, and they were still performing on radio in the 1970's. For over twenty years the pair entertained fans with their impersonations and sketches.[23]

Bob and Ray brought a freshness to radio comedy in its twilight years with their brilliant satires on America's institutions and customs. They especially enjoyed ribbing radio programs and personalities. Bob Elliott played the absentminded radio interviewer Wally Ballou and the sportscaster Steve Bosco. Their parodies included skits called "Jack Headstrong, The All-American American," "Mary Backstayge, Noble Wife," and "One Feller's Family"—takeoffs on soap operas. They also lampooned commercials and giveaway programs. Goulding signed off by reminding listeners "to write if you get work." "And to hang by your thumbs," said Elliott. Bob and Ray continued a comic tradition dating back to the song-and-patter teams of the 1920's. They perpetuated the uproarious sounds of American humor on the airwaves.[24]

Notes

Abbreviations Used in the Notes

BA   George Burns and Gracie Allen Collection, Department of Special Collections, Doheny Library, University of Southern California, Los Angeles.

BBC   Ben Blue Collection, Miscellaneous Radio Scripts, Research Library, Department of Special Collections, University of California, Los Angeles.

EWS   Ed Wynn Scrapbooks, Research Library, Department of Special Collections, University of California, Los Angeles.

FA   Original Radio and Television Scripts of Fred Allen, microfilm copy, Manuscript Division, Library of Congress, Washington, D.C.

JBC   Jack Benny Collection, Research Library, Department of Special Collections, University of California, Los Angeles.

LBC   Lawrence G. Blochman Collection, Division of Rare Books and Special Collections, William Robertson Coe Library, University of Wyoming, Laramie.

MJC   Milton Josefsberg Collection, Jack Benny and Bob Hope Scripts, Division of Rare Books and Special Collections, William Robertson Coe Library, University of Wyoming, Laramie.

NBC   National Broadcasting Company Papers, 1923–60. Mass Communications History Center, Division of Archives and Manuscripts, State Historical Society of Wisconsin, Madison.

PPB   Pacific Pioneer Broadcasters, Hollywood, California.

PRP   Paul Rhymer Papers, Mass Communications History Center, Division of Archives and Manuscripts, State Historical Society of Wisconsin, Madison.

RB   *Radio Broadcast* Magazine.
RL   *Radio Life* Magazine.
RSC   Miscellaneous Radio Script Collection, Department of Special
      Collections, Doheny Library, University of Southern California,
      Los Angeles.
STSS *Same Time . . . Same Station*, a series of interviews with radio
      entertainers on Los Angeles station KRLA from December 26,
      1971, to January 28, 1973. John Price producer.
USC   *Amos 'n' Andy* Scripts and Scrapbooks, Department of Special
      Collections, Doheny Library, University of Southern California,
      Los Angeles.
WRMC Will Rogers Memorial Commission, Claremore, Oklahoma.

Notes to Chapter 1

1. Irving Settel, *A Pictorial History of Radio* (New York, 1960), 41. See
   also Erik Barnouw, *Tube of Plenty: The Evolution of American Television* (New York, 1975), 35, 41; Erik Barnouw, *A Tower in Babel: A
   History of Broadcasting in the United States to 1933* (New York, 1966),
   85.
2. 1923 WJZ radio logs, NBC.
3. "The Listeners Speak for Themselves," *RB*, 8 (Apr. 1926), 669-70.
4. Jack Gaver and Dave Stanley, *There's Laughter in the Air!: Radio's
   Top Comedians and Their Best Shows* (New York, 1945), 6-8.
5. *Ibid.* 5-9.
6. *RB*, 11 (May 1927), 31. See also Ben Gross, *I Looked and I Listened:
   Informal Recollections of Radio and Television* (New Rochelle, N.Y.,
   1970), 70-71.
7. Gaver and Stanley, *There's Laughter in the Air!* 11. Gross, *I Looked
   and I Listened*, 96-97.
8. Gaver and Stanley, *There's Laughter in the Air!* 2-3; Barnouw, *A
   Tower in Babel*, 86; Edgar H. Felix, *Using Radio in Sales Promotion*
   (New York, 1927), 160-61.
9. Radiola Records, MR-1001, "The Happiness Boys," *Jest Like Old
   Times*; Felix, *Using Radio in Sales Promotion*, 244.
10. Radiola, MR-1001, *Jest Like Old Times*; Felix, *Using Radio in Sales
    Promotion*, 162.
11. John Dunning, *Tune in Yesterday: The Ultimate Encyclopedia of Old-
    Time Radio, 1925–1976* (Englewood Cliffs, N.J., 1976), 235.
12. Felix, *Using Radio in Sales Promotion*, 162.
13. Gross, *I Looked and I Listened*, 101. See also Robert Campbell, *The
    Golden Years of Broadcasting: A Celebration of the First 50 Years of
    Radio and TV on NBC* (New York, 1976), 29, 31.
14. Frank Buxton and Bill Owen, *The Big Broadcast, 1920–1950* (New
    York, 1973), 187, 205; James C. Young, "Broadcasting Personality,"

RB, 5 (July 1924), 246-50. Dunning, *Tune in Yesterday*, 187, 524-25; Barnouw, *A Tower in Babel*, 159, 191.

15. John Wallace, "Why It Is Difficult To Be Funny Over the Radio," *RB*, 9 (June 1926), 134.

16. *Ibid.* 134. See also Barnouw, *A Tower in Babel*, 87, 102-4.

17. Wallace, "Why It Is Difficult To Be Funny Over the Radio," 133.

18. Gaver and Stanley, *There's Laughter in the Air!* 10; *ibid.* 134. See also Douglas Gilbert, *American Vaudeville: Its Life and Times* (1940; rpt. New York, 1963), 255-58, 278-82.

19. Barnouw, *Tube of Plenty*, 36-38; Barnouw, *A Tower in Babel*, 187; William E. Leuchtenburg, *The Perils of Prosperity, 1914–32* (Chicago, 1958), 196; George Soule, *Prosperity Decade: From War to Depression: 1917–1929* (1947; rpt. New York, 1968), 147-51; Frederick Lewis Allen, *Only Yesterday: An Informal History of the 1920's* (1931; rpt. New York, 1964), 137-38.

Notes to Chapter 2

1. Biographical information on Gosden and Correll derives from Charles Correll and Freeman Gosden, *All About "Amos 'n' Andy" and Their Creators Correll and Gosden* (New York, 1929); author's interview with Freeman Gosden, October 13, 1977; miscellaneous articles in the *Amos 'n' Andy* scrapbooks, USC; Gaver and Stanley, *There's Laughter in the Air!* 138-41.

2. Freeman F. Gosden, "Amos Looks at Andy," *RL* (Oct. 10, 1943), 32.

3. Douglas Gilbert, "Touring Southern States as Theatrical Performers," magazine clipping, *Amos 'n' Andy* Scrapbooks, USC.

4. Charles Correll discusses *Amos 'n' Andy*, *STSS*, Jan. 14, 1973.

5. Henry Selinger interview, conducted by Les Tremayne, Jan. 10, 1973, tape PPB; *Ibid.*

6. Correll, *STSS*, Jan. 14, 1973; Selinger interview, Jan. 10, 1973, PPB.

7. Russel Nye, *The Unembarrassed Muse: The Popular Arts in America* (New York, 1970), 220.

8. Ann Webb, "The Making of 'Amos's' Philosophy," *Winston-Salem* (N.C.) *Journal and Sentinel*, May 4, 1930, newspaper clipping, *Amos 'n' Andy* Scrapbooks, USC. See also Correll and Gosden, *All About "Amos 'n' Andy,"* 21, 47.

9. Robert C. Toll, *Blacking Up: The Minstrel Show in Nineteenth-Century America* (New York, 1974), 53-55; Robert C. Toll, *On With the Show: The First Century of Show Business in America* (New York, 1976), 81-109.

10. Toll, *On With the Show*, 308-9, 324-26; Gilbert, *American Vaudeville*, 278-82; Barnouw, *A Tower in Babel*, 230; Joe Laurie, Jr., *Vaudeville: From the Honky-Tonks to the Palace* (New York, 1953), 139-42; George M. Frederickson, *The Black Image in the White Mind: The*

Debate on Afro-American Character and Destiny, 1817–1914 (New York, 1972), 327-28.

11. Columbia Records, Moran and Mack, PPB. See also Leonard Maltin, *Movie Comedy Teams* (New York, 1970), 318-22; Gilbert, *American Vaudeville*, 84, 142; Laurie, *Vaudeville*, 84, 142.

12. Script #1128 (Nov. 3, 1931), p. 3, USC.

13. Harrison B. Summers, *A Thirty-Year History of Programs Carried on National Radio Networks in the United States, 1926–1956* (Columbus, Ohio, 1958) *passim;* Correll and Gosden, *All About "Amos 'n' Andy,"* 109; Buxton and Owen, *The Big Broadcast,* 57, 212-13.

14. Correll and Gosden, *All About "Amos 'n' Andy,"* 84.

15. Charles Correll and Freeman Gosden, *Sam 'n' Henry* (Chicago, 1926), 9.

16. *Ibid.* 63, 30.

17. "Sam 'n' Henry, W-G-N's Comic Story Makes Hit with Fans," clipping, *Sam 'n' Henry* Scrapbook, USC. See also Barnouw, *A Tower in Babel,* 226; Correll, *STSS,* Jan. 14, 1973.

18. Barnouw, *A Tower in Babel,* 225.

Notes to Chapter 3

1. Correll and Gosden, *All About "Amos 'n' Andy,"* 10-11, 39-40; Correll, *STSS,* Jan. 14, 1973; interview with Freeman Gosden, Oct. 13, 1977; Barnouw, *A Tower in Babel,* 226.

2. Quoted from Correll and Gosden, *All About "Amos 'n' Andy,"* 43-44. Publicity articles are in the General Publicity Scrapbook, USC. The legend is perpetuated in "The Life Story of Amos 'n' Andy," *25th Anniversary Program,* Feb. 14, 1953, CBS; on Radiola Records, 2 MR-2526, Release #25 Side A, *The Amos 'n' Andy Story.*

3. Max Eastman, *Enjoyment of Laughter* (New York, 1948), 28, 41.

4. Script #499 (Oct. 30, 1929), p. 1, USC.

5. "It's the 'Repression'!" *Decatur* (Ill.) *Herald,* Aug. 8, 1931, clipping, *Amos 'n' Andy* Scrapbooks, USC.

6. Script #502A (Nov. 3, 1929), pp. 1-2, USC.

7. Script #1539 (Mar. 7, 1933), pp. 1, 4, USC; quoted from University of Southern California publicity statement on the *Amos 'n' Andy* collection. See also interview with Gosden, Oct. 13, 1977.

8. Script #1537 (Mar. 3, 1933), p. 4, USC.

9. Script #1115 (Oct. 19, 1931), p. 1, USC.

10. Hadley Cantril and Gordon W. Allport, *The Psychology of Radio* (New York, 1935), 24.

11. Script #23 (Apr. 19, 1928), pp. 4-5, USC.

12. Script #1 (Mar. 19, 1928), p. 3; #806 (Oct. 23, 1930), p. 3, USC.

13. Script #52 (May 25, 1928), pp. 2-3, USC.

14. Script #1 (Mar. 19, 1928), p. 1; #1243 (Mar. 16, 1932), p. 4; #29 (Apr. 27, 1928), p. 2, USC.

15. Script #518 (Nov. 19, 1929), p. 4; #1108 (Oct. 10, 1931), p. 1, USC.
16. Script #1210 (Feb. 6, 1932), p. 4, USC.
17. Script #836 (Nov. 27, 1930), pp. 3-4, USC. See also #1148 (Nov. 26, 1931).
18. Script # 859 (Dec. 24, 1930), pp. 4-5, USC.
19. Charles J. Correll and Freeman F. Gosden, *Here They Are—Amos 'n' Andy* (New York, 1931), 149, 151-53.
20. Robert S. Lynd and Helen Merrell Lynd, *Middletown: A Study in Contemporary Culture* (New York, 1929), 271; *Middletown in Transition: A Study in Cultural Conflicts* (New York, 1937), 263-64.
21. Morgan E. McMahon, *A Flick of the Switch, 1930–1950* (Palos Verdes Peninsula, Calif., 1975), 2, 41, 88, 100-101, 150.
22. Cantril and Allport, *The Psychology of Radio*, 85-87.
23. "Amos 'n' Andy Moral Influence," *Newark* (Ohio) *Leader*, Feb. 27, 1930; "Lessons from Amos 'n' Andy," *Everett* (Wash.) *News*, Feb. 21, 1930; "Our Kind of Fun," *Greensburg* (Ky.) *Record-Herald*, Apr. 23, 1930, newspaper clippings, *Amos 'n' Andy* Scrapbooks, USC; Bill Hay, *Amos 'n' Andy* broadcast (Apr. 3, 1939), tape PPB.
24. Lynd, *Middletown in Transition*, 264; Cantril and Allport, *The Psychology of Radio*, 260.
25. "Our Public Gods," *Dunkirk* (Ohio) *Standard*, July 2, 1931; "Amos 'n' Andy Rise to Fame Outdoes Alger Story Hero," *Minneapolis* (Minn.) *Journal*, Apr. 16, 1930; "Amos 'n' Andy's Big Income," *Danvers* (Ill.) *Independent*, May 1, 1931; "The Seven O'Clock Calm," *McKeesport* (Pa.) *News*, Mar. 14, 1930, newspaper clippings, *Amos 'n' Andy* Scrapbooks, USC.
26. James Brown, "Lowell Thomas, A Living Treasure in History," *Los Angeles Times Calendar*, Oct. 17, 1976, 30; George Frazier, "Amos & Andy, Two Angels in Blackface," *Coronet*, 23 (Mar. 1948), 91. See also Thomas Meehan, "WEAF, 7:00-7:15—'Ow wah, ow wah, ow wah,'" *New York Times Magazine* (Dec. 31, 1972), 5-7, 26, 28, 31; Summers, *A Thirty-Year History*, 21, 27; "Amos 'n' Andy Hit Phone Co.," *Perth Amboy* (N.J.) *Evening News*, Apr. 8, 1930, clipping, *Amos 'n' Andy* Scrapbooks, USC.
27. Bill Hay interviewed by Frank Bresee on *The Golden Days of Radio*, KGIL, Sept. 5, 1976; Reginald Marsh, "The Angelus," *The New Yorker* (Jan. 3, 1931), 14-15. See also George E. Mowry (ed.), *The Twenties: Fords, Flappers & Fanatics* (Englewood Cliffs, N.J., 1963), 64.
28. Clyde B. Davis, "Secretary of State Sends Wire Objecting to 5 P.M. Broadcasting of Feature," *Rocky Mountain News*, Nov. 15, 1929, clipping, *Amos 'n' Andy* Scrapbooks, USC.
29. Frazier, "Amos & Andy, Two Angels in Blackface," 92; Correll, STSS, Jan. 14, 1973.
30. A. L. Ashby to Correll and Gosden, Jan. 14, 1931, *Amos 'n' Andy* Scrapbooks, USC; "Amos 'n' Andy Creators Took All Parts in Trial," *Shaw-*

nee (Okla.) *Evening Star,* Mar. 31, 1931, clipping, *Amos 'n' Andy* General Publicity Scrapbook, USC.

31. Correll and Gosden, *All About "Amos 'n' Andy,"* 51-59.
32. Correll, *STSS,* Jan. 14, 1973.
33. Correll and Gosden, *All About "Amos 'n' Andy,"* 83, 98-99, 113.
34. *Ibid.* 88-91.
35. "Amos 'n' Andy Dialect Rules Wherever Groups Congregate," *Norfolk* (Va.) *Pilot,* Apr. 27, 1930, clipping, *Amos 'n' Andy* Scrapbooks, USC.
36. Letter from F. M. Hander and family, entitled "An Appreciation," Aug. 19, 1929, *Amos 'n' Andy* Scrapbooks, USC.
37. Letter from Mary Justine Dutt, *Amos 'n' Andy* General Publicity Scrapbook, USC.
38. "Creators of Amos 'n' Andy Know Harlem," Houston (Tex.) *Chronicle,* Aug. 30, 1929; Douglas Gilbert, "Amos 'n' Andy," *El Paso* (Tex.) *Herald,* Apr. 10, 1930, newspaper clippings, *Amos 'n' Andy* Scrapbooks, USC.
39. Letter from Charles F. Allen in "Views on Many Topics," *Chicago Daily News,* n.d., newspaper clipping, *Amos 'n' Andy* Scrapbooks, USC. See also "Amos 'n' Andy," *Christian Science Monitor,* Feb. 20, 1929; "To Sign Books for their Fans," *Chicago Daily News,* Mar. 7, 1929; "Amos 'n' Andy and Harlem," *Boston Transcript,* Apr. 26, 1930, newspaper clippings, *Amos 'n' Andy* Scrapbooks.
40. "Would Abolish *Amos 'n' Andy,*" *Utica* (Ohio) *Herald,* Sept. 17, 1931, newspaper clipping, *Amos 'n' Andy* Scrapbooks, USC.

Notes to Chapter 4

1. The copy of *Radio Broadcasting News* is in the archives of WRMC. See also Richard M. Ketchum, *Will Rogers: His Life and Times* (New York, 1973), 175; Settel, *A Pictorial History of Radio,* 1, 47. A note in binder 005, WRMC, states that Rogers made his KDKA broadcast on Feb. 25, 1922.
2. "When Will Rogers Explained Why He Could Not Broadcast," *New York Times,* Aug. 21, 1927, Section 7, p. 10, binder 005, WRMC.
3. Radio Industries Banquet Address, Sept. 16, 1925, binder 005, WRMC.
4. *The Golden Days of Radio Television Special, KCET,* Los Angeles, Dec. 14, 1976; various *New York Times* articles, Nov. 14 to Nov. 21, 1926, binder 005, WRMC; Gleason L. Archer, *History of Radio to 1926* (New York, 1938), 347; Dunning, *Tune in Yesterday,* 187.
5. Donald Day (ed.), *Sanity Is Where You Find It: An Affectionate History of the United States in the 20's and 30's by America's Best-Loved Comedian Will Rogers* (Boston, 1955), 93.
6. *Ibid.* 93-94.
7. Calvin Coolidge to Will Rogers, Jan. 11, 1928, copy, box 5, WRMC; *Ibid.* 95.

8. Gulf radio broadcast, June 11, 1933, p. 1, binder 005, WRMC; "The Radio Scares Mr. Rogers," *Tulsa World*, Jan. 29, 1928, p. 2, binder 4, WRMC.

9. Gulf radio broadcasts, June 11, 1933, p. 3, binder 005, WRMC; July 8, 1934, p. 1, folder marked Gulf radio broadcasts, copies of original MS, WRMC.

10. Gulf radio broadcasts, May 7, 1933, p. 1; May 14, 1933, p. 1, binder 005, WRMC.

11. Gulf radio broadcasts, May 14, 1933, p. 4; June 6, 1935, p. 5, binder 005, WRMC.

12. Gulf radio broadcast, May 7, 1933, p. 1, binder 005, WRMC.

13. Gulf radio broadcast, June 11, 1933, p. 1, binder 005, WRMC.

14. Quoted by Homer Croy, *Will Rogers: Homespun Humorist: An Intimate Portrait of an Endearing Comic Philosopher*, cassette tape #431, The Center for Cassette Studies, copy, Doheny Library, University of Southern California; "Statement of J. Franklin Drake, then President of Gulf Oil Co., May 18, 1966," binder 005, WRMC. The broadcast occurred Mar. 4, 1934.

15. Interviews with Homer Croy and Will Rogers, Jr., *Will Rogers: Home-Spun Humorist*.

16. Donald Day (ed.), *The Autobiography of Will Rogers* (Boston, 1949), 39; Will Rogers, *Twelve Radio Talks Delivered by Will Rogers During the Spring of 1930 through the Courtesy of E. R. Squibb and Sons* (1930), 3.

17. Gulf radio broadcast, May 2, 1935, pp. 1-2, binder labeled verbatim transcriptions radio broadcasts, Apr. 30, 1933–June 9, 1935, WRMC.

18. President Charles L. O'Donnell of the University of Notre Dame to Will Rogers, Box 5, WRMC. Rogers discussed the Rose Bowl contest in the Gulf broadcasts of Dec. 23, 1934, Dec. 30, 1934, and Jan. 6, 1935. Quoted from the Gulf broadcast, Nov. 12, 1933, pp. 1, 3, binder 006, WRMC.

19. Day (ed.), *The Autobiography of Will Rogers*, 79.

20. Fred Allen, *Will Rogers: Homespun Humorist*; Gulf radio broadcast, May 14, 1933, p. 3, binder 005, WRMC.

21. See E. Paul Alworth, *Will Rogers* (New York, 1974), 93-124; Walter Blair, *Horse Sense in American Humor* (Chicago, 1952); Jennette Tandy, *Crackerbox Philosophers in American Humor and Satire* (New York, 1925); Norris Yates, *The American Humorist: Conscience of the Twentieth Century* (Ames, Iowa, 1964).

22. Gulf radio broadcasts, May 12, 1935, p. 5; June 4, 1933, p. 1; May 21, 1933, p. 3; Nov. 26, 1933, p. 1, binder 005 and binder labeled verbatim transcriptions, WRMC.

23. Gulf radio broadcasts, Apr. 14, 1935, p. 1; Apr. 28, 1935, p. 4, binder labeled verbatim transcriptions, WRMC.

24. Gulf radio broadcasts, May 7, 1933, p. 3; Oct. 29, 1933, p. 2, binder 005, WRMC.

25. Gulf radio broadcast, June 11, 1933, p. 1, binder 005, WRMC; Fred Allen, *Will Rogers: Homespun Humorist.*

26. Gulf radio broadcast, Apr. 28, 1935, p. 3, binder labeled verbatim transcriptions, WRMC. See also J. L. Dillard, *American Talk: Where Our Words Come From* (New York, 1976); Constance Rourke, *American Humor: A Study of the National Character* (1931; rpt. New York, 1953), 15-69.

27. Gulf radio broadcasts, Apr. 14, 1935, p. 2, binder labeled verbatim transcriptions; June 4, 1933, p. 2, binder 005, WRMC.

28. Gulf radio broadcasts, June 4, 1933, p. 1; June 2, 1935, p. 2, binder 005, WRMC.

29. Rogers, *Twelve Radio Talks*, 14; Gulf radio broadcast, Apr. 14, 1935, p. 3, binder labeled verbatim transcriptions, WRMC.

30. "Will Rogers To Receive $77,000 for 13 Programs over Columbia Stations," *Hackensack* (N.J.) *Record*, Mar. 31, 1930, clipping, *Amos 'n' Andy* Scrapbooks, USC.

31. "Will Rogers To Become Regular Radio Star in Weekly Broadcasts," Squibb publicity material, binder 005, WRMC; Rogers, *Twelve Radio Talks*, 8, 35.

32. "Rogers Tells 'Em in Radio Speech," *Beverly Hills Citizen*, Oct. 23, 1931, copy, binder 005, WRMC; radio address, Oct. 18, 1931, reprinted in Ketchum, *Will Rogers*, 298-99.

33. Gulf radio broadcasts, Nov. 5, 1933, pp. 2-3, binder 005; Dec. 30, 1934, p. 5, binder labeled verbatim transcriptions, WRMC.

34. Gulf radio broadcasts, Oct. 29, 1933, p. 1, binder 005; Dec. 23, 1934, p. 1, binder labeled verbatim transcriptions; Apr. 30, 1933, p. 1, binder 005, WRMC.

35. *Time* (May 1, 1939), 44; see also *The Journal of Applied Psychology* (Feb. 1939). Hazel A. Sawyer to Rogers and Richard H. Van Esselstyn to Rogers, Feb. 5, 1934, Box 6, WRMC.

36. "Will Rogers To Become Regular Radio Star in Weekly Broadcasts," Squibb publicity material; Gulf radio broadcast, May 7, 1933, p. 2, binder 005, WRMC.

37. Gulf radio broadcast, May 7, 1933, p. 2, binder 005, WRMC.

38. Gulf radio broadcast, Apr. 30, 1933, pp. 2, 5, binder 005, WRMC.

39. Gulf radio broadcasts, Aug. 27, 1933, p. 2; Jan. 14, 1934, p. 4, binder 005, WRMC.

40. Gulf radio broadcasts, Jan. 14, 1934, p. 4, folder labeled Gulf radio broadcasts, copies of original 1934 MS; Feb. 3, 1935, p. 1, binder labeled verbatim transcriptions, WRMC.

41. Gulf radio broadcast, Apr. 21, 1935, pp. 1, 3, binder labeled verbatim transcriptions, WRMC.

42. Gulf radio broadcast, Apr. 28, 1935, p. 2, binder labeled verbatim transcriptions, WRMC.

43. Gulf radio broadcast, Apr. 21, 1935, p. 2, binder labeled verbatim transcriptions, WRMC.
44. Gulf radio broadcasts, Nov. 26, 1933, p. 1; Jan. 6, 1935, p. 1, binder 005, WRMC. The "Death of the Republican Party" was broadcast Nov. 11, 1934.
45. Gulf radio broadcast, May 12, 1935, pp. 4-5, binder labeled verbatim transcriptions, WRMC.
46. Gulf radio broadcast, May 21, 1933, pp. 1-2, binder 005; telegram in WRMC.
47. See Gulf radio broadcasts, Jan. 13, 1935, pp. 4-5; Jan. 28, 1934, p. 2; Mar. 4, 1934, p. 5, binder 005, WRMC.
48. President Franklin D. Roosevelt to Walter M. Harrison, secretary, Will Rogers Memorial Commission, Oct. 15, 1938, Box 5, WRMC.

Notes to Chapter 5

1. Robert J. Landry, *This Fascinating Radio Business* (New York, 1946), 159-60; Fred Allen, *Treadmill to Oblivion* (Boston, 1954), 12-14; Gilbert Seldes, *The Great Audience* (1950; rpt. Westport, Conn., 1970), 126; Gilbert, *American Vaudeville*, 214; Barnouw, *A Tower in Babel*, 244-45; Nye, *The Unembarrassed Muse*, 170-71; Albert F. McLean, Jr., *American Vaudeville as Ritual* (Lexington, Ky., 1965), 106-37.
2. Eddie Cantor with Jane Kesner Ardmore, *Take My Life* (Garden City, N.Y., 1957), 213-43; Gaver and Stanley, *There's Laughter in the Air!* 114-18.
3. Cantor, *Take My Life*, 216; Summers, *A Thirty-Year History*, 31, 37.
4. Carroll Carroll, *None of Your Business: Or My Life with J. Walter Thompson (Confessions of a Renegade Radio Writer)* (New York, 1970), 37; Eddie Cantor and David Freedman, *My Life Is In Your Hands* (New York, 1932), 307-9.
5. Carroll, *None of Your Business*, 34-35; Alan Reed interview, STST, May 28, 1972.
6. Quoted from Keenan Wynn, Introduction to *Ed Wynn, The Fire Chief as the Perfect Fool*, Mark 56 Records #621, a George Garabedian production. Biographical details on Wynn derive from Keenan Wynn, *Ed Wynn's Son* (Garden City, N.Y., 1959) *passim*; Gaver and Stanley, *There's Laughter in the Air!* 153-57; Gilbert, *American Vaudeville*, 251-53; Larry Wilde, *The Great Comedians Talk About Comedy* (New York, 1968), 369-82; clippings, EWS.
7. Wilde, *The Great Comedians Talk About Comedy*, 370.
8. Gilbert, *American Vaudeville*, 251.
9. *Ibid.* 253.
10. *Ibid.* 252.
11. Archer, *History of Radio to 1926*, 243; Sam J. Slate and Joe Cook, *It Sounds Impossible* (New York, 1963), 30.

12. Allen, *Treadmill to Oblivion*, p. 13; Wynn, *Ed Wynn's Son*, 89; Buxton and Owen, *The Big Broadcast*, 50; Dunning, *Tune in Yesterday*, 207.

13. Eddie Cantor, *Take My Life* (1930; rpt. Garden City, N.Y., 1957), 214; Cantril and Allport, *The Psychology of Radio*, 100-103.

14. Ed Wynn, *The Fire Chief as the Perfect Fool*; Ogden Mayer, "Backstage at a Broadcast," *Radio Stars* (Jan. 1933), clipping in EWS.

15. Richard B. O'Brien, "After a Year Ed Wynn Finds Being Funny on the Radio a Difficult Task," *New York Times*, Apr. 23, 1933, clipping, EWS. See also Wynn, *Ed Wynn's Son*, p. 90; *Worcester* (Mass.) *Gazette*, Jan. 12, 1933, clipping, EWS.

16. Robert West, *The Rape of Radio* (New York, 1941), 259-60.

17. *Ibid.* 260-61.

18. Ed Wynn, "My Friend Graham," *Radio Guide* (July 11, 1936), 43, clipping, EWS. *The Fire Chief Program*, Feb. 12, 1935, tape, PPB.

19. Ed Wynn, *The Fire Chief as the Perfect Fool*; "Flashes of Fun," *Radio Guide* (Nov. 10, 1934), clipping, EWS.

20. *The Fire Chief Program*, Feb. 12, 1935, tape, PPB.

21. *The Fire Chief Program*, Feb. 21, 1933, tape, PPB.

22. Gaver and Stanley, *There's Laughter in the Air!* 158-60.

23. West, *The Rape of Radio*, 237-38. *The Fire Chief Program*, Jan. 22, 1935, tape, PPB.

24. *The Fire Chief Programs*, Aug. 9, 1932, Aug. 30, 1932, tapes PPB; Wynn, "My Friend Graham," 10.

25. Wilde, *The Great Comedians Talk About Comedy*, 376. Keenan Wynn, Introduction to Ed Wynn, *The Fire Chief as the Perfect Fool*.

26. Gaver and Stanley, *There's Laughter in the Air!* 154; *Worcester* (Mass.) *Gazette*, Jan. 12, 1933, clipping, EWS.

27. *Boston* (Mass.) *Record*, Sept. 29, 1932, and *Cleveland* (Ohio) *Press*, Dec. 15, 1932, clippings, EWS; Gaver and Stanley, *There's Laughter in the Air!* 157; Keenan Wynn, *Ed Wynn's Son*, 86-91.

28. *The Fire Chief Programs*, Jan. 22, 1935, Jan. 10, 1932, tapes, PPB. Gaver and Stanley, *There's Laughter in the Air!* 160.

29. Wilde, *The Great Comedians Talk About Comedy*, 375; *The Fire Chief Program*, Feb. 12, 1935, tape, PPB.

30. Keenan Wynn, *Ed Wynn's Son*, 86; Ed Wynn Radio Script, Apr. 10, 1934, 13, David Freedman Collection, Theatre Arts Library, University of California, Los Angeles; *The Fire Chief* program, Feb. 21, 1933, tape, PPB.

31. *Milwaukee Journal*, clipping, EWS; the 1932 *Nation* article is reprinted in Cantril and Allport, *The Psychology of Radio*, 40; see also various clippings, EWS.

32. Summers, *A Thirty-Year History*, 31, 37, 43. The C.A.B., or Crossley ratings, was the first service to be widely used in the industry (from 1929–30 through 1936–37). Ratings were secured either in the first week of February or the first week of April. Telephone calls were made

to listeners in various cities by Crossley, Inc., a private research organization.
33. "Ed Wynn To Return to Air," clipping, EWS.
34. West, *The Rape of Radio*, 224; Summers, *A Thirty-Year History*, 6, 59. The rating service of C. E. Hooper, Inc., was widely used in the industry from 1935–36 through 1948–49. The Hooper ratings were based on telephone calls made in 28 to 36 cities. Summers quotes the ratings for the first week in January of each year.
35. Keenan Wynn, *Ed Wynn's Son*, 92-93; Gaver and Stanley, *There's Laughter in the Air!* 155.
36. Keenan Wynn, Introduction to *Ed Wynn, The Fire Chief as the Perfect Fool*.
37. Clippings, Scrapbook marked "Personals," EWS.
38. Summers, *A Thirty-Year History*, 123; Dunning, *Tune in Yesterday*, 207-8.
39. Wilde, *The Great Comedians Talk About Comedy*, 378.

Notes to Chapter 6

1. For biographical information on Penner see Dunning, *Tune in Yesterday*, 330-31; Joe Penner interviewed by Dale Armstrong, *Radiolio Program*, KFI, Feb. 15, 1935, tape, PPB.
2. *NBC Silver Jubilee Show*, Sept. 30, 1951, tape, PPB; Rudy Vallee and Gil McKean, *My Time Is Your Time: The Rudy Vallee Story* (New York, 1962), 87; Vallee interviewed by Frank Bresee, *The Golden Days of Radio*, tape, PPB.
3. *The Bakers' Broadcast* script, Oct. 15, 1933, pp. 5-8, Parke Levy Collection, Division of Rare Books and Special Collections, William Robertson Coe Library, University of Wyoming.
4. Summers, *A Thirty-Year History*, 37; Dunning, *Tune in Yesterday*, 331.
5. Summers, *A Thirty-Year History*, 43, 67, 75, 83.
6. For biographical information on Pearl see Richard Lamparski, *Whatever Became of?* (New York, 1967), 188-89; Laurie, *Vaudeville*, 86; Dunning, *Tune in Yesterday*, 323; Jack Pearl interviewed by Richard Lamparski on the *Whatever Became of?* radio program, Feb. 1966, tape, PPB.
7. Summers, *A Thirty-Year History*, 31, lists his rating at 47.2.
8. For ethnic characterizations on the stage see Toll, *On With the Show*, 105, 185, 289.
9. Radiola Records, Jack Pearl, *Jest Like Old Times*.
10. Summers, *A Thirty-Year History*, 37, 59; Irving A. Fein, *Jack Benny: An Intimate Biography* (New York, 1977), 63.
11. Quoted from Gaver and Stanley, *There's Laughter in the Air!* 285-86. See also Slate and Cook, *It Sounds Impossible*, 124-25. John Barry,

"Harvard Men Write Radio Skits," *Boston Globe*, July 20, 1930, clip-ping, *Amos 'n' Andy* Scrapbooks, USC; Buxton and Owen, *The Big Broadcast*, 64; Dunning, *Tune in Yesterday*, 150-51.

12. Gaver and Stanley, *There's Laughter in the Air!* 285, 288.
13. *Ibid.* 285, 291.
14. *Ibid.* 284.
15. Andrew Bergman, *We're in the Money: Depression America and Its Films* (New York, 1972), 41.
16. Groucho Marx with Hector Arce, *The Secret Word Is Groucho* (New York, 1976), 1. See also Dunning, *Tune in Yesterday*, 656-58.
17. John Lahr, *Notes on a Cowardly Lion: The Biography of Bert Lahr* (New York, 1970), 171-72.
18. Gaver and Stanley, *There's Laughter in the Air!* 183-88; Dunning, *Tune In Yesterday*, 571-73.
19. Gaver and Stanley, *There's Laughter in the Air!* 183.
20. *Ibid.* 184.
21. *Ibid.* 186.
22. *Ibid.* 193-95.
23. *Ibid.* 194-95.

Notes to Chapter 7

1. Leo Rosten, "Jack Benny, America's Favorite 'Fall Guy,' " *Look*, XIV (May 9, 1950), 55.
2. Martin Grotjahn, *Beyond Laughter* (New York, 1957), 22.
3. For biographical information on Benny see Mary Livingstone Benny and Hilliard Marks with Marcia Borie, *Jack Benny* (Garden City, N.Y., 1978); Irving A. Fein, *Jack Benny: An Intimate Biography* (New York, 1976); Milt Josefsberg, *The Jack Benny Show: The Life and Times of America's Best-Loved Entertainer* (New Rochelle, N.Y., 1977).
4. Jack Benny, "The Best Advice I Ever Had," *Reader's Digest*, LXXIV (Mar. 1959), 78.
5. Benny and Marks, *Jack Benny*, 28-29. Josefsberg states that it was the actor Pat O'Brien who walked on stage, not Wolff (*The Jack Benny Show*, 30-31).
6. Walter Walker, "Jack Benny—He Has To Be Loved," *Look*, IX (May 13, 1945), 35.
7. Fein, *Jack Benny*, 33.
8. Jack Benny, "The Best Advice I Ever Had," 77. See also Benny and Marks, *Jack Benny*, 113.
9. Fein, *Jack Benny*, 33; Cantor, *Take My Life*, 113.
10. Benny and Marks, *Jack Benny*, 35-36; Cantor, *Take My Life*, 227.
11. Frederick Van Ryn, "This is Jack Benny—Who Cares?" *Reader's Digest*, XLII (June 1943), 88; Ed Sullivan, *Jack Benny Tribute Radio Show*,

May 9, 1941, NBC, tape, PPB; Maurice Zolotow, *No People Like Show People* (New York, 1951), 185; Benny and Marks, *Jack Benny*, 55; Dunning, *Tune in Yesterday*, 316-17.

12. Zolotow, *No People Like Show People*, 185; *Ben Bernie Show* script, Oct. 2, 1938, p. 2, Parke Levy Collection, Division of Rare Books and Special Collections, William Robertson Coe Library, University of Wyoming.

13. *Canada Dry Ginger Ale Program*, script #1, Vol. I (May 2, 1932), p. 1, JBC; also tape, PPB.

14. On Boasberg see George Burns, *Living It Up or They Still Love Me in Altoona* (New York, 1976), 168-70; *Canada Dry Ginger Ale Program*, script #1, Vol. I (May 2, 1932), pp. 1, 6, JBC.

15. *Canada Dry Ginger Ale Program*, script #4, Vol. I (May 11, 1932), p. 1, JBC.

16. *Canada Dry Ginger Ale Program*, script #1, Vol. I (May 2, 1932), p. 5; tape, PPB. See also Benny and Marks, *Jack Benny*, 56; Josefsberg, *The Jack Benny Show*, 322.

17. "First draft, synoptic outline, and several comedy sequences for new Canada Dry Jack Benny programs," David Freedman Collection, Theatre Arts Library, University of California, Los Angeles.

18. On Conn see Burns, *Living It Up*, 163-64.

19. *The Chevrolet Program*, script #23, Vol. III (Mar. 11, 1934), p. 2; script #22, Vol. III (Mar. 4, 1934), p. 2, JBC.

20. *The Chevrolet Program*, script #22, Vol. III (Mar. 4, 1934), p. 12, JBC.

21. Wilde, *The Great Comedians Talk About Comedy*, 45.

22. Benny and Marks, *Jack Benny passim*; Mary Livingstone Benny, "My 48-Year Love Affair with Jack Benny," *McCall's* (Feb. 1978), 113, 198, 200, 203-4, 207, 209.

23. See *The Chevrolet Program*, script #23, Vol. III (Mar. 11, 1934); *The General Tire Program*, script #19, Vol. IV (Aug. 3, 1934), p. 3, JBC. For a discussion of Jewish stage caricatures see Toll, *On With the Show*, 289-90; Laurie, *Vaudeville*, 175-76; Gilbert, *American Vaudeville*, 290-92.

24. Summers, *A Thirty-Year History*, 37; Zolotow, *No People Like Show People*, 185; Fein, *Jack Benny*, 62; Benny and Marks, *Jack Benny*, 58; Kenneth M. Goode, *What About Radio?* (New York, 1937), 133-34.

25. *The General Tire Program*, script #7, Vol. IV (May 18, 1934), pp. 8-9, JBC.

26. Ann Comar, "Don Wilson: Toasty Brown Malty-Rich," *RL* (Jan. 9, 1944), 4-5, 34; Don Wilson interviewed on *The Merv Griffin Show*, Jan. 28, 1976.

27. *The General Tire Program*, script #8, Vol. IV (May 25, 1934), p. 2; script #4, Vol. IV (Aug. 27, 1934), p. 2, JBC.

28. Josefsberg, *The Jack Benny Show*, 159, 258-59; Fein, *Jack Benny*, 65-67.

29. *The Jell-O Program*, script #2, Vol. V (Oct. 21, 1934), pp. 5-6; script

#38, Vol. VII (June 20, 1937), p. 3; script #13, Vol. VII (Dec. 27, 1936), p. 10, JBC.

30. Fein, *Jack Benny*, 70-71; Benny and Marks, *Jack Benny*, 93.

31. *The Jell-O Program*, script #30, Vol. VII (Apr. 25, 1937), p. 2; script #21, Vol. VII (Feb. 21, 1937), p. 3, JBC.

32. Frank del Olmo, "Eddie Anderson, Famed 'Rochester,' Dies at 72," *Los Angeles Times*, Mar. 1, 1977, Part I, 3, 12; Richard Lamparski, *Whatever Became of?* 4th series (New York, 1972), 110-11; Benny and Marks, *Jack Benny*, 76-77; Thomas Cripps, *Slow Fade to Black: The Negro in American Film, 1900–1942* (New York, 1977), 258-60.

33. *The Jell-O Program*, script #38, Vol. VII (Mar. 28, 1937), pp. 6-7, 10-11, JBC.

34. del Olmo, "Eddie Anderson, Famed 'Rochester,' Dies at 72," 3.

35. *The Jell-O Program*, script #38, Vol. VII (June 20, 1937), p. 6. See also Joseph Boskin, "The National Jester in the Popular Culture," *The Great Fear: Race in the Mind of America*, eds. Gary B. Nash and Richard Weiss (New York, 1970), 180.

36. *The Jell-O Program*, Apr. 12, 1942, p. 9, RSC.

37. *The Jell-O Program*, script #38, Vol. VII (June 20, 1937), pp. 12-13, JBC.

38. Estelle Edmerson, "A Descriptive Study of the American Negro in United States Professional Radio, 1922–1953" (unpubl. Master's essay, 1954, University of California, Los Angeles), 185; Milton Josefsberg, comments on the Jack Benny script collection, p. 8, MJC.

39. Edmerson, "A Descriptive Study of the American Negro in . . . Radio," 61, 186.

40. Gaver and Stanley, *There's Laughter in the Air!* 45, 51, 59, 67, 75.

41. Summers, *A Thirty-Year History*, 43.

Notes to Chapter 8

1. Fred Allen, *NBC Biography in Sound*, "A Portrait of Fred Allen," May 31, 1956, tape, PPB; Fred Allen, *Much Ado About Me* (Boston, 1956) traces his childhood and vaudeville career.

2. Zolotow, *No People Like Show People*, 281.

3. *Town Hall Tonight*, June 22, 1938, p. 16, FA.

4. *NBC Biography in Sound*.

5. *Ibid.* Zolotow, *No People Like Show People*, 282, 282n.

6. Allen, *Much Ado About Me*, 177, 202, 205; Gilbert, *American Vaudeville*, 263.

7. Allen, *Much Ado About Me*, 202; *NBC Biography in Sound*; Gaver and Stanley, *There's Laughter in the Air!* 20.

8. Allen, *Treadmill to Oblivion*, 3.

9. *Ibid.* 4-5.

10. Arnold M. Auerbach, *Funny Men Don't Laugh* (Garden City, N.Y., 1965), 125; *Ibid.* 5.

11. Allen, *Treadmill to Oblivion*, 7.
12. *Ibid.* 14.
13. *Linit Bath Club Revue*, Oct. 30, 1932, p. 3, FA. See also Radio Archives Records, LP 1002, *Fred Allen, Linit Bath Club Revue*, Side 1, Dec. 25, 1932.
14. Allen, *Treadmill to Oblivion*, 16; *Linit Bath Club Revue*, Oct. 23, 1932, p. 17, FA.
15. *Linit Bath Club Revue*, Feb. 19, 1933, p. 1; Oct. 23, 1932, p. 5; Mar. 5, 1933, p. 2; Jan. 22, 1933, p. 3, FA.
16. Roger White, producer of the Linit Show, comments on *NBC Biography in Sound*.
17. Fred Allen to Jack Mulcahy, *Fred Allen's Letters*, ed. Joe McCarthy (Garden City, N.Y., 1965), 195. See also Allen, *Treadmill to Oblivion*, 30; Goode, *What About Radio?* 198-99.
18. Allen, *Treadmill to Oblivion*, 155.
19. Auerbach, *Funny Men Don't Laugh*, 143-44. See also Allen, *Treadmill to Oblivion*, 154-59; Auerbach, 118-75.
20. Goodman Ace remarked on the *NBC Biography in Sound* that Allen made the statement about California in a letter to him.
21. *NBC Biography in Sound*.
22. Author's interview with Sylvester (Pat) Weaver, June 14, 1977, Santa Barbara, Calif.
23. Auerbach, *Funny Men Don't Laugh*, 162; Allen, *Treadmill to Oblivion*, 155.
24. Interview with Pat Weaver.
25. *Town Hall Tonight*, Jan. 30, 1935, p. 1; Mar. 13, 1935, pp. 2-3, FA.
26. *Town Hall Tonight*, June 1, 1938, p. 3, FA. See also Allen, *Treadmill to Oblivion*, 33-34.
27. *Town Hall Tonight*, May 15, 1935, p. 11; June 22, 1938, p. 13, FA. See also Auerbach, *Funny Men Don't Laugh*, 133.
28. *Town Hall Tonight*, Apr. 17, 1935, p. 7, FA.
29. *Town Hall Tonight*, Jan. 23, 1935, pp. 6-7, FA.
30. *Town Hall Tonight*, June 22, 1938, pp. 10-11, LBC.
31. *Town Hall Tonight*, June 15, 1938, p. 6, FA.
32. Allen, *Treadmill to Oblivion*, 41; Zolotow, *No People Like Show People*, 274-75.
33. *Town Hall Tonight*, Apr. 19, 1939, p. 4, LBC; Feb. 6, 1935, p. 5, FA. *The Fred Allen Show*, Oct. 20, 1946, p. 3; Apr. 14, 1946, p. 2; Feb. 28, 1943, p. 16, LBC. See also Steve Allen, *The Funny Men* (New York, 1956), 54-59.
34. Allen, *Treadmill to Oblivion*, 68; *Town Hall Tonight*, Dec. 7, 1938, in *Best Broadcasts of 1938–39*, ed. Max Wylie (New York, 1939), 223-24.
35. *Town Hall Tonight*, Mar. 23, 1940, tape, PPB; Allen, *Treadmill to Oblivion*, 123, 125, 128.
36. Allen, *Treadmill to Oblivion*, 131-32.
37. *Ibid.* 46-48.

38. *Town Hall Tonight*, May 1, 1935, p. 11, FA; May 8, 1935, p. 11, FA; May 15, 1935, p. 12, FA; Feb. 23, 1938, pp. 18, 18A, LBC.
39. *Town Hall Tonight*, Apr. 17, 1935, p. 11, FA.
40. *Town Hall Tonight*, May 25, 1938, pp. 35-36, FA. See also Auerbach, *Funny Men Don't Laugh*, 133.
41. Wilde, *The Great Comedians Talk About Comedy*, 45.
42. *NBC Silver Jubilee Show*, Oct. 7, 1951, tape, PPB.
43. Elizabeth Ribben, "A Conversation with Jack Benny," n.d., tape, JBC.
44. For Benny's version see Radiola Records, 2 MR-2930, *The Radio Fight of the Century, Jack Benny vs. Fred Allen*; Allen, *Treadmill to Oblivion*, 54.
45. *The Jell-O Program*, Jan. 3, 1937, tape, JBC; *The Radio Fight of the Century*.
46. *The Jell-O Program*, script #15, Vol. VII (Jan. 10, 1937), pp. 1-3, JBC.
47. *Town Hall Tonight* (addition), Jan. 20, 1937, p. 1, FA; *The Jell-O Program*, script #37, Vol. VII (Jan. 24, 1937), p. 5, JBC.
48. *The Jell-O Program*, script #18, Vol. VII (Jan. 31, 1937), p. 14, JBC; *Town Hall Tonight*, Feb. 3, 1937, pp. 1-2, FA; *The Jell-O Program*, script #19, Vol. VII (Feb. 7, 1937), p. 13, JBC.
49. *Town Hall Tonight*, Feb. 17, 1937, pp. 2-3; Feb. 3, 1937, p. 13, FA; *The Radio Fight of the Century*.
50. *The Jell-O Program*, Mar. 7, 1937, tape, PPB; *Town Hall Tonight*, Mar. 10, 1937, p. 31-A, FA.
51. *The Jell-O Program*, Mar. 14, 1937, tape, PPB; *The Radio Fight of the Century*.
52. *Town Hall Tonight*, Feb. 8, 1939, p. 32; Feb. 22, 1939, p. 29, LBC.
53. *Town Hall Tonight*, Mar. 23, 1938, p. 22, FA; Mar. 30, 1938, pp. 22-23, FA; Apr. 13, 1938, p. 30, FA; Mar. 1, 1939, p. 37, LBC. *The Jell-O Program*, Mar. 27, 1938, tape, PPB. *The Jack Benny Program*, Feb. 4, 1945, p. 17, MJC; Dec. 31, 1944, tape, PPB.
54. *The Fred Allen Show*, Feb. 4, 1945, p. 17, LBC; *The Jell-O Program*, Mar. 27, 1938, tape, PPB; *The Jack Benny Program*, May 19, 1946, p. 20, MJC.
55. *The Jack Benny Program*, June 27, 1948, p. 17, MJC; Josefsberg, *The Jack Benny Show*, p. 242.
56. *The Radio Fight of the Century*, May 26, 1946. See also the script in the Nat Hiken Collection, Mass Communications History Center, State Historical Society of Wisconsin.
57. Summers, *A Thirty-Year History*, pp. 43, 59, 67, 75; interview with Pat Weaver.

Notes to Chapter 9

1. For a discussion of vaudeville mixed acts see Laurie, *Vaudeville*, 226-31.
2. For biographical information pertaining to the Aces see Mark Singer,

"Profiles—Goody," *The New Yorker* (Apr. 4, 1977), 41-80; Gaver and Stanley, *There's Laughter in the Air!* 196-200.

3. Singer, "Profiles—Goody," 44-45.

4. *Ibid.* 46.

5. *Ibid.* 49.

6. Summers, *A Thirty-Year History*, 33.

7. Their ratings registered between 7 and 8; see Summers, *A Thirty-Year History*, 54, 61, 69, 77, 86, 94, 102.

8. Goodman Ace discusses *Easy Aces, STSS*, May 14, 1972; Larry Wilde, *How the Great Comedy Writers Create Laughter* (Chicago, 1976), 14.

9. Wilde, *How the Great Comedy Writers Create Laughter*, 13, 15.

10. Goodman Ace, *Ladies and Gentlemen, Easy Aces* (Garden City, N.Y., 1970), 58; see also 33-57, 139-61.

11. Singer, "Profiles—Goody," 44-45; Gaver and Stanley, *There's Laughter in the Air!* 199; Wilde, *How the Great Comedy Writers Create Laughter*, 10.

12. See George Burns with Cynthia Hobart Lindsay, *I Love Her, That's Why!* (New York, 1955) *passim*; George Burns, *Living It Up or They Still Love Me in Altoona, passim*; Benny and Marks, *Jack Benny*, 35.

13. Burns, *I Love Her, That's Why!* 5. See also Irving Howe, *World of Our Fathers: The Journey of the East European Jews to America and the Life They Found and Made* (New York, 1976), 210n, 556, 558, 560, 562.

14. Joyce Haber, "George Burns Still Not Acting His Age," *Los Angeles Times Calendar*, Aug. 24, 1975, 31; Burns, *Living It Up*, 162. See also Laurie, *Vaudeville*, 45.

15. Wilde, *The Great Comedians Talk About Comedy*, 137.

16. *Ibid.* 138-39.

17. Stage routine, Box #1, BA; *Living It Up*, 57.

18. Bill Smith, *The Vaudevillians* (New York, 1976), 84.

19. Burns, *Living It Up*, 52-55.

20. Burns, *I Love Her, That's Why!* 137.

21. Gracie Allen guest spot, *The Chase and Sanborn Hour*, Nov. 15, 1931, BA.

22. Burns, *Living It Up*, 182; see also 172-85.

23. Carroll Carroll, *None of Your Business*, 48.

24. *The Robert Burns Panatela Program*, script #6 (Mar. 28, 1932), 7, BA; *Burns and Allen Show*, Jan. 13, 1937, tape, BA.

25. *The White Owl Program*, Sept. 6, 1934, tape, PPB; *The Robert Burns Panatela Program*, script #2 (Feb. 29, 1932), pp. 6-8, BA.

26. *Burns and Allen Show*, Jan. 13, 1937, tape, BA; *The Robert Burns Panatela Program*, script #37 (Nov. 2, 1932), p. 3, BA.

27. Burns and Allen Joke Books, Joke #61, BA; see *The Robert Burns Panatela Program*, script #6 (Mar. 28, 1932), p. 12, BA.

28. Burns and Allen Joke Books, Jokes #203, #1747, BA; *The Robert Burns Panatela Program*, script #3 (Mar. 7, 1932), p. 6, BA.

29. *The N.R.A. Program,* Box #1 (1931–1937), pp. 1-2, BA.
30. George Burns interviewed by Frank Bresee, *The Golden Days of Radio,* KGIL, Nov. 28, 1976; Carroll, *None of Your Business,* 45. See also Burns, *I Love Her, That's Why!* 149-51.
31. Summers, *A Thirty-Year History,* 75, 83, 91; Wilde, *The Great Comedians Talk About Comedy,* 148-49.

Notes to Chapter 10

1. For biographical information pertaining to the Jordans see Gaver and Stanley, *There's Laughter in the Air!* 83-88; Jim Harmon, *The Great Radio Comedians* (Garden City, N.Y., 1970), 23-32; Dunning, *Tune in Yesterday,* 200-206.
2. Jim Jordan interviewed by Frank Bresee, *The Golden Days of Radio,* KGIL, Nov. 14, 1976.
3. Author's telephone interview with Jim Jordan, Jan. 25, 1977; Madeleine Edmondson and David Rounds, *The Soaps: Day Time Serials of Radio and TV* (New York, 1973), 27.
4. *The Golden Days of Radio,* Nov. 14, 1976; Summers, *A Thirty-Year History,* 21.
5. Summers, *A Thirty-Year History,* 59, 115.
6. Gaver and Stanley, *There's Laughter in the Air!* 87.
7. *Fibber McGee and Molly* Script Summaries, Apr. 16, 1935; Apr. 23, 1935, PPB.
8. *Ibid.* Apr. 23, 1935; Sept. 30, 1935, PPB.
9. *Ibid.* Oct. 7, 1935, PPB.
10. *Ibid.* Mar. 25, 1941; Jan. 1, 1946, PPB.
11. *Fibber McGee and Molly* script, May 14, 1940, pp. 16-17, PPB.
12. Constance Rourke, *American Humor,* 48-49; John Truesdell, "Tain't Funny McGee!" *Cincinatti Enquirer,* Feb. 9, 1941, clipping, Billy Mills Scrapbook, Vol. I, PPB; Richard M. Dorson, *American Folklore* (Chicago, 1959), pp. 216-26, 232-36.
13. *Fibber McGee and Molly* scripts, Jan. 6, 1942, p. 20, RSC; Dec. 26, 1944, pp. 4-5, PPB.
14. *Fibber McGee and Molly* script, Nov. 9, 1948, p. 12, PPB; Jim Jordan interviewed by Les Tremayne, Feb. 7, 1973, tape, PPB.
15. See the *Fibber McGee and Molly* script, Aug. 26, 1935, PPB.
16. Arthur Asa Berger, *The Comic-Stripped American: What Dick Tracy, Blondie, Daddy Warbucks, and Charlie Brown Tell Us About Ourselves* (Baltimore, 1974), 102-11.
17. *Fibber McGee and Molly* script, Dec. 26, 1944, p. 5, PPB.
18. *Ibid.* Mar. 15, 1940, pp. 4-5, 23-25, PPB.
19. *Ibid.* Feb. 2, 1943, p. 10, PPB.
20. *Fibber McGee and Molly* broadcast excerpt, "Top Ten Albums," 1947, tape PPB; *Fibber McGee and Molly* script, Mar. 25, 1941, p. 4, PPB.

21. *Fibber McGee and Molly* script, Nov. 11, 1941, p. 23, PPB.
22. *Ibid.* Jan. 28, 1941, p. 5, PPB.
23. *Ibid.* Mar. 25, 1941, p. 6, PPB; *Fibber McGee and Molly* broadcast, June 1, 1948, tape, PPB.
24. Dunning, *Tune in Yesterday*, 205.
25. *The Golden Days of Radio*, Nov. 14, 1976.
26. *Fibber McGee and Molly* script, June 21, 1938, p. 6, PPB.
27. *Ibid.* May 14, 1940, p. 15, PPB; Feb. 3, 1942, p. 16, RSC.
28. *Fibber McGee and Molly* script, Apr. 22, 1941, p. 21, PPB.
29. *Fibber McGee and Molly* script, Apr. 14, 1942, pp. 21-22, RSC.
30. *Fibber McGee and Molly* script, June 11, 1940, p. 20; Jan. 24, 1939, p. 16, PPB.
31. *Ibid.* Oct. 25, 1938, pp. 4-6, PPB; *Fibber McGee and Molly* script, reprinted in *Best Broadcasts of 1940–41*, ed. Max Wylie (New York, 1942), 96.
32. *Fibber McGee and Molly* script, Oct. 26, 1948, p. 22, PPB.
33. *Fibber McGee and Molly* broadcasts, May 25, 1945; June 1, 1948, tapes, PPB; script, Apr. 3, 1935, p. 23, PPB.
34. Gaver and Stanley, *There's Laughter in the Air!* 241. See also Harold Peary discusses *The Great Gildersleeve*, STSS, Dec. 26, 1971.
35. *Fibber McGee and Molly* scripts, Dec. 29, 1939, p. 24; Oct. 17, 1939, p. 8, PPB.
36. *Ibid.* Sept. 30, 1941, pp. 14, 24, PPB. See also Dunning, *Tune in Yesterday*, 249-53.
37. *Fibber McGee and Molly* script, Feb. 1, 1944, p. 20, PPB. See also "Is It True What They Say About Beulah!" *RL* (Nov. 4, 1945), 28-31.
38. *Fibber McGee and Molly* scripts, Nov. 11, 1941, p. 4; Feb. 7, 1938, p. 18, PPB.
39. *Fibber McGee and Molly* broadcast, Sept. 5, 1939, author's tape.

Notes to Chapter 11

1. For biographical details pertaining to Rhymer see Mary Frances Rhymer, Introduction to *The Small House Half-Way Up in the Next Block: Paul Rhymer's Vic and Sade* (New York, 1972), xvii-xxii; "Vic & Sade," *Time* (Dec. 27, 1943), 42.
2. William Idelson, Pacific Pioneer Broadcasters Nostalgia Night, Jan. 23, 1975, tape, PPB. See also Rhymer, *The Small House Half-Way Up the Next Block*, xix; Harmon, *The Great Radio Comedians*, 44.
3. William Idelson interviewed by Richard Lamparski, *Whatever Became of Vic and Sade?* Nov. 2, 1971, tape, PPB.
4. William Idelson discusses *Vic and Sade*, STST, Jan. 23, 1972.
5. Quoted from untitled clipping, PRP.
6. STST, Jan. 23, 1972; Don Weldon, "Paul Rhymer, Madcap Marquis of Vic and Sade," *Los Angeles Times Calendar*, Apr. 11, 1976, 32.

7. John Gihon to Paul Rhymer, Mar. 20, 1933, Box 36, correspondence folder, PRC.

8. Jean Shepherd, Foreword to *Vic and Sade: The Best Radio Plays of Paul Rhymer*, ed. Mary Frances Rhymer (New York, 1976), xiii. See also *STST*, Jan. 23, 1972.

9. Buxton and Owen, *The Big Broadcast*, 250; Rhymer, *The Small House Half-Way Up in the Next Block*, 39; Rhymer, *Vic and Sade*, 176, 136.

10. Rhymer, *The Small House*, 149, 131, 40; Rhymer, *Vic and Sade*, 100; *Time* (Dec. 27, 1943), 42.

11. Rhymer, *Vic and Sade*, 131-34.

12. *Ibid.* 75, 77.

13. *Vic and Sade* broadcast, Jan. 4, 1943, tape, PPB.

14. *Vic and Sade* broadcasts, Sept. 20, 1943, June 16, 1942, May 28, 1937, tapes, PPB.

15. Rhymer, *Vic and Sade*, 60, 64.

16. *Vic and Sade* broadcast, "Missing Person," n.d., tape, PPB; *Vic and Sade* script, Feb. 4, 1935, p. 1, Box 8, PRC.

17. *Vic and Sade* broadcasts, n.d., tapes, PPB.

18. Rhymer, *Vic and Sade*, 95.

19. Pacific Pioneer Broadcasters Nostalgia Night, Jan. 23, 1975; *STST*, Jan. 23, 1972; *Whatever Became of Vic and Sade?* Nov. 2, 1971.

20. Rhymer, *Vic and Sade*, 136, 197.

21. *Ibid.* 115; Rhymer, *The Small House*, 169.

22. Rhymer, *The Small House*, 202.

23. *Ibid.* 101-102, 106.

24. *Whatever Became of Vic and Sade?* Nov. 2, 1971.

25. Betty Hammer, "It's Great To Be Old," *RL* (Dec. 29, 1946), 8.

26. Rhymer, *The Small House*, 299.

27. Shepherd, Foreword to *Vic and Sade*, xi; see also 105-13.

28. *Vic and Sade* broadcast, Sept. 29, 1944, author's tape.

Notes to Chapter 12

1. Mary Jane Higby, *Tune in Tomorrow* (New York, 1968), 20-22; Cripps, *Slow Fade to Black*, 269.

2. Erik Barnouw, *The Golden Web: A History of Broadcasting in the United States, 1933 to 1953* (New York, 1968), 103-5; Dunning, *Tune in Yesterday*, 282-83, 378-79; Abel Green and Joe Laurie, Jr., *Show Biz From Vaude to Video* (New York, 1951), 537; *Variety Radio Directory, 1937–1938* (New York, 1937), 184-85.

3. Cripps, *Slow Fade to Black*, 269; Barnouw, *The Golden Web*, 104; Maltin, *Movie Comedy Teams*, 163-83, 333-35.

4. Summers, *A Thirty-Year History*, 109; also 69, 89, 94, 102.

5. Carlton Cheney, "Blackface is a Big Business," clipping dated Oct. 1947, *Amos 'n' Andy* Scrapbooks, USC; Summers, *A Thirty-Year History*, 118.

6. Cabell Phillips, *The 1940s: Decade of Triumph and Trouble* (New York, 1975), 189; Richard R. Lingeman, *Don't You Know There's a War On?: The American Home Front, 1941–1945* (New York, 1970), 272.
7. John Morton Blum, *V Was for Victory: Politics and American Culture During World War II* (New York, 1976), 16-17, 53; Geoffrey Perrett, *Days of Sadness, Years of Triumph: The American People, 1939–1945* (Baltimore, 1973), 299; Robert K. Merton, *Mass Persuasion: The Social Psychology of a War Bond Drive* (New York, 1946) *passim*; Lingeman, *Don't You Know There's a War On?* 175; Dunning, *Tune in Yesterday*, 415, 615.
8. Barnouw, *The Golden Web*, 159-60, 196-97; Theodore Stuart DeLay, Jr., "An Historical Study of the Armed Forces Radio Service to 1946" (unpubl. Ph.D. dissertation, Dept. of Speech, University of Southern California, 1951) *passim*; Edward M. Kirby and Jack W. Harris, *Star-Spangled Radio* (Chicago, 1948), 59.
9. Theodore S. DeLay, Jr., "A Historical Study of the Radio Series *Command Performance*" (unpubl. research paper, Dept. of Speech, University of Southern California, June 1950) *passim*; Kirby and Harris, *Star-Spangled Radio*, 42-51; Barnouw, *The Golden Web*, 159-60; Dunning, *Tune in Yesterday*, 145-46.
10. Kirby and Harris, *Star-Spangled Radio*, 50; DeLay, "A Historical Study of the Radio Series *Command Performance*," 53.
11. DeLay, "An Historical Study of the Armed Forces Radio Service to 1946," 132, 246-47, 674; DeLay, "A Historical Study of the Radio Series *Command Performance*," 41; Barnouw, *The Golden Web*, 108, 194; Red Skelton, *Mike Douglas Show*, CBS-TV, Mar. 31, 1977.
12. DeLay, "An Historical Study of the Armed Forces Radio Service to 1946," 246, 674; DeLay, "A Historical Study of the Radio Series *Command Performance*," 75 Barnouw, *The Golden Web*, 109.
13. DeLay, "An Historical Study of the Armed Forces Radio Service to 1946," 247-49, 674-79; DeLay, "A Historical Study of the Radio Series *Command Performance*," 75-80; Barnouw, *The Golden Web*, 245.
14. Phillips, *The 1940s*, 186; Kirby and Harris, *Star-Spangled Radio*, 225; Dunning, *Tune in Yesterday*, 127.
15. Navy Enlistment Broadcast, Jan. 24, 1942, Radio and Stage Scripts, File #3 (1940–42), BA.
16. See *The Jack Benny Program*, Jan. 21, 1945; *Texaco Star Theatre*, Dec. 31, 1941; Lingeman, *Don't You Know There's A War On?* 226.
17. Johnny Lee, "Radio Chatter," *Schenectady* (N.Y.) *Gazette*, Nov. 30, 1942; "Amos 'n' Andy Get New Honor, 'Essential to Morale,'" *Niagara Falls* (N.Y.) *Gazette*, Nov. 21, 1942, clippings, *Amos 'n' Andy* Scrapbooks, USC; *Amos 'n' Andy* broadcast, Dec. 24, 1941; tape, PPB.
18. *Fibber McGee and Molly* broadcast, Dec. 9, 1941, tape, PPB; script, Dec. 16, 1941, p. 22, PPB; broadcast, June 6, 1944, tape, PPB.
19. Mileage Rationing Show, n.d., pp. 5-6, Box #4, BA.

20. Allen, *Treadmill to Oblivion*, 102; *Texaco Star Theatre*, Jan. 3, 1943, p. 7, FA.
21. *The Jack Benny Program*, Aug. 29, 1944; Feb. 4, 1945, tapes, PPB. See also Josefsberg, *The Jack Benny Show*, 472.
22. *Texaco Star Theatre*, May 16, 1943, p. 2, LBC; *Texaco Star Theatre*, Dec. 13, 1942, p. 4, FA; *Fibber McGee and Molly*, Jan. 6, 1942, p. 6, RSC. See also Blum, *V Was for Victory*, 46.

Notes to Chapter 13

1. For biographical details pertaining to Hope see Bob Hope, *Have Tux, Will Travel: Bob Hope's Own Story* (New York, 1954); Bob Hope and Bob Thomas, *The Road to Hollywood: My Forty-Year Love Affair with the Movies* (Garden City, N.Y., 1977); Joe Morella, Edward Z. Epstein, and Eleanor Clark, *The Amazing Careers of Bob Hope, From Gags to Riches* (New Rochelle, N.Y., 1973).
2. Hope, *Have Tux, Will Travel*, 27-28.
3. *Ibid.* 6.
4. *Ibid.* 49.
5. *Ibid.* 66.
6. Wilde, *The Great Comedians Talk About Radio*, 271.
7. *Ibid.* 73, 75, 89, 86.
8. Campbell, *The Golden Years of Broadcasting*, 10; see also Morella *et al.*, *The Amazing Careers of Bob Hope*, 72-73; Hope, *Have Tux, Will Travel*, 104-5.
9. Bob Hope, *They've Got Me Covered* (Hollywood, Calif., 1941), 38, 40; Hope, *Have Tux, Will Travel*, 109.
10. Campbell, *The Golden Years of Broadcasting*, 10.
11. William Robert Faith, "Bob Hope and the Popular Oracle Tradition in American Humor" (unpubl. Ph.D. dissertation, Dept. of Communications, University of Southern California, June 1976), 107; Summers, *A Thirty-Year History*, 51.
12. Hope, *Have Tux, Will Travel*, 214.
13. *Ibid.* 135; *Bob Hope's 60th Birthday Party* broadcast, May 11, 1963, tape, PPB.
14. Hope, *Have Tux, Will Travel*, 209; Campbell, *The Golden Years of Broadcasting*, 13.
15. Hope, *Have Tux, Will Travel*, 234.
16. Hope and Thomas, *The Road to Hollywood*, 29.
17. Wilde, *How the Great Comedy Writers Create Laughter*, 149; see also Jack Douglas, *A Funny Thing Happened to Me on the Way to the Grave* (New York, 1962), 53-55; Hope, *Have Tux, Will Travel*, 213-14; Faith, "Bob Hope and the Popular Oracle Tradition in American Humor," 113-14.
18. *The Pepsodent Show*, Sept. 27, 1938, scene 10, p. 1, MJC.

19. *The Pepsodent Show,* Oct. 13, 1942, p. 8-5, Box 3, BBC; *The Pepsodent Show* broadcast, June 4, 1946, tape, PPB.
20. *The Pepsodent Show,* Jan. 8, 1946, pp. 1-A-1, 1-A-2, Box 16, BBC.
21. Hope and Thomas, *The Road to Hollywood,* 30-31; Morella *et al., The Amazing Careers of Bob Hope,* 86.
22. *The Pepsodent Show,* Nov. 21, 1939, pp. 9-3, 9-4, MJC.
23. Marcia Sinclair, "The Transformation of Miss Vera Vague," *RL,* 8 (Nov. 28, 1943), 33; *The Pepsodent Show,* May 5, 1941, p. 8-5, MJC. See also Milton Josefsberg's comments on the MJC, pp. 2-3.
24. Hope, *Have Tux, Will Travel,* 214; *The Pepsodent Show,* Sept. 27, 1938, scene 2, p. 1; Apr. 20, 1943, scene 2, p. 1, MJC.
25. *The Pepsodent Show,* Sept. 27, 1938, scene 2, pp. 1-3, MJC.
26. Hope, *Have Tux, Will Travel,* 214; *The Pepsodent Show,* Oct. 18, 1938, scene 2, pp. 1-2, MJC. The laugh lines were marked by Josefsberg. See also Faith, "Bob Hope and the Popular Oracle Tradition in American Humor," 117.
27. Hope, *Have Tux, Will Travel,* 257-58.
28. *The Bob Hope Show* broadcast, Nov. 9, 1948, tape, PPB. See also Faith, "Bob Hope and the Popular Oracle Tradition in American Humor," 120-21, 271.
29. Hope, *Have Tux, Will Travel,* 248.
30. J. Anthony Lukas, review of *The Road to Hollywood, New York Times Book Review* (July 17, 1977), 13, 30; "Comedian As Hero," *Time* (Dec. 22, 1967), 59.
31. *The Pepsodent Show,* Jan. 5, 1943, pp. 2-2, 2-3, MJC; Dec. 29, 1942, p. 2-2, Box 4, BBC.
32. *The Pepsodent Show,* Mar. 11, 1941, pp. 5-5, 5-6, Box 3, BBC; Oct. 6, 1947 (preview), p. 5-1, Box 16, BBC.
33. Hope, *Have Tux, Will Travel,* 103.
34. *The Bob Hope Show* broadcast, Dec. 7, 1948, tape, PPB; *The Pepsodent Show,* Mar. 18, 1940, p. S-3, MJC; *Bob Hope's 60th Birthday Party* broadcast, May 11, 1963, tape, PPB.
35. Hope, *Have Tux, Will Travel,* 189.
36. *The Pepsodent Show,* Mar. 31, 1941, p. 2-1; Mar. 3, 1941, p. 2-1; Apr. 20, 1943, pp. 2-1, 2-2; Dec. 1, 1941, p. 2-1, MJC.
37. *The Pepsodent Show,* Dec. 16, 1941, p. 2A-1; Apr. 20, 1943, scene 9, MJC.
38. Bob Hope, *I Never Left Home* (New York, 1944) *passim;* Campbell, *The Golden Years of Broadcasting,* 14; "Hope for Humanity," *Time* (Sept. 20, 1943), 43.
39. Hope, *I Never Left Home,* 114-15; Bob Hope, "Sure-Fire Gags for the Fox Hole," *New York Times,* May 28, 1944, 16.
40. Hope, "Sure-Fire Gags for the Fox Hole," 16; Hope, *I Never Left Home,* 205-6; see also Faith, "Bob Hope and the Popular Oracle Tradition in American Humor," 140-47.

41. Summers, *A Thirty-Year History*, 75, 83, 91, 99, 107, 123.
42. *Ibid.* 157.

Notes to Chapter 14

1. Josefsberg, *The Jack Benny Show*, 122-29; George Balzer talk, Braille Institute, Los Angeles, Apr. 13, 1977, tape, PPB.
2. Mary Benny and Hilliard Marks, *Jack Benny*, 99-100, 167-68; Balzer talk, Braille Institute, Apr. 13, 1977; Gaver and Stanley, *There's Laughter in the Air!* 48.
3. George Balzer talk, Pacific Pioneer Broadcasters Nostalgia Night, Mar. 31, 1977, tape, PPB; Radiola Records, 2MR-4546, *The Jack Benny Story* Record; Gross, *I Looked and I Listened*, 128.
4. *The Jack Benny Program*, Mar. 28, 1948, p. 22, MJC; Josefsberg, *The Jack Benny Show*, 147; see also pp. 146, 475-76; Benny and Marks, *Jack Benny*, 171.
5. Elizabeth Ribben, "A Conversation with Jack Benny," tape, JBC; *The Jack Benny Program*, Feb. 13, 1949, pp. 19-20, MJC.
6. *The Jack Benny Program*, Mar. 4, 1945, p. 12, MJC; broadcast, May 15, 1949, tape, PPB.
7. *The Jack Benny Program*, Apr. 1, 1951, pp. 15-16, MJC.
8. *The Jack Benny Program*, Jan. 7, 1945, p. 17; MJC.
9. *Ibid.* pp. 14-17, 19.
10. Ann Comar, "We Nominate for Radio Stardom: Mel Blanc, Man of Many Voices," *RL* (Jan. 2, 1944), pp. 6-7, 35; Dunning, *Tune in Yesterday*, 405-6.
11. Josefsberg, *The Jack Benny Show*, 103.
12. *The Jack Benny Program*, Nov. 14, 1948, pp. 2-3, MJC. See also Mel Blanc interview, *The Merv Griffin Show*, Aug. 12, 1977.
13. *The Jack Benny Program*, May 27, 1945, p. 2; Apr. 29, 1945, pp. 11-12, MJC.
14. *Ibid.* Sept. 23, 1951, p. 19, MJC.
15. Henry Popkin, "The Vanishing Jew of Our Popular Culture," *Commentary*, 14 (July 1952), 46-55; Josefsberg, *The Jack Benny Show*, 107-8; *The Jack Benny Program*, Jan. 6, 1946, pp. 16-17, MJC.
16. *The Jack Benny Program* broadcast, Dec. 2, 1945, tape, PPB.
17. Benny and Marks, *Jack Benny*, 105-10; Josefsberg, *The Jack Benny Show*, 86-87; Dennis Day interview, *Merv Griffin Show*, Aug. 12, 1977.
18. *The Jack Benny Program*, Feb. 25, 1951, pp. 6-7, MJC.
19. Dunning, *Tune in Yesterday*, 156.
20. *Ibid.* 479-82.
21. Fein, *Jack Benny*, 121-23.
22. Robert Metz, *CBS: Reflections in a Bloodshot Eye* (Chicago, 1975), 137-48.
23. Eugene Lyons, *David Sarnoff: A Biography* (New York, 1966), 286.

24. "The Benny Tug O' War," *Newsweek* (Dec. 6, 1948), 58; *Ibid.*
25. *The Jack Benny Program*, Dec. 26, 1948, pp. 20-21, MJC.
26. Fein, *Jack Benny*, 123; see also *The Jack Benny Program*, Jan. 2, 1949.

Notes to Chapter 15

1. Allen, *Treadmill to Oblivion*, 105-06.
2. *Ibid.* 164.
3. *Ibid.* 179.
4. *Ibid.* 180; Summers, *A Thirty-Year History*, 67, 75, 83, 91, 99, 107.
5. *Texaco Star Theatre*, Dec. 6, 1942, p. 4, LBC.
6. Allen, *Treadmill to Oblivion*, 152; Alan Reed interview, *STSS*, Jan. 9, 1972. See also "Rites Pending for Actor Alan Reed," *Los Angeles Times*, June 16, 1977, Pt. III, 13.
7. *The Fred Allen Show*, Mar. 17, 1946, p. 11; June 27, 1946, p. 11, LBC; *STSS*, Jan. 9, 1972.
8. *Texaco Star Theatre*, Jan. 10, 1943, pp. 4-5, LBC; Allen, *Treadmill to Oblivion*, 181.
9. "Here's Mrs. Nussbaum!" *Tune In* (Feb. 1946), 16-17.
10. *The Fred Allen Show*, Jan. 13, 1946, p. 6; Nov. 4, 1945, p. 8; June 2, 1946, pp. 10-11; Radiola Records, MR-1008, *Down in Allen's Alley*, Dec. 28, 1947.
11. Allen, *Treadmill to Oblivion*, 192; Dunning, *Tune in Yesterday*, 221; Kenny Delmar, *NBC Biography in Sound*, May 31, 1956, tape, PPB.
12. *The Fred Allen Show*, Nov. 4, 1945, p. 4; Feb. 24, 1946, p. 5; Jan. 13, 1946, pp. 3-4, LBC.
13. *Ibid.* May 15, 1949, pp. 4-6, LBC.
14. *Ibid.* Jan. 13, 1946, pp. 3-4, LBC.
15. *Ibid.* May 15, 1949, p. 10; LBC. See also Toll, *On With the Show*, 105-6, 183, 185-86.
16. *The Fred Allen Show*, Mar. 16, 1947, p. 9, LBC; Allen, *Treadmill to Oblivion*, 193-94.
17. *The Fred Allen Show*, Mar. 17, 1946, pp. 7-9, LBC.
18. Allen, *Treadmill to Oblivion*, 220.
19. *The Fred Allen Show*, Oct. 27, 1946, pp. 22-24, LBC.
20. *Ibid.* pp. 27-28, 30.
21. Allen, *Treadmill to Oblivion*, 27.
22. Fred Allen to Al Maister, June 20, 1941, *Fred Allen's Letters*, 231; *Town Hall Tonight*, Mar. 29, 1939, pp. 2-3, LBC. See also *Ibid.* 29; Cantril and Allport, *The Psychology of Radio*, 56; Carroll, *None of Your Business*, 132.
23. Interdepartment correspondence, Feb. 9, 1946, Fred Allen file, NBC; Gross, *I Looked and I Listened*, 131-32.
24. Interdepartment correspondence, Oct. 19, 1946; Mar. 5, 1947; Feb. 22, 1947; Nov. 26, 1945; Fred Allen File, NBC.

25. Auerbach, *Funny Men Don't Laugh,* 150.
26. Allen, *Treadmill to Oblivion,* 213; Harmon, *The Great Radio Comedians,* 174-75.
27. *Town Hall Tonight,* Mar. 22, 1939, p. 2; *The Fred Allen Show,* June 2, 1946, pp. 3-4, LBC.
28. Joseph Julian, *This Was Radio: A Personal Memoir* (New York, 1975), 220-21; see also interdepartment correspondence, Apr. 21, 1947, Fred Allen File, NBC.
29. Letter of Niles Trammell, May 5, 1947, Fred Allen File, NBC.
30. Joe McCarthy, Introduction to *Fred Allen's Letters,* p. ix; Herman Wouk to the Editor of *New York Times,* Mar. 18, 1956, *Fred Allen's Letters,* 358.

Notes to Chapter 16

1. Edgar Bergen interviewed by Les Tremayne, Nov. 15, 1972, tape, PPB; Smith, *The Vaudevillians,* 38-49; Gaver and Stanley, *There's Laughter in the Air!* 65-74.
2. Laurie, *Vaudeville,* 113; Bergen interview, Nov. 15, 1972; see also Smith, *The Vaudevillians,* 43; Laurie, *Vaudeville,* 114-17, 321, 441.
3. Bergen interview Nov. 15, 1972; Smith, *The Vaudevillians,* 39; Gaver and Stanley, *There's Laughter in the Air!* 66; Marshall Berges, "Frances and Edgar Bergen," *Los Angeles Times Home Magazine,* Feb. 12, 1978, 38.
4. Berges, "Frances and Edgar Bergen," 38.
5. Smith, *The Vaudevillians,* 39-40; Bergen interview, Nov. 15, 1972.
6. Smith, *The Vaudevillians,* 44.
7. Bergen interview, Nov. 15, 1972; Berges, "Frances and Edgar Bergen," 40.
8. *Royal Gelatin Hour,* Dec. 17, 1936, tape, PPB; Berges, "Frances and Edgar Bergen," 40.
9. Buxton and Owen, *The Big Broadcast,* 76-77.
10. Edgar Bergen interview, *Candid Session,* KABC, Oct. 24, 1960, tape, Dept. of Special Collections, Doheny Library, University of Southern California; Berges, "Frances and Edgar Bergen," 41.
11. Gaver and Stanley, *There's Laughter in the Air!* 69-70.
12. "The Birth of Charlie McCarthy," *Radio Guide* (Dec. 4, 1937), 21-23; Dunning, *Tune in Yesterday,* 126; *ibid.* 69-70.
13. *The Chase and Sanborn Hour,* Dec. 29, 1940, p. 2, RSC.
14. *Ibid.* Sept. 25, 1938, p. 6; June 15, 1941, p. 5, RSC.
15. Nye, *The Unembarrassed Muse,* 216-21; Berger, *The Comic-Stripped American,* 23-46.
16. *The Chase and Sanborn Hour,* Apr. 6, 1941, p. 19, RSC; *The Edgar Bergen and Charlie McCarthy Show,* n.d., tape, PPB.
17. Ronald J. Fields (ed.), *W. C. Fields by Himself: His Intended Auto-*

biography with Hitherto Unpublished Letters, Notes, Scripts, and Articles (Englewood Cliffs, N.J., 1973), 201-3.

18. Robert Lewis Taylor, *W. C. Fields: His Follies and Fortunes* (Garden City, N.Y., 1949), 309; Smith, *The Vaudevillians*, 48-49; Bergen interview, *Candid Session*, Oct. 24, 1960; Carlotta Monti with Cy Rue, *W. C. Fields and Me* (New York, 1971), 148.

19. Fields, *W. C. Fields by Himself*, 243-44; *The Chase and Sanborn Hour*, Nov. 8, 1942, pp. 12, 17A, Box 19, BBC; Monti, *W. C. Fields and Me*, 152.

20. Fields, *W. C. Fields by Himself*, 255, 260.

21. Excerpt reprinted in *The Strenuous Decade: A Social and Intellectual Record of the Nineteen-Thirties*, eds. Daniel Aaron and Robert Bendiner (Garden City, N.Y., 1970), 289; Mae West, *Goodness Had Nothing To Do with It* (New York, 1970), 182.

22. H. B. Summers, *Radio Censorship* (New York, 1939), 29; Warren Susman (ed.), *Culture and Commitment, 1929–1945* (New York, 1973), 110-11.

23. Aaron and Bendiner, *The Strenuous Decade*, 384, 390-91.

24. West, *Goodness Had Nothing To Do with It*, 183.

25. Smith, *The Vaudevillians*, 48; *The Edgar Bergen and Charlie McCarthy Show*, Mar. 23, 1947, p. 9, Box 20, BBC.

26. *The Chase and Sanborn Hour*, Nov. 5, 1939, p. 5, RSC.

27. The show was rated the top comedy program in January of 1938, 1939, 1940, and 1942. See Summers, *A Thirty-Year History*, 67, 75, 83, 91, 95. See also Buxton and Owen, *The Big Broadcast*, 57, 242; Dunning, *Tune in Yesterday*, 180, 471, 611-13.

28. Norman Katkov, *The Fabulous Fanny: The Story of Fanny Brice* (New York, 1953) *passim*; Gaver and Stanley, *There's Laughter in the Air!* 163-66; Toll, *On With the Show*, 321-24.

29. Katkov, *The Fabulous Fanny*, 244-45; "Baby Snooks is 25!" *RL* (Apr. 7, 1946), 28.

30. Katkov, *The Fabulous Fanny*, 243, 244, 287.

31. *Ziegfeld Follies of the Air*, Jan. 27, 1936, pp. 5-8, David Freedman Collection, Theatre Arts Library, University of California, Los Angeles.

32. *Ibid.* Apr. 4, 1936, p. A, David Freedman Collection, Theatre Arts Library, University of California, Los Angeles.

33. *The Baby Snooks Show*, May 29, 1951, tape, PPB; see also Dunning, *Tune in Yesterday*, 51-54, 216, 240-41.

34. Culbreth Sudler, "Sitting in on a Skelton Rehearsal," *RL* (Jan. 23, 1944), 4-5, 35; Harmon, *The Great Radio Comedians*, 14-17.

35. Summers, *A Thirty-Year History*, 99, 107, 131, 141, 149, 157, 165, 193; Settel, *A Pictorial History of Radio*, 140.

36. *The Raleigh Cigarette Program*, Nov. 8, 1942, p. 29, Box 6, BBC.

37. *Ibid.* Jan. 20, 1942, p. 30, Box 6, BBC.

38. *Ibid.* Apr. 30, 1946, pp. 21-22, RSC.

39. *Ibid.* May 19, 1946, pp. 7-8, Box 20; Dec. 26, 1942, pp. 9-10, Box 7, BBC.
40. Red Skelton interview, *Voices in the Wind*, May 14, 1977, National Public Radio, KUSC Los Angeles.

Notes to Chapter 17

1. Allen, *The Funny Men*, 13, 14; see also Barnouw, *The Golden Web*, 285.
2. Gilbert Seldes, "Notes and Queries," *Esquire*, 25 (Mar. 1946), 78. Shortly afterward Seldes appeared on Benny's show and they did a dull skit in which the characters were overly nice to one another.
3. Summers, *A Thirty-Year History*, 149, 157; Allen, *Treadmill to Oblivion*, 214-19.
4. Allen, *Treadmill to Oblivion*, 238-40; *Time* (Dec. 1948), p. 37.
5. Joseph C. Gulden, *The Best Years, 1945–1950* (New York, 1976), 176. See also Barnouw, *The Golden Web*, 284-86, 295; Barnouw, *Tube of Plenty*, 103; Nye, *The Unembarrassed Muse*, 405-6.
6. Summers, *A Thirty-Year History*, 157, 175, 193; Barnouw, *The Golden Web*, 286; Barnouw, *Tube of Plenty*, 114.
7. Lee Israel, *Tallulah Bankhead* (New York, 1972), 271. See also Tallulah Bankhead, *Tallulah: My Autobiography* (New York, 1952), 293-94; Summers, *A Thirty-Year History*, 175, 185; Dunning, *Tune in Yesterday*, 66-67; Mark Singer, "Profiles—Goody," *The New Yorker* (Apr. 4, 1977), 41-80.
8. Israel, *Tallulah Bankhead*, 271; *The Fred Allen Show*, Feb. 6, 1949, pp. 2-3, LBC; Joe McCarthy, "What Do You Think of Television, Mr. Allen?" *Life* (July 4, 1949), 72.
9. Max Wilk, *The Golden Age of Television: Notes from the Survivors* (New York, 1976), 55; "You Can Do Better, Mr. Allen," *Life* (Oct. 23, 1950), 86.
10. Allen, *The Funny Men*, 43.
11. Milton Berle with Haskel Frankel, *Milton Berle* (New York, 1975), 210; see also 207, 208-9, 222-24, 261.
12. Berle, *Milton Berle*, 294.
13. Smith, *The Vaudevillians*, 73; Charles Champlin, "Reunion of Uncle Miltie's Million-Member Family," *Los Angeles Times Calendar*, Mar. 26, 1978, 47.
14. Champlin, "Reunion of Uncle Miltie's Million-Member Family," 47.
15. Wilk, *The Golden Age of Television*, 85.
16. Barnouw, *Tube of Plenty*, 314.
17. Hope, *Have Tux, Will Travel*, 237-38; Campbell, *The Golden Years of Broadcasting*, 15-16.
18. "Benny Tries TV; Old Vaudeville Gags Come in Handy as He Wows Los Angeles Audience," *Life* (Apr. 4, 1949), 50.
19. *The Jack Benny Television Show*, Oct. 28, 1950, tape, PPB; Benny and Marks, *Jack Benny*, 182-83; Summers, *A Thirty-Year History*, 213.

20. Josefsberg, *The Jack Benny Show*, 383, 388-406.
21. Dunning, *Tune in Yesterday*, 428-29; Nye, *The Unembarrassed Muse*, 406-16.
22. Richard Lamparski, *Whatever Became Of?* 5th series (New York, 1974), 206-7; Barnouw, *The Golden Web*, 297.
23. Barnouw, *The Golden Web*, 288; see also Buxton and Owen, *The Big Broadcast*, 35-36; Dunning, *Tune in Yesterday*, 81-83.
24. Bob Elliott and Ray Goulding, *Write If You Get Work: The Best of Bob & Ray* (New York, 1975) *passim*.

Index